Polish Film and the Holocaust

Polish Film and the Holocaust

Politics and Memory

Marek Haltof

berghahn
NEW YORK · OXFORD
www.berghahnbooks.com

Published in 2012 by
Berghahn Books
www.berghahnbooks.com

©2012, 2014 Marek Haltof
First paperback edition published in 2014

All rights reserved. Except for the quotation of short passages for the purposes of criticism and review, no part of this book may be reproduced in any form or by any means, electronic or mechanical, including photocopying, recording, or any information storage and retrieval system now known or to be invented, without written permission of Berghahn Books.

Library of Congress Cataloging-in-Publication Data

Haltof, Marek.
  Polish film and the Holocaust : politics and memory / Marek Haltof.
    p. cm.
  Includes bibliographical references and index.
  Includes filmography.
  ISBN 978-0-85745-356-3 (hardback) -- ISBN 978-1-78238-496-0 (paperback) -- ISBN 978-0-85745-357-0 (ebook)
  1. Holocaust, Jewish (1939–1945), in motion pictures. 2. Motion pictures--Poland--History--20th century. I. Title.
  PN1995.9.H53H35 2011
  791.43'658405318--dc23
                                                            2011020655

British Library Cataloguing in Publication Data

A catalogue record for this book is available from the British Library.

Printed on acid-free paper

ISBN: 978-0-85745-356-3 hardback
ISBN: 978-1-78238-496-0 paperback
ISBN: 978-0-85745-357-0 ebook

Contents

List of Illustrations   vii

Acknowledgments   xi

Acronyms and Abbreviations   xiii

Introduction   1

Chapter 1   Postwar Poland: Geopolitics and Cinema   11

Chapter 2   Wanda Jakubowska's Return to Auschwitz: *The Last Stage* (1948)   28

Chapter 3   Commemorating the Warsaw Ghetto Uprising in *Border Street* (1949)   53

Chapter 4   Images of the Holocaust during the Polish School Period (1955–1965)   74

Chapter 5   Years of Organized Forgetting (1965–1980)   115

Chapter 6   Return of the Repressed: "The Poor Poles Look at the Ghetto" (1981–)   139

Chapter 7   Andrzej Wajda Responds: *Korczak* (1990) and *Holy Week* (1996)   187

Chapter 8   Documentary Archaeology of the Holocaust and Polish-Jewish Past   211

Afterword   227

Filmography   230

Select Bibliography   250

Index   265

List of Illustrations

1.1 Henryk Szweizer as a hiding Jew in *Forbidden Songs* (1947)   23
1.2 *Forbidden Songs*. Henryk Szweizer   23
1.3 Zofia Mrozowska as a Jewish street singer in *Forbidden Songs*   23
1.4 Zofia Mrozowska in *Forbidden Songs*   23
1.5 Jewish shoemaker Leon (Jacek Woszczerowicz) in *Two Hours* (1946/1957)   24
2.1 Wanda Jakubowska on the set of *The Last Stage*. Courtesy Filmoteka Narodowa in Warsaw   29
2.2 Wanda Jakubowska's *The Last Stage* (1948). (From the left) Serb Dessa (Alina Janowska), German Anna (Antonina Górecka), Polish Helena (Wanda Bartówna), and Russian Nadia (Maria Winogradowa)   30
2.3 (From the left) Tatjana Górecka (Russian Doctor), Stefan Śródka (Bronek), Antonina Górecka (Anna), and Wanda Bartówna (Helena)   30
2.4 Barbara Drapińska as Marta   33
2.5 Helena (Wanda Bartówna) and Marta (Barbara Drapińska)   33
2.6 Barbara Rachwalska as *Kapo* Elza   36
2.7 Anna (Antonina Górecka) and SS Doctor (Edward Dziewoński)   36
2.8 Russian Doctor (Tatjana Górecka)   37
2.9 Marta (Barbara Drapińska) and Tadeusz (Stanisław Zaczyk)   40
2.10 Lech Skolimowski as Henryk (center) in Wanda Jakubowska's *The End of Our World* (1964)   47
3.1 Aleksander Ford in 1958. Courtesy Filmoteka Narodowa in Warsaw   54
3.2 Nathan Rapoport's Warsaw Ghetto Monument   57
3.3 (From the left) Władek Wojtan (Dionizy Ilczenko), Jadzia Białek (Maria Broniewska), and Bronek Cieplikowski (Tadeusz Fijewski) in Aleksander Ford's *Border Street* (1949)   63
3.4 Dawidek (Jerzy Złotnicki) in *Border Street*   63

3.5	Kazimierz Wojtan (Jerzy Pichelski)	64
3.6	Władysław Godik as Liberman	65
3.7	The Warsaw Ghetto Uprising. Natan (Stefan Śródka)	66
3.8	Natan (Stefan Śródka)	66
3.9	Poles look at the Warsaw Ghetto Uprising. (Center) Tadeusz Fijewski as Bronek	68
4.1	Tadeusz Janczar as Jasio Krone in Andrzej Wajda's *A Generation* (1955)	79
4.2	Jasio (Tadeusz Janczar) and his Jewish friend Abram (Zygmunt Hobot)	80
4.3	Escape from the burning ghetto through the city sewers in *A Generation*. Tadeusz Łomnicki as Stach helps a Jewish fighter	81
4.4	Stach (Tadeusz Łomnicki) helps the communist Sekuła (Janusz Paluszkiewicz)	81
4.5	*A Generation*. A carousel near the wall of the burning Warsaw Ghetto	82
4.6	(From the left) Jasio (Tadeusz Janczar), Mundek (Roman Polański), Stach (Tadeusz Łomnicki), and Jacek (Ryszard Kotys) meet near the ghetto wall in *A Generation*	82
4.7	*The Beater* (1964) by Ewa and Czesław Petelski. Michał (Bronisław Pawlik) and a Hungarian Jewish Woman (Maria Wachowiak)	91
4.8	The Jewish girl Mirka (Beata Barszczewska) leaves her hiding in Stanisław Różewicz's *Birth Certificate* (1961)	95
4.9	*Birth Certificate*. Mirka's POV	96
4.10	Beata Barszczewska as Mirka in *Birth Certificate*	96
4.11	A scene from *Birth Certificate*. (From the left) Zygmunt Zintel, Emil Karewicz, and Mariusz Dmochowski. Courtesy Filmoteka Narodowa in Warsaw. © Film Studio "Tor"	96
4.12	A scene from Jerzy Zarzycki's *White Bear* (1959). (From the left) Rudof von Henneberg (Adam Pawlikowski), Henryk Fogiel (Gustaw Holoubek) in a white bearskin, and Henneberg's wife (Liliana Niwińska)	97
4.13	Gustaw Holoubek (Henryk) and Adam Pawlikowski (Major Henneberg) in *White Bear*	99
4.14	Andrzej Munk (1921–1961). *The Passenger* (1963)	100
4.15	Andrzej Munk's *The Passenger*. Aleksandra Śląska as Liza watches the newly arrived Jewish transport	102
4.16	A scene from *The Passenger*	102
4.17	A scene from *The Passenger*	102
4.18	A scene from *The Passenger*	103

4.19	(From the left) Anna Ciepielewska as Marta, Marek Walczewski as Tadeusz, and Aleksandra Śląska as Liza in *The Passenger*	103
4.20	Anna Ciepielewska as Marta in *The Passenger*	104
4.21	Jerzy Kawalerowicz's *Mother Joan of the Angels* (1961). Father Suryn (Mieczysław Voit)	108
4.22	The Rabbi (Mieczysław Voit) in *Mother Joan of the Angels*	108
5.1	Daniel Olbrychski as Tadeusz in Andrzej Wajda's *Landscape after Battle* (1970)	120
5.2	Nina (Stanisława Celińska) and Tadeusz (Daniel Olbrychski) in *Landscape after Battle*	121
5.3	Nina's death in *Landscape after Battle*	121
5.4	Ryszard Filipski as the writer Andrzej Miller in Jerzy Ziarnik's *A Journey into the Unknown* (1968)	123
5.5	A scene from *A Journey into the Unknown*	124
5.6	(From the left) Józef Duriasz as Zygmunt Korsak and Ryszard Pietruski as blue policeman Wasiak in Janusz Nasfeter's *The Long Night* (1967/1989)	127
5.7	Zygmunt Hobot as the hiding Jew in *The Long Night*	127
5.8	A scene from *The Long Night*. (From the left) Mrs. Piekarczyk (Ryszarda Hanin), her daughter Marta (Jolanta Wołłejko), and Katarzyna (Anna Ciepielewska)	128
5.9	Jan Rybkowski's *Ascension Day* (1969)	131
5.10	Małgorzata Braunek as Raisa Goldstein and Andrzej Antkowiak as Sebastian Goldstein in *Ascension Day*	132
5.11	The wedding in *Ascension Day*. (From the right) Mrs. Goldstein (Zofia Mrozowska), Raisa (Małgorzata Braunek), and Sebastian (Andrzej Antkowiak)	133
5.12	*Ascension Day*. Małgorzata Braunek as Raisa	133
6.1	Stanisław Różewicz's *Lynx* (1982). Jerzy Radziwiłowicz (Priest Konrad) and Franciszek Pieczka (Alojz). Courtesy Filmoteka Narodowa in Warsaw. © Film Studio "Tor"	141
6.2	The innkeeper Tag (Franciszk Pieczka) in Jerzy Kawalerowicz's *Austeria* (1983)	142
6.3	A scene from Jerzy Hoffman's *According to the Decrees of Providence* (1984). Courtesy Filmoteka Narodowa in Warsaw	145
6.4	Chaja (Ernestyna Winnicka) and Piotr (Maciej Kozłowski) in Juliusz Janicki's *There Was No Sun That Spring* (1984). Courtesy Filmoteka Narodowa in Warsaw	147
6.5	Bożena Adamek as Zofia (left) and Róża Chrabelska as Róża in Wojciech Żółtowski's *In the Shadow of Hatred* (1986)	150

x List of Illustrations

6.6	*In the Shadow of Hatred*. Ewa (Aleksandra Cezarska) and Zofia's Aunt (Wanda Łuczycka)	151
6.7	Teresa Marczewska as Elżbieta in Krzysztof Kieślowski's *Decalogue 8* (1988)	152
6.8	Ryszarda Hanin as Mrs. Kulgawcowa in Jan Łomnicki's *Just Beyond this Forest* (1991)	158
6.9	*Just Beyond this Forest*. Rutka (Joanna Friedman) and Mrs. Kulgawcowa (Ryszarda Hanin)	158
6.10	*Just Beyond this Forest*. (From the left) Rutka (Joanna Friedman), Mrs. Kulgawcowa (Ryszarda Hanin), and the German soldier (Bogusław Sochnacki)	159
6.11	Erasing the camp number. Jan Jakub Kolski's *Pornography* (2003)	171
6.12	Krzysztof Majchrzak as Fryderyk in Jan Jakub Kolski's *Pornography*	171
6.13	Jan Kurnakowicz as Rafalski in Jerzy Zarzycki's *Unvanquished City* (1950)	176
6.14	Adrien Brody as Szpilman (center) and his family in Roman Polański's *The Pianist* (2002)	178
6.15	A scene from *The Pianist*	178
6.16	Szpilman (Adrien Brody). *The Pianist*	179
6.17	A scene from *The Pianist*	179
6.18	Adrien Brody as Szpilman in *The Pianist*	180
7.1	Andrzej Wajda on the set of *Korczak* (1990). © Film Studio "Perspektywa"	187
7.2	Wojciech Pszoniak as Dr. Korczak in Andrzej Wajda's *Korczak*. © Film Studio "Perspektywa"	192
7.3	The Polish city tram conductor (Olaf Lubaszenko) is executed for giving bread to the Jews in Andrzej Wajda's *Korczak*. © Film Studio "Perspektywa"	193
7.4	Ewa Dałkowska as Stefania Wilczyńska in *Korczak*. © Film Studio "Perspektywa"	196
7.5	A scene from Andrzej Wajda's *Korczak*. © Film Studio "Perspektywa"	196
7.6	The ending of *Korczak*. © Film Studio "Perspektywa"	197
8.1	Samuel Willenberg tells his story of survival in Michał Nekanda-Trepka's *The Last Witness* (2002)	219
8.2	An archival image in *The Last Witness*	219
8.3	Samuel Willenberg (left) and a Polish helper in *The Last Witness*	219
8.4	Elżbieta Ficowska in Michał Nekanda-Trepka's *A Teaspoon for Life* (2004)	222
8.5	Irena Sendler in Michał Nekanda-Trepka's *A Teaspoon for Life*	222

Acknowledgments

I gratefully acknowledge the help of Northern Michigan University in Marquette for supporting my research and this work with a generous grant—the Peter White Scholar Award—and with sabbatical leave. In the course of researching and writing this book, I received help from a number of individuals. Special thanks go to Adam Wyżyński, Krzysztof Berłowski, and Helena Damętka of the National Film Archive (Filmoteka Narodowa) in Warsaw for their kind assistance. My thanks also go to Bogdana Pilichowska at the Andrzej Wajda Archive in Kraków and to Andrzej Wajda himself for allowing me to do research at his archive.

I am grateful to Polish film directors Michał Bukojemski, Wojciech Majewski, and Michał Nekanda-Trepka for conversations as well as for their assistance with films. Also, I wish to acknowledge the invaluable contribution of Professor Piotr Zwierzchowski, who helped me to obtain a number of films. This work could not have been produced without him.

Several colleagues at Northern Michigan University provided important, generous comments on various parts of the early versions of the manuscript, among them Dr. Gabriel Brahm, Dr. Stephen Burn, and Dr. Toby Rose. I am also grateful to Professor Shravan Rajagopal for his help with editing images from films. Special thanks go to Dr. David Boe for his unvarying assistance regarding the complexities of the English language and comments on parts of the manuscript. Also, I very much appreciated conversations with Dr. Alan Rose and his comments on several chapters of the book.

A number of valuable comments on draft chapters of *The Last Stage* and *Border Street* were provided by my graduate class at NMU (Emily Aho, Brenda Bancroft, Joshua Biron, Harger Boal, Elizabeth Faucett, Kristin Fautsch, Adam Gray, Amanda Paulus, Veronica Pepe, Jason Pilarski, Gillian Podkomorka, Michelle Rozga, Emily Schneeberger, Sean Schoenherr, Mary Stimac, Scott Stone, and Kevin Pearson). I greatly appreciate their feedback. Special thanks also go my graduate student at NMU, William Provost, for his editorial assistance.

In addition, I would like to thank Dr. Allan Reid, Dr. Wacław Osadnik, Dr. Bohdan Nebesio, and Professor Alicja Helman for support. Also, I would like to thank Dr. Joanna Preizner, Dr. Daria Mazur, and Dr. Elżbieta Ostrowska for assisting in the preparation of this book in various ways, and Berghahn's anonymous readers for comments.

The book incorporates still frames from several films. Other images are courtesy of the National Film Archive in Warsaw, Irena Strzałkowska and the Film Studio "Tor" (*Birth Certificate* and *Lynx*), and the Film Studio "Perspektywa" (*Korczak*). An earlier version of chapter 2 was published as "Return to Auschwitz: Wanda Jakubowska's The Last Stage (1948)" in *The Polish Review* 55 (1) 2010: 7–34. Reprinted with permission. I would like to thank Dr. Charles S. Kraszewski for his insightful comments.

Always, with love to my wife Margaret and my daughter Alma.

Acronyms and Abbreviations

AAN	Archiwum Akt Nowych (Archive of Contemporary Documents)
AK	Armia Krajowa (Home Army)
AL	Armia Ludowa (People's Army)
CKŻP	Centralny Komitet Żydów Polskich (Central Committee of Polish Jews)
CŻKH	Centralna Żydowska Komisja Historyczna (Central Jewish Historical Commission)
FIPRESCI	International Federation of Film Critics (Fédération Internationale de la Presse Cinématographique)
FN	Filmoteka Narodowa (National Film Archive in Warsaw)
FPFF	Festival Polskich Filmów Fabularnych (Festival of Polish Films), Gdynia
GG	Generalgouvernement (the central part of German-occupied Poland)
GL	Gwardia Ludowa (People's Guard)
GUKPPiW	Główny Urząd Kontroli Prasy, Publikacji i Widowisk (Main Office for the Control of the Press, Publications, and Public Performances)
IPN	Instytut Pamięci Narodowej (Institute of National Remembrance), Warsaw
KOS	Komisja Ocen Scenariuszy (Committee for the Evaluation of Scripts)
LWP	Ludowe Wojsko Polskie (Polish People's Army)
MBP	Ministerstwo Bezpieczeństwa Publicznego (Ministry of Public Security)
MO	Milicja Obywatelska (People's Militia)
NIK	Najwyższa Izba Kontroli (Supreme Chamber of Control)
NSZ	Narodowe Siły Zbrojne (National Armed Forces)

NZK	Naczelny Zarząd Kinematografii (Main Board of Cinema)
PFDKF	Polska Federacja Dyskusyjnych Klubów Filmowych (Polish Federation of Film Clubs)
PISF	Polski Instytut Sztuki Filmowej (Polish Film Institute), Warsaw
PKF	Polska Kronika Filmowa (Polish Newsreel)
PPR	Polska Partia Robotnicza (Polish Communist Party)
PPS	Polska Partia Socjalistyczna (Polish Socialist Party)
PRL	Polska Rzeczpospolita Ludowa (Polish People's Republic)
PRON	Patriotyczny Ruch Odrodzenia Narodowego (Patriotic Movement for National Rebirth)
PWSFTviT	Państwowa Wyższa Szkoła Filmowa, Telewizyjna i Teatralna im. Leona Schillera (Łódź Film School), Łódź
PZPR	Polska Zjednoczona Partia Robotnicza (Polish United Workers' Party)
RP	Rzeczpospolita Polska (Polish Republic)
RPŻ	Rada Pomocy Żydom (aka Żegota; Polish Council for Aid to the Jews)
SE-MA-FOR	Studio Małych Form Filmowych (Short Film Studio Semafor), Warsaw
SFP	Stowarzyszenie Filmowców Polskich (Polish Filmmakers Association)
TVP	Telewizja Polska (Polish Television)
UBP	Urząd Bezpieczeństwa Publicznego (Public Security Office)
UW	Uniwersytet Warszawski (Warsaw University)
WAiF	Wydawnictwa Artystyczne i Filmowe (Film and Art Publishers)
WFDiF	Wytwórnia Filmów Dokumentalnych i Fabularnych (Documentary and Feature Film Studio)
WFF	Warszawski Festiwal Filmowy (Warsaw Film Festival)
WFO	Wytwórnia Filmów Oświatowych (Educational Film Studio)
ZBOWiD	Związek Bojowników o Wolność i Demokrację (Union of Fighters for Freedom and Democracy)
Żegota	Rada Pomocy Żydom (Council for Aid to the Jews)
ŻIH	Żydowski Instytut Historyczny (Jewish Historical Institute)
ŻOB	Żydowska Organizacja Bojowa (Jewish Combat Organization)
ŻZW	Żydowski Związek Wojskowy (Jewish Military Union)

Introduction

The vibrant, multicultural mosaic of prewar Polish culture was destroyed during World War II. Poland lost more than six million inhabitants, almost 22 percent of the entire population. That number includes about three million Polish Jews, approximately 90 percent of Polish Jewry, who perished during the war in the ghettos and extermination camps built by Nazi Germany in occupied Polish territories.[1]

In a dispute with several historians who argued that Polish anti-Semitism and the indifference of Polish "bystanders" determined the fate of the Jewish population, Lucy S. Dawidowicz declares in her book, *The Holocaust and the Historians*, that "the Germans used Poland as their gigantic laboratory for mass murder, not (as has sometimes been wrongly charged) because the Nazis counted on Polish anti-Semitism, but because that was where most of Europe's Jews were concentrated and where the Germans expected to settle for a long time."[2] James E. Young perceptively comments in a similar manner in his acclaimed book *The Texture of Memory*: "That the death camps were located on Polish soil suggests to the Poles not their national complicity, but their ultimate violation: it was one thing to be ravaged outside one's land, another to be occupied and enslaved at home. In this view, the killing centers in Poland were to have begun with the Jews and ended with the Poles."[3] Today, there are probably no more than ten thousand Jews living in Poland, compared with 3.3 million before the war. Like other European countries, Poland was subsequently able to rebuild its economy and to redevelop its culture. With the war, however, as Eric Goldman writes, "Poland ceased to be one of the great centres of Yiddish life and culture; instead it became its burial ground."[4]

Like members of other nations, Poles construct their own national memory. Also, as in any other nation, Poles mourn their dead differently. Similar to the Jews, Poles often see themselves as victims of history. In Polish historiography, World War II started with the invasion of Poland by Nazi Germany on 1 September 1939, and its effects lasted for generations due to the Yalta agreement and Poland's postwar occupation by the Soviets until the return of democracy in 1989. The murdered Polish Jews had been incorporated into the Polish collective memory of its citizens who were killed during the war; the Polish Jews became part of the Polish national martyrdom.

Nonetheless, every act of capturing memory, as Andrew Charlesworth observes, "can by its exclusivity push aside the claims of others or their own collective rights and identities."[5] Historian Piotr Wróbel fittingly emphasizes the presence of "double memory" in Poland—different memories of the same event depending on the ethnicity of the witness.⁶ Journalist Konstanty Gebert also writes about the "two-sided nature of Holocaust memory in Poland," providing the following explanation of the different, Polish and Jewish, memories of World War II atrocities:

> For both Polish and Jewish nations, their very real suffering plays a major role in their self-images—in the very way they define themselves—and this influences the way they now see each other. If 3 out of the 6 million of Poland's war dead were Jewish, the other 3 million were ethnically Polish. It is hard for the Poles to see a substantial difference between these two fates ... Whether consciously or not, the Poles have thus conflated the suffering of Poles and Jews, claiming the Holocaust as part of Polish heritage.⁷

Thus, we are dealing with two competing versions of history and two competing national memories, with two groups in a way claiming to be the true victims of history. In Polish historiography, the discourse of Poland as a European martyr country, often labeled the "Christ among Nations," has a long tradition, which originated during the period of partition (1795–1918), when Poland was eliminated from the map of Europe by its powerful neighbors. The Polish romantic poets, in particular, made this image the most important element of the national identity of a stateless people.

The image of a martyr nation, victimized by the Germans, returned powerfully after 1945. For several decades, the Polish wartime experiences were subjected to a communist interpretation of history. The underground Polish nationalist forces, who distinguished themselves fighting the Germans and the Soviets, were physically persecuted after the war. In postwar communist history their role was either ridiculed or silenced, and is barely known abroad; for example, the role of the Council for Aid to the Jews (Rada Pomocy Żydom; code name Żegota), the only such institution in German-occupied Europe, is rarely recognized.⁸ The importance of the Polish left-wing underground, largely organized and controlled by the Soviets, was exaggerated and elevated to suit the dominant ideology. In an attempt to legitimize the communists' leading political role, the Communist Party falsified history to create its own legend. In both versions of history, the nationalist and the communist, the occupation of Poland had been seen as a heroic armed struggle with the occupier(s), a period marked by resistance and martyrdom. There was no room for Jewish martyrology in that version of Polish national history.

The return of democracy in 1989 has enabled filmmakers in Poland to freely explore areas that were taboo under the previous political order. The recovery of the common Polish-Jewish heritage and the incorporation of Jewish culture into Polish national memory necessitate the disturbing confrontation with the past. The recognition of Poland's Jewish history and the struggle with the legacy of the Holocaust involves an unavoidable process of re-defining the Polish national character, of negotiating Polishness.

The post-1989 years have also brought unique opportunities, as well as challenges, for scholars and researchers. The end of the communist period has yielded a wealth of information and resources that were largely unavailable for nearly half a century. Polish scholars are no longer restricted in the scope or substance of their research regarding the Holocaust, and this has resulted in an unprecedented number of meticulously researched and thought-provoking academic studies.

***

For the purpose of this book, the Holocaust is defined as the premeditated murder of European Jews by Nazi Germany during World War II. A full exploration of the complexities of Polish-Jewish relationships before and after the Holocaust is outside of the scope of this book, although these matters are being, and have to be, taken into account. Several recently published studies perceptively address this issue, for example, *Bondage to the Dead: Poland and the Memory of the Holocaust* written by Michael C. Steinlauf, *Rethinking Poles and Jews*, edited by Robert Cherry and Annamaria Orla-Bukowska, and *Imaginary Neighbors: Mediating Polish-Jewish Relations after the Holocaust* edited by Dorota Głowacka and Joanna Zylinska.[9]

For a number of historians, the Holocaust has become the most important event of the twentieth century, an event that is traumatic, unique, inexplicable, and beyond representation. It tends to overshadow other aspects of World War II. "The Holocaust has been both repressed and 'canonized' in the recent past," writes Dominick LaCapra.[10] For many filmmakers and theorists, to represent the Holocaust is to attempt to represent the unrepresentable; visual images seem incapable of portraying its horror. Some of them seem to share Claude Lanzmann's much-quoted concern that there are things that "cannot and should not be represented,"[11] or Elie Wiesel's assertion that "Auschwitz cannot be explained nor can it be visualized."[12] However, as historian Peter Novick notes, "the assertion that the Holocaust is unique—like the claim that it is singularly incomprehensible or unrepresentable—is, in practice, deeply offensive. What else can all of this possibly mean except 'your catastrophe, unlike ours, is ordinary; unlike ours is comprehensible; unlike ours is representable.'"[13]

Despite the "unrepresentable" nature of the Holocaust, hundreds of films have been made thus far, and certainly more will be made. Some films undeniably present the Holocaust in a highly conventionalized form, and Polish cinema is no exception. Given the complexities of the Polish past, it comes as no surprise that memories of World War II have haunted Polish cinema, and, like many other traumatic experiences, these memories have returned powerfully on the screen. Polish filmmakers who initially confronted the theme of the Holocaust faced the same difficulties as filmmakers elsewhere: Is it better to speak or to remain silent? Is it possible to create a cinematic language adequate to convey the enormity of human suffering, a language that will in no way trivialize the Holocaust?

Polish filmmakers also faced problems relevant to Poland's political situation after 1945, chiefly the pressure of the harsh political censorship. Willingly or not, they were serving the communist state; time and again their works were compromised by the dominant ideology and the propagandist goals of the communist authorities. Thus, Polish films about the Holocaust, and about Polish-Jewish relations in general, reflect the postwar political status quo and the changing historical and political circumstances more than historical truth. They reflect the changing policy of the Communist Party concerning Polish-Jewish issues as well as relations between Poland and Israel. As Bożena Szaynok puts it in the title of her perceptive study in Polish, this is a subject with history and Moscow in the background.[14]

Any book dealing with the representation of the Holocaust in any national cinema, especially if the country being studied was struggling with a communist system, has to take into account the political context. The present book is no exception. Another important factor has to do with the changing Holocaust memory worldwide, which also affected Polish films, especially after the return of democracy in 1989.

Despite the importance of the topic, the representation of the Holocaust in Polish cinema is still a domain which has not been the focus of systematic study, and awaits its historian. The present work is a contribution to this important though neglected field of study. Without venturing into theoretical debates concerning the issue of "Polish cinema," I have decided to adopt a functional definition of Polish film. I examine films that fulfill at least two of the following criteria: works made in Poland (with significant Polish involvement), in the Polish language, and by Polish filmmakers (regardless of their nationality).

This book primarily considers Polish fiction films made after 1945 that deal with the Holocaust in a direct manner. Attention is also paid to major short films and documentary films pertaining to the topic, some of which are classic works outside of the context of Polish cinema. Films made before World War II, both in Polish and Yiddish, and sometimes analyzed in the spirit of Siegfried Kracauer as sensitive barometers of things to come, are outside the scope of this book. Several notable contemporary films, such as Jerzy Kawalerowicz's *Austeria* (aka *The Inn*, 1983) and Wojciech Jerzy Has's *Hospital under the Hourglass* (*Sanatorium pod klepsydrą*, 1973), both being evocations of the lost Jewish world, are not discussed at length in this book, but are taken into account.

Given my working definition of Polish film, this book does not offer an extensive commentary on films made by Polish diasporic filmmakers outside of Poland and without the involvement of the Polish film industry, for example Agnieszka Holland's German-made film *Angry Harvest* (*Bittere Ernte*, 1985) and *Europa, Europa* (1991, a French and German co-production). Excluded also are several foreign (mostly documentary) productions about the Holocaust made on location in Poland, sometimes with noticeable Polish participation, as is the case, for example, of Steven Spielberg's *Schindler's List* (1993).

Although the occupied Polish territories were the site of a number of German concentration and extermination camps, it is surprising to learn that not a single book (in English or in Polish) has addressed the representation of the Holocaust in Polish cinema. Several problems of a cinematic, historical, and ethical nature have been, however, discussed in great depth by other scholars. For instance, readers may find discussion of a number of better known Polish films in books written by Annette Insdorf (*Indelible Shadows: Film and the Holocaust*), Ilan Avisar (*Screening the Holocaust: Cinema's Images of the Unimaginable*), Omer Bartov (*The "Jew" in Cinema: From* The Golem *to* Don't Touch My Holocaust), and Lawrence Baron (*Projecting the Holocaust into the Present: The Changing Focus of Contemporary Holocaust Cinema*), among others.[15] Several articles in English were also written on this subject, for example by Paul Coates, Stuart Liebman, Elżbieta Ostrowska, and Michael Stevenson (see Bibliography). Although exemplary, these articles, however, do not offer broader historical and cultural perspectives of the problem due to their limited scope.

It has to be also stressed that, regrettably, several English anthologies dealing with the reception of various classic films on the Holocaust neither include texts written by the historians of Polish cinema nor pay any particular attention to the Polish historical and cultural contexts. For example, the renowned anthologies on the reception of Steven Spielberg's *Schindler's List* and Alan Resnais' *Night and Fog* (1955), albeit dealing with films partly made on location in Poland and referring to events that happened on Polish soil and witnessed by Poles, almost entirely overlook the Polish aspect of these films.[16] Historian Omer Bartov in his insightful essay on "Eastern Europe as the Site of Genocide" thoroughly and eloquently addresses the problem of ignoring this very important (not only for Holocaust Studies) geopolitical context:

> Eastern Europe is thus not merely the site of the Holocaust in the physical sense that most of Europe's Jews lived there and were murdered there. It was and remains the heart of the Holocaust in that it was where Jewish and Christian civilizations formed a long, though troubled, tradition of living side by side, and where that social and cultural fabric was ultimately shattered in World War II and the Holocaust.[17]

Polish Film and the Holocaust is the first book-length study on the subject. My goal is to present the most comprehensive and up-to-date discussion relying chiefly on Polish archival findings and published sources. As with my earlier book on *Polish National Cinema*,[18] my hope is that more studies, possibly theoretically minded ones, focusing on selected filmic examples, will follow. The above goal explains my intention to take into account all relevant films, not only a few well-known selected examples, some of them already renowned outside of Poland.

During World War II, Poles witnessed mass murders committed on Polish soil and also were victims of unspeakable crimes. The Jewish diaspora in

Poland, a visible and important part of Polish society, vanished in front of their eyes. Given the uniqueness of the Polish experience of the Holocaust, it comes as no surprise to see that the majority of locally produced films depict the Holocaust through the prism of Polish-Jewish relationships. This distinctive feature of Polish films dealing with the Holocaust, part of coming to terms with the troubled past, delineates the difference between the treatment of the Holocaust in Polish and other national cinemas.

The unique Polish experience of the Holocaust undoubtedly invites approaches focusing on the traumatic impact of the past as well as on the traumatic aspect of the witnessing. It is not my goal, however, to engage in theorizing about the much-discussed, in recent years, concepts such as "trauma theory," "posttraumatic cinema," or "national memory." They were eloquently elaborated by scholars such as Joshua Hirsch, Alan Mintz, and Janet Walker.[19] Their sophisticated and nuanced monographs, however, refer to a relatively small number of films, and demonstrate depth rather than breadth as far as filmic examples are concerned. Instead of limiting the study to a few textual analyses, I prefer to discuss a wide range of Polish films chronologically, and to situate each film in the context of Polish historical and political circumstances that shaped the screen representation of the Holocaust in Poland.

***

This book's first chapter discusses "Postwar Poland: Geopolitics and Cinema." It summarizes the losses among Polish filmmakers (filmmakers of Jewish origin in particular), comments on the gradual Sovietization of Polish life after 1945, and stresses attempts by the communist regime to create a new national identity by rewriting Polish history from the communist perspective. The chapter also briefly outlines the postwar organization of the nationalized Polish film industry and comments on Polish-Jewish relations immediately after the war. In addition, this portion of the book also discusses films made by the Jewish cooperative Kinor. The chapter ends with a commentary on the first Polish narrative films that made reference to the Holocaust, such as Leonard Buczkowski's *Forbidden Songs* (*Zakazane piosenki*, 1947).

The next two chapters deal with two classic films released in the late 1940s, Wanda Jakubowska's *The Last Stage* (*Ostatni etap*, 1948) and Aleksander Ford's *Border Street* (*Ulica Graniczna*, 1949), which established images discernible in later Holocaust narratives, and which also serve as examples of the Polish communist regime's efforts to commemorate the war and the Holocaust. The chapter titled "Wanda Jakubowska's Return to Auschwitz: *The Last Stage* (1948)" analyzes the film made by an Auschwitz survivor on location in Auschwitz-Birkenau. The focus is on the political, ideological, and cultural contexts of Jakubowska's film, which was made in line with the ideological requirements of the time and Jakubowska's own communist beliefs. Her film also reflects the status of the postwar debates about Auschwitz. Although the leading character in the film is Jewish, the camp's largest group of victims is not the main focus. The film reflects the efforts of the communist government to internationalize Auschwitz and to make it a memorial to those who fought against fascism. The chapter ends with comments on three lesser-known films by Jakubowska, made after *The Last Stage*, in which she also returns to her camp experiences: *Meetings in the Twilight* (*Spotkania w mroku*, 1960), *The End of Our World* (*Koniec naszego świata*, 1964), and *Invitation* (*Zaproszenie*, 1985).

Chapter 3, "Commemorating the Warsaw Ghetto Uprising in *Border Street* (1949)," addresses the cinematic portrayal of the 1943 uprising and Jewish-Polish relations in occupied Warsaw. Aleksander Ford's film accentuates the need for unity, common struggle, and heroism on both sides of the wall dividing the city, and it offers a heroic representation of the uprising. This segment of the book comments on Ford's background, his struggles to produce the film, and the government's pressure to make an ideologically correct film. The political context of the commemorations of the Warsaw Ghetto Uprising is also in the center of this chapter. The premiere of Ford's film, along with the unveiling of memorials and the release of documentary films and literary works paying tribute to the ghetto insurgents, coincided with the suppression of any reference, not to mention official memorialization, pertaining to the 1944 Warsaw Rising and the nationalist Home Army (AK). The film's release in 1949 also corresponded to the beginning of "the struggle with Zionism" within the communist bloc.

The next chapter, "Images of the Holocaust during the Polish School Period (1955–1965)," discusses the most vibrant phase in the history of Polish cinema. The political thaw after 1956 enabled young filmmakers to move away from the dogma of socialist realism and to produce several well-known films about Poland's recent history. The revival of Polish cinema, helped by a number of organizational changes within the film industry, comprises also a number of films dealing with the Holocaust, including Andrzej Munk's psychological drama *The Passenger* (*Pasażerka*, 1963), Ewa and Czesław Petelski's *The Beater* (*Naganiacz*, 1964), and Andrzej Wajda's *A Generation* (*Pokolenie*, 1955) and *Samson* (1961). The chapter also discusses lesser-known films, such as *White Bear* (*Biały niedźwiedź*, 1959), directed by Jerzy Zarzycki, and films with references to the Holocaust and featuring characters of Jewish origin, such as Stanisław Różewicz's *Three Women* (*Trzy kobiety*, 1957).

Chapter 5, "Years of Organized Forgetting (1965–1980)," deals with the period during which, due to the pressure of politics, only a small number of films were released about Polish-Jewish relations or the Holocaust. The chapter discusses the late 1960s in Poland, characterized by the gradual demise of Władysław Gomułka's communist faction and the rise of communist nationalists led by General Moczar. It takes into account the deterioration of relations between Poland and Israel following the Six-Day War in 1967, an open anti-Semitic campaign under the disguise of an "anti-Zionist" campaign, and, as a result, a forced emigration of a number of Polish citizens of Jewish origin, among them several prominent filmmakers. The downfall of Gomułka in 1970 led to the appearance of the more pragmatic Silesian communists, led by Edward Gierek, who dominated the 1970s. The chapter looks at the period between 1965 and 1980 in Polish cinema, which is characterized by the "organized silence" regarding sensitive Polish-Jewish relations. The example of Janusz Nasfeter's *The Long Night* (*Długa noc*, produced in 1967, released in 1989) is at the heart of this chapter. Other films include Jan Rybkowski's *Ascension Day* (*Wniebowstąpienie*, 1969) and Wajda's *Landscape after Battle* (*Krajobraz po bitwie*, 1970), among others.

The following chapter, "Return of the Repressed: 'The Poor Poles Look at the Ghetto' (1981–)," analyzes films produced during the last decade of communist rule in Poland and films made after the return of democracy in 1989. It stresses the beginning of a national debate on the memory of the Holocaust that was propelled by the television screening of Claude Lanzmann's *Shoah* (1985) and the publication of an essay by Jan Błoński, "The Poor Poles Look at the Ghetto," which appeared in 1987 in the Catholic weekly *Tygodnik Powszechny*.[20] This first part of the chapter focuses, among others, on three films released in 1984, *A Postcard from the Journey* (*Kartka z podróży*, 1984, Waldemar Dziki), *According to the Decrees of Providence* (*Wedle wyroków twoich*, 1984, Jerzy Hoffman), and *There Was No Sun That Spring* (*Nie było słońca tej wiosny* 1984, Juliusz Janicki). It also considers several documentary and television films, including the internationally known *Decalogue 8* (*Dekalog 8*, 1988) by Krzysztof Kieślowski. Liberated from the constraints of communist censorship, after 1989 Polish filmmakers produced a group of important films about Jewish-Polish history, including *Warszawa. Année 5703* (1992) by Janusz Kijowski, *Farewell to Maria* (*Pożegnanie z Marią*, 1993) by Filip Zylber, *Just Beyond this Forest* (*Jeszcze tylko ten las*, 1991) by Jan Łomnicki, *Deborah* (*Debora*, 1996) by Ryszard Brylski, and *Keep Away from the Window* (*Daleko od okna*, 2000) by Jan Jakub Kolski.

The final segment of chapter 6 deals with Roman Polański's celebrated Holocaust drama, *The Pianist* (*Pianista*, 2002), based on the memoirs written by the Jewish-Polish composer and pianist Władysław Szpilman, and published for the first time in 1946. *The Pianist* is discussed as Polański's first cinematic return to his own war-time childhood experiences in occupied Poland. In addition, this portion of the chapter also discusses an earlier attempt to adapt Szpilman's story of survival, namely Jerzy Zarzycki's postwar project called *The Warsaw Robinson* (*Robinson Warszawski*), which was mutilated by censors and released in 1950 as *Unvanquished City* (*Miasto nieujarzmione*), a film obeying the rules of socialist realist cinema.

The book's chapter 7, "Andrzej Wajda Responds," is devoted to films by Wajda that left their mark on discussions about the screen portrayal of the Holocaust and gained international attention: *Korczak* (1990) and *Holy Week* (*Wielki Tydzień*, 1996). While acknowledging the controversies stirred by *Korczak* in

France, this chapter pays particular attention to the Polish context of the film and to Korczak's importance in both Polish and Jewish traditions. The chapter also discusses earlier attempts to portray his life in literary works and on screen. *Holy Week* continues Wajda's examination of Polish-Jewish relations during the war. It is based on a short novel written soon after the Warsaw Ghetto Uprising by the prominent Polish writer Jerzy Andrzejewski, which is arguably the first literary attempt to examine the behavior of Poles facing the Holocaust.

Chapter 8, "Documentary Archaeology of the Holocaust and Polish-Jewish Past," offers a concise survey of documentary films that, without a doubt, warrants more scholarly attention and a separate study. The chapter discusses first postwar documentaries about the war atrocities and the Holocaust. It contains comments on documentary classics made during the Polish School period, such as *Requiem for 500,000* (*Requiem dla 500 000*, 1963) by Jerzy Bossak and Wacław Kaźmierczak. The chapter also briefly addresses the representation of the Holocaust in a number of significant documentary films made in recent years, for example *Birthplace* (*Miejsce urodzenia*, 1992, Paweł Łoziński), *Chronicle of the Warsaw Ghetto Uprising according to Marek Edelman* (*Kronika powstania w getcie warszawskim wg Marka Edelmana*, 1993, Jolanta Dylewska), and *Photographer* (*Fotoamator*, 1998, Dariusz Jabłoński).

The book ends with a short Afterword, Filmography of Polish films dealing with the Holocaust, as well as with a Bibliography of works in English and Polish.

Notes

1. The estimated figures concerning Polish and Jewish losses during World War II differ slightly in various historical accounts. The majority of historians write about six million deaths, including three million Polish Jews. For example, this is the figure provided by Lucy S. Dawidowicz in her *The Holocaust and the Historians* (Cambridge: Harvard University Press, 1981), 6–7. M. B. Biskupski provides the same figures in his concise *The History of Poland* (Westport: Greenwood Press, 2000), 108.
2. Dawidowicz, *The Holocaust and the Historians*, 92–93.
3. James E. Young, *The Texture of Memory: Holocaust Memorials and Meaning* (New Haven: Yale University Press), 123.
4. Eric A. Goldman, *Visions, Images, and Dreams: Yiddish Film Past and Present* (Ann Arbor: UMI Research Press, 1983), 109.
5. Andrew Charlesworth, "Contesting Places of Memory: The Case of Auschwitz," *Environment and Planning D: Society and Space* 12 (1994): 579.
6. Piotr Wróbel, "Double Memory: Poles and Jews after the Holocaust," *East European Politics and Societies* vol. 11, no. 3 (1997): 560–574.
7. Konstanty Gebert, "The Dialectics of Memory in Poland," in *The Art of Memory: Holocaust Memorials in History*, ed. James E. Young (New York: Prestel, 1994), 121.
8. See Irene Tomaszewski and Tecia Werbowski, *"Żegota": The Council for Aid to Jews in Occupied Poland, 1942–45* (Montreal: Price-Patterson, 1994). New, 2010 edition by Praeger is entitled *Code Name: Żegota. Rescuing Jews in Occupied Poland, 1942–1945*.
9. Michael C. Steinlauf, *Bondage to the Dead. Poland and the Memory of the Holocaust* (Syracuse: Syracuse University Press, 1997); Robert Cherry and Annamaria Orla-Bukowska, eds., *Rethinking Poles and Jews: Troubled Past, Brighter Future* (Lanham: Rowman and Littlefield,

2007); Dorota Głowacka and Joanna Zylinska, eds., *Imaginary Neighbors: Mediating Polish-Jewish Relations after the Holocaust* (Lincoln: University of Nebraska Press, 2007).
10. Dominick LaCapra, *Representing the Holocaust: History, Theory, Trauma* (Ithaca and London: Cornell University Press, 1994), xi.
11. Claude Lanzmann, "Why Spielberg Has Distorted the Truth," *Guardian Weekly* (April 9, 1994): 14–15.
12. Elie Wiesel quoted in Libby Saxton, *Haunted Images: Film, Ethics, Testimony and the Holocaust* (London: Wallflower Press, 2008), 6. Originally published in 1978 in *New York Times*.
13. Peter Novick, *The Holocaust in American Life* (Boston: Houghton Mifflin, 1999), 9.
14. Bożena Szaynok, *Z historią i Moskwą w tle. Polska a Izrael 1944–1968* (Warsaw: Instytut Pamięci Narodowej, 2007).
15. Annette Insdorf, *Indelible Shadows: Film and the Holocaust* (Cambridge and New York: Cambridge University Press, 1989); Ilan Avisar, *Screening the Holocaust: Cinema's Images of the Unimaginable* (Bloomington: Indiana University Press, 1988); Omer Bartov, *The "Jew" in Cinema: From The Golem to Don't Touch My Holocaust* (Bloomington: Indiana University Press, 2005); Lawrence Baron, *Projecting the Holocaust into the Present: The Changing Focus of Contemporary Holocaust Cinema* (Lanham: Rowman and Littlefield, 2005).
16. Yosefa Loshitzky, ed., *Spielberg's Holocaust: Critical Perspectives on Schindler's List* (Bloomington: Indiana University Press, 1997); Ewout van der Knaap, ed., *Uncovering the Holocaust: The International Reception of Night and Fog* (London: Wallflower Press, 2006). The book on Alain Resnais's classic film, for example, deals with this film's reception in France, Germany, Israel, Britain, the Netherlands, and the USA.
17. Omer Bartov, "Eastern Europe as the Site of Genocide," *Journal of Modern History* vol. 80, no. 3 (2008): 593.
18. Marek Haltof, *Polish National Cinema* (New York: Berghahn Books, 2002).
19. Joshua Hirsch, *Afterimage: Film, Trauma, and the Holocaust* (Philadelphia: Temple University Press, 2004), Alan Mintz, *Popular Culture and the Shaping of Holocaust Memory in America* (Seattle: University of Washington Press, 2001), and Janet Walker, *Trauma Cinema: Documenting Incest and the Holocaust* (Berkeley: University of California Press, 2005).
20. Jan Błoński, "Biedni Polacy patrzą na getto," *Tygodnik Powszechny* vol. 41, no. 2 (11 January 1987): 1 and 4.

Chapter 1

POSTWAR POLAND:
GEOPOLITICS AND CINEMA

The Polish state ceased to exist in September of 1939.[1] In accordance with the Nazi German-Soviet Union (Ribbentrop-Molotov) Pact, Nazi German forces invaded Poland on 1 September 1939, and then Soviet armies attacked from the east on 17 September, thus completing another partition of Poland. Unlike a number of other European countries whose film production was maintained at the prewar level, or had even increased at the beginning of the 1940s, Poland had no feature film production during the occupation.

During the war, a number of established Polish filmmakers lost their lives. Actor Eugeniusz Bodo (Bogdan Junod, 1899–1943), a symbol of commercial Polish cinema of the 1930s, was arrested by the Soviet secret police in 1941 and killed in a Soviet concentration camp. Ina Benita (Janina Ferow-Bułhak, 1912–1944), the blond femme fatale of prewar Polish cinema, died with her baby son during the Warsaw Rising in the city underground sewers while trying to escape the fighting. The legend of Polish cinema, Kazimierz Junosza-Stępowski (1882–1943), was killed by members of the Polish Home Army (AK) while trying to protect his wife, a Gestapo informer. The scientist and inventor Kazimierz Prószyński (1875–1945), also the producer of the first Polish narrative film, *The Return of a Merry Fellow* (*Powrót birbanta*, 1902), died in the Mauthausen concentration camp on 13 March 1945. The list of losses is extensive and includes film people also killed in concentration camps, for example Henryk Korewicki (1899–1943), Witold Zacharewicz (1914–1943), and Władysław Bugayski-Prus (1906–1943), and those killed in action or shot by the Germans, such as Mieczysław Krawicz (1893–1944), Tadeusz Frenkiel (1896–1943), and Franciszek Brodniewicz (1892–1944).

The losses were particularly high with regard to Polish filmmakers of Jewish origin. Henryk Szaro (Szapiro, 1900–1942), one of the leading prewar directors, was killed in the Warsaw Ghetto in June of 1942. He shared his fate in the ghetto with, among others, film producer Maria Hirszbejn (1889–1942?), actor, producer, and director of Polish and German films Danny Kaden (Daniel Kirschenfinkel, 1884–1942), and the popular composer and author of musical scores for Polish films Szymon Kataszek (1898–1943). Several filmmakers were killed by the Gestapo, among them the producer of a number of classic Polish films Józef Rosen (1902–1942) and the most accomplished prewar set designer Jacek Rotmil (1888–1944), who was arrested and killed at the infamous Pawiak prison in Warsaw. The list of victims also includes actors such as Michał Znicz (Michał Feiertag (1888–1943) and Ajzyk Samberg (Samborek, 1889–1943), directors such as Aleksander Marten (Marek Tennenbaum, 1898–1942) and Aleksander Reich (1887–1942), writers and screenwriters such as Jadwiga Migowa (literary pseudonym: Kamil Norden, 1890–1942), Andrzej Marek (Marek Arnstein, 1878–1943), and Alter Kacyzne (1885–1941), and directors who died in the Soviet Union, such as Leon Trystan (Chaim Lejb Wagman, 1899–1941) and Juliusz Gardan (Gradstein, 1912–1944).[2]

The new political system that was forcefully imposed on the Polish state by the Soviet Union after 1945 replaced one dreaded system with another. Traditionally disliked and feared, Poland's eastern neighbor and its communist ideology started to leave a mark on Polish life. This led to gradual Sovietization, to Poles being subjected to the rules of the communist minority operating under the strict control of the Soviet Union, and to the rejection of any links with the prewar, "bourgeois Poland."

In addition, the Polish borders changed dramatically. Poland moved to the west, at least geographically. It lost its eastern territories, the so-called *Kresy*, places immortalized in patriotic tales by, among others, the Nobel Prize winner for Literature in 1905, Henryk Sienkiewicz, in his epic historical novels. As compensation, Poland gained new territories in the west and the north, with new borders set on the Odra (Oder) and Nysa Łużycka (Neisse) Rivers, the so-called Recovered Lands (Ziemie Odzyskane) or Western Lands (Ziemie Zachodnie). Due to migration from the east to the west, from villages to cities, the Polish people needed to be incredibly mobile. The migration, the changed borders, and the losses caused by the war visibly altered the Polish landscape. After the war, Poland became an almost homogeneous society ethnically: the majority of Polish Jews had been killed, the Germans were forced to resettle behind the Odra River border, and the Ukrainians and other nationals who populated the eastern provinces were now part of the Soviet Union. Poland started to become an ethnic and religious monolith, with the majority of the population being Roman Catholic. (Poland had previously been a multinational society, with Poles comprising 68.9 percent of the total population in 1931.)[3]

Attempts to create a new national identity began with the rewriting of Polish history from the communist (Marxist-Leninist) perspective. This became a history that stressed the "progressive" tendencies of the Polish past and presented a new, politically correct, version of troubled Polish-Russian relations. In spite of attempts to erase traces of traditional Polish identity and to reinterpret Polish history, there were certain aspects important for national distinctiveness which still remained. Arguably, the most important aspect continued to be the role of the Roman Catholic Church in preserving Polish national identity, especially during the earlier period of Poland's partition (1795–1918). The Roman Catholic religion played a significant role in defining and strengthening the Polish character. Throughout the ages, Poles fought with a number of enemies representing different religions, from Islamic Turks to Orthodox Russians. Polish nationalism, identified with the Roman Catholic Church, always focused on national freedom being paramount, to be defended at all costs; it demanded personal sacrifice for national causes. The communist authorities fought a losing battle trying to change the nature of Polish nationalism. They failed to replace nationalism with internationalism, religion with ideology, and Polish romanticism with revolutionary spirit.

Postwar Poland, renamed as the Polish People's Republic (Polska Rzeczpospolita Ludowa, PRL), started its existence by gradually erasing links with prewar Poland. Reliable information about the prewar period had virtually disappeared from school curricula and was replaced by accounts of the class struggle and the larger-than-life communist movement. The silence over certain nationally sensitive issues and the harsh criticism of others created a conviction that everything was to begin anew in a social and cultural void. The same applied to cinema. The negation of prewar achievements paralleled the mythologization of certain marginal, yet politically more appropriate, trends that were in line with the communist ideology.

Some major filmmakers survived the occupation in Poland, including scriptwriter Ludwik Starski, director Leonard Buczkowski, and actor Adolf Dymsza, but the majority left the country after the September campaign of 1939. Michał Waszyński, Seweryn Steinwurzel, Ryszard Ordyński, Józef Lejtes, and Jadwiga Smosarska, among others, found themselves in the West. In the new geopolitical situation after the war, these and other filmmakers chose permanent emigration rather than return to a Soviet-dominated Poland. As a consequence of their decision to remain abroad, their postwar careers were rarely mentioned in Poland. Others, mostly filmmakers associated with prewar leftist groups, survived the war in the Soviet Union. In 1943, they created the Polish Army Film Unit Czołówka (Czołówka Filmowa Wojska Polskiego) within the Polish Tadeusz Kościuszko First Division, part of the Red Army. Its task was to document struggles of Polish soldiers fighting alongside the Red Army. Headed by Aleksander Ford, the Czołówka (Vanguard) members, including Jerzy Bossak, Stanisław Wohl, and Ludwik Perski (all of them assimilated Polish Jews), returned with the Red Army as officers in the First Polish Army.

Immediately after the war there was only one Polish film organization in existence, namely the Polish Army Film Unit (Wytwórnia Filmowa Wojska Polskiego), an extension of Czołówka, which was attached to the political department of the Polish army. Its task had been not only to provide documentation of war activities (frequently biased and unreliable), but also to capture film equipment and film stock left by the Germans, and to take care of the surviving movie theaters.[4] Polish filmmakers who affiliated themselves with the Polish army, which had come from the east, were able to take some advantage of the German studio UFA's technical supplies, both in Berlin and the Lower Silesia, where the Germans had stored their film equipment. The equipment and confiscated films enabled the establishment of a film studio in Łódź (the only major Polish city with an intact infrastructure).[5] By the end of 1945, the studio in Łódź was ready to produce films.

Although Ford and other leading postwar film figures started their careers before the war, they attacked the prewar film industry and the dominant film culture of that period. Leonard Buczkowski became the only established prewar film director to be able to make films in communist Poland. Interestingly, some of the first and most popular postwar films were made by the prewar professionals who had associated with the *filmowa branża* (film business), much criticized by Ford and other members of the Society for the Promotion of Film Art (Stowarzyszenie Propagandy Filmu Artystycznego, START), established in Warsaw in 1930 by, among others, film historian Jerzy Toeplitz, and filmmakers Wanda Jakubowska, Eugeniusz Cękalski, Jerzy Zarzycki, and Stanisław Wohl. Officially known from 1931 as The Society of Film Art Devotees (Stowarzyszenie Miłośników Filmu Artystycznego), the START members began their careers by attacking commercial Polish productions while promoting art cinema. Regarding cinema as more than just entertainment, they were united by "the struggle for films for the public good," which was the START slogan from 1932. After the disintegration of the START group in 1935, its former members attempted to make films that reflected their interest in a socially committed cinema. In 1937, some of the START members, including Ford, Cękalski, and Wohl, established the Cooperative of Film Authors (Spółdzielnia Autorów Filmowych, SAF). Their two productions, *The Ghosts* (*Strachy*, 1938), directed by Cękalski and Karol Szołowski, and *The People of the Vistula* (*Ludzie Wisły*, 1938), directed by Ford and Zarzycki, were among the finest achievements in prewar Polish cinema. After World War II, the former START members immediately seized power, imposed their vision of cinema, which was much in line with that of the communist authorities, and practically controlled the nationalized post-1945 Polish film industry, both as decision makers and filmmakers.

The Polish film industry was nationalized on 13 November 1945. Film Polski (Polish Film; the National Board of Polish Film) was established as the sole body producing, distributing, and exhibiting films in Poland. From 1945 to 1947, Aleksander Ford was the head of the organization, which operated within the Ministry of Information and Propaganda. Ford accumulated power, and, thanks to his high-ranking political and military connections with the communist leaders, he ran the board in an almost dictatorial manner. After 1947, Film Polski was headed by Stanisław Albrecht and operated within the newly formed Ministry of Culture and Arts (Ministerstwo Kultury i Sztuki), which replaced the Ministry of Information and Propaganda.

Following the Soviet example, the Polish communist government paid particular attention to the "cinefication" (kinofikacja) of rural areas by building new cinema theaters and creating mobile cinemas (kina objazdowe). The ambitions of the communist government and Film Polski were very high, yet very few feature films were made within the first ten years after the war. No feature films were released in 1945–1946, largely due to censorship and the impossibility of dealing with certain sensitive issues, such as the 1944 Warsaw Rising and the role of the underground Home Army (AK).[6]

Poland after Auschwitz

Several published works, while justly stressing some anti-Semitic attitudes in Poland during and after the war, typically provide a one-dimensional picture of the Polish postwar reality that is often not substantiated by serious archival research. Less common works, such as Michael Steinlauf's insightful *Bondage to the Dead: Poland and the Memory of the Holocaust*, offer a nuanced analysis of the history of Polish-Jewish relations after 1945 by stressing a unique nature of the conflict, deeply rooted in history, and taking into account the complexity of Polish-Jewish relations during and immediately after the war.[7]

Despite the recent opening of archives in Poland and other countries in the region (referred to as "opening Pandora's Box"[8]), the history of the Holocaust and the postwar Polish-Jewish relations still pose a number of problems for scholars and require more extensive research. "We don't have a history of the Holocaust that is set in the Eastern European lands where the victims died, and that describes the interactions of the German invaders, the Jewish inhabitants, and the peoples among whom the Jews lived," writes Timothy Snyder.[9] Given the importance of Poland and the whole region for Holocaust Studies, scholars seems to agree, regardless of their political, ethnic, and other possible differences, that the postwar period should be re-conceptualized in new terms. According to the American-Polish historian Marek Jan Chodakiewicz, it is essential to get rid of the "Stalinist framework" that earlier had prevented scholars from considering "other factors behind anti-Jewish violence besides anti-Semitism." He writes in the introduction to his 2003 book, *After the Holocaust*, that Soviet criminal policy, in particular the magnitude of Soviet terror after 1944, is "left unresearched" and rarely debated in the context of Polish-Jewish relations.[10] In a recently published decisive study, *Bloodlands: Europe between Hitler and Stalin*, Timothy Snyder pays particular attention to the complexity of "political mass murder" occurring in the territories ranging from central Poland to western Russia, and including the Baltic States, Ukraine, and Belarus. These "bloodlands," as Snyder calls the killing fields of Europe, claimed almost fourteen million victims when Hitler and Stalin were in power.[11] Sharing the above concerns, Omer Bartov forcefully argues:

> Hence the very idea that a historian could presume to write the history of the Holocaust without much knowledge of the cultures, languages, traditions, and politics of the people that was murdered, or of the peoples in whose midst the killing took place, or of the lands in which the majority of the victims had resided is truly remarkable. And yet, this is probably the single most obvious characteristic, the

most easily identifiable common denominator, of the scholarship on the Holocaust. In a certain sense, this one-sided view of the event reveals much more about the scholars involved in reconstructing it than about the nature of the event itself, although it is also related to the enormous geographical scale of this genocidal undertaking ... Generalizing assertions about gentile antisemitism or rescue, collaboration or resistance, can be found both in accusatory and in apologetic works; but systematic analyses of the triangular relationship between Jews, local gentiles, and the German perpetrators are quite rare. Testimonies and other personal accounts are normally employed as anecdotal evidence rather than being subjected to a more rigorous examination and thus, unsurprisingly, tend to sustain otherwise contradictory interpretations. The fact that the mass of the gentile population was often hardly a unified bloc, but was divided into different and not seldom conflicting ethnic groups, religious affiliations, and classes (related in large part to the differences between the urban and rural populations), is again often missed in this literature.[12]

Returning to Poland after the war, Polish Jews tried to rebuild their life, but, unlike the majority of Poles, some of them judged the forcefully imposed communist system as offering some hope for the future. The initial politics of the communist government certainly reinforced such hopes. Unlike other national minorities, Polish Jews enjoyed a short-lasting period of relative freedom after the war. They had their own political parties and cultural and educational organizations whose programs were not necessarily in line with the official communist policy. Jewish journals and newspapers were published in Polish, Yiddish, and Hebrew. The activities of Jewish organizations were coordinated by the Central Committee of Polish Jews (Centralny Komitet Żydów w Polsce, CKŻP), founded in 1944. In 1949, with the rapid Stalinization of Poland, the autonomy of Jewish organizations was abruptly terminated by the communist authorities.[13] In light of recent archival research, it would perhaps be unjust to ascribe some anti-Semitic sentiments to the Polish Communist Party (Polska Partia Robotnicza, PPR) immediately after the war. As August Grabski writes, the Jewish Faction of the PPR was the only ethnic section of the Communist Party. In its published programs and manifestoes, the Communist Party often singled out the Jewish ethnic minority as deserving special treatment due to its terrible plight during the war.[14] The communist paper *Głos Ludu* stated, in 1945, in an article commemorating the second anniversary of the Warsaw Ghetto Uprising: "Our party, the Polish Workers' Party, is proud that its military wing, the People's Guard detachments, were leading those, who on the 'Polish' side of the ghetto wall were helping the heroic defenders of the Warsaw Ghetto. Our Party, the Polish Workers Party, knows and teaches the working masses that anti-Semitism is fascism; it is the enemy of Polish people and Poland."[15]

As expected, the official policy of the Communist Party, linking anti-Semitism not only with fascism, but also with the prewar "bourgeois Poland," found its way to Polish screens in numerous films, not necessarily those dealing primarily with the Holocaust. It is discernible, for example, in Jerzy Kawalerowicz's socialist-realist classic, *Under the Phrygian Star* (*Pod gwiazdą frygijską*, 1954), a film set in the late 1930s about a peasant's son who works in a cellulose factory, gains "class consciousness," and becomes a communist activist. In a scene where workers go on strike protesting the unjust labor practices, a police agent sends two informers (later identified as nationalists) to disrupt the workers' rally and advises them: "Just in case, let it focus on the Jews." After their failed attempt to divert the attention of the striking workers by delivering an anti-Semitic tirade, they are promptly rebuked by some vigilant communist activists.

In the summer of 1946 there were approximately 245,000 Jews in Poland, mostly repatriates from the Soviet Union (157,420 according to the CKŻP figures) who, as Jaff Schatz writes, faced economic hardships, anti-Semitism, and the fact that Poland had become "a gigantic Jewish cemetery."[16] After the war, the Polish communists tried to "depict themselves as the sole protectors of the Jews, while imputing to their opponents a genocidal brand of anti-Semitism."[17] The communist regime used the postwar pogroms in Kraków (11 August 1945) and Kielce (4 July 1946) to portray the nationalist forces as anti-Semites, while emphasizing the role of the left-wing underground in helping the Jews during the war.[18] The official position of several Jewish organizations supported that policy. For example, in February 1945, the CKŻP declared that "the saved Jews will never forget help provided by friends, and often completely unknown Poles, who endangered their lives. They will also never forget criminals from the NSZ [Narodowe Siły Zbrojne/National Armed Forces] and the AK [Armia Krajowa/Home Army] who, serving the Hitlerite bandits, actively participated in murdering the defenseless Jewish population and killed the Jewish partisans."[19]

Despite equating anti-Semitism with fascism and with the opponents of the communist system, and declaring the need to fight any anti-Semitic sentiments among the Polish population, the overrepresentation of Jews in the Communist Party, and particularly in the higher echelons of the security apparatus, was a source of concern for the communist leader, Władysław Gomułka (1905–1982), a person disliked by several Jewish communist activists. (Interestingly, his wife Zofia/Liwa Szoken was from an assimilated Jewish family.) The frequent incidents of Polonization of Jewish names, which were encouraged by the Communist Party in order to blend into rather than to provoke the Polish nationalists, may testify that this was a sensitive issue.

The Jewish-Polish researcher Aleksander Smolar writes about the postwar "consolidation of two traditional stereotypes, the 'Polish-Catholic' on the one hand, the 'Judeo-Communist' on the other. Both seemed to gain credibility like never before. A Polish-Catholic was now, as always, a defender of the fatherland—with its tradition, culture, and religion—against the communist power imposed by the Soviets and exercised on their behalf by the Jews."[20] Smolar has commented on the overrepresentation of Jews (often adopting Polish names) in positions of leadership in postwar Poland, in particular in the state security apparatus. He states that the situation "seemed to be a resumption and indeed a continuation of the Soviet occupation of Eastern Poland in 1939–1941, but also a continuation of the 'cold civil war' between the 'Polish element' and the 'Jewish element,' which in the minds of right-wingers had been waged in Poland even before the war. Official posters, appearing in April 1946, read 'Honor to the heroic defenders of the ghetto,' and 'Shame to the fascist knaves of the AK army' ... To many Poles, it seemed as though the Jews had 'won.'"[21]

For many Poles, the postwar situation resembled the earlier collaboration of several Polish Jews with the Soviet regime between 17 September 1939 (the Red Army's invasion of eastern Poland) and 22 June 1941 (Nazi Germany's attack on the Soviet Union), which had greatly impacted Jewish-Polish relations during the war. As Richard C. Lukas writes in his book, symptomatically titled *Forgotten Holocaust: The Poles under German Occupation 1939–1944*, "Jews in cities and towns displayed Red flags to welcome Soviet troops, helped to disarm Polish soldiers, and filled administrative positions in Soviet occupied Poland. One report estimated that 75 percent of all the top administrative posts in the cities of Lwów, Białystok, and Łuck were in Jewish hands during the Soviet occupation. The Soviets with Jewish help shipped off the Polish intelligentsia to the depths of the Soviet Union."[22] The situation in the Soviet-occupied Polish eastern provinces strengthened the stereotype of a "pro-communist Jewish traitor," a collaborator with the Soviet aggressor.

Polish historian Krzysztof Jasiewicz carefully examined the complexity of Polish-Jewish relations in the Soviet-occupied part of Poland between 1939 and 1941. Jasiewicz's meticulous research in the Polish and former Soviet archives enabled him to see the intricacy of that period and, to a large degree, to challenge the existing stereotypes, for example concerning the number of Polish Jews actively engaged in pro-Soviet activities. In his opinion, the collaboration with the Soviets was widespread among the different ethnic groups involved.[23] However, his most recent book in Polish, *The Soviet Reality 1939–1941 in the Testimonies of Polish Jews* (2009), clearly demonstrates that anti-Jewish feelings and pogroms that occurred after June 1941 should be treated as Polish responses to the extensive Jewish collaboration with the Soviets.[24]

There are also published studies that have been offering a somewhat different picture from that of a non-loyal Polish citizen of Jewish descent—works emphasizing the participation of Polish Jews in the 1939 September campaign and their losses as soldiers and officers fighting in the Polish army. These studies accentuate that Polish officers of Jewish origin shared a similar fate after their capture by the Soviets. According to Simon Schochet, among the approximately 22,000 Polish officers that were murdered on Stalin's order by the Soviet NKVD at Katyń and other camps, between 700 and 800 were of Jewish origin. Among them was the chief rabbi of the Polish armed forces, Major Baruch Steinberg, as well as several high-ranked officers whose careers began during World War I.[25]

Most historians, however, agree that the Jewish-Polish communists who survived the war in the Soviet Union were visibly overrepresented in the leadership of the Communist Party, in the government, and in the oppressive state security apparatus—Urząd Bezpieczeństwa (UB), an extension of the Soviet secret police. During the postwar years, the Jews and people of Jewish origin made up no more than 1 percent of Poland's population, but they comprised 37.1 percent of the higher strata of the feared Ministry of Public Security (Ministerstwo Bezpieczeństwa Publicznego, MBP).[26] The examination of the personal files of top functionaries of the Polish security apparatus by a group of researchers affiliated with the Institute of National Remembrance (Instytut Pamięci Narodowej) in Warsaw concluded that between 1944 and 1954 the security apparatchiks consisted mostly of Poles (chiefly prewar communists and members of the communist armed organizations during the war) at 59.1 percent, while Jews accounted for 37.1 percent (34.5 percent between 1954 and 1956), and Soviet officers 10.2 percent.[27] The Polish security force was trained by the Soviets and formed an integral part of the Soviet security apparatus. Between 1944 and 1956, not only the Polish security apparatus, but also virtually every aspect of political life was tightly controlled by Soviet advisers, usually the high ranking officers.

The high number of functionaries of Jewish origin in the postwar security apparatus is a highly controversial topic to this day, and helped strengthen the stereotypical negative image of the so-called Żydokomuna (Judeo-Communism/Judeo-Bolshevism), a Jewish-communist conspiracy blamed for the imposition of the Stalinist rule in post-1945 Poland, a stereotype that certainly was not a Polish invention but had functioned earlier in Europe and America. The actions of several infamous names of high-ranking security officers, such as Julia Brystiger, Anatol Fejgin, Józef Różański (Goldberg), and Józef Światło (Izak Fleischfarb), contributed to that stereotype. The presence of Jewish communists was also visible in the higher cadres of the PPR and then, after the incorporation of the Polish Socialist Party (Polska Partia Socjalistyczna, PPS) in December 1948, in the Polish United Workers' Party (Polska Zjednoczona Partia Robotnicza, PZPR). The PPR leader, Paweł Finder (1904–1944), who was killed during the occupation by the Germans, was Jewish. Also Jewish were two Polish Stalinists, Jakub Berman (1901–1984), responsible for ideology and security, and Hilary Minc (1905–1974), in charge of the economy, both leading figures in postwar Poland before their dismissal in 1956.[28]

Discussing the postwar situation in Poland, Joanna Michlic rightly points out that this state of affairs, "the presence of Polish Jews like Minc, Berman, and Zambrowski in high state and party positions in the early postwar period must have been seemed to many ethnic Poles a 'reversal of the natural order.' The presence of Jews in post-1945 government positions constituted a sharp contrast with the 'natural order' of the prewar period. In pre-1939 Poland, among six hundred persons who held high diplomatic and governmental positions, no more than two were ethnically Jewish."[29] Władysław Bartoszewski, the wartime member of Żegota, the Polish Council for Aid to the Jews, writes about "the public activity of those Jewish communists who played an important role in the security apparatus, at a time when the majority of Polish society was inclined to see this activity as pursued in the direct interests of the USSR." He emphasizes, however, that "there was a dangerous, and morally absolutely unacceptable tendency to blame the Jews in Poland *en masse* for the complete suppression of human rights by the new authorities and for the misfortune of the nation which felt it had lost its independence, despite nominally winning the war against Germany as one of the Allies."[30] The researchers affiliated with the Institute of National Remembrance (IPN) appropriately conclude that "it would be a considerable simplification to treat the Jewish nationals working in the security apparatus as one group, unified and maintaining its national identity. Those people considered themselves as primarily communists. Many, which is documented in their own biographies, considered themselves also as Poles, trying not to remember about their Jewish roots. Some of them learned about their Jewish origin as late as in 1968."[31]

Kinor

In postwar Poland there were several attempts to document Jewish life and to confront the Holocaust by the remaining Jewish filmmaking community. Producers Saul and Izak Goskind, director Natan Gross, and the camera operator brothers Adolf and Władysław Forbert tried to seek the help of the head of Film Polski, Aleksander Ford, whom they had known since before the war (Saul produced two films directed by Ford). Despite Ford's Jewish origin (his true name was Mosze Lifszyc[32]), and his prewar interests in Jewish political and cultural affairs, he was reluctant to offer support. According to Natan Gross, Ford responded in the following way when asked by Saul Goskind for help: "What do you need Jewish films for? There are no Jews anymore."[33]

Not disheartened by Ford's negative stance, in 1947 the Jewish filmmaking community secured the help of the American Joint Distribution Committee for the Aid of Jews (simply known as Joint) and the CKŻP. With Ford's eventual approval, they re-established the cooperative Kinor (an abbreviation of *Kino-Organizacja*/Cinema-Organization). Working with a small budget, the Goskinds and their friends started to produce short films in Yiddish about Jewish issues, capturing on film several important events happening in postwar Warsaw, such as the uncovering of Emmanuel Ringelblum's archives and the ceremony of the handing over of Torah scrolls that had survived the destruction of the Warsaw Ghetto. The filmmakers also recorded the funeral of the victims of the 1946 anti-Semitic pogrom in Kielce along with numerous images of the surviving Polish Jews returning home. They also captured various cultural events on camera, including the visit of an American Yiddish cinema star, Molly Picon, known for her work in prewar classics made by Joseph Green in Poland, such as *Yiddle with His Fiddle* (*Yidl mitn fidl*, 1936).

Several of Kinor's documentary fragments were later used in a full-length film, *We Are Still Alive* (*Mir, lebngeblibene*, 1947), produced by Saul Goskind, directed by Gross, and photographed by the Forbert brothers. The film acknowledges the horrors of the near past but focuses on the present situation. As Ira Konigsberg emphasizes in his illuminating account titled "*Our Children and the Limits of Cinema: Early Jewish Responses to the Holocaust*," *We Are Still Alive* "almost seems to be arguing that a better Poland is the result of the past horrors," and "buys into the utopianism of Poland's movement toward a Communist state ... Jewish workers feel wanted in the new Poland, we are told, and are working together with Poles to produce civilization acceptable to both." That reconciliatory tone of the film, argues Konigsberg, was "a vision that was all too utopian: anti-Semitism was still very much a part of Poland and the documentary was not approved for screening by the Polish government."[34]

While agreeing with Konigsberg's perceptive comments and not denying the anti-Semitic sentiments of several Poles, one can nevertheless raise several points pertinent to the issue. First, due to the geopolitical situation, several other films made during the postwar period, both documentary and narrative works, experienced similar treatment. All scripts were subjected to severe criticism and endless rewrites. Others were produced and immediately shelved. For example, *Two Hours* (*Dwie godziny*), directed by Stanisław Wohl and Józef Wyszomirski, was made in 1946, but did not have its premiere until 1957. There were also frequent cases of films released in heavily re-edited versions, as it happened, for example, with Jerzy Zarzycki's *Unvanquished City* (*Miasto nieujarzmione*, 1950, see chapter 6). Second, in the developing political climate of the cold war, the participation of a philanthropic Jewish organization, Joint, in the Kinor activities proved to be difficult to accept by the state authorities. In 1950, the actions of Joint in Poland were terminated after the accusation of spying, a charge often used during Stalinist times. Third, the underfunded Kinor proved to be a success compared to the feeble Film Polski. Natan Gross comments that there was some jealousy involved on the part of the Film Polski authorities. They wanted to "hide the fact that the Jews were able to produce films, while the state production company faced big difficulties, mostly of political nature."[35]

In 1948, Saul Goskind produced the first postwar narrative film in Yiddish, and the first narrative film made in Poland about the Holocaust, *Our Children* (*Unzere Kinder*), once again directed by Gross and with the participation of two comic actors, Szymon Dzigan and Israel Szumacher, who had returned to Poland earlier that year from the Soviet Union. In the film, Dzigan and Szumacher perform their prewar numbers for a group of Jewish orphans, who do not appreciate the references to the occupation. Later, the comedians perform once again, this time in the orphanage, and their performance brings back tragic war memories. The film was not approved for general screening by the Polish authorities and was shown in Poland only once, at a closed screening for invited guests. It premiered in Tel Aviv in 1951. For Konigsberg, *Our Children* serves as the first film to "confront the issue of whether the Holocaust is a suitable subject for art":

In light of the enormous evil that had been unleashed against the Jews, the film asks whether remembering is beneficial and whether it is even possible to deal with this subject in art … In raising these questions so soon after the Holocaust, the film provides important insights into the thinking and spiritual state of the Jews in Poland immediately after the war. But, in its inability, ultimately, to confront the reality of the past, the film also announces the decades of silence that are to follow.[36]

After the creation of the state of Israel in 1948 and the implementation of Stalinist restrictions on cinema in 1949, there was no place for Kinor in communist Poland. The majority of its members, including the Goskind brothers and Natan Gross, emigrated to Israel.[37]

First Polish Premieres

Leonard Buczkowski's *Forbidden Songs* (*Zakazane piosenki*, 1947) is generally regarded as the first postwar Polish film. It was made by a group of leading prewar filmmakers: directed by Buczkowski, who had made nine feature films before the war, scripted by Ludwik Starski, and photographed by the experienced Adolf Forbert. This film fulfilled the expectations of Polish audiences and had 10.8 million viewers within the first three years of its release (the average attendance at the time was high, at five million viewers per film). Today, *Forbidden Songs* remains one of the most popular Polish films ever, with fifteen million total viewers. This episodic film narrates an anthology of songs popular in Warsaw during the occupation. Although well liked by audiences, *Forbidden Songs* was reproached by communist authorities and film critics for its lack of political involvement and for the stereotyped and false picture of the occupation it projected. As a result, it was taken off the screens, remade, and then re-released in 1948. The new version embraced stronger political views and portrayed a darker picture of the occupation (with an emphasis on German brutality), stressed the role of the Red Army in the "liberation" of Warsaw, and provided better developed psychological motivation for the characters' actions.

Among its various subplots and characters, *Forbidden Songs* also depicts the first postwar Jewish character in a Polish narrative film. In one of the film's best episodes, which is also present in the 1947 version of the film, Henryk Szweizer plays a nameless Jew who has been hiding on the Aryan side of the ghetto wall for almost two years (Figure 1.1). He says to his friendly Polish neighbor that "good people" are helping him. "Without them I would starve to death," he adds. In a different scene, he approaches the window of his apartment to look at a young female Jewish singer in the courtyard (Zofia Mrozowska), an escapee from the ghetto who is singing a poignant song about "My Warsaw" ("Warszawo ma") (Figures 1.2, 1.3, and 1.4). While she sings, the presence of the hiding Jew is discovered by a female *Volksdeutsch* (ethnic German living in Poland).[38] She reports him to a Polish policeman. The next scene, short and deprived of dialogue, shows the hiding man being blackmailed. For her deeds, the

Figure 1.1: Henryk Szweizer as a Jew in hiding in *Forbidden Songs* (1947)

Figure 1.2: *Forbidden Songs*. Henryk Szweizer

Volksdeutsch is later killed by a Polish underground unit. Although uneven, and chiefly remembered in Poland for being the first postwar film, *Forbidden Songs* contains some outstanding scenes. The song "My Warsaw," with lyrics by Ludwik Starski, performed to the melody of a famous prewar song "Mein Shtetele Belz/ Miasteczko Bełż" is such an example. In Mrozowska's masterful interpretation, the song and the scene are among the most memorable in Polish cinema.

Like *Forbidden Songs*, other postwar Polish films also dealt primarily with the war. Mostly due to political censorship, some projects were either not released or had their premieres delayed, for example *Dead Track* (*Ślepy tor*, aka *Powrót*, 1948/1991), directed by Czech filmmaker Boživoj Zeman, and *Two Hours*, directed by Józef Wyszomirski and Stanisław Wohl (who was also responsible for the expressionistic cinematography). In the melodramatic *Dead Track*, a concentration camp survivor, Elżbieta Gruszecka (Irena Eichlerówna), returns home and searches for her missing child. Scripted by Adam Ważyk, the film did not meet the expectations of the film authorities and was never theatrically released due to heavy criticism at the 1949 Congress of Filmmakers at Wisła.

Two Hours, a panoramic view of the traumatized and demoralized postwar Polish society, is more interesting in the context of the present book. This

Figure 1.3: Zofia Mrozowska as a Jewish street singer in *Forbidden Songs*

Figure 1.4: Zofia Mrozowska in *Forbidden Songs*

episodic film is set in a small town and its screen time matches the actual time, two evening hours from 9 P.M. to 11 P.M.[39] The film opens with a scene on a train coming from Germany to Poland with several ex-prisoners returning home from labor camps and concentration camps. Some passengers are still wearing striped camp attire, a recurrent image throughout the film. As in two other popular films from that period, *Forbidden Songs* and *Treasure* (*Skarb*, 1949), the viewer meets a young lead couple, played by Danuta Szaflarska and Jerzy Duszyński. More noteworthy, however, are the characters who cannot put their camp past behind them: the former *Kapo* from Majdanek, Filip (Władysław Hańcza), and his brutalized victim, the shoemaker Leon (Jacek Woszczerowicz), who is most probably Jewish, although his nationality is never clearly defined (Figure 1.5). *Kapo* Filip is introduced in the opening scene when he throws another prisoner who recognized him off the moving train. Visibly disturbed, Leon is haunted by images of Majdanek where he had been assigned to search for gold in victims' shoes. In one scene, addressing two little girls, he relives his camp experience by telling them a tale: "From afar, from the east, from the west, under the cover of night, people came to this huge square. They didn't want it—who would have wanted it. They had to come ... And there was a stinking smoke in the air. The sweet stench of death. To meet death one has to go barefoot. The shoes stay behind. And later those old, damaged shoes were turned into brand new shoes for the murderers. I did it myself." In the film's highly dramatic final scenes, Leon kills the *Kapo*, while his wife gives birth to their son.

The film's dark messages, expressionistic look, and stylized acting of Woszczerowicz and Hańcza prevail over the optimistic message of "living against all odds," intended by the film's original writer Ewa Szelburg-Zarembina. This happens despite the recurrent musical motif, a song stressing in a joking manner that "whatever will be, will be." When the film was released in 1957, it was barely noticed by critics and viewers, who were at that time embracing new cinematic approaches to the war offered by Andrzej Wajda, Andrzej Munk, and Kazimierz Kutz.

Polish films with references to the war and concentration camps and featuring camp survivors attempting to rebuild their lives represented the main trend of

Figure 1.5: Jewish shoemaker Leon (Jacek Woszczerowicz) in *Two Hours* (1946/1957)

Polish postwar cinema. These films were deprived of direct references to the plight of Polish Jews, although some of them featured Jewish characters. For example, among the characters in Antoni Bohdziewicz's war drama, *Others Will Follow* (*Za wami pójdą inni*, 1949), is a hiding Warsaw Jew, Jakub (Józef Kostecki), an escapee from the ghetto. Two major films released in the late 1940s, Wanda Jakubowska's *The Last Stage* (*Ostatni etap*, 1948) and Aleksander Ford's *Border Street* (*Ulica Graniczna*, 1949), established images that influenced the way subsequent filmmakers looked at Auschwitz and the Warsaw Ghetto Uprising.

Notes

1. Portions of the first paragraphs were previously published in my *Polish National Cinema* (New York: Berghahn Books, 2002). That book contains chapters dealing with the postwar situation, socialist-realist cinema, and the Polish School phenomenon, among other topics.
2. For a book-length discussion about Polish filmmakers during World War II see, for example, Stanisław Ozimek, *Film polski w wojennej potrzebie* (Warsaw: Państwowy Instytut Wydawniczy, 1974) and Stanisław Jewsiewicki, *Polscy filmowcy na frontach II wojny światowej* (Warsaw: Państwowy Instytut Wydawniczy, 1972). For detailed biographies of filmmakers in English see my *Historical Dictionary of Polish Cinema* (Lanham: Scarecrow Press, 2007) and a Polish source by Jerzy Maśnicki and Kamil Stepan, *Pleograf: Słownik biograficzny filmu polskiego 1896–1939* (Kraków: Staromiejska Oficyna Wydawnicza, 1996).
3. Norman Davies, *Heart of Europe: A Short History of Poland* (New York: Oxford University Press, 1984), 104.
4. Alina Madej, "100 lat kina w Polsce: 1938–1945," *Kino* 4 (1998): 50.
5. Alina Madej writes that the main UFA studio was captured by the Soviets. The Polish emissaries seized film materials from small private companies. Ibid., 50.
6. For the sake of clarity, I will be referring to the 1944 Polish Warsaw Uprising (Powstanie Warszawskie) as the Warsaw Rising. The 1943 Jewish uprising in the Warsaw Ghetto will be discussed as the Warsaw Ghetto Uprising.
7. Michael C. Steinlauf, *Bondage to the Dead. Poland and the Memory of the Holocaust* (Syracuse: Syracuse University Press, 1997).
8. Omer Bartov's label for the opening of archives in Eastern Europe in his in-depth study "Eastern Europe as the Site of Genocide," *Journal of Modern History* vol. 80, no. 3 (2008): 566.
9. Timothy Snyder, "What We Need to Know about the Holocaust," *The New York Review of Books* 14 (September 30, 2010): 76.
10. Marek Jan Chodakiewicz, *After the Holocaust: Polish-Jewish Conflict in the Wake of World War II* (Boulder: East European Monographs, 2003), 9.
11. Timothy Snyder, *Bloodlands: Europe between Hitler and Stalin* (New York: Basic Books, 2010), vii–viii.
12. Bartov, "Eastern Europe as the Site of Genocide," 561–562.
13. Grzegorz Berendt, August Grabski, and Albert Stankowski, *Studia z Historii Żydów w Polsce po 1945 r.* (Warsaw: Żydowski Instytut Historyczny, 2000), 9, 67.
14. August Grabski's chapter, "Kształtowanie się pierwotnego programu żydowskich komunistów w Polsce po Holokauście," in Berendt, Grabski, and Stankowski, *Studia z Historii Żydów w Polsce po 1945 r.*, 68–70.
15. Quoted from Grabski, ibid., 70. Originally published in *Głos Ludu* (19 April 1945). As Lucy S. Dawidowicz writes, however, communist historiography neglected to stress that "several GL unit leaders were Jews passing as 'Aryans' and that their participation in these forays could scarcely be characterized as help rendered by the Poles to the Jews." Lucy Dawidowicz, *The Holocaust and the Historians* (Cambridge: Harvard University Press, 1981), 105.

16. Jaff Schatz, *The Generation: The Rise and Fall of the Jewish Communists of Poland* (Berkeley: University of California Press, 1991), 203.
17. Chodakiewicz, *After the Holocaust*, 2. The practice of associating anti-Semitism with the opponents of communism had been initiated by the Polish communist press during the war. See Peter Klaus Friedrich, "Nazistowski mord na Żydach w prasie polskich komunistów (1942-1944)," *Zagłada Żydów: Studia i Materiały* 2 (2006): 54-75.
18. For more information about the Kraków pogrom, see Anna Cichopek, *Pogrom Żydów w Krakowie 11 sierpnia 1945 r.* (Warsaw: Żydowski Instytut Historyczny, 2000). The Kielce pogrom is discussed by Bożena Szaynok, *Pogrom w Kielcach 4 lipca 1946* (Wrocław: Bellona, 1992).
19. August Grabski, *Żydowski ruch kombatancki w Polsce w latach 1944-1949* (Warsaw, 2002), 21. Quoted from: Dariusz Libionka, "Polskie piśmiennictwo na temat zorganizowanej i indywidualnej pomocy Żydom (1945-2008)," *Zagłada Żydów: Studia i Materiały* 4 (2008): 18.
20. Aleksander Smolar, "Jews as a Polish Problem," *Daedalus* 116, no. 2 (1987): 50.
21. Ibid., 50.
22. Richard C. Lukas, *Forgotten Holocaust: The Poles under German Occupation 1939-1944* (New York: Hippocrene Books, 2005), 128. See also Jan T. Gross, *Revolution from Abroad: The Soviet Conquest of Poland's Western Ukraine and Western Belorussia* (Princeton: Princeton University Press, 1988), 29, 31-33.
23. Krzysztof Jasiewicz, *Pierwsi po diable: Elity sowieckie w okupowanej Polsce, 1939-1941* (Warsaw: Rytm and Instytut Studiów Politycznych PAN, 2002). Also, Jasiewicz's *Tygiel narodów: Stosunki społeczne i etniczne na dawnych ziemiach wschodnich Rzeczpospolitej 1939-1953* (Warsaw: Instytut Studiów Politycznych PAN, 2002).
24. Krzysztof Jasiewicz, *Rzeczywistość sowiecka 1939-1941 w świadectwach polskich Żydów* (Warsaw: Rytm, 2009).
25. Simon Schochet, "Polish Jewish Officers Who Were Killed in Katyń: An Ongoing Investigation in Light of Documents Recently Released by the USSR," in *The Holocaust in the Soviet Union: Studies and Sources on the Destruction of the Jews in the Nazi-Occupied Territories of the USSR, 1941-1945*, ed. Lucjan Dobroszycki and Jeffrey S. Gurock (Armonk: M.E. Sharpe, 1993): 238 and 243. See also Beniamin Majerczak (Benjamin Meirtchack), *Żydzi—żołnierze wojsk polskich polegli na frontach II wojny światowej* (Warsaw: Dom Wydawniczy Bellona, 2001).
26. Krzysztof Szwagrzyk, ed., *Aparat bezpieczeństwa w Polsce. Kadra kierownicza 1944-1956* (Warsaw: Instytut Pamięci Narodowej, 2005), 59.
27. See Szwagrzyk, ed., *Aparat bezpieczeństwa w Polsce*, 59. Also 53-54 and 61-62. These figures vary in several studies published earlier. For example, Krystyna Kersten states that in November 1945, Polish Jews accounted for only 13 percent of the prominent functionaries in the security apparatus. Krystyna Kersten, *Polacy. Żydzi. Komunizm. Anatomia półprawd, 1939-1968* (Warsaw: Niezależna Oficyna Wydawnicza, 1992), 81.
28. The stereotype of the communist Jew also functioned in Poland before World War II. The overrepresentation of Polish Jews in the Communist Party of Poland (KPP) was used by the right-wing political forces to identify Jews as communist agents. For example, in 1937 Warsaw, Poles of Jewish origin constituted a clear majority with 806 members out of 1,215 in the KPP. After the dissolution of the KPP in 1938 by Stalin and the subsequent purges, several Jewish communists perished in the Soviet Union. Piotr Wróbel, "An NKVD Residentura (Residency) in the Warsaw Ghetto, 1941-42," in *Secret Intelligence and the Holocaust*, ed. David Bankier (New York: Enigma Books, 2006), 252. See also Stefan Korboński's chapter, "The Jews in Postwar Poland" in his *The Jews and the Poles in World War II* (New York: Hippocrene Books, 1989), 71-86.
29. Joanna Michlic, *Poland's Threatening Other: The Image of the Jew from 1880 to the Present* (Lincoln: University of Nebraska Press, 2006), 201.
30. Władysław Bartoszewski, "The Founding of the All-Polish Anti-Racist League in 1946," *Polin* 4 (1989): 245.
31. Szwagrzyk, ed., *Aparat bezpieczeństwa w Polsce*, 63.

32. Natan Gross, *Film żydowski w Polsce* (Kraków: Rabid, 2002), 12.
33. Ibid., 118. This fragment relies on Gross' first-hand account, 118-133.
34. Ira Konigsberg, "*Our Children* and the Limits of Cinema: Early Jewish Responses to the Holocaust," *Film Quarterly* vol. 52, no. 1 (1998): 12.
35. Gross, *Film żydowski w Polsce*, 131. The banning of a film sometimes had to do with the rapidly changing internal political situation. This happened, for example, with the 1948 documentary, *Der finfter jorcajt fun ojfsztand in warszewer geto* (*The Fifth Anniversary of the Warsaw Ghetto Uprising*), banned because it featured a speech by a Polish General, Marian Spychalski (1906-1980), who in 1949 was removed from his position and imprisoned. This thirty-minute film was scripted and directed by Natan Gross, photographed by Adolf Forbert, and produced by Saul Goskind for Kinor. See Gross, 125-126.
36. Konigsberg, "*Our Children* and the Limits of Cinema," 13.
37. Jewish life and culture during the Stalinist period is discussed, among others, by Grzegorz Berendt, *Życie żydowskie w Polsce: Z dziejów Towarzystwa Kulturalnego Żydów w Polsce* (Gdańsk: Wydawnictwo Uniwersytetu Gdańskiego, 2006).
38. *Volksdeutsch* is a complex term basically referring to ethnic Germans. During the war (and even to this day) this word is synonymous in Poland with "traitor" or "treason."
39. One of the earlier versions of *Two Hours* was titled *From 9 pm to 11 pm* (*Od 9-tej do 11-tej*). Due to ideological pressures, the length of the final version, released in 1957, was reduced to a mere 68 minutes. Protesting the changes, the film's co-scriptwriter, Ewa Szelburg-Zarembina, withdrew her name from the credits. Her letter is published in *Film* 4 (1946): 2, and was reprinted in other Polish magazines. See Tadeusz Lubelski's discussion in his *Strategie autorskie w polskim filmie fabularnym lat 1945-1961* (Kraków: Universitas, 1992): 65-71.

Chapter 2

WANDA JAKUBOWSKA'S RETURN TO AUSCHWITZ: THE LAST STAGE (1948)

In her landmark film, *The Last Stage* (*Ostatni etap*, also known under the title *The Last Stop*, 1948), Wanda Jakubowska (1907–1998) depicted the monstrosity of *Konzentrationslager Auschwitz-Birkenau* and drew on her firsthand experiences to portray the "factory of death." With its dramatization of the camp experience, *The Last Stage* established several images easily discernible in later Holocaust narratives: the dark, "realistic" images of the camp (the film was shot in Auschwitz-Birkenau); the passionate moralistic appeal; and the clear divisions between victims and victimizers.[1]

In film criticism, *The Last Stage* is often discussed as "the mother of all Holocaust films,"[2] which "provided a model for other numerous, ideologically oriented representations of victimhood and heroism under Nazi rule."[3] In addition, Jakubowska's name is almost exclusively associated with this work, despite the fact that she directed thirteen feature films, and her career spanned almost fifty years. In historical accounts on Polish film, *The Last Stage* also marks the birth of the Polish post-1945 cinema (although it was the third film released in People's Poland), and was received as such after its much-anticipated premiere on 28 March 1948.[4] With more than 7.8 million viewers, the film is number thirty on the list of the biggest box-office successes on Polish screens from 1945 to 2000, and it was exported to dozens of countries.[5] (See Figure 2.1.)

The Last Stage opens with a brief, quasi-documentary pre-credit scene of a German raid on a Warsaw street, which results in the arrest of several people, including one of the film's leading characters, Helena (Wanda Bartówna). Another scene, over the credits, moves the action to Auschwitz by portraying a train loaded with Polish Jews arriving at the camp. Throughout *The Last Stage* Jakubowska depicts the nightmarish conditions in Auschwitz—recurrent roll calls, random executions and selections, images of powerless people being herded to the gas chambers, and the terrifying efficiency of Auschwitz run by SS guards and camp administrators, both groups portrayed as the embodiment of evil. The filmmaker's objective, however, is not so much to portray the repelling reality of the concentration camp, as it is to show the women's solidarity in their suffering as well as in their struggle against fascism. Jakubowska focuses on carefully chosen female inmates, mostly communists

Figure 2.1: Wanda Jakubowska on the set of *The Last Stage*. Courtesy Filmoteka Narodowa in Warsaw

and supporters of the communist resistance in the camp, who represent different oppressed nationalities and groups of people. The Auschwitz Babel of tongues (Polish, German, Russian, French, Romany, and Serbian are all spoken on screen—but no Yiddish) is chiefly represented by the following characters: a Russian physician Eugenia (Tatjana Górecka) and a nurse Nadia (Maria Winogradowa); a German nurse Anna (Antonina Górecka); a Polish woman Helena (Wanda Bartówna) who lost her newborn baby in the camp; a French patriot Michele (Huguette Faget); a Jewish-Polish interpreter Marta (Barbara Drapińska); a Serb prisoner of war (POW) Dessa (Alina Janowska); and a Gypsy singer (Zofia Mrozowska). (See Figures 2.2 and 2.3.)

The film was scripted by Jakubowska and another Auschwitz survivor, German communist Gerda Schneider.[6] Jakubowska was captured by the Gestapo in 1942, spent six months in the infamous Pawiak prison in Warsaw, and then, from 28 April 1943 to 18 January 1945, was incarcerated in the women's concentration camp at Auschwitz-Birkenau. Her camp number was 43513. For the remaining months of the war she was imprisoned at Ravensbrück.

As stated by Jakubowska on several occasions, she was thinking about a film documenting her camp experience while still at Auschwitz: "The decision to make a film about Auschwitz originated as soon as I crossed the camp's gate."[7] She started working on the script immediately after the war and finished the first draft in December 1945. For her, this was a personal duty as a camp survivor and as a filmmaker to bear witness to history and to register the enormity of evil.[8] In addition, the making of this film became an almost

Figure 2.2: Wanda Jakubowska's *The Last Stage* (1948). (From the left) Serb Dessa (Alina Janowska), German Anna (Antonina Górecka), Polish Helena (Wanda Bartówna), and Russian Nadia (Maria Winogradowa)

Figure 2.3: (From the left) Tatjana Górecka (Russian Doctor), Stefan Śródka (Bronek), Antonina Górecka (Anna), and Wanda Bartówna (Helena)

therapeutic endeavor on the part of Jakubowska, as revealed in the very title of an interview with her, published after the film's premiere: "I Remained in the Camp until 1948."[9]

Jakubowska intended her film to be based exclusively on authentic events (a fact stressed in a commentary at the beginning of the film) that were witnessed either by herself or by her fellow inmates. To reflect the reality of the camp appropriately, she decided to produce her film, initially named just *Oświęcim* (*Auschwitz*), on location in Auschwitz. She made the film with the participation of the local population (the inhabitants of the town of Oświęcim) and Red Army personnel, also making use of German prisoners of war as extras.[10] Several episodic roles were played by the camp's former inmates, for example Elżbieta Łabuńska, who in a sense were forced to relive their Auschwitz experiences. According to Jerzy Kawalerowicz, an assistant director on Jakubowska's film (and later one of the leading Polish directors), these actresses "were wiser than all assistant directors; they knew everything from experience. They saw it. Those former inmates were returning to their places."[11] Moreover, the majority of the film's crew had survived the terror of the occupation in Poland, were knowledgeable about the history of the camps, and some also experienced incarceration in concentration camps, as was the case of the set designer Czesław Piaskowski.

The postwar appearance of Auschwitz-Birkenau had little to do with the images that Jakubowska carefully preserved in her memory and wanted to portray on the screen: heavy smoke over the crematorium, ever-present mud, and shabby barracks surrounded by barbed wire. After the war, the former Nazi camp Auschwitz-Birkenau came under the supervision of the underfunded Ministry of Culture and Art, administered by a group of Polish former prisoners. The place was routinely vandalized; the rumors about hidden valuables attracted plunderers from outside. A lesser-known aspect of Auschwitz, only recently documented by historians but important for the preservation of the site, was the fact that parts of it were used by the Soviet troops, and then by the Polish army for at least a year, as a concentration camp for German prisoners of war, *Volksdeutsche*, and civilians from Silesia. For many of them, Auschwitz served as an internment center before deportations to Soviet gulags and slave labor.[12] In his important contribution to our knowledge about those early days of Auschwitz-Birkenau museum, Jonathan Huener writes that,

> To the Polish government, to former prisoners working at the site, and to the Polish public at large, Auschwitz *was* a "sacred space;" yet the size, character, and remaining "evidence" of what had transpired there was subject to legal, political, and, not least, financial limitations. The Birkenau barracks, for example, were not always the victims of plunder. Eighteen of them were sold to members of the local population in July 1946, with each barracks divided among five villagers ... The dismantling of artifacts such as these reveals the perceived, or perhaps genuine, inability of the Polish state to preserve and protect much of what was left of the Auschwitz camp complex, and also illustrates even more graphically what appear today as rather reckless, if practical, measures taken by the local population in a period of extreme material want.[13]

Conflicting ideas about the future of the camp site and the chronic lack of funds to maintain the vast grounds of the memorial site resulted in a deterioration of the camp, of Birkenau (Auschwitz II) in particular. The decision issued on 2 July 1947 by the Polish parliament declared the site of the former concentration camp at Auschwitz-Birkenau to be under state control, serving as "a monument to the martyrdom and struggle of the Polish and other peoples."[14] However, in the spring of 1946, Jakubowska was surprised to see a different aspect of the camp: "I was shocked because I saw daisies of monstrous proportions and exuberant, indescribable vegetation on the soil that was fertilized by blood and sweat."[15] Apart from removing the vegetation before the shooting in May of 1947, Jakubowska also restored part of the camp. On 1 October 1947 the magazine *Film* reported from the set of Jakubowska's production that the "film's crew made their home in the former SS quarters, and Wanda Jakubowska decided to stay in the house belonging to the former commander of the camp, the recently hanged Rudolf Höss."[16] This same report also contained information about the German POWs who volunteered to appear in the film: "It is worth seeing how the self-effacing German POWs, when they obtain the almost new SS uniforms and put them on, immediately regain their former haughtiness; they seem to be truly dangerous. First and foremost, this makes the director happy, who wants to portray the Germans the way we all know them."[17]

The idea of shooting the film on location in Auschwitz-Birkenau not only contributed to its quasi-documentary appeal but also had an enormous impact on the film's crew. For example, actress Maria Redlichówna (Urszula) states that during the making of *The Last Stage* the actors lived in the authentic barracks of Auschwitz, and their "clothes were the authentic striped clothing of prisoners that, although disinfected, still contained blood stains … The air was filled with a characteristic unpleasant smell that had a depressing effect on us."[18]

Despite Jakubowska's loyalty, which bordered on devotion, to the communist cause, and despite the theme of international solidarity, anti-fascist and pacifist messages, and the stress on the communist resistance in the camp, *The Last Stage* encountered several problems while being made. On several occasions, Jakubowska stressed that the head of Film Polski, Aleksander Ford, who was privately on friendly terms with her, proved to be an obstacle for her project. She labeled him *Tematenfresser*, a person stealing other people's ideas for his own films.[19] Also, the communist authorities in Poland were evidently afraid of similarities between the Soviet and German concentration camps, and preferred not to touch the sensitive topic.[20] According to Jakubowska, at the beginning of 1946 she went to Moscow with a forty-page long filmic novella translated into Russian and met with Mikhail Kalatozov, who was then responsible for the Soviet cinema. Several years later, at the Moscow Film Festival, she learned from Kalatozov that he cried while reading her text. Afraid, however, to support her, since this was the first film script dealing with the camps and nobody knew how to tackle the problem, Kalatozov sent the script to Andrei A. Zhdanov (who earlier, in 1934, formulated the tenets of socialist realist art). He was also deeply affected by the text and passed it on to Stalin. Stalin's personal approval (allegedly, he was also moved to tears) made it possible for Jakubowska to pursue her project. In several interviews, she hypothesized that Stalin was probably touched by the scenes in her script "showing that Soviet female prisoners in the camp were almost praying to Stalin … As a result, he realized that the topic was timely."[21] Despite the Soviet blessing, however, Jakubowska's script had been revised a number of times, and the Artistic Committee (Komisja Artystyczna) of Film Polski also sought opinions from outsiders, including political activists, writers, and former Auschwitz prisoners.

Jakubowska also faced aesthetic problems while making this first major film about the horror of Nazi concentration camps. For example, she tried to reach large audiences at the expense of naturalistic scenes. She commented that "the camp's reality was human skeletons, piles of dead bodies, lice, rats, and various disgusting diseases. On the screen, this reality would certainly cause dread and repulsion. It was necessary to eliminate those elements which, although authentic and typical, were unbearable for the postwar viewer."[22] For this reason, Jakubowska tried to avoid explicit imagery and, instead, appealed to the viewer's knowledge of the mechanisms of death camps. For example, frequent shots of smoke and the flames indicate rather than depict the true nature of the "factory of death"—the extermination process. In one scene, the camera tracks over the piles of belongings left after one of the Jewish transports. In another scene, Jakubowska cuts from an image of Jewish children walking toward the crematorium, unaware of their fate, to an image of burning grass and the SS men returning to their barracks. Explicit scenes showing the brutality of the camp are employed sporadically, such as the execution of a young female prisoner, who is singing a joyful song, by an SS guard. He forces her to move near the barbed wire, then arbitrarily kills her, and is rewarded for his deed with three days of leave.

While depicting Auschwitz-Birkenau, *The Last Stage* suffers from several weaknesses inherent in many later projects that aimed at re-creating the horror of the Holocaust, including the melodramatization of situations and characters due to a dependence on mainstream narrative patterns, and the use of inspiring endings. The incorporation of some Hollywood conventions is chiefly seen in the last, much-discussed scene of the film. Portrayed with a low angle shot, Marta Weiss, the heroic Polish-Jewish woman working as an interpreter in the camp and involved in the communist resistance, dies a martyr's death while warning others: "You must not let Auschwitz be repeated" (Figure 2.4). "It will not be repeated," responds Helena, who is holding her dying friend (Figure 2.5). Marta's last words are juxtaposed with the image of (presumably Soviet) planes over Auschwitz, creating havoc among the SS guards, including the lagerkommandant, who is almost ridiculed in a performance by the theatrical actor Władysław Brochwicz.[23] The pompous music by Roman Palester makes this ending even more blatantly heroic, bordering on the hysterical.

The optimistic ending, which from today's perspective looks perhaps like a mockery of happy endings ("a complete fantasy" writes Ilan Avisar[24]), was expected by audiences and encouraged by the state authorities at that time. In a private letter dated 9 April 1948, the renowned Hungarian film theorist Béla Balázs, who advised Film Polski, for political, artistic, and also, interestingly, commercial reasons, strongly suggested that Jakubowska include an optimistic ending designed chiefly for foreign viewers: "Another [after the camp orchestra] very important image must be made for the export version: for the translator should not die in the final moments. Especially since one has the impression—I myself did—that she was shot down by the Russian airplanes. As the women

Figure 2.4: Barbara Drapińska as Marta

Figure 2.5: Helena (Wanda Bartówna) and Marta (Barbara Drapińska)

must stream out into freedom, the translator must also be brought out on a stretcher with a smiling, hopeful face."[25] Despite his privately expressed reservations, in a published review, entitled "Concerning the Great Polish Auschwitz Film," Balázs stressed the documentary nature of the film ("a film of authentic photographs," "historical document") in which "the most horrible reality in mankind's history crashes over our brains and hearts as a landslide of photographed documents."[26]

Jakubowska's vision of the camp clearly differed from that portrayed in several acclaimed literary accounts published in Poland immediately after the war. This prominent group included, among others, *Medallions* (*Medaliony*, 1945) by Zofia Nałkowska (1884–1954), *Smoke over Birkenau* (*Dymy nad Birkenau*, 1945) by Seweryna Szmaglewska (1916–1992), *I Survived Auschwitz* (*Przeżyłam Oświęcim*, 1946) by Krystyna Żywulska (1914–1992), and *Farewell to Maria* (*Pożegnanie z Marią*, 1947) by Tadeusz Borowski (1922–1951).[27] In particular, this last-mentioned collection of short stories, offering a classic account of life in Auschwitz written by an eyewitness, provides no distinction between good and evil, and presents a brutal, matter-of-fact narration that is deprived of authorial commentary and uplifting messages, portraying instead all characters as infected by the devastating degeneration of human values. The factual, despairing picture by Borowski, a writer frequently accused of cynicism and moral indifference, is replaced in *The Last Stage* by the vision of human solidarity in the face of evil and the strong anti-fascist and pro-communist (pro-Stalinist) messages.

Unlike Borowski, for whom Auschwitz revealed the repulsive side of contemporary civilization, Jakubowska (who privately praised Borowski as a writer)[28] became a propagator of a different set of images that stressed dignity, solidarity, and friendship among those who suffered in the camp.[29] The author of a seminal book on Borowski, Andrzej Werner, writes that, as is typical for subjective narrations, regardless of their ideological positions, "the idealization of human relationships in the camp, if they go beyond the prisoner–perpetrator relation, results in a portrayal that becomes, in a sense, softened; as a rule, examples of solidarity, fraternity, compassion, and sacrifice are elevated."[30] Werner emphasizes that, from today's perspective, Jakubowska's film, notwithstanding its objective ("to show the truth about Auschwitz and to stir up a feeling of hatred toward fascism"), and despite the fact that it was received after its premiere as an almost documentary work, portrays not representative, but mythologized reality.[31]

In her pioneering book on Polish cinema between 1944 and 1949, Alina Madej discusses the political and cultural contexts of Jakubowska's film and explains that Borowski's representation of Auschwitz, which is deprived of martyrological and heroic gestures, "simply did not conform to the image of terrorized and suffering society," which was then expected by the authorities and audiences alike. Madej concludes her essay by saying that "*The Last Stage* became truly successful in Europe because nobody was waiting for a different truth about Nazi concentration camps."[32] Similarly to Madej, Stuart Liebman aptly summarizes the postwar political climate around 1948 that prompted the production of films such as *The Last Stage*:

> The Western Allies' efforts to rehabilitate Western Germany as a bulwark against communism and the ensuing onset of the Cold War provided the Communist-dominated regimes in Poland, East Germany, and Czechoslovakia with ideological inspiration to find ways of embarrassing the Western Allies. One particularly glaring moral lapse that could be exploited involved the Allies' lackluster denazification efforts. Films recalling and rendering palpable the horrible epicenter of Nazi evil— especially those that highlighted determined communist resistance to it—therefore offered a subtle, effective means with which to wage the propaganda battle for world opinion. The filmmakers' expressive needs and state policy converged.[33]

The proximity of the traumatic experience, Jakubowska's own Marxist beliefs, and the policy of the new communist regime trying to find its own national voice within the tightly controlled Soviet eastern bloc, all influenced the final shape of the film. At the meeting of the Commission for Film Approval (Komisja Kolaudacyjna) on 11 April 1948 in Łódź, the film was evaluated as "very good," which was the highest rating on the scale.[34] The Commission, chaired by the head of Film Polski, Stanisław Albrecht, and including film theorist Bolesław W. Lewicki (an Auschwitz survivor), applauded the film's "social usefulness." The "social usefulness" and adherence to the reigning communist ideology were also appreciated at the third Karlovy Vary International Film Festival where *The Last Stage* received the Grand Prize.

The clear divisions between good and evil, the pacifist tone of the film, combined with the use of mainstream narrative principles, contributed to the film's critical acclaim in Poland and its success at international film festivals abroad. Negative criticism of the film, rare and usually meekly voiced by the Auschwitz survivors, concerned its alleged anti-Polish bias (apart from the German staff of the camp, a few Polish characters—portrayed as inept, brutal, or both—collaborate with the Germans), and the fact that naturalism in the camp scenes was sacrificed at the altar of ideological needs and cinematic conventions. Former Auschwitz inmates also wrote about several crucial elements of the camp life that were either missing on the screen (the desperate fight for survival, the ever-present hunger and fear, and the terrible sounds of the camp), or misrepresented (the focus on the privileged—mostly political— prisoners at the expense of the struggling and dehumanized masses). Satisfied at seeing an attempt at portraying the reality of Auschwitz, some former inmates, such as Seweryna Szmaglewska, Krystyna Żywulska, and Henryk Korotyński, openly voiced, however, their reservations concerning Jakubowska's visualization of the camp.[35]

The above-mentioned Auschwitz survivors particularly singled out for emphasis the negative portrayal of several Polish characters, mostly brutal and primitive camp *Kapos*, chiefly the vicious block *Kapo* Elza (Barbara Rachwalska)

(Figure 2.6), and a pharmacist's wife who is pretending to be a doctor, "Lalunia" (Halina Drohocka). Much stronger words to describe the film were employed by a prominent Polish writer, Maria Dąbrowska, who wrote in her diary (published in 1996) that the film is clearly "anti-Polish." *The Last Stage*, according to Dąbrowska, favors the communists (Jews and Russians) at the expense of Poles who are portrayed as "depraved" and as "louts." She concluded that "ideologically, this is pro-Soviet propagandist kitsch, not a film about the tragedy of the Polish nation and not a film about Auschwitz."[36]

Despite Jakubowska's extensive research, which included interviews with some of the SS guards from Auschwitz,[37] from today's perspective the Germans are portrayed in a stereotypical manner, bordering on the grotesque—repulsive, sadistic, and lacking human qualities. Even a German child, wearing a Hitlerjunge uniform, is shouting in the presence of the commandant (and causing only laughter): "Shut up you *Muselmann* [exhausted, close to death prisoner]! Stand up in the line or you'll go through the chimney!" The only "good German" in the film, not surprisingly, is the communist political prisoner Anna, possibly modeled on the ordeal of the co-scriptwriter, Gerda Schneider (Figure 2.7). Looking at the formulaic German characters on the screen, however, one has to take into account the "Nazis" that peopled earlier European films, for example in the celebrated *Rome, Open City* (*Roma città aperta*, 1945) by Roberto Rossellini. The portrayal of the Gestapo chief, Major Bergmann (Harry Feist), also bordered on caricature, in particular when juxtaposed with the masculine, laconic communist resistance leader Giorgio Manfredi (Marcello Pagliero). It is safe to assume, however, that Jakubowska was not familiar with Rossellini's film, since it was released in Poland only in 1949.

Interestingly, in an interview with Alina Madej, Jakubowska pointed out that she insisted on working with Schneider (although in the postwar atmosphere in Poland this was an unusual and unwelcome partnership, which had to be approved at the highest level), because she wanted a proper representation of the Germans, "as it should be, not as they were represented in, for example, Soviet films, that mostly featured caricatures."[38] Another reason for Jakubowska's

Figure 2.6: Barbara Rachwalska as *Kapo* Elza

Figure 2.7: Anna (Antonina Górecka) and SS Doctor (Edward Dziewoński)

close collaboration with Schneider and her extensive postwar research had to do perhaps with the fact that she spent "only" several weeks at Birkenau before being moved to the Rajsko sub-camp of Auschwitz. Rajsko, where Jakubowska worked as a photographer, was a relatively privileged experimental agricultural branch that, among other things, was raising the kok-saghyz plant for the production of rubber.

Certainly, *The Last Stage* presents an ideologically correct version suited to the times by emphasizing the role of the Soviet army in the liberation of the camp, by stressing the role of the communist resistance in Auschwitz, and by introducing the dignified figure of a brave female Russian doctor (Figure 2.8). (According to several accounts, the brave doctor who tried to reveal the real nature of Auschwitz to the Red Cross delegation was Polish.)[39] Although not present on the screen, Stalin seems to be the true hero of the film. Female prisoners mention his name with reverence, almost religiously; he seems to be their only hope and their only protector. Despite the fact that the Soviets became the aggressors in 1939 and oppressors (not liberators) after 1945, several scenes were carefully constructed to depict an ideologically correct situation full of pro-Soviet sympathies. In one scene, Helena reads a manifesto that is circulating in the camp about "the liberation of Europe from Hitler's tyranny," and she is almost radiant when mentioning its author's name—Stalin. Other prisoners also worship the communist leader. As pointed out by several Polish scholars, one scene in particular perfectly illustrates the worship of Stalin and the communist ideology: a group of Polish inmates starts a prayer, then another group begins to sing the Polish patriotic song, "The Song of Warsaw" (Warszawianka), composed during the anti-Russian "November Uprising" of 1831, only to be silenced by the Russian women singing the Soviet war song, "Sacred War" (Vstavai strana ogromnaya! [Arise, colossal land!]), which also engages an older Polish woman, who earlier intoned a prayer.[40]

In the introduction to Jakubowska's published script, her former START colleague, Jerzy Toeplitz, wrote the following: "The value of the film lies in the ideological stand of its maker, who put her great talent and all her strength into the effort to fight fascism, to unmask its genocidal method."[41] Throughout the

Figure 2.8: Russian Doctor (Tatjana Górecka)

film, as Tadeusz Lubelski fittingly writes, the pro-Soviet attitude is forcefully imposed on the viewer, for example, by attributing anti-Soviet comments to dishonest characters collaborating with the Germans. Only negative Polish characters in the film may utter anti-Soviet comments, such as "I would prefer ten years in the camp to living under the Bolsheviks." Jakubowska, according to Lubelski, clearly favors communist agitation at the expense of the self-proclaimed "strategy of a witness."[42]

Undoubtedly, *The Last Stage* reflects more the postwar political atmosphere, and less the reality of the camp. After the film's premiere, several Polish papers published "letters from concerned viewers" that were painfully in line with the current state of affairs, such as this one: "The film shows fascism. Fascism, Auschwitz, death factories—all this is the last reserve that the capitalist system mobilizes in the moment of utmost danger ... American imperialism offers fascism a safe haven."[43]

Today, in spite of its powerful imagery, *The Last Stage* may seem archaic and artificial, in line with the official cultural policy and the dominant aesthetic modes of the late 1940s. Contemporary critics emphasize the employment of traditional cinematic conventions and the use of proper lighting and make-up not appropriate for the circumstance. Tadeusz Lubelski attributes the "overaesthetization" of several camp images to a Russian cinematographer, Boris Monastyrski, who had filmed equally "unreal" images of war in Mark Donskoi's *Rainbow* (*Raduga*, 1943).[44] When *The Last Stage* was released, however, several critics praised Monastyrski, among them writer Jalu Kurek, who called him "an artist of the camera!" and singled out for emphasis scenes with "the forest of women in striped uniforms during the penal roll call that are waving like a field of corn propelled by the wind; this is the picture of despair reaching a mystical dimension."[45] In critical appraisals of the film, often neglected is the role played by two set designers, Czesław Piaskowski, who knew the reality of the concentration camps first hand, and Roman Mann, one of the most accomplished set designers working in Polish cinema.[46]

The images of camp life in *The Last Stage* (for example, morning and evening roll calls on the *Appellplatz*, the arrival of new transports, images of the camp orchestra playing classical music that are juxtaposed with the images of selections to the gas chambers) reinforced the depiction of Nazi concentration camps and are present in a number of subsequent American films, including, as noted by several scholars, *Sophie's Choice* (1982, Alan Pakula) and *Schindler's List* (1993, Steven Spielberg). Scenes from *The Last Stage* are also present (without acknowledgment and, interestingly, as actual footage from the camp), in several films such as Alain Resnais's classic documentary essay on memory—*Night and Fog* (*Nuit et Brouillard*, 1955). They include the scene of a train with Jewish prisoners arriving at night to awaiting SS men with their dogs, and the image of a truck transporting victims to the gas chamber.[47] Certainly, to this day *The Last Stage* remains a "definitive film about Auschwitz,"[48] a seminal film about the Nazi Holocaust, and a prototype for future Holocaust cinematic narratives.

***

As Jakubowska stated on several occasions, after the film's premiere some of the Polish concentration camp survivors did not appreciate the fact that the leading character in her film, Marta Weiss, is Jewish. Such a representation, she said, "was my moral duty. Only Jews went straight to the gas from the transports."[49] Indeed, during the war Jakubowska was perfectly aware of the plight of Polish Jews. The Warsaw Ghetto Uprising started while she was being held by the Gestapo at the Pawiak prison, which was situated inside the ghetto. During the Uprising, the prison building was used as an attack base for the Germans. Jakubowska recalled the following in an interview done shortly before her death in 1998:

> The Germans were burning the ghetto, and they kept pouring water on us. The smoldering pieces were falling through the window into our prison cell. Through the window we could see the burning flames; in the prison cell—high temperatures, terrible stench. When, after half a year of my stay at Pawiak, they were taking us to Auschwitz, I have to tell you that the very fact of leaving this inferno gave us a sense of relief, despite our knowledge of where we were going.[50]

As elaborated by many writers and scholars, including former Auschwitz inmates, the character of Marta is modeled on Mala (Malka) Zimetbaum (1918–1944), a Polish-born Jewish woman who, at the age of ten, moved with her family to Belgium. Fluent in several languages, in Auschwitz she became a translator (her camp number was 19,880), and played an active part in the camp's underground. She is remembered by many eyewitnesses for her spirit and aid to other prisoners. In June 1944, she escaped from Auschwitz with a young Polish prisoner, but was caught after two weeks, and hanged in a public execution at Auschwitz. Primo Levi commented that in Auschwitz "the flight of even a single prisoner was considered the most grievous fault on the part of all surveillance personnel." He adds that the capture of an escapee was "punished by public hanging, but this hanging was preceded by a ceremony that varied each time but was always of an unheard of ferocity, an occasion for the imaginative cruelty of the SS to run amok."[51] Levi provides the following account of Mala Zimetbaum that is similar to several other testimonies:

> In Birkenau she acted as an interpreter and messenger and as such enjoyed a certain freedom of movement. She was generous and courageous; she had helped many of her companions and was loved by all of them. In the summer of 1944 she decided to escape with Edek, a Polish political prisoner ... [After her capture] she had managed to conceal a razor blade on her body. At the foot of the gallows, she cut the artery on one of her wrists, the SS who acted as executioners tried to snatch the blade from her and Mala, under the eyes of all the women in the camp, slapped his face with the bloodied hand. Enraged, other guards immediately came running: a prisoner, a Jewess, a woman, had dared defy them! They trampled her to death; she expired, fortunately for her, on the cart taking her to the crematorium.[52]

Although it is now generally agreed that Zimetbaum escaped with her lover, Edward (Edek) Galiński (1923–1944), according to another Auschwitz survivor, Krystyna Żywulska, the character of Tadeusz (Tadek), played by Stanisław Zaczyk (Figure 2.9), is based on a prewar right-wing nationalist activist, Jan Mosdorf (1904–1943), imprisoned at Auschwitz in January 1941, who "underwent an ideological change in the camp."[53] The published script by Jakubowska contains a scene supporting the above claim, which never made it fully to the final version of the film. This scene shows that the characters knew each other before the war. Tadeusz is surprised by Marta's presence in the camp, to which she responds bitterly, "You should be happy. Everything here is the way you wanted it to be in your university leaflets. 'Down with the Jews!' 'Beat the Jews!' And so on ... There is only one thing that you did not predict—that you also will end up here ... together with me."[54] Mala's Polish lover, Galiński, was one of the first inmates at Auschwitz, where he was sent in June 1940 and received the very low camp number 531. The story of Zimetbaum and Galiński's love, their escape, capture, and heroic death featured prominently in numerous camp memoirs, in particular in Wiesław Kielar's book, *Anus Mundi: Five Years in Auschwitz*, an honest, factual account of his ordeal as well as his friendship with Galiński.[55]

Leaving the historical aspect aside, in the film Marta is portrayed in line with the ideological requirements of the postwar era and Jakubowska's own communist convictions. Although *The Last Stage* was made before the official advent of the socialist realist doctrine in Poland, the Stalinist model unmistakably imprinted its mark on this film. It is seen, for example, in the development of Marta's character, who undergoes a desired ideological change. At the beginning of the film, she is personally chosen by the camp's commander to serve as an interpreter. At first, she displays a complete ignorance of the surroundings. "What is this factory?"—she asks pointing at the crematorium covered in dense smoke. Her ideological change from a middle-class character to a communist martyr takes place quickly. During the first conversation with Tadek, Marta says that "only here, in the camp, have I learned how to think ... I owe it to my comrades." Stuart Liebman aptly labels her a typical socialist

Figure 2.9: Marta (Barbara Drapińska) and Tadeusz (Stanisław Zaczyk)

realist character, and comments: "Over the course of the film, however, Marta's role evolves into that of a stock Socialist Realist heroine for whom the camp barriers pose no problem as she slips out past an armed guard carrying the German liquidation plans for the camp to the standard-issue Socialist Realist resistance chief."[56] Likewise, however, depicted is another convert to communism, a Polish woman, Helena. She is portrayed as a suffering "Polish Mother" who symbolizes "the suffering and heroism experienced by the whole nation."[57] After losing her baby, Helena undergoes a swift ideological change. In the film's final scene, which invites symbolic interpretation, she is holding a dying Marta in her arms, and promises her that Auschwitz will never be repeated.

Ironically, given the ideological stand of *The Last Stage*, during the 1949 congress of filmmakers at a small mountain resort Wisła, Jakubowska's film was subjected to criticism for a lack of "revolutionary spirit." The same criticism also faced other successful postwar films, such as *Forbidden Songs*, *Border Street*, and *Treasure* (*Skarb*, 1949).[58] The Wisła Congress enforced the doctrine of socialist realism in Polish cinema. The doctrine demanded the adherence to the Communist Party line, the necessary portrayal of the class struggle (the struggle between old and new), the emphasis on class-based images, the rewriting of history from the Marxist perspective, and the elimination of "reactionary bourgeois" ideology.[59]

In the introduction to the script of *The Last Stage*, published in 1955, Jakubowska writes about being perfectly aware that her choice of a small group, which resists and fights instead of suffering silently, was not representative of the whole concentration camp.[60] In line with her own, and the communist state's ideological goals, one of the early versions of her script was entitled, in a military fashion, *The Birkenau Front Reports* (*Odcinek Birkenau melduje*).

The heroic aspect of Jakubowska's portrayal of Auschwitz was expected by several former Auschwitz inmates, who applauded *The Last Stage* for being "a tribute to the dead and the murdered in the camp, precisely because the film does not expose passivity before death, but shows a noble attitude by celebrating struggle, not martyrdom."[61] The same portrayal was expected by the Communist Party Politburo members who watched the hastily edited film before its final approval for general screening. According to Jakubowska, the communist leader Bolesław Bierut immediately embraced the film, as did Józef Cyrankiewicz, the prime minister of People's Poland. Jakubowska later recalled that Cyrankiewicz, himself a former political prisoner in Auschwitz from 1942 to 1945 (number 62,993), "was of great help ... After all, there was that Auschwitz connection between us."[62] The postwar secretary general of the Polish Socialist Party (Polska Partia Socjalistyczna, PPS), in 1948 Cyrankiewicz merged the collaborationist wing of his party with the communist Polish Workers' Party (Polska Partia Robotnicza, PPR) into the Polish United Workers' Party (Polska Zjednoczona Partia Robotnicza, PZPR). This cunning politician with a long political life ahead of him (he served as Prime Minister until 1970), was carefully building his image as an anti-fascist leader at Auschwitz. In Cyrankiewicz's version of history, also propagated by Jakubowska, only the communists were able to build a resistance network in the camp. As an extension of this, only they could liberate Auschwitz and Poland from fascism.

The Auschwitz experience, more precisely the legend surrounding the "fight with fascism," was later used to legitimize communist rule, and to propel the careers of Cyrankiewicz and other members of the communist resistance after the war. Information about the Home Army (AK) members inside the camp and their role in the resistance was suppressed in Poland before 1989. With the publication outside of Poland of books such as Józef Garliński's *Fighting Auschwitz: The Resistance Movement in the Concentration Camp* (1974),[63] a more complete picture of the Auschwitz resistance started to emerge. In recent years, thanks to the sifting of communist archives, we have learned about several unknown heroes of the resistance, such as Witold Pilecki (1901–1948), the prewar cavalry officer, member of the AK, who in 1940 volunteered to be incarcerated at Auschwitz (number 4,859) in order to provide the Western Allies with information.[64] In the camp, Pilecki organized the resistance network and worked closely with Cyrankiewicz. In 1943, he escaped from the camp and later took part in the 1944 Warsaw Rising. Imprisoned by the communists after the war and accused of espionage, he was executed in 1948 after a show trial.

***

After the collapse of communism, several scholars perceptively discussed the politics surrounding the postwar history of Auschwitz and tried to address the issue of the postwar attempts at internationalizing the camp.[65] For the communist regime, Auschwitz symbolized Polish martyrdom and the victory over fascism. In his book, *Auschwitz, Poland, and the Politics of Commemoration, 1945–1979*, Jonathan Huener lists three "dominant modes of collective memory at the memorial site":

> First, Auschwitz was presented and groomed as a site of Polish national martyrdom. Second, the plight and struggle of the political prisoner, often styled as a socialist hero or resistance fighter, was elevated over the fate of the Jewish victim of genocide at Auschwitz. Third, the memorial site, through its exhibitions and commemorative events, was often used by the Polish state and its representative to gain political currency and at times was even instrumentalized as a stage for political propaganda.[66]

Huener stresses that both the Catholic Church and the communist state used the commemorative site for their own political purposes, in some cases in an "exclusionary manner, understating or even excluding the memory of nearly a million Jews killed at Auschwitz—some 90 percent of the camp's victims."[67]

While describing the symbolic meaning of the former death camp, and the communist attempts at memorialization, some scholars stress the fact that the communist regime's efforts were also targeting the "Polish aspect" of the camp. For example, Andrew Charlesworth, a political geographer, persuasively argues that "by emphasizing its international character and ignoring the fact the victims were Jewish, the Communists linked Poland through the memorialisation of Auschwitz to the other Warsaw Pact countries, both as past and potential victims of German aggression and as present beneficiaries of their liberation by the Red Army and of their continuing defence by the Soviet Union."[68] In Charlesworth's words, the communist authorities "succeeded to a large extent in de-Polonising as well as almost totally de-Judaizing Auschwitz."[69]

At the beginning of her film, Jakubowska introduces a statement about the authenticity of presented scenes ("the film is based on authentic events"), a disclaimer that they "represent only a small fraction of the truth about the concentration camp in Auschwitz," and an inflated figure (in accordance with the knowledge of the day[70]) about the number of victims ("4,500,000"), who are described as "people from all countries under the Nazi occupation." Jakubowska also selects for emphasis those moments in the camp's history that, albeit true, were certainly not representative, such as the heroic death of Marta/Mala, the portrayal of the French prisoners who are singing "La Marseillaise" while being led to the gas chamber, and the death of a Serb prisoner of war, Dessa. As Omer Bartov shrewdly comments about the outcome, "Watching this film more than half a century after it was made, one cannot but be struck by the fact that the exposure of the lies and fabrications that underlay Nazi ideology and policies was already predicated on a new series of lies and fabrications meant to facilitate the reestablishment of Polish nationalism and to legitimize communist domination."[71]

In the preface to their book, *We Were in Auschwitz*, published in 1946, Tadeusz Borowski and two other Auschwitz survivors, Janusz Nel-Siedlecki and Krystyn Olszewski, warned against future falsifications of the camp experience:

> Auschwitz, the meeting place of the whole Europe, a sliver of earth where the living were gassed and the dead burned. We were united by commonplace, pitiless death, not death on behalf of the nation or honor, but death for worn-out flesh, boils, typhus, swollen legs. Years of lying to death, cheating her, slipping by her stealthily, bind us tightly together as if we'd fought battles in the same trench, even though these were not heroic years ... Confinement in the camp, destitution, torture, and death in the gas chamber are not heroism, are not even anything positive. It was defeat, the almost immediate abandonment of ideological principles. A primeval battle remained waged by the solitary, debased prisoner for his existence against the equally debased SS and against the terrible force of the camp. We stress this strongly because myths and legends will arise on both sides. We did not fight for the concept of nation in the camp, nor for the inner restructuring of man; we fought for a bowl of soup, for a place to sleep, for women, for gold and watches from the transports.[72]

We Were in Auschwitz opens with a note "From the Publisher" by Anatol Girs (another ex-prisoner of Auschwitz), who emphasizes the documentary aspect of the book and bluntly states that "false legends are being created around many aspects of this war. This book removes one of them: the legend of the concentration camp."[73] Jakubowska's film strives for an impossible goal of representing a truthful reality about the camp while faithfully following the tenets of the communist ideology. The result is a legend convenient for the communist state. A Polish production made with the help of an international contingent (Russian cinematographer, German co-scriptwriter, and actresses from Russia and France), *The Last Stage* lays emphasis on the international aspect of Auschwitz. Although the viewer watches some Jewish prisoners (wearing the Star of David), and their plight is also addressed, albeit not explicitly, in several scenes, the film refers to "people," and the nationality of screen characters is of minor importance. For example, Marta's "cosmopolitan looks," multi-lingual abilities, and proper communist convictions make her a model protagonist, who symbolizes the "fighting Auschwitz" that the communist regime wished to represent on the screen.

Jakubowska's film also reflects the status of the postwar debates about Auschwitz, namely the emphasis on the victims' country of origin (the nation-state), rather than their respective nationality or ethnicity. As discussed by historian Marek Kucia, this approach originated with the findings of the Soviet commission that inspected the site of the concentration camp soon after its liberation by the Red Army.[74] The Soviets categorized the victims of Auschwitz according to their state affiliations, which resulted in the absence of the category "Jews." Their approach certainly impacted subsequent Polish attempts at documenting Auschwitz. Instead of reflecting the camp's true fabric, the language used in the official documents, as well as in several early literary accounts, relied on universal categories such as "people," "victims," and "men, women, and children." The efforts by the Polish communist government to internationalize Auschwitz, and to make it a memorial to those who fought with fascism, led to the absence or the marginalization of the camp's largest group of victims—the Jews.

One also finds a similar absence of Jewish suffering in those postwar Polish literary works which were mentioned earlier, describing the horror of Auschwitz. Zofia Nałkowska, for example, a member of the Main Commission for the Investigation of Nazi Crimes in Poland (Główna Komisja Badania Zbrodni Hitlerowskich w Polsce), deals mostly with the plight of the Jewish people in her masterpiece, a collection of short stories *Medallions*. Despite that, her references are mainly to generic "people," in line with the motto to her book: "People dealt this fate to people."[75]

References to people of all nations being the victims of Nazi Germany and the lack of singling out for emphasis Jewish victims is not a Polish phenomenon. For example, as Peter Novick explains, "the words 'Jew' and 'Jewish' do not appear in Murrow's broadcast about Buchenwald, nor do they appear in Margaret Bourke-White's account of photographing the camp."[76] Several postwar documentary and narrative films made outside of Poland also did not mention specifically the Jewish victims, although they dealt with their suffering.

The classic documentary by Alan Resnais, *Night and Fog*, which includes only four scenes featuring prisoners with the Star of David, might serve here as one of the examples.

Jakubowska after *The Last Stage*

In books on Polish cinema, Jakubowska's name is almost exclusively associated with *The Last Stage*. The silence over Jakubowska's films produced later has to do largely with her staunch involvement with communist ideology (she was a dedicated communist throughout her entire life, even after the collapse of communism), which resulted in several painfully didactic and propagandistic films promoting the communist cause. Some of Jakubowska's films, for example *The Soldier of Victory* (*Żołnierz zwycięstwa*, 1953), are classic examples of blatant communist propaganda—and as such were praised and awarded prizes immediately after their release, while becoming objects of ridicule for contemporary audiences.

It has to be noted that later in her career Jakubowska returned to her camp experiences in three films: *Meetings in the Twilight* (*Spotkania w mroku*, 1960), *The End of Our World* (*Koniec naszego świata*, 1964), and *Invitation* (*Zaproszenie*, 1985). These films, rarely seen and virtually ignored in discussions on the filmic representation of the Holocaust, are set in the present and rely on the flashback structure to tell the story of Auschwitz. All three films are scripted by Jakubowska, and they also feature familiar characters and situations—concentration camp survivors, mostly communists, strong-willed professionals who are unable, however, to free themselves from the shadow of their wartime experiences. Jakubowska's films also contain explicit denunciation of fascism, praise of human solidarity, as well as criticism of Western-style consumerism and the "touristy" approach to life.

In the Polish-East German production *Meetings in the Twilight*, made at the peak of the Polish School phenomenon and photographed by Kurt Weber, Jakubowska developed a contemporary story with wartime references. Based on *Let Us Shout* (*Pozwólcie nam krzyczeć*), a novel by Stanisława Fleszarowa-Muskat, who also served as co-scriptwriter, the film introduces a Polish pianist Magdalena (Zofia Słaboszowska) who, while performing in West Germany, remembers her imprisonment in a labor camp. The main character in *Invitation*, Anna Górska, is a successful, self-sacrificing pediatrician. After meeting her first love, Piotr (Kazimierz Witkiewicz), they travel together to places she cannot erase from her memory: Auschwitz, Sachsenhausen, and Ravensbrück. It is not a coincidence that Anna is played by Antonina Gordon-Górecka, who earlier appeared as the German nurse Anna in *The Last Stage*.

The End of Our World, the film Jakubowska considered her best,[77] is arguably the most accomplished of all her camp films. She made this film in the mid-1960s, when Auschwitz became widely known in the West as the site of Jewish extermination. The film was made after the capture of Adolf Eichmann by Israeli Mossad agents in Argentina, his historic trial in 1961, and his conviction and execution in Jerusalem. The film also coincided with the much publicized Frankfurt Auschwitz Trial of twenty-two SS guards from Auschwitz (1963–1965). For the world, the meaning of Auschwitz had broadened in the 1960s from that of an East-Central European emblem of German atrocities, a place hidden behind the Iron Curtain and used for propaganda purposes, to a site of international significance, the symbol of the Holocaust. Notwithstanding the lack of official diplomatic relations between West Germany and Poland, the Polish authorities assisted the Frankfurt investigation, for example they allowed the German judge and other officials to inspect the site of the concentration camp at Auschwitz. Despite the Polish state award for Jakubowska, her film was barely noticed by critics and (particularly) audiences in Poland; it also remained virtually unknown in the West.

Jakubowska's film is based on a novel of the same title published for the first time in 1958 by writer and a communist political activist Tadeusz Hołuj (1916–1985), who is also cast in the film as Adam. This was one of Hołuj's several returns to his own experiences in Auschwitz, where he was imprisoned in 1942. Jakubowska and Hołuj, however, were not the only Auschwitz survivors who worked on this film. Assistant to the camera operator, Wiesław Kielar (see endnote 55), and costume designer, Marian Kołodziej, came to Auschwitz in 1940 with the first transport of Polish political prisoners (camp numbers 290 and 432 respectively).[78]

The End of Our World focuses on a former (communist) political prisoner at Auschwitz, Henryk (Lech Skolimowski). Several years after the war, he becomes a reluctant guide at the camp for two American tourists—a young woman Julia, whose father perished there, and her male companion, who is reduced in the film to an almost cartoonish "Western character" familiar from communist propaganda, thanks to his touristy approach, his ignorance, and his lack of compassion.

Henryk's presence at the State Museum in Auschwitz brings back his own camp memories. The film depicts Henryk being captured on the streets of Warsaw for helping a Polish mother and her child who were being mistreated by a German policeman. For this deed, he is sent to Auschwitz. Unusually for Jakubowska, the initial scenes at Auschwitz resemble the representation of the camp by Borowski.[79] The stress is on the monstrous, bordering on a grotesque aspect of camp life, which will later be developed more fully in Leszek Wosiewicz's *Kornblumenblau* (1989). Jakubowska depicts Henryk's miraculous survival as a *Muselmann*, his brush with death, the help he receives from other inmates (mostly political prisoners), and the change of his camp identity (Figure 2.10). The second part of the film is more conventional and utilizes elements of melodrama coupled with the ideology present in *The Last Stage*. Henryk learns that his wife Maria (Teresa Wicińska), who was convinced about his death, has married his friend Jan Smolik. Later Smolik is imprisoned at

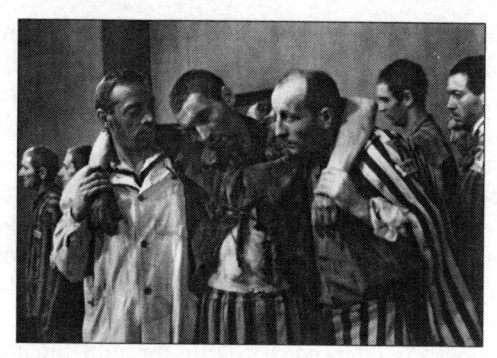

Figure 2.10: Lech Skolimowski as Henryk (center) in Wanda Jakubowska's *The End of Our World* (1964)

Auschwitz, where he quickly perishes. Maria also finds herself in Auschwitz. Despite Henryk's connections and help, Maria dies with a group of children she is taking care of in the Gypsy Family Camp.

Once again, the most important aspect of Jakubowska's film is the protagonist's gradual involvement with the camp's resistance. Henryk becomes a reluctant *Kapo* at the request of other political prisoners. With a hidden camera, he captures images of extermination inside the camp. He even helps the Jewish *Sonderkommando* (Special Commando) to destroy the crematoria, and later participates in the *Sonderkommando*'s uprising on 7 October 1944.

Writing about Henryk's heroic exploits, Hanno Loewy rightly states that "Jakubowska is turning the history of the camp's resistance upside down."[80] The "heroic version of the Auschwitz resistance" was, however, strongly advocated not only by Jakubowska, but also by scriptwriter Hołuj, for whom "the camp had fought and won the battle. Auschwitz was not only martyrology, but struggle as well."[81] Hołuj defends this way of representing the camp by saying that "the issue of the camp resistance was shown in the film well, faithfully and truthfully, albeit sometimes not in line with the fixed ideas [about the camp]." He admits that the history of the *Sonderkommando* uprising proved to be the most difficult to represent: "We don't have a single witness of the very uprising itself. However, recently uncovered documents from the rubble of the crematoria confirm the whole process of preparations [for the uprising]."[82] Hołuj emphasizes that a framework was needed to link the first scene—Henryk defending a Polish mother—with the scene when the protagonist helps those who "fight alone."[83] The symbolic image of a communist Pole helping Jewish insurgents in their suicidal fight, although distorting the historical reality, was the one the communist state as well as the makers of the film wanted to preserve and to elevate.

Stylistically, Jakubowska utilizes a similar set of images to that which she developed in *The Last Stage*. Working with cinematographer Kazimierz Wawrzyniak, Jakubowska cuts from the shot of a Jewish transport to a long shot of smoke over the crematoria. She also portrays the women's orchestra playing classical music near the gate leading to the camp. Furthermore, she stresses the multinational aspect of the camp (several languages are spoken, including Polish, German, Russian, Yiddish, Slovak, Roma, and Italian), and portrays the political (mostly communist) prisoners at Auschwitz as heroic members of the resistance. Since the main protagonist is a well-connected *Kapo*, he moves relatively freely within the camp, enabling the viewer to witness the different sub-camps of Auschwitz. Jakubowska uses archival footage as well, such as photographs of Jewish transports taken inside the camp. In addition, she models some scenes on remaining documentary photographs.

Despite Jakubowska's often-voiced desire for authenticity and the semi-autobiographical (and quasi-documentary) nature of her camp films, her embracing of communist ideology resulted in a shallow and politicized image of Auschwitz, more a testament to cold war politics than to the reality of the camp. Despite the aforementioned criticism, it is nonetheless not difficult to agree with Jan Alfred Szczepański who, reviewing *The End of Our World* in 1964, stated that, regardless of their filmic value, the Auschwitz films by Jakubowska would serve as a point of reference for other camp films.[84]

Notes

1. Due to the outbreak of World War II, *The Last Stage* became Jakubowska's first theatrically released film. Her much-expected prewar adaptation of Eliza Orzeszkowa's canonical novel, *On the Niemen River* (*Nad Niemnem*, 1939), was finished shortly before the war, but never had its premiere, which had been scheduled for 5 September 1939. All of the film's prints were destroyed during the war.
2. Hanno Loewy, "The Mother of All Holocaust Films? Wanda Jakubowska's Auschwitz Trilogy," *Historical Journal of Film, Radio and Television* vol. 24, no. 2 (2004): 179.
3. Omer Bartov, *The "Jew" in Cinema: From* The Golem *to* Don't Touch My Holocaust (Bloomington: Indiana University Press, 2005), 169.
4. For example, Jan Nepomucyn Miller, "Nowy etap polskiego filmu," *Warszawa: Niezależny dwutygodnik literacki* 4 (1948): 1, Ryszard Matuszewski, "Martwy punkt polskiego kina—przełamany," *Kuźnica* 15 (1948): 5, and Aleksander Kulisiewicz, "Triumf polskiej kinematografii," *Film* 6 (1948): 10.
5. Krzysztof Kucharski, *Kino plus. Film i dystrybucja kinowa w Polsce w latach 1990–2000* (Toruń: Oficyna Wydawnicza Kucharski, 2002), 388. It is necessary to remember that box-office figures before 1950 are estimated. Also, very few Polish films were released between 1945 and 1950, for example only two, including *The Last Stage*, in 1948.
6. Gerda Schneider, German communist and political prisoner at Auschwitz, is credited as a co-writer of the script. Jerzy Kawalerowicz, the first assistant director on *The Last Stage*, remembers that Schneider's role was more prominent than just serving as a co-scriptwriter. He recalls that Schneider basically co-directed the whole film. See Łukasz Figielski and Bartosz Michalak, *Prywatna historia kina polskiego* (Gdańsk: słowo/obraz terytoria, 2006), 18. Alina Madej argues that Schneider most probably wrote the first version of the script in German. Considering the postwar political sensitivities, it almost bordered on provocation. Alina Madej, "Wanda Jakubowska wygrywa ostatni etap," in *Historia kina polskiego*, ed. Tadeusz Lubelski and Konrad Zarębski (Warsaw: Fundacja Kino, 2006), 68.

7. Wanda Jakubowska, "Kilka wspomnień o powstaniu scenariusza (na marginesie filmu *Ostatni etap*)," *Kwartalnik Filmowy* 1 (1951): 40.
8. See, for example, Barbara Mruklik, "Wierność sobie. Rozmowa z Wandą Jakubowską," *Kino* 5 (1985): 7.
9. "Tkwiłam w lagrze do 1948 roku. Rozmowa z Wandą Jakubowską po premierze *Ostatniego etapu*," *Głos Ludu* 91 (1948). Quoted from Alina Madej, *Kino, władza, publiczność. Kinematografia polska w latach 1944–1949* (Bielsko-Biała: Wydawnictwo Prasa Beskidzka, 2002), 157.
10. The German POWs were also used in the summer of 1946 during the production of the first postwar Polish film, *Forbidden Songs* (released in 1947). See, for example, Piotr Śmiałowski, "Pierwszy na zawsze," *Kino* 1 (2007): 56. The production of *The Last Stage* is abundant with interesting anecdotes. For example, Edward Zajiček comments that the film's producer, Mieczysław Wajnberger, used as extras a group of unsuspecting Jewish-French tourists, whom he offered a free train ride from Auschwitz to Birkenau. He kept them for several hours in the heat of a summer day locked in a cattle train. When the doors opened, the tourists faced the SS-guards with their dogs. Although the filmmakers were very pleased with the verisimilititude of the scene, Zajiček writes, the tourists were not, nor were the French Embassy and the Polish Foreign Service. Edward Zajiček, *Poza ekranem. Kinematografia polska 1918–1991* (Warsaw: Filmoteka Narodowa and Wydawnictwa Artystyczne i Filmowe, 1992), 85.
11. Figielski and Michalak, *Prywatna historia kina polskiego*, 20.
12. Several sub-camps of Auschwitz, mostly located in Upper Silesia, were used for a number of years after the war by the communist regime as slave labor centers for, among others, members of the Polish underground that opposed the communist rule.
13. Jonathan Huener, *Auschwitz, Poland, and the Politics of Commemoration, 1945–1979* (Athens: Ohio University Press, 2003), 64–65. The early years of the Auschwitz-Birkenau State Museum are also discussed by Jacek Lachendro in his *Zburzyć i zaorać ...? Idea założenia Państwowego Muzeum Auschwitz-Birkenau w świetle prasy polskiej 1945–1948* (Oświęcim: Państwowe Muzeum Auschwitz-Birkenau, 2007).
14. Kazimierz Smoleń, "Auschwitz Today: The Auschwitz-Birkenau State Museum," in *Auschwitz: A History in Photographs*, ed. Teresa Świebocka, English edition prepared by Jonathan Webber and Connie Wilsack (Oświęcim: Auschwitz-Birkenau State Museum, 1993), 261.
15. Alina Madej, "Jak powstawał *Ostatni etap*" [interview with Jakubowska], *Kino* 5 (1998): 16.
16. Z.P., "Widma niedawnych lat: Oświęcim na ekranie," *Film* 26 (1947): 8.
17. Ibid., 8. Jakubowska comments on using the German POWs as extras in Madej, "Jak powstawał *Ostatni etap*," 16.
18. Andrzej Waligórski, "Jak nakręcano film *Ostatni etap*," *Słowo Polskie* (20 April 1948): 7.
19. Tadeusz Lubelski, "Dwa debiuty oddzielone w czasie: Rozmowa z Wandą Jakubowską," in *Debiuty polskiego kina*, ed. Marek Hendrykowski (Konin: Wydawnictwo "Przegląd Koniński," 1998), 19. Similar comments about Aleksander Ford can be found in other sources. For example, Edward Zajiček writes that Ford used to reserve interesting projects for himself. As a result of his policy, several scripts waited for years to go into production. In Zajiček, *Poza ekranem*, 85.
20. See Tadeusz Lubelski, "Generalissumus płakał" [interview with Wanda Jakubowska], *Film* 18–19 (1990): 3–4.
21. Lubelski, "Dwa debiuty oddzielone w czasie," 22; Also, Lubelski, "Generalissimus płakał," 4; Madej, "Jak powstawał *Ostatni etap*," 16. Jakubowska tells a similar version of this story to Stuart Liebman, "I Was Always in the Epicenter of Whatever Was Going On ... An Interview with Wanda Jakubowska," *Slavic and East European Performance* vol. 17, no. 3 (1997): 22.
22. Jakubowska, "Kilka wspomnień o powstaniu scenariusza," 43. Considering the postwar sensitivities, one has to agree with Jakubowska's comment. Films were often subjected to censorship not necessarily on political, but mostly on moral grounds. For example, as insightfully discussed by Janina Struk, the screening of *Night and Fog* (1955) in England encountered several problems with the censor. A number of graphic shots, for example,

depicting piles of corpses, were removed by the British Board of Film Classification (BBFC). The whole film, with the scenes reintroduced by the BBFC, was released in 1990. See Janina Struk, *Photographing the Holocaust: Interpretations of the Evidence* (London: I.B. Tauris, 2004), 168.
23. According to the film's logic ("Hold on! The Red Army is near!" shouts Marta when she is about to be hanged), the planes must be Soviet. Jakubowska, however, comments that these were the bombers of the United States. See, for example, Liebman, "I Was Always in the Epicenter of Whatever Was Going On," 25.
24. Ilan Avisar, *Screening the Holocaust: Cinema's Images of the Unimaginable* (Bloomington: Indiana University Press, 1988), 37.
25. Béla Balázs, "A Letter to Wanda Jakubowska," trans. Stuart Liebman, in "Béla Balázs on Wanda Jakubowska's *The Last Stop*: Three Texts," trans. Stuart Liebman and Zsuzsa Berger, *Slavic and East European Performance* vol. 16, no. 3 (1996): 65.
26. Béla Balázs, "Concerning the Great Polish Auschwitz Film," quoted from Stuart Liebman and Zsuzsa Berger, trans. "Béla Balázs on Wanda Jakubowska's *The Last Stop*: Three Texts," *Slavic and East European Performance* vol. 16, no. 3 (1996): 67-69.
27. The books are available in English: Zofia Nałkowska, *Medallions* (Evanston: Northwestern University Press, 2000); Seweryna Szmaglewska, *Smoke over Birkenau* (New York: Henry Holt, 1947), Krystyna Zywulska, *I Came Back* (London: Dennis Dobson, 1951), and Tadeusz Borowski, *This Way for the Gas, Ladies and Gentleman* (New York: Penguin, 1992).
28. Lubelski, "Dwa debiuty oddzielone w czasie," 27.
29. In several interviews Jakubowska emphasized the heroic aspect of Auschwitz marked by friendship and solidarity. See, for example, Barbara Mruklik, "Wierność sobie," 8.
30. Andrzej Werner, *Zwyczajna apokalipsa. Tadeusz Borowski i jego wizja świata obozów* (Warsaw: Czytelnik, 1971), 21.
31. Ibid., 22.
32. Madej, *Kino, władza, publiczność*, 170 and 180.
33. Stuart Liebman, "Wanda Jakubowska's *The Last Stop (Ostatni etap)*," *Slavic and East European Performance* vol. 16, no. 3 (1996): 56.
34. "Protokół Komisji Kwalifikacyjnej Filmów: *Jasne Łany*, reż. E. Cękalskiego, *Ostatni etap*, reż. W. Jakubowskiej, *Stalowe serca*, reż S. Urbanowicza," 11 April 1948, National Film Archive (Filmoteka Narodowa), A-329/A8.
35. See, for example, published opinions expressed by the following Auschwitz survivors: Seweryna Szmaglewska, "Dzieło czy arcydzieło," *Gazeta Filmowa* 16 (1 June 1948): 2; Krystyna Żywulska, "Nareszcie film," *Odrodzenie* 12 (21 March 1948): 8; Henryk Korotyński, "Oczyma Oświęcimiaka," *Film* 7 (1948): 7.
36. Maria Dąbrowska, *Dzienniki powojenne. T 1: 1945-1949* (Warsaw: Czytelnik, 1996), 209-210. Quoted from Madej, *Kino, władza, publiczność*, 163-164.
37. Madej, "Jak powstawał *Ostatni etap*," 15.
38. Ibid., 15.
39. For example, the Auschwitz survivor Halina Birenbaum writes the following about the character portrayed by Jakubowska as Eugenia, a Russian doctor: "The woman in charge of the sick bay, a Polish doctor, paid for her courage immediately after the delegates departed by torture in the *Gestapo* dungeons in Auschwitz. People said she died with outstanding heroism, and she certainly knew what awaited her when she told the Red Cross delegates the whole horrible truth about the Auschwitz tortures. This woman doctor, like the runner Mala, became to us the personification of human dignity and courage." Halina Birenbaum, *Hope is the Last to Die: A Personal Documentation of Nazi Terror* (Oświęcim: State Museum in Oświęcim, 1994), 192.
40. See, for example, Tadeusz Lubelski, *Strategie autorskie w polskim filmie fabularnym lat 1945-1961* (Kraków: Wydawnictwo Uniwersytetu Jagiellońskiego, 1992), 82; Marta Wróbel, "*Ostatni etap* Wandy Jakubowskiej jako pierwszy etap polskiego kina ideologicznego," *Kwartalnik Filmowy* 43 (2003): 13.
41. Jerzy Toeplitz, "Introduction" to Wanda Jakubowska, *Ostatni etap* (Warsaw: FAW, 1955), 9.

42. Lubelski, *Strategie autorskie w polskim filmie fabularnym 1945-1961*, 80 and 82.
43. B.W. "Patrząc na ekran," *Życie Warszawy* (4 April 1948). Quoted from Wróbel, "Ostatni etap Wandy Jakubowskiej," 10.
44. Lubelski, *Strategie autorskie w polskim filmie fabularnym 1945-1961*, 81.
45. Jalu Kurek, "*Ostatni etap* od strony filmowej," *Warszawa: Niezależny Dwutygodnik Literacki* 4 (1948): 4. Apart from critical praise, Boris Monastyrski also received Polish state honors, including one of the highest Polish medals (*Krzyż Oficerski Orderu Polonia Restituta*), which he received on 8 October 1948 at the Polish embassy in Moscow.
46. Roman Mann (1911-1960) worked on thirty-six films, including the Polish School classics, such as Andrzej Wajda's war trilogy—*A Generation* (1955), *Kanal* (1957), and *Ashes and Diamonds* (1958)—Andrzej Munk's *Man on the Tracks* (1956), Aleksander Ford's *Teutonic Knights* (1960), and Jerzy Kawalerowicz's *Mother Joan of the Angels* (1961).
47. Stuart Liebman also points out that "George Stevens used some of Jakubowska's images for *The Diary of Anne Frank* (1959). More recently, in 1995 Steven Spielberg incorporated shots of the selection and the work brigades in his hour-long promotional television program for his 'Survivors of the Holocaust' project without any acknowledgment that these were Jakubowska's fictional reconstructions and not documentary images." In Liebman, "Wanda Jakubowska's *The Last Stop* (*Ostatni etap*)," 63.
48. Annette Insdorf, *Indelible Shadows: Film and the Holocaust* (Cambridge: Cambridge University Press, 2003), 20.
49. Maria Kornatowska, "Kto ratuje jedno życie," *Kino* 10 (1994): 37. See also Madej, "Jak powstawał *Ostatni etap*," 17.
50. Lubelski, "Dwa debiuty oddzielone w czasie: Rozmowa z Wandą Jakubowską," 17.
51. Primo Levi, *The Drowned and the Saved*, trans. Raymond Rosenthal (New York: Summit Books, 1988), 154-155.
52. Ibid., 156.
53. Żywulska, "Nareszcie film," 8.
54. Jakubowska, *Ostatni etap*, 83.
55. Wiesław Kielar, *Anus Mundi: Five Years in Auschwitz* (New York: Penguin Books, 1982). Kielar was one of the first prisoners at Auschwitz (camp number 290). After the war, he studied cinematography at the Łódź Film School, and later worked as a camera operator on, among others, Czesław Petelski's classic film *Damned Roads* (*Baza ludzi umarłych*, 1959). *Anus Mundi* was published in Polish for the first time in 1966, and since then reprinted numerous times.
56. Liebman, "Pages from the Past," 60. Jakubowska claimed that Marta'a character dominates the screen partly due to bad casting on her part. Barbara Drapińska (Marta) proved to be a much stronger actress than the prewar actress Wanda Bartówna (Helena). Had she, as originally planned, cast the rising Polish postwar star, Danuta Szaflarska, in the role of Helena, this could be a film with a different emphasis. See, Madej, "Jak powstawał *Ostatni etap*," 17.
57. Elżbieta Ostrowska, "Filmic Representations of the 'Polish Mother' in Post-Second World War Polish Cinema," *European Journal of Women Studies* vol. 5, no. 3-4 (1998): 424.
58. See Alina Madej, "Zjazd filmowy w Wiśle, czyli dla każdego coś przykrego," *Kwartalnik Filmowy* 18 (1997): 207-214.
59. See my chapter on socialist realist films in Poland, "The Poetics of Screen Stalinism," in my book on *Polish National Cinema* (New York: Berghahn, 2002): 56-72. Piotr Zwierzchowski extensively discusses Polish socialist realist films in his books: *Zapomniani bohaterowie. O bohaterach filmowych polskiego socrealizmu* (Warsaw: Wydawnictwo Trio, 2000) and *Pęknięty monolit. Konteksty polskiego kina socrealistycznego* (Bydgoszcz: Wydawnictwo Uniwersytetu Kazimierza Wielkiego w Bydgoszczy, 2005).
60. Jakubowska, "Introduction," *Ostatni etap* (Warsaw: FAW, 1955), 17.
61. Żywulska, "Nareszcie film," 8.
62. Lubelski, "Dwa debiuty oddzielone w czasie," 24.

63. Józef Garliński's book was first published in Polish in 1974 as *Oświęcim walczący* (London: Odnowa). It was translated into English in 1975 as *Fighting Auschwitz: The Resistance Movement in the Concentration Camp* (London: Fawcett Books). Garliński was imprisoned in Auschwitz in May 1943 (number 121,421). After the war he settled in England.
64. See Konstanty R. Piekarski, *Escaping Hell: The Story of a Polish Underground Officer in Auschwitz and Buchenwald* (Toronto: Dundurn Press, 1989); Adam Cyra, *Ochotnik do Auschwitz: Witold Pilecki 1901–1948* (Oświęcim: Chrześcijańskie Stowarzyszenie Rodzin Oświęcimskich, 2000); Wincenty Gawron (former Auschwitz inmate), *Ochotnik do Oświęcimia* (Oświęcim: Państwowe Muzeum w Oświęcimiu, 1992). Ryszard Bugajski, of *Interrogation* (1982/1989) fame, directed a television play about the heroics of Pilecki entitled *The Death of Cavalry Captain Pilecki* (*Śmierć Rotmistrza Pileckiego*) that was aired on 15 May 2006.
65. For example, Andrew Charlesworth, "Contesting Places of Memory: The Case of Auschwitz," *Environment and Planning D: Society and Space* 12 (1994), 579–593; Tim Cole, chapter "Auschwitz" in his *Selling the Holocaust: From Auschwitz to Schindler* (New York: Routledge, 1999), 97–120; James E. Young, chapter "The Rhetoric of Ruins: The Memorial Camps at Majdanek and Auschwitz" in his *The Texture of Memory: Holocaust Memorials and Meaning* (New Haven: Yale University Press, 1993), 119–154; and, quoted earlier, Huener, *Auschwitz, Poland, and the Politics of Commemoration, 1945–1979*.
66. Huener, *Auschwitz, Poland, and the Politics of Commemoration, 1945–1979*, xiv.
67. Ibid., xvi.
68. Charlesworth, "Contesting Places of Memory," 583.
69. Ibid., 584.
70. As Jonathan Huener writes, after the war there was no consensus regarding the number of Auschwitz victims. Figures provided in 1945 by different sources, ranging from the Red Army to the Polish Main Commission for the Investigation of German Crimes, were high, usually citing four million estimated victims. See Huener, *Auschwitz, Poland, and the Politics of Commemoration, 1945–1979*, 42–44.
71. Bartov, *The "Jew" in Cinema*, 169.
72. Tadeusz Borowski, Janusz Nel-Siedlecki, and Krystyn Olszewski, *Byliśmy w Oświęcimiu* (Monachium, Oficyna Warszawska, 1946). English translation by Alicia Nitecki as *We Were in Auschwitz* (New York: Welcome Rain Publishers, 2000), 3–4. As stated in the English edition, part of the original 1946 edition in Polish "was bound in concentration camp 'stripes' cut from original prison garments" (p. 197).
73. Anatol Girs, "From the Publisher," in *We Were in Auschwitz*, 1.
74. Marek Kucia, "'Jews'—The Absence and Presence of a Category in the Representations of Auschwitz in Poland, 1945–1985," *Studia Judaica* 2 (2006): 328–329.
75. Zofia Nałkowska, *Medallions*, trans. Diana Kuprel (Evanston, Il: Northwestern University Press, 2000).
76. Peter Novick, *The Holocaust in American Life* (Boston: Houghton Mifflin, 1999), 64.
77. Kornatowska, "Kto ratuje jedno życie," 37; Barbara Hollender, "Nie można nikogo nauczyć żyć," *Rzeczpospolita* 11 (1997): 25.
78. Marian Kołodziej (1921–2009) was a distinguished set designer and painter who survived Auschwitz by adopting the name of a deceased prisoner. He kept this name after the war. This aspect of his life perhaps influenced the story presented by Jakubowska.
79. Borowski's influence is noticed by, among others, Hanno Loewy in his insightful text, "The Mother of All Holocaust Films?" 199.
80. Ibid., 189.
81. Quoted from Huener, *Auschwitz, Poland, and the Politics of Commemoration, 1945–1979*, 93.
82. Tadeusz Hołuj, "Jak powstawał *Koniec naszego świata*," *Film* 14 (1964): 6.
83. Ibid., 6.
84. Jan Alfred Szczepański, "*Koniec naszego świata*," *Film* 14 (1964): 7.

Chapter 3

COMMEMORATING THE WARSAW GHETTO UPRISING IN *BORDER STREET* (1949)

Aleksander Ford (1908–1980), the controversial organizer of Polish postwar cinema, released his first film, *Border Street* (*Ulica Graniczna*), on 23 June 1949. The much-awaited film dealt with the wartime predicament of Polish Jews, and for the first time represented on the screen the Warsaw Ghetto Uprising (19 April–16 May 1943). The film had been produced mostly at the well-equipped Czech Barrandov studio (sometimes labeled the "Slavic Hollywood") and with the Czech contingent—cinematographer Jaroslav Tuzar, editor Jiřina Lukešová, and art director Štěpán Kopecký, among others. The straightforward and realistic (although studio-made) *Border Street* shows the partitioning of Warsaw by the Germans into Jewish and Aryan quarters and gives a vast panorama of Jewish and Polish characters living in a building on the street that becomes the border of the ghetto. This "cinematic monument to a trauma that was barred from any celluloid representation"[1] received many awards, including the Golden Medal at the International Film Festival in Venice in 1948. With more than eight million viewers, Ford's film is also number twenty-six on the list of the biggest box-office successes on Polish screens from 1945 to 2000.[2] (See Figure 3.1)

***

Ford was very well-prepared for the task. He started his career before the war with a series of documentary films in 1928. In 1930, he became a co-founder of START—a dynamic cine-club that promoted ambitious and artistic cinema. His much praised narrative debut (now lost), *The Legion of the Street* (*Legion ulicy*, 1932), was voted the best film of the year by the readers of film journal *Kino*. It was one of the first Polish films showing images of everyday life coupled with elements of social commentary. Ford's film, which focused on Warsaw street boys who sell newspapers, was well narrated, realistic (featuring non-professional actors), and devoid of the stereotypical sentimental features that permeated prewar Polish narratives. The young director was hailed by the leftist press in particular (he was a known communist, member of the KPP—the Communist Polish Party) as the most promising Polish director.[3]

Figure 3.1: Aleksander Ford in 1958. Courtesy Filmoteka Narodowa in Warsaw

In the 1930s Ford also made two films in Yiddish about Jewish life—*Sabra* (1933) and *Children Must Laugh* (aka *The Road of the Youth*; *Mir kumen on/ Droga młodych*, 1936). The quasi-documentary *Sabra* was made on location in Palestine and portrayed the harsh living conditions of Jewish settlers and their struggles with hostile Arabs. Initially planned by Ford as a warning against the politics of resettling in Palestine, the final version of the film included optimistic, poster-like images of the emerging Jewish state.[4] *Children Must Laugh*, a film financed by the Jüdischer Arbeiter Bund and produced by Saul Goskind, dealt with the Medem Sanatorium for children with tuberculosis in Miedzeszyn. The film encountered problems with the censor for allegedly spreading communist propaganda (helped by the notoriety of Wanda Wasilewska as a co-scriptwriter), and was never released theatrically (it was only shown at small private gatherings).[5]

After the 1939 September campaign, during which Ford actively participated in the defense of Warsaw against the advancing German troops, he moved to the Soviet-occupied part of Poland, to the town of Białystok. In Białystok, he offered his services to the Soviet film authorities and worked on Soviet political propaganda films. After the outbreak of the German-Soviet war in June of 1941, Ford and his studio were moved to Tashkent.[6] It has to be stated that Ford was not the only Polish filmmaker of Jewish origin who had worked for the Soviets. Stanisław Wohl, Adolf Forbert and his brother Władysław, Leon Jeannot

(Lejbele Katz), and Ludwik Perski gathered toward the end of 1939 in Lvov and later in Kiev, where they found work in Soviet cinema. They contributed to several Soviet films that were clearly of anti-Polish nature.[7] For obvious political reasons, the issue of collaboration with the Soviet occupier was never mentioned in postwar Poland, although several Polish filmmakers who collaborated with the Nazi German regime were chastised by the Polish underground during the war, and punished by the communist film authorities after 1945.[8]

Ford survived the war in the Soviet Union. In the summer of 1943, he co-created the Film Unit Czołówka within the Polish Tadeusz Kościuszko First Division, part of the Red Army. He returned to Poland with the Red Army as an officer in the Polish division and, thanks to his political connections, became the most important figure in the postwar Polish film industry. From 1945 to 1947, he was the head of Film Polski, then artistic director of two film units—"Blok" (1948–1949) and "Studio" (1955–1968), and teacher at the Łódź Film School from its foundation in 1948 until 1968. Roman Polański calls Ford "the real power broker during the immediate postwar period … who established a small empire of his own."[9]

Border Street was carefully planned as Ford's first postwar film. The first version of the script was written in 1946. In February of the next year, Ford was shooting at the Barrandov studio where he learned about his replacement by Stanisław Albrecht as the head of Film Polski. Accused of mismanagement and rapidly losing his political footing, Ford had been closely watched by his successor and the Communist Party functionaries.[10] Since Ford never submitted a detailed script of his film and never sought advice about the project from proper authorities (although he claimed otherwise), Poland's chief ideologue Jakub Berman sent Albrecht to Barrandov to inspect the progress of Ford's film. According to Albrecht, Berman (who was on friendly terms with Ford) was afraid that Ford was making a quasi-religious film.[11] After seeing the footage of *Border Street*, Albrecht filed a short critical report, where he pointed out some of the film's weaknesses, mostly of a political nature, such as a lack of characters who are attempting to implement new, communist ideas in line with the Marxist ideology.[12]

The postwar political situation, with its forceful implementation of the communist system, the persecution of the Home Army members, and the suppression of any unbiased portrayal of the nationalists' struggle, proved to be a major obstacle for Ford who seemed, however, to be fully aware of the problems his project was going to encounter. He was making a film about the Warsaw Ghetto Uprising when not one film, whether documentary or fictional, addressed the issue of the Warsaw Rising (1 August–2 October 1944) or the plight of the nationalist Home Army.[13] Ford knew that for political reasons he would have to wait with the premiere of his film. In a letter to the Film Polski Artistic Council, dated 2 February 1947, he wrote that he had discussed his project with several influential people who said that his film should be released "neither first nor second" in 1947.[14] Most probably this had to do with the fact that communist leaders, some of them of Jewish origin, tried to avoid any association with the concept of *Żydokomuna* (Jewish-communist conspiracy). They also considered the timing very inappropriate, following the anti-Semitic violence in Kielce, known as the Kielce Pogrom (July of 1946), in which forty-one Jews were killed and several wounded.

A number of negative comments about *Border Street* had already appeared in the Polish press during the film's production. For example, the weekly *Przekrój* compared the new film by Ford to a sequel of the much criticized, albeit very popular, first postwar film, *Forbidden Songs*, and reported the following: "We have just received first pictures from our new full-length Polish film titled *Border Street*, made by director Ford in Prague ... One should expect just another martyrological kitsch."[15] A number of other reports presented only veiled information about the film's focus. They emphasized the humanistic aspect of Ford's project and stressed the epic scope of this Polish-Czech production.[16]

To understand the difficulties faced by Ford, it is imperative to see the political context of his film, namely how the Warsaw Ghetto Uprising had been commemorated in Poland. The first memorial was unveiled in Warsaw on 16 April 1946, and was placed where the uprising started. Designed by Polish architect Leon Marek Suzin, the monument was dedicated (in Polish, Yiddish, and Hebrew) "To the memory of those who died in unparalleled and heroic struggle for the dignity and freedom of the Jewish nation, for free Poland, and for the liberation of mankind—the Jews of Poland."[17] Nathan Rapoport's Warsaw Ghetto Monument, which was unveiled to full military honors on 19 April 1948, five years after the uprising began, is arguably better known. The heroic-tragic figures on the front of this eleven-meter-high monument represent different ghetto fighters (Figure 3.2). The composition clearly emphasizes armed resistance and martyrdom rather than the memory of those who were exterminated in the ghetto and in the concentration camps. The inscription on it, "To the Jewish nation—to its fighters and its martyrs," makes this notion apparent. The reverse side of the monument, sometimes missed by visitors, represents the suffering, deportations, and death.[18]

It has to be stressed that the first memorial commemorating the 1944 Warsaw Rising was built as late as 1989, after the fall of communism. This fact certainly did not help Polish-Jewish relations. A Warsaw-based journalist Konstanty Gebert aptly writes that "these Jewish memorials reminded many of the Poles of the monument to the Warsaw Uprising of 1944, one year after the Ghetto Uprising, which had *not* been built. The 1944 struggle, led by the non-communist underground army (Armia Krajowa, AK), had become almost a nonevent in Polish communist historiography. The speedy commemoration of the Jewish Uprising, coupled with the official non recognition of the Polish one, provided grounds for years of bitter feelings."[19] Taking this into account, one may only agree with Omer Bartov who fittingly writes that Ford's *Border Street* served "two contradictory purposes": "First, it was an opportunity to extol

Figure 3.2: Nathan Rapoport's Warsaw Ghetto Monument

Jewish heroism, showing that the Jews were 'just as heroic' as the Poles and asserting that Jews and Poles had united in resisting the Germans. Second, it served as an ersatz depiction of what most Poles experienced as a far more traumatic, but equally heroic event, the Polish Warsaw Uprising of August 1944."[20] Released in 1957, Andrzej Wajda's breakthrough *Kanal* (*Kanał*) became the first film about the Warsaw Rising, narrating the story of a Home Army unit that manages to escape German troops via the only route left—the city sewers—in which the majority of the fighters meet their deaths.

The Warsaw Ghetto Monument reflects a general attitude toward martyrdom and victimhood in the late 1940s. Writing about the American attitudes toward the Holocaust, Peter Novick states: "Whereas nowadays the status of victim has come to be prized, in the forties and fifties it evoked at best the sort of pity mixed with contempt. It was a label actively shunned."[21] He also notes that in the late 1940s several prominent American Jewish organizations objected to a proposed Holocaust memorial in New York City: "They were concerned that such a monument would result in Americans' thinking of Jews as victims: it would be 'a perpetual memorial to the weakness and defenselessness of the Jewish people'; it would 'not be in the best interests of Jewry.'"[22]

Border Street became the first cinematic monument to the Ghetto Uprising, yet the Warsaw Ghetto was featured prominently in Polish literary works published during and shortly after the war. For example, the writings of Jerzy

Andrzejewski, Tadeusz Borowski, Maria Dąbrowska, Zofia Nałkowska, Kazimierz Brandys, and Adolf Rudnicki (the last two being of Jewish descent) belong to the most discussed in Poland. Władysław Broniewski, Antoni Słonimski, Jerzy Ficowski, Miron Białoszewski, Czesław Miłosz, and several other poets also devoted their works to the plight of Polish Jews.[23] The 1944 collection of poems, *From the Abyss* (*Z otchłani*), published in three thousand copies by an underground press in occupied Warsaw and dedicated to the Warsaw Jews, featured works in Polish written by poets living on both sides of the wall.[24] In 1947, director of the Jewish Historical Commission (Żydowska Komisja Historyczna) in Kraków, Michał Borwicz, edited another anthology, *The Song Will Survive: An Anthology of Poems about Jews under the German Occupation* (*Pieśń ujdzie cało. Antologia wierszy o Żydach pod okupacją niemiecką*) that includes poems by Czesław Miłosz, Mieczysław Jastrun, Michał Borwicz, and several other Polish and Jewish poets.[25]

***

Like *Forbidden Songs*, the first released postwar film, *Border Street* also had been made by some prewar professionals. The film was scripted by Ford, the experienced Ludwik Starski (1903–1984), and Jan Fethke (1903–1980, credited as Jean Forge). Starski, an assimilated Polish Jew, was a prolific prewar screenwriter and author of lyrics to several popular Polish songs composed by Henryk Wars, among others, which are popular in Poland to this day. Starski also scripted some of the most popular postwar Polish films directed by Leonard Buczkowski. They include *Forbidden Songs*, the comedy *Treasure* (*Skarb*, 1949) and the classic socialist realist comedy, *An Adventure at Marienstadt* (*Przygoda na Mariensztacie*, 1954).[26] Fethke, a Polish-German screenwriter and director born in Upper Silesia, worked for German UFA in the 1920s, and published novels in Esperanto under the pseudonym Jean Forge. He co-scripted *Mother Krause's Journey to Happiness* (*Mutter Krauses Fahrt ins Glück*, 1929), a proletarian melodrama directed by Piel Jutzi. In the mid-1930s, he moved to Warsaw where he was a scriptwriter and later a film director. During the war, Fethke worked as a director for German film studios. After 1945, he continued his career in Poland, directing three films during the period of socialist realist cinema.[27]

Since both screenwriters and the director were not familiar with the situation in the Warsaw Ghetto, they sought the advice of a psychologist and writer Rachela Auerbach (1901–1976), credited as the film's consultant. She lived in the Warsaw Ghetto during the war (where she worked together with Emmanuel Ringelblum), and later escaped to the "Aryan side," and was active in Polish Żegota (Council for Aid to the Jews). After the war, she documented the Holocaust through several publications including two books, among them the first book about the extermination camp at Treblinka. In 1950, she left Poland for Israel and worked for the Yad Vashem Institute.

The original screenplay of *Border Street* stressed the hostile attitude of Poles toward Jews.[28] The final version of the screenplay, modified by Ford after severe criticism of his project, presented not so much the division, but the solidarity between Jews and Poles across the real and symbolic wall dividing the city. The two versions of the film were commented upon by a prominent Polish writer, Maria Dąbrowska, in her *Diaries*. She called the first version, which she saw in January 1949, "a scandal" and "veiled anti-Polish propaganda." After seeing the modified, final version, she remarked that this was a "very good and at times moving Jewish film. Not Polish, but no longer offending the feelings of the Polish nation, as the first version did."[29]

The anti-Semitic sentiments of many Poles, however, are not suppressed in the final version of the film. In addition to images of Poles risking their lives to help the ghetto dwellers and to support the Ghetto Uprising, *Border Street* also shows Poles denouncing Jews to the Germans out of malice or in the hope of getting their vacated apartments. Ford succeeds when portraying the extermination of his fellow countrymen. Like Wanda Jakubowska in *The Last Stage*, he soothes the pessimistic tone of the film with an edifying final voice-over urging the solidarity of all people as the means of destroying man-made barriers.

The Commission for Film Approval's (Komisja Kwalifikacyjna) record of the meeting held in Warsaw at the beginning of June 1948 clearly demonstrates how Ford's film was viewed by the film authorities.[30] Headed by the Film Polski director Stanisław Albrecht, the committee members had no problems with purely cinematic aspects of the film. They praised its "artistic value," although they disliked the "prewar acting mannerism" and the reliance on much criticized prewar narrative conventions. They also evaluated the "technical aspect of the film" (its quality) as "very good" (the highest on the scale). The real discussion began with the issue of the "social usefulness" (użyteczność społeczna) of Ford's film. Several voices objected to Ford's portrayal of anti-Semitic Poles as not being representative of the historical reality. Bolesław W. Lewicki, then the Artistic Director of Film Polski, pointed out that the previously released film, *The Last Stage*, was considered by many viewers as anti-Polish. He added that "reminders of the sins from the occupation period irritate the viewer ... Certain sensitive topics ought to be covered with silence; only in ten or fifteen years one can return to them."[31] For Albrecht, the film lacked the Marxist perspective and was devoid of "patriotism that is built on class consciousness."[32] Interestingly, Albrecht considered that *Border Street* played a useful role outside of Poland. In a different document, issued toward the end of 1948, Albrecht explicitly stated that it is evident after viewing the film that its author "was not an eyewitness of events presented in his film, and that he did not tackle appropriately the problem of the fight for freedom among Jews and Poles during the Ghetto Uprising."[33]

Aleksander Ford had to wait until June 1949 to have his film released. As Alina Madej's research reveals, the Communist Party finally decided to release the film after test screenings for factory workers and after instructing reviewers how to interpret the film. Thus, as Madej writes, reviews and comments published after the film's premiere cannot be taken as a valid historical source. Rather, they testify to the official policy of the Communist Party toward Ford's film. They also reflect the state of Polish-Jewish relations.[34] By and large, the published reviews emphasized the universal nature of the film. Comments stressing the common Polish-Jewish struggle, such as this one—"the victimized Jews represent here all free people fighting with injustice," dominated the discussion.[35] Infrequent voices, like the one belonging to critic Leon Bukowiecki, referred to Polish anti-Semitism and praised Ford for tackling the problem with the help of "simple, truthful images." In his review, the title of which serves as a paraphrase of the French title of the film ("Truth has no borders"), Bukowiecki writes: "Ford chose Poland, chose Polish film as a tribute to the suffering of the millions."[36]

Ford's film was released one year after the declaration of Israel's independence on 14 May 1948, when the remaining Jews were leaving Poland. The immigration to Israel was at full speed. During the period when Ford started working on his project in 1946 and the release of his film in June of 1949, more than two-thirds of the surviving Polish Jews left the country (approximately thirty thousand from 1948 to 1950).[37] Alina Madej justly notes that due to its timing, "Ford's film did not thus have its targeted audiences who could watch the film through the prism of their own tragic experiences."[38] Apart from the above circumstances, the policy toward the state of Israel and Jews in general also began to change rapidly. Following the Soviet example, Poland officially recognized the Jewish state on 18 May 1948. In the fall of 1948, however, once again following the developments in the Soviet Union, there were the first signs marking the beginning of an anti-Semitic campaign under the umbrella term of the "struggle with Zionism." Stalin's campaign against Jews accelerated after the official closure of the Jewish Anti-Fascist Committee in November 1948, and was followed by violent persecutions of "Zionist conspirators" and purges of Jewish cultural life.[39]

***

Border Street opens with credits over the shots of wartime Warsaw ruins. After the credits the camera continues to capture images of destruction. The voice-over commentary introduces the setting of the film:

> Streets changed into cemeteries. Ruins, burned down places. So many of them you can still find in Warsaw. The action of our film takes place on one such street. Let us call it Border Street, although it could be Długa, Bielańska or Świętokrzyska. We don't want to determine its real name. We do intend only to show a small fragment of its history, the history of its modest inhabitants, little people, children, or practically children.

This initial comment suggests that "Border Street" is a fictional street that could be anywhere in Warsaw, thus enhancing a deeply symbolic, universal meaning of the film. There was, however, a real "Border Street" (Ulica Graniczna) in Warsaw, situated alongside the ghetto wall, and close to one of the entrances to the ghetto.[40]

The film's action moves briefly to a period preceding the September 1939 invasion of Poland and swiftly introduces several different Polish and Jewish families living in a Warsaw apartment building on Border Street. Among them is the Polonized Jewish doctor Józef Białek (Jerzy Leszczyński) and his daughter Jadzia (Maria Broniewska); a bank employee Kazimierz Wojtan (Jerzy Pichelski) with family, who is portrayed as a proud nationalist Pole; Kuśmirak, an opportunist shopkeeper who runs a café with his family; the good natured, working-class Cieplikowski (Władysław Walter) with his son Bronek. The basement of the building is inhabited by the Libermans: an orthodox Jewish tailor Liberman (Władysław Godik) and his family, including an assimilated socialist worker Natan (Stefan Śródka) and his nephew Dawidek (Jerzy Złotnicki).

The initial scenes of Ford's film also introduce the anti-Jewish attitudes of several Poles. For example, Dawidek is victimized by Polish boys when he clumsily tries to join them for a soccer game. Wojtan also comments that "of course, there will be no war. Hitler will never dare. The Jews only encourage such gossip to make better business," and forbids his son, Władek, to play with Dawidek. However, Wojtan's wife defends Dawidek by saying that he "is a good child although he is Jewish," and she calls the Libermans "decent people."

With the war imminent, Wojtan puts on his officer's uniform and is surprised to see Natan also wearing a Polish soldier's uniform. In another scene, Cieplikowski's comment, "I'm telling you: there will be no war," is followed by images of German planes over Warsaw. An abrupt cut moves the action to occupied Warsaw and introduces a symbolic image, often employed in Polish cinema, of a wounded Polish soldier watching the victorious German troops marching on the streets of Warsaw. The subsequent occupation changes relations among the families on Border Street. In an almost farcical scene, Kuśmirak (played by a Czech actor Josef Muncliger) defines himself as a *Volksdeutsch* in purely visual terms at a barber store, by trimming his Piłsudski-like moustache and changing his hairstyle to resemble Hitler ("The times have changed," he proclaims to a surprised barber). Later, Kuśmirak (now Kushmirak) takes advantage of his privileged position and blackmails Dr. Białek, threatening to reveal his Jewish identity. He forces him to move to the ghetto and takes over his spacious apartment.

While showing differences between the treatment of Poles and Jews by the Germans, Ford constantly accentuates the need for unity and common struggle with the occupier. Wojtan comes to the conclusion that "the Jews are not all alike, and we have our own Kuśmiraks, too." When Liberman comments that "terrible times are coming for the Jews," Natan responds emphatically, "not only for the Jews." After learning about the creation of the ghetto, Liberman says that "maybe it will be better for the Jews to be separate." When his daughter supports him ("But at least in the ghetto, we shall all be equal"), Natan responds in the following way: "Oh yes, they will exterminate all of us equally. Don't you see? They want to separate us from the Poles. It will be easier to eliminate us and the Pole … It is their policy. In the POW camp people were saying that we should be together. To fight!" When the fatalistic Liberman ridicules Natan's desire to fight, he responds that the Jews will fight even with bare fists (and his gesture looks as if taken from a propagandist war poster): "The Poles will surely fight and we should go with them."

Writer Bogdan Wojdowski once observed that "The wall divided people. That is why it was built."[41] Ford portrays the two sides of the division, the two sides of the wall. As in several of his earlier films, children are at the center of *Border Street*. Like their families, they represent a cross-section of Warsaw. Led by Cieplikowski's teenage son Bronek (played by Tadeusz Fijewski who debuted in Ford's first film, *The Legion of the Street*), they display the same qualities as their parents. For example, like his father, Władek Wojtan (Dionizy Ilczenko) evolves from an anti-Semite to a member of the resistance. He gives Dawidek his most precious possession—a pistol given to him by his father who was executed for his underground activities. Fredek Kuśmirak collaborates with the Germans and becomes a member of Hitlerjugend. Bronek Cieplikowski, who survives by smuggling food (and also helping Dawidek who supports his family by going to the Aryan side), displays the same working-class charm as his father. As in a number of Italian neorealist films (that later influenced the Polish School generation), children represent hope for the future. The ending of *Border Street*, with Fredek mistakenly killed by a German soldier (who takes him for a fleeing Jewish child) and Dawidek returning to fight in the ghetto, portrays a working-class Bronek, a changed middle-class Władek, and a half-Jewish Jadzia standing "united as the seeds of new 'positive' Polish society"[42] (Figure 3.3).

In the final scene of *Border Street*, Dawidek waves to the camera in the Warsaw sewers and starts moving back to the ghetto (Figure 3.4). After Bronek comforts Jadzia that Dawidek "cannot die; he will not die," the images of Dawidek are accompanied by a voice-over narrator, who concludes: "Farewell Dawidek. We also believe that you won't die, that on the other side of the Border Street Bronek and Władek will be fighting, and surely all those who know the truth cannot have borders, that there are no borders between the people." Looking at the uplifting ending of *Border Street*, Ilan Avisar remarks that "David's joining of the other Jewish fighters can be interpreted as Ford's tribute to the contemporary Jewish struggle in Israel to establish an independent state."[43] Perhaps Avisar is right in looking at Dawidek as an emblem of the Jewish struggle for statehood, but the film's script ends on a pessimistic note, with the death of Dawidek during his escape from the ghetto. Also in the script Jadzia is killed by Fredek, whom she wants to denounce to the police for his wartime activities. In turn, Fredek dies in the ruins while being chased by

Commemorating the Warsaw Ghetto Uprising in Border Street (1949)   63

Figure 3.3: (From the left) Władek Wojtan (Dionizy Ilczenko), Jadzia Białek (Maria Broniewska), and Bronek Cieplikowski (Tadeusz Fijewski) in Aleksander Ford's *Border Street* (1949)

Bronek and Władek.[44] Although the released version of the film certainly invites interpretations such as the one by Avisar, it is worth noting that the original (scripted) versions of not only *Border Street*, but also of the prewar *Sabra*, end in tragedy and are deprived of optimistic, nation-building images.

The ending of Ford's film unmistakably shows a new inclusive Poland where people can live together. A similar dream was visualized by a renowned Polish poet of Jewish descent, Julian Tuwim, in his manifesto and lament on the destruction of Polish Jewry, *We Polish Jews …*, written in 1944 in the United States:

> Upon the armbands which you wore in the ghetto the Star of David was painted. I believe in a future Poland in which that star of your armbands will become the highest order bestowed upon the bravest among Polish officers and soldiers. They will wear it proudly upon their breast next to the old Virtuti Militari … And there shall be in Warsaw and in every Polish city some fragment of the ghetto standing and preserved in its present form in all its horror of ruin and destruction. We shall surround that monument to the ignominy of our foes and to the glory of our tortured heroes with chains wrought from captured Hitler's guns, and every day

Figure 3.4: Dawidek (Jerzy Złotnicki) in *Border Street*

shall twine fresh live flowers into its iron links, so that the memory of the massacred people shall remain forever fresh in the minds of the generations to come, and also as a sign of our undying sorrow for them.[45]

As mentioned earlier, Ford did not experience the wartime occupation of Poland first hand. Arguably, this is the reason why the ghetto scenes are reduced to a necessary minimum, and the film largely presents an external perspective—from the Aryan side. There are no scenes of starvation, disease, and mass deportations from the transfer point, the *Umschlagplatz*, to the Treblinka extermination camp. Sporadically, Ford incorporates fragments of documentary newsreels to enhance the realism of the ghetto street scenes but, apart from the portrayal of the uprising, he reduces the reality of the ghetto to several universalizing scenes such as Dr. Białek dying of typhoid fever and the execution of an old Jewish worker. When Jadzia is sent out of the ghetto by the Libermans and wanders on the streets of "Aryan Warsaw," Ford cuts to an image of a street loudspeaker announcing: "Attention! Jewish children are escaping from the ghetto. Attention! The presence of Jewish children in the Aryan part of the city is forbidden by law. Anybody who helps the Jewish children, gives them shelter, or feeds them, is subjected to the death penalty. The Jewish children transmit typhoid fever and spread epidemics ... should be immediately given to the police." The same approach applies to the portrayal of the other side of the wall. When Wojtan is captured in a restaurant while meeting his son, Ford cuts abruptly to a short scene of his execution. Portrayed against the wall in a medium shot, Wojtan shouts "Long live Poland!" before a bandage is put on his mouth (Figure 3.5). In an attempt at a universalizing metaphor, Ford's camera pans to the right to reveal other Poles who are sharing Wojtan's fate.

Ford's portrayal of the horrors of the ghetto and tense Polish-Jewish relations are nonetheless weakened by the film's reliance on melodramatic conventions. As mentioned by some members of the Commission for Film Approval, an "operetta-like image of the war and occupation" and an old-fashioned manner of acting make *Border Street* look like a prewar film. Although the commission members praised the role of old Liberman played by Godik (a theatrical actor

Figure 3.5: Kazimierz Wojtan (Jerzy Pichelski)

active in Jewish theater before the war; see Figure 3.6), they pointed out the theatrical acting of Leszczyński and Pichelski and unconvincing child actors (with the exception of Fijewski and Złotnicki) as the film's weaknesses.[46]

Like his fellow START member Jakubowska, despite being a prewar avant-garde filmmaker who attacked the cinematic establishment (so-called *branża*—film trade), Ford relied on mainstream narrative conventions in his first postwar film. Like Jakubowska's *The Last Stage*, Ford's film also had to follow the tenets of the communist ideology as it was released during the year of rapid Stalinization of Poland. Several speakers at the 1949 congress of filmmakers at Wisła condemned previously made films, including *The Last Stage* and *Border Street*, for their cosmopolitan and bourgeois tendencies and lack of "revolutionary spirit." The Communist Party official film critic, Irena Merz, commented in her review that "given its noble premises, *Border Street* lost its social goal, limiting its impact to generate pity."[47] Another critic, Marian Warszałłowicz, pointed out that Ford neglects to emphasize the important help that the ghetto fighters received from the Communist Party. Also, according to the same reviewer, *Border Street* does not depict the unity between Polish and Jewish underground workers and their common goals.[48]

The issue of common Polish-Jewish struggle was of utmost importance for the communist authorities, certainly more important than the homage to the victims of the Holocaust. The portrayal of Polish-Jewish unity in a country rebuilding itself from the destructions of war, from moral as well as material wounds, was encouraged and expected by the communist regime. The communists also expected to see themselves represented on the screen as leading the struggle in the ghetto. Ford's task was thus enormous, almost unattainable, although some critics praised Ford for doing the impossible. Reviewing the film after its premiere, Leon Bukowiecki wrote about "an anti-Semitic complex that weighed down on Polish society," and that "Aleksander Ford with simple, truthful images undid that complex, showing its meaninglessness."[49]

Among several scenes showing the unified front against the Germans, two set themselves apart. In an early scene in Dr. Białek's apartment, a group of

Figure 3.6: Władysław Godik as Liberman

children, supervised by Jadzia's teacher, Miss Klara,[50] is singing the song "Warszawskie dzieci" (We, Warsaw Children), which begins with the stanza stressing that "We shall go together toward victory/When the nation stands together shoulder to shoulder." And the song continuous with this refrain:

> We, Warsaw children, we shall fight a battle,
> For every stone of yours, the Capital, we shall spill our blood!
> We, Warsaw children, we shall fight a battle,
> When you give the order, we shall carry our wrath to our enemies!

In the film, the song appears before the establishment of the ghetto in November 1940. "We, Warsaw Children," however, was composed shortly before the 1944 Warsaw Rising by Andrzej Panufnik to the lyrics of Stanisław Ryszard Dobrowolski (writing under the pseudonym of Goliard). Later it became the emblematic song of the Warsaw Rising. This was also the first song of the Rising that was featured in postwar Polish cinema. In her book on *Polish Film Music* Iwona Sowińska observes:

> Even though one can only speculate about the reasons why the makers of the film risked this discrepancy with facts, they present themselves quite clearly. This tactic conceivably had to serve identifying the two uprisings in social consciousness. The film argued that all "Warsaw children," regardless of their roots, fought for the same cause. Although not always shoulder to shoulder.[51]

In another scene emphasizing the common struggle, the Jewish fighter Natan is portrayed in a heroic pose, on top of a partly destroyed apartment building, throwing a hand grenade at the German soldiers (Figures 3.7 and 3.8). Behind him the viewer can see two waving Polish flags (white and red). The medium shot of Natan with the Polish flag in the background made the cover of the Polish weekly *Film* in 1948.[52] The symbolic framing of Natan between the two flags certainly invites interpretations that this image is ideologically, but not historically, correct. For example, discussing Natan ("Jew as Polish hero"), prominent historian Omer Bartov writes the following: "married to Liberman's

Figure 3.7: The Warsaw Ghetto Uprising. Natan (Stefan Śródka)

Figure 3.8: Natan (Stefan Śródka)

daughter, a veteran soldier in the Warsaw Ghetto, throws his last grenade at the advancing Germans, flanked by two Polish national flags. Such flags were never flown by the Jewish resisters, who felt betrayed by the Polish underground's reluctance to supply them with arms."[53]

According to several historical accounts, however, the Polish national flag was indeed displayed in the ghetto, hanging above Muranowska Street 7 after the beginning of the uprising.[54] Marek Edelman, one of the leaders of the Ghetto Uprising and also the narrator of one of the most powerful literary accounts of that struggle, Hanna Krall's book *Shielding the Flame*, talks about Polish and Jewish banners displayed during the uprising: "They'd been hanging over the Ghetto from the first day of the uprising: white and red, and blue and white. They provoked an outpouring of affection on the Aryan side, and the Germans finally took them down, with the greatest difficulty and the greatest satisfaction, as war trophies."[55] The ghetto historian Emmanuel Ringelblum writes in a similar manner:

> We shall not describe here in detail the course of the fighting with the Germans in April 1943. Separate groups were fighting in the Ghetto, in the bristle workshops in Świętojerska Street, on the terrain of the Schultz and Toebbens workshops, etc. There was fighting on the roofs of blocks where Polish and Zionist (blue-white) flags were fluttering. From the fourth floor of 32 Nalewki Street I was an eye witness of fighting like this at Muranowska Street during the afternoon hours of Monday the 18th of April. In the headquarters of the Order Service the Germans proudly displayed their trophies—captured flags—and gloried in their seizure.[56]

The poster-like image of Natan, an assimilated Jew fighting for "your freedom and ours"[57] and calling his fellow Jews to arms ("Brothers, the Jewish Combat Organization calls you to fight!"), not only was in line with the view of the communist regime in Poland, but was also commonly accepted in the West and in the Jewish state of Israel. In an introduction to his *Resistance: The Warsaw Ghetto Uprising*, Israel Gutman writes: "The Warsaw Ghetto Uprising is a historical event, but it also has become a symbol of Jewish resistance and determination, a moment in history that has transformed the self-perception of the Jewish people from passivity to active armed struggle. The Uprising has shaped Israel's national self-understanding."[58]

Discussing the emblematic nature of the ghetto uprising, Janina Struk notices,

> During the Cold War, The Warsaw Ghetto Uprising became a symbolic event for both East and West, albeit for different political reasons. No nation wanted victims but everyone wanted heroes, a point exemplified by the large number of books and pamphlets published about the ghetto fighters on both sides of the Iron Curtain. Apart these commemorations of the Warsaw Ghetto Uprising, there were to be no more displays of Nazi atrocity photographs in the West for two decades. Only when, as communism crumbled and the world order began to change again, did the murder of the 6 million Jews in the Western world, by then unambiguously referred

to as the Holocaust, become of prime importance. The Jewish question, which Western nations had colluded in suppressing for thirty years, would become central to memories of the Second World War and, crucially, its representation would shift from one of heroes to that of victims.[59]

The Polish authorities wanted to see a film about heroism on both sides of the wall. Particularly, they favored images of assistance provided for the ghetto fighters by the units of People's Guard (Gwardia Ludowa, GL), the Communist Party armed wing founded in 1942 and renamed People's Army (Armia Ludowa, AL) in January 1944. Ford included only a brief scene of a Polish fireman, who is killed for putting out the fire in the ghetto, and shots of some unidentified fighters (one of whom speaks with a foreign, perhaps Russian, accent) moving to the ghetto through the city sewers. Although views, such as Bartov's, that "in reality, the Jews fought and the Poles watched,"[60] are prevalent in historical accounts written outside of Poland, the Polish aid for the ghetto, albeit limited, is a historical fact. The commander of the German forces fighting the ghetto insurgency, SS General Jürgen Stroop, commented on the participation of Poles ("Polish bandits") in his report dated 23 April 1943.[61] Some units of AK and GL smuggled weapons and explosives into the ghetto, provided the military training, attacked the German posts near the ghetto walls, briefly participated in the uprising, and assisted some ghetto fighters in their escape from the ghetto. Several of the surviving Jewish fighters, including Edelman, later participated in the Warsaw Rising (see Figure 3.9).[62]

In the light of the political situation in the late 1940s, it is indeed surprising that Ford was able to produce and release his film without paying a customary tribute to the communist underground.[63] A later film by Andrzej Wajda, *A Generation* (*Pokolenie*, 1955), which is discussed in the next chapter, addressed the issue of communist help for the ghetto in a more direct manner.

***

Figure 3.9: Poles look at the Warsaw Ghetto Uprising. (Center) Tadeusz Fijewski as Bronek

Despite problems Ford faced while making *Border Street*, he maintained his leading position in the Polish film industry and continued his career with a socialist-realist biographical film, *The Youth of Chopin* (*Młodość Chopina*, 1952). In 1954, he made his first film in color, *Five Boys from Barska Street* (*Piątka z ulicy Barskiej*), for which he won the Best Director award at the Cannes Film Festival. The film focused on juvenile delinquency, a theme previously untouched in Polish cinema. For Polish viewers, however, Ford is chiefly known as the maker of the most successful (at the box-office) Polish film ever, the historical epic *The Teutonic Knights* (*Krzyżacy*, 1960). The events of 1968 (the anti-Semitic campaign orchestrated by a nationalistic faction of the Communist Party in order to remove some seasoned party and security force members, many of whom were Jewish, from their privileged positions) isolated Ford as both a person of Jewish origin and an activist linked with the group removed from power. He was removed from the party and his Film Unit "Studio" was disbanded in December 1968. As a result, in 1969 Ford migrated from Poland and tried to continue his career in West Germany, Denmark, and the United States. In Germany he directed *The First Circle* (*Den Foerste Kreds*, 1971) and *Dr. Korczak, the Martyr* (*Sie Sind Frei, Dr. Korczak*, 1974, West Germany-Israel). The latter, as Ilan Avisar writes, "due to a weak story line, poor acting, and excessive sentimentality ... is a regrettable failure, even though it borrows much from the remarkable *Border Street*."[64] In 1980, at the age of 72, Ford committed suicide in Naples, Florida. His death was barely noticed by Polish papers.[65]

Notes

1. Omer Bartov, *The "Jew" in Cinema: From* The Golem *to* Don't Touch My Holocaust (Bloomington: Indiana University Press, 2005), 180.
2. Krzysztof Kucharski, *Kino plus. Film i dystrybucja kinowa w Polsce w latach 1990–2000* (Toruń: Oficyna Wydawnicza Kucharski, 2002), 388. *Border Street* is listed eighteen on the list of the biggest Polish box-office successes. Another film by Ford, *The Teutonic Knights* tops the list with more than 33 million viewers.
3. Barbara Armatys, Leszek Armatys, and Wiesław Stradomski, *Historia filmu polskiego 1930–1939* (Warsaw: Wydawnictwa Artystyczne i Filmowe, 1988), 223–224.
4. Alina Madej, *Kino, władza, publiczność. Kinematografia polska w latach 1944–1949* (Bielsko-Biała: Wydawnictwo "Prasa Beskidzka," 2002), 182–183.
5. On 20 August 1942, the children from Miedzeszyn and their teachers were sent to Treblinka. Joanna Preizner, "Aleksander Ford—car PRL-owskiego kina," *Autorzy kina polskiego*, ed. Grażyna Stachówna and Bogusław Żmudziński (Kraków: Wydawnictwo Uniwersytetu Jagiellońskiego, 2007): 21. Ford's three ventures into mainstream cinema made between 1930 and 1935 were not successful. The authors of the second volume of the *History of Polish Cinema* note that the combination of the conventions of traditional cinema and communist messages produced a "pretentious style" that was "anachronistic in its modernist avant-gardism." In 1938, Ford and Jerzy Zarzycki directed *The People of the Vistula* for the Cooperative of Film Authors, a continuation of the START group. The film received critical acclaim and became known for its realistic portrayal of the marginalized groups of society. The melodramatic aspect of this film focused on Anna (Ina Benita), the daughter of the barge

owner on the Vistula River, in love with a handsome petty thief from the shore, Aleksy (Jerzy Pichelski). This film was set in the milieu of Jean Vigo's *L'Atalante* (1934) and also had some features of Vigo's masterpiece: glimpses of social conditions, a love story on a river barge, and the life on the shore contrasted with that on the barge. See Armatys, Armatys, and Stradomski, *Historia filmu polskiego 1930-1939*, 226.

6. Jolanta Lemann-Zajiček, *Kino i polityka. Polski film dokumentalny 1945-1949* (Łódź: PWSFTviT, 2003), 16.
7. Ibid., 19. Also, Alicja Mucha-Świeżyńska, "Powikłane drogi" (interview with Stanisław Wohl), *Kino* 11 (1984): 6.
8. The Polish underground tried to discourage people from visiting movie theaters, but also punished filmmakers and actors who collaborated with the Germans during the war. For instance, Igo Sym, a popular prewar actor, was executed for spying, acting in Gustav Ucicky's anti-Polish *Heimkehr* (*Return Home*, 1941), and recruiting other Polish actors to appear in this film. In retaliation, the Germans sent a group of distinguished Polish actors, including Leon Schiller and Stefan Jaracz, to Auschwitz. After the war, a small group of Polish filmmakers and actors, including Bogusław Samborski, who appeared in *Heimkehr* (and left Poland after the war), were put on trial for collaborating with the Germans. Others, for example Adolf Dymsza who performed in Warsaw's theaters during the war, underwent verifications and sometimes symbolic punishment. The issue of collaboration of artists with German and Soviet regimes is insightfully discussed by Tomasz Szarota in "Kolaboracja z okupantem niemieckim i sowieckim w oczach Polaków—wówczas, wczoraj i dziś," included in his anthology *Karuzela na Placu Krasińskich. Studia i szkice z lat wojny i okupacji* (Warsaw: Oficyna Wydawnicza Rytm, 2007), 71-145.
9. Roman Polanski, *Roman by Polanski* (New York: William Morrow, 1984), 104.
10. See Edward Zajiček, *Poza ekranem. Kinematografia polska 1918-1991* (Warsaw: Filmoteka Narodowa and Wydawnictwa Artystyczne i Filmowe, 1992): 62-66; Madej, *Kino, władza, publiczność*, 186-190.
11. Alina Madej, "Wielka gra" [interview with Stanisław Albrecht], *Kwartalnik Filmowy* 6 (1994): 207-208.
12. Stanisław Albrecht, "Ocena filmu 'Ulica graniczna' (na podstawie niezmontowanego materiału)," Archive of Contemporary Documents (Archiwum Akt Nowych), PPR/295/XVII-7/19. I owe the information about the existence of this document to Alina Madej's research. Madej, *Kino, władza, publiczność*, 189-190. The document is reprinted in *Kwartalnik Filmowy* 6 (1994): 216.
13. See discussion about the memory of the Warsaw Rising and the Home Army in Andrzej Waśkiewicz, "The Polish Home Army and the Politics of Memory," *East European Politics and Societies* vol. 24, no. 1 (2010): 44-58.
14. "Minutes from the Meeting of the Artistic Council (Rada Artystyczna)," National Film Archive in Warsaw, S-587, p. 2.
15. Kasp. [pseudonim], "Zakazane piosenki nr 2 i 3," *Przekrój* 122 (1948).
16. For example, Aleksander Suchcicki, "Kręcimy w Pradze polski film 'Hranicni Ulice'! Zvuk Cislo!" *Film* 18 (1947): 8-9; Zbigniew Kuźmiński, "Pracowity dzień najmłodszych gwiazd," *Film* 20 (1947): 5; Z.P. [Zbigniew Pitera], "Dziwna ulica," *Film* 29 (1947): 4.
17. Quoted from Konstanty Gebert, "The Dialectics of Memory in Poland," *The Art of Memory: Holocaust Memorials in History*, ed. James E. Young (New York: Prestel, 1994), 122.
18. See Gebert, "The Dialectics of Memory in Poland," 124. For an illuminating discussion on the history and meaning of the Warsaw Ghetto Monument see also James E. Young's chapter, "The Biography of a Memorial Icon: Nathan Rapoport's Warsaw Ghetto Monument," in his *The Texture of Memory: Holocaust, Memorials, and Meaning* (New Haven: Yale University Press, 1993), 155-184.
19. Gebert, "The Dialectics of Memory in Poland," 126.
20. Bartov, *The "Jew" in Cinema*, 180.
21. Peter Novick, *The Holocaust in American Life* (Boston: Houghton Mifflin, 1999), 121.

22. Ibid., 123. Peter Novick cites the 1947 comment by Jules Cohen of NCRAC (National Community Relations Advisory Council).
23. See Irena Maciejewska, "Getto warszawskie w literaturze polskiej," *Literatura wobec wojny i okupacji*, ed. Michał Głowiński and Janusz Sławiński (Wrocław: Ossolineum, 1976), 135–162. See also Maciejewska's excellent anthology of works in Polish dealing with Jewish suffering, *Męczeństwo i zagłada Żydów w zapisach literatury polskiej* (Warsaw: Krajowa Agencja Wydawnicza, 1988).
24. Rafael F. Scharf comments that "considering the circumstances in which these poems were written and came to see the light of day, I have no hesitation in calling the appearance of that little volume an event unique in the history of literature." Rafael F Scharf, "Literature in the Ghetto in the Polish Language: Z otchłani—From the Abyss," in *Holocaust Chronicles: Individualizing the Holocaust through Diaries and Other Contemporaneous Personal Accounts*, ed. Robert Moses Szapiro (Ktav Publishing House, 1999), 31.
25. Michał Borwicz, ed., *Pieśń ujdzie cało. Antologia wierszy o Żydach pod okupacją niemiecką* (Warsaw: Centralna Żydowska Komisja, 1947).
26. In the 1950s, Starski wrote the script for Jan Rybkowski's satire *Nikodem Dyzma* (1956) and Fethke's comedy *Irena, Go Home! (Irena do domu!*, 1955). In addition to writing, Starski headed film units Warszawa (1948–1949) and Iluzjon (1955–1963). He is the father of an Oscar-winning set designer Allan Starski, who worked on Steven Spielberg's *Schindler's List* and also, among others, on several Polish Holocaust dramas, such as Andrzej Wajda's *Korczak* (1990) and *Holy Week* (1996), and Roman Polański's *The Pianist* (2002).
27. In 1961 Fethke migrated to West Berlin where (as Jan Fethge) he produced the script for *The Thousand Eyes of Dr. Mabuse (Tausend Augen des. Dr. Mabuse*, 1960), directed by Fritz Lang.
28. Alina Madej, "100 lat kina w Polsce: 1945–1948," *Kino* 5 (1998): 49–50.
29. Maria Dąbrowska, *Dzienniki powojenne, 1945–1965* (Warsaw: Czytelnik, 1996), 373 and 442. Interestingly, Dąbrowska's friend/lover, Stanisława Blumenfeld, who perished during the war, was Jewish.
30. "Ulica Graniczna. Protokół z posiedzenia Komisji Kwalifikacyjnej w dniach 1 i 2 czerwca 1948 roku," National Film Archive A-329/1. Reprinted in Piotr Litka, "Polacy i Żydzi w *Ulicy Granicznej*," *Kwartalnik Filmowy* 29–30 (2000): 68–74. Quoted from Litka.
31. Ibid., 72–73.
32. Stanisław Albrecht, "Tezy ideologiczne filmu polskiego," Archive of Contemporary Documents in Warsaw (Archiwum Akt Nowych), PPR/295/XVII-8/5. Quoted from Madej, *Kino, władza, publiczność*, 191.
33. Ibid., 191.
34. Madej, *Kino, władza, publiczność*, 192–193.
35. Litka, "Polacy i Żydzi w *Ulicy Granicznej*," 60–61. Litka cites a review published in *Gazeta Robotnicza* in 1949.
36. Leon Bukowiecki, "Prawda nie zna granic. *Ulica Graniczna* Aleksandra Forda," *Kuźnica* 14 (1949).
37. Piotr Wróbel, "Double Memory: Poles and Jews after the Holocaust," *East European Politics and Societies* vol. 11, no. 3 (1997): 572. See also Józef Adelson, "W Polsce zwanej Ludową," *Najnowsze dzieje Żydów w Polsce*, ed. Jerzy Tomaszewski (Warsaw: Państwowy Instytut Wydawniczy, 1993) and Bożena Szaynok, "The Impact of the Holocaust on Jewish Attitudes in Postwar Poland," *Contested Memories: Poles and Jews during the Holocaust and Its Aftermath* (New Brunswick: Rutgers University Press, 2003).
38. Madej, *Kino, władza, publiczność*, 185.
39. Arno Lustiger, *Stalin and the Jews. The Red Book: The Tragedy of the Anti-Fascist Committee and the Soviet Jews* (New York: Enigma Books, 2003), 182–215.
40. Gunnar S. Paulsson, *Secret City. The Hidden Jews of Warsaw 1940–1945* (New Haven: Yale University Press, 2002), xiii.
41. Bogdan Wojdowski, *Chleb rzucony rannym* (Warsaw 1971). Quoted from Maciejewska, "Getto warszawskie w literaturze polskiej," 148.

42. Ilan Avisar, *Screening the Holocaust: Cinema's Images of the Unimaginable* (Bloomington: Indiana University Press, 1988), 40.
43. Ibid., 40.
44. See Stanisław Janicki, *Aleksander Ford* (Warsaw: Wydawnictwa Artystyczne i Filmowe, 1967), 54; Madej, *Kino, władza, publiczność*, 197–198.
45. Julian Tuwim, *My Żydzi polscy ... /We, Polish Jews ...*, ed. Chone Shmeruk (Jerusalem: Magnes Press, 1984), 19. Like Ford, Tuwim was an assimilated Polish Jew. He also learned about the Holocaust outside of Poland, during his exile in New York. Due to this experience, he started identify himself with Jewish suffering.
46. Litka, "Polacy i Żydzi w *Ulicy Granicznej*," 70 and 73. Concerning acting, it is worth noting the participation of Ida Kamińska (1899–1980), who plays Helena, Jadzia's aunt (not credited). Later she became known for her role of Mrs. Lautmann in an Oscar-winning Czechoslovak film about the Holocaust, *The Shop on Main Street* (*Obchod na Korze*, 1965, Jan Kádár and Elmar Klos). In 1949, Andrzej Munk, then a student at the Łódź Film School, produced an essay analyzing acting in *Border Street*. The text, "Analiza filmowa. Gra aktorów w filmie *Ulica Graniczna*," was published in *Images* (Poland) 5, no. 9–10 (2007): 102–105.
47. Irena Merz, "5 lat filmu polskiego. Od *Zakazanych piosenek* do *Czarciego żlebu*," *Film* 23/24 (1949): 7.
48. Marian Warszałłowicz, "Ulica Graniczna," *Film* 12 (1949): 8–9.
49. Bukowiecki, "Prawda nie zna granic."
50. Miss Klara is played by Mieczysława Ćwiklińska, one of the icons of prewar Polish cinema. This was her only appearance in postwar cinema.
51. Iwona Sowińska, *Polska muzyka filmowa 1945–1968* (Katowice: Wydawnictwo Uniwersytetu Śląskiego, 2006), 75.
52. *Film* 8 (1948). Stefan Śródka (Natan) earlier played proletarian heroes in *The Last Stage* and *Forbidden Songs*.
53. Bartov, *The "Jew" in Cinema*, 185.
54. August Grabski in his Polish-language text titled, "Czy Polacy walczyli w powstaniu w Getcie? Rzecz o polskich sojusznikach Żydowskiego Związku Wojskowego, *Kwartalnik Historii Żydów* 4 (2007): 422–434. See also Israel Gutman, *Resistance: The Warsaw Ghetto Uprising* (Boston: Houghton Mifflin, 1994), 207.
55. Hanna Krall, *Zdążyć przed Panem Bogiem* (Kraków: Wydawnictwo Literackie, 1977). I am quoting from the English translation, *Shielding the Flame: An Intimate Conversation with Dr. Marek Edelman, the Last Surviving Leader of the Warsaw Ghetto Uprising*, trans. Joanna Stasinska and Lawrence Weschler (New York: Henry Holt, 1986), 107–108.
56. Emmanuel Ringelblum, *Polish-Jewish Relations During the Second World War* (Evanston: Northwestern University Press, 1992), 175–176.
57. The common Polish-Jewish struggle is also emphasized in the very title of Jerzy Kuryluk's review, "Za wolność waszą i naszą" [For Your Freedom and Ours], *Film* 4 (1949): 8–9.
58. Gutman, *Resistance. The Warsaw Ghetto Uprising*, xii.
59. Janina Struk, *Photographing the Holocaust: Interpretations of the Evidence* (London: I.B. Taurus, 2004), 171.
60. Bartov, *The "Jew" in Cinema*, 186.
61. Richard C. Lukas, *Forgotten Holocaust: The German Occupation 1939–1944* (New York: Hippocrene Books, 2005), 180.
62. While stressing that the Home Army (AK) commanders did not support the idea of an uprising, Marek Edelman also admits that during the uprising AK was helping the ghetto fighters. See, "Campo di Fiori—obraz dzisiejszego świata, *Tygodnik Powszechny* (1 May 2005). Quoted from http://www.dialog.org/dialog_pl/campo-di-fiori.html. Elsewhere, Edelman admits that before the uprising started "we had sixty guns at that point, from the Polish Workers' Party and from the Home Army, and that was all the guns there were." See Edelman's account in Krall, *Shielding the Flame*, 62, 93–94. See Stefan Korboński's books, *The Polish Underground State: A Guide to the Underground, 1939–1945* (New York: Hippocrene Books,

1981), 120-139 and *The Jews and the Poles in World War II* (New York: Hippocrene Books, 1989), 56-64. Also, Lukas, *Forgotten* Holocaust, 171-181. The issue of Polish help for the ghetto insurgents is discussed recently by Grabski, "Czy Polacy walczyli w powstaniu w getcie?", 422-434.

63. It has to be also added that Ford's film was approved for general screening despite its portrayal of some darker aspects of the occupation, such as the issue of collaboration and *szmalcowniks* (persons blackmailing hiding Jews or those who helped them). Several recently published books in Poland deal with these sensitive and repressed issues of the occupation in an explicit manner, for example, Jan Grabowski, *"Ja tego Żyda znam!": Szantażowanie Żydów w Warszawie 1939-1945* (Warsaw: IFiS PAN, 2004) and Barbara Engelking, *"Szanowny Panie Gistapo": Donosy do władz niemieckich w Warszawie i okolicach w latach 1940-1941* (Warsaw: IFiS PAN, 2003). The issue of denunciation of Polish Jews during the war is discussed by Sławomir Buryła, "Literatura polska o donosach i donosicielach," *Zagłada Żydów. Studia i Materiały* 2 (2006): 76-98. The mass looting ("the looting frenzy") in postwar Poland of unattended property is discussed by Marcin Zaremba, "Gorączka szabru," *Zagłada Żydów. Studia i Materiały* 5 (2009): 193-220.

64. Avisar, *Screening the Holocaust*, 39. See chapter 7 for more information about Janusz Korczak and early attempts to produce his screen biography.

65. After Ford left Poland, his name was blacklisted and rarely mentioned in official Polish publications. Details of his eventful life are covered in Stanisław Janicki's informative and aptly titled documentary, *Loved and Hated: The Tragedy of Life and Death of the Maker of the Teutonic Knights* (*Kochany i znienawidzony. Dramat życia i śmierci twórcy Krzyżaków*, 2002).

Chapter 4

IMAGES OF THE HOLOCAUST DURING THE POLISH SCHOOL PERIOD (1955–1965)

Several important developments in Poland were propelled by the political thaw after Stalin's death in March 1953, particularly after a speech by Nikita Khrushchev in February 1956, in which he criticized Stalin and condemned the personality cult. The escape from Poland in December 1953 of a high ranking officer of the Ministry of Public Security, Józef Światło, and his broadcasts via Radio Free Europe after fall 1954 embarrassed the communist authorities by revealing the inner workings of the Polish security apparatus. Światło's disclosure of Stalinist crimes led to several changes within the communist apparatus that culminated in 1956. The death (under mysterious circumstances) of Polish President Bolesław Bierut during his visit to the Soviet Union in March 1956 symbolically marked the end of the Stalinist period in Poland. It was followed by general amnesty in April 1956 and workers' strikes in Poznań in June 1956 (the so-called "Poznań events") that were violently crushed by the security forces. The real danger of the Soviet military involvement led to a dramatic meeting in Warsaw in October of 1956 between Gomułka and the high-level Soviet delegation led by Khrushchev, which resulted in the Soviet's reluctant approval of Gomułka as the new Polish communist leader.

Initially Gomułka was supported by the majority of Poles as a communist who understood Polish national aspirations, especially after his speech in Warsaw on 24 October 1956 addressed to almost 400,000 people. Quickly, however, this widespread support for Gomułka turned into disenchantment with his politics. This was clearly visible from the beginning of the 1960s, the period ironically labeled in Poland as the 1960s "small stabilization" (mała stabilizacja), which lasted until 1970, when Gomułka was removed from power by Edward Gierek.

During the de-Stalinization process in Poland the Jewish-Polish secret service functionaries were blamed for the Stalinist crimes. Several of them were removed from the dreaded security service. Jaff Schatz explains it in his thorough study of Polish-Jewish left-wing activists, *The Generation: The Rise and Fall of the Jewish Communists of Poland*:

When the might of the security apparatus was curtailed, the blame for its previous misdeeds was almost solely put on its Jewish functionaries. This was demonstrated when a special committee appointed by the politburo in 1954 to investigate the activity of Department Ten [created in 1948 to keep an eye on the communist elite—MH] found only three culprits, all of them Jewish. Similarly, in the party's central committee resolution of May 1957, there was one ethnic Pole but six Jews mentioned as responsible for the 'errors and distortions.' Neither the Soviet officials and 'advisors' nor the non-Jewish leaders, functionaries, and politicians responsible for the security sector were mentioned. Thus Jewish security men were singled out and made scapegoats.[1]

Despite Gomułka's proclamations that there is no place for anti-Semitism within the Communist Party, the blaming of the Jewish communists and security apparatchiks for the Stalinist crimes and for the so-called "period of mistakes and blunders" (epoka błędów i wypaczeń) only increased anti-Semitic sentiments among Communist Party members as well as among the Polish population. Coupled with more relaxed emigration laws after 1956, this increased the exodus of Polish Jews, mostly to Israel, toward the end of the 1950s.

Since the mid-1950s, the Soviet bloc supported the Arab states in their conflict with Israel. Interestingly, despite the Soviet support for the Arab countries, from 1953 to early 1960s one can observe good relations between Poland and the state of Israel, which led to the creation of full diplomatic relations at the rank of embassies in 1962.[2]

Although subjected to heavy political censorship, Polish cinema attempted to reflect the political changes. The eruption of artistic energy and the emergence of the new wave of filmmakers in Poland after 1956 are usually described as the Polish School phenomenon. The disappointment with the Stalinist period, the urge to represent reality's complex nature, and the desire to confront issues that had functioned as taboos in Polish political and cultural life created a stimulating atmosphere for a new generation of filmmakers, known as the "generation of Columbuses" (*Kolumbowie*). The political changes introduced after the "Polish October" of 1956 enabled the young filmmakers to move away from the socialist realist dogma and, to a large extent, to build their films around their own experiences. For inspiration they turned to works written after 1946 by their contemporaries—Jerzy Andrzejewski, Kazimierz Brandys, Bohdan Czeszko, Józef Hen, Marek Hłasko, and Jerzy Stefan Stawiński. The images of Polish history and present-day reality that they produced for the screen often disturbed communist authorities.[3]

The revival of Polish cinema in the late 1950s was certainly helped by a number of organizational changes that had already begun before the "Polish October" of 1956. Starting in May 1955, the film industry in Poland was based on a Film Units (Zespoły Filmowe) system, a new and efficient way of managing film production. Each film unit was composed of film directors, scriptwriters, and producers (along with their collaborators and assistants), and was supervised by an artistic director, with the help of a literary director and a production manager. Film units were considered state enterprises, yet had some rudimentary freedoms; thanks to them, a number of the Łódź Film School graduates quickly achieved strong positions in the national film industry.

The artistic formation known as the Polish School was open, multifaceted, and created by many authors (including directors, scriptwriters, cinematographers, actors, composers, and set designers). Film historians often distinguish the "romantic" tendency represented at its best in the films of Andrzej Wajda, *Kanal* (*Kanał*, 1957), *Ashes and Diamonds* (*Popiół i diament*, 1958), and *Lotna* (1959); the "rationalistic" tendency embodied in the films by Andrzej Munk, *Eroica* (1958) and *Bad Luck* (*Zezowate szczęście*, 1960); the "psychological-existential" trend present in the films of Wojciech J. Has, Stanisław Lenartowicz, and Jerzy Kawalerowicz; and the "plebeian" cinema of Kazimierz Kutz. The young emerging filmmakers, trained at the Łódź Film School, believed in a genuine depiction of vital national themes. Unlike older filmmakers, including Aleksander Ford and Wanda Jakubowska, who opted for cinema imitating the Soviet epic models, the young filmmakers clearly favored the Italian neorealist approach, which offered them a chance to break with their predecessors and reflect the spirit of the de-Stalinization period.

During the Polish School period the primary concern remained history, World War II in particular. In several films made during this period there are also direct and indirect references to the Holocaust. In the mid-1950s, Jewish characters peopled several war films, for example in *The Hours of Hope* (*Godziny nadziei*, 1955) by Jan Rybkowski, a film heralding the Polish School phenomenon. The war often served as a point of departure for dramas focusing on the psychology of their characters. Stanisław Różewicz's *Three Women* (*Trzy kobiety*, 1957) is considered by critic Aleksander Jackiewicz a continuation of Jakubowska's *The Last Stage*.[4] It is a realistic story of three women of different ages—the youngest of them, eighteen-year-old Celinka (Anna Ciepielewska), is Jewish—who are liberated from a concentration camp. Unable to rebuild their lives in the destroyed Warsaw, they settle in a small town in the Polish Regained Lands (western Poland). Różewicz is interested in friendships that survived the harsh reality of the concentration camp but now are tested by everyday life; he examines a difficult return to normality. The film does not focus on the nature of Polish-Jewish relations although Celinka was adopted during the war by a Polish family. "I am looking at you. Your eyes are as if they have never seen evil," declares a Polish boy who falls in love with her.

Polish psychological war dramas usually narrate their stories with two planes of action. Set in the present, they stress the effects of the war: the inability to live normal life, to communicate, and to love as a result of traumatic war experiences. Memories of the war often return as nightmarish flashbacks, and prevent burned-out protagonists from completely returning to life. Jerzy Kawalerowicz's *The True End of the Great War* (*Prawdziwy koniec wielkiej wojny*, 1957) serves as a good example of this narrative strategy. It is a psychological study of a Polish woman, Róża (Lucyna Winnicka), and the two men in her life—her emotionally disturbed husband, a concentration camp survivor, and the man she turned to when she thought her husband was dead. Róża no longer loves her husband, yet she tries to take care of him out of pure compassion. This situation, hopeless for her and the two men involved, ends with her husband's suicide. The realistic scenes, set in postwar conditions, are interrupted by flashbacks into the past, done in an almost expressionistic manner. In the opening sequence, Róża's reminiscences of a happier past are juxtaposed with her husband's recollections of the death camp. The reality of the camp, portrayed from his point of view, is nightmarish and deformed—a reflection of his suffering as well as his psychological and physical disintegration.

Kazimierz Kutz's *People from the Train* (*Ludzie z pociągu*, 1961), based on a short story by Marian Brandys, is narrated in a similar manner. It portrays an "average day" during the occupation and deals with the psychology of the crowd and accidental heroism. Prompted by an unusual incident (somebody throws a bouquet of flowers from a passing train), a station-master tells his assistant what happened there in 1943 when, due to a technical problem, a group of passengers was stranded at the provincial train station. Kutz presents the mosaic of intertwined incidents and the broad spectrum of Polish society, depicts gestures devoid of pathos, and relies on detailed observations that may foreshadow the "small realism" of the Czechoslovak cinema in the 1960s. Unlike Wajda, he deheroicizes the protagonists (Kutz's trademark throughout his career) and narrates their stories in a realistic manner, eschewing symbols and metaphors. Among many characters in the train station is a Polish war widow (Danuta Szaflarska) who is hiding a young Jewish girl, Marylka. They are endangered not only by the presence of a German SS patrol, but also by a Polish *szmalcownik* (blackmailer). Later, when the Germans discover a machine gun in the station's waiting room that, unknown to them, belongs to a drunken German railway policeman (*Bahnschutz*), they threaten to kill every fifth passenger. In a symbolic scene, the Polish widow steps forward without hesitation and replaces the Jewish girl, who is one of those marked by death. Their lives are eventually spared by events combining fortuitous acts of heroism and dark comedy. A teenage boy tries to save his fellow passengers by claiming the gun and, before long, the drunken policeman is found by the station-master. The SS soldiers move away after severely beating the boy—the quiet hero of "an ordinary wartime day."

The second part of Kutz's debut, the three-part *Cross of Valor* (*Krzyż Walecznych*, 1959), which is titled *The Dog* (*Pies*), portrays another "ordinary scene" from World War II. A group of Polish soldiers encounters a stray German shepherd. Later, when the dog tries to attack two concentration camp survivors (in all probability from Auschwitz), they realize that the dog was used by the SS guards in the concentration camp to control and kill inmates. Outraged, they decide to kill the dog, but are unable to carry it out.

The Polish School period is abundant not only with films about the war, but also with films specifically referring to the Holocaust. At the beginning of the 1960s, Wanda Jakubowska returned to the memories of Polish suffering and resistance at Auschwitz in *Meetings in the Twilight* (1960) and *The End of Our World* (1964), both films being a continuation of her *The Last Stage* (discussed in chapter 2). The same structure (a contemporary incident triggers the flow of past, often suppressed, memories) and the same setting (Auschwitz) is employed in Andrzej Munk's psychological drama *The Passenger* (*Pasażerka*, 1963). The motif of Jewish hiding and Polish responses to the Holocaust are present in Andrzej Wajda's *Samson* (1961) and in two lesser known films: *White Bear* (*Biały niedźwiedź*, 1959), directed by Jerzy Zarzycki, and *The Beater* (*Naganiacz*, 1964), directed by Ewa and Czesław Petelski.

Wajda's *A Generation* and *Samson*

Discussions of the Polish School Period usually start with Andrzej Wajda's directorial debut, *A Generation* (*Pokolenie*), which premiered in January 1955. Essentially a "coming-of-age" story set during the war, this film also significantly tackled Jewish-Polish relations from the perspective of the left-wing underground. The film's protagonist, Stach (Tadeusz Łomnicki), an ordinary streetwise character from a poor district of Warsaw, joins the communist resistance when he meets and falls in love with an underground communist activist, Dorota (Urszula Modrzyńska). In the film's finale Stach leads the underground unit after Dorota is arrested by the Gestapo.

Originally, Aleksander Ford was assigned to make *A Generation*. Most probably due to some reservations expressed at the script stage, he passed this project to Wajda—his assistant in 1954 on *Five Boys from Barska Street*. Wajda secured the help of Jerzy Lipman, the cinematographer whose name is associated with several great achievements of the Polish School and who, like Wajda, also started his career on Ford's film.[5]

A Generation is a work tainted by political compromise. Despite its stylistic freshness, it remains by and large a socialist realist film influenced by the Italian neorealist style. Wajda's film is based on Bohdan Czeszko's novel about the People's Guard (Gwardia Ludowa, GL), the communist military resistance formed in 1942. Like Czeszko's novel, the film is heavily stereotyped and rewrites recent Polish history from the communist perspective. It contains a distorted picture of the occupation in Poland with its black-and-white portrayal of the different factions of the underground. The nationalist Home Army members (present on the screen although not named as such) are stereotyped as "collaborators" and "pseudo patriots" and the communist People's Guard members are represented as "true patriots."[6] The film also reverses the proportions of the Polish underground: the role of the communist underground, portrayed as the only political power helping the Warsaw Jews, is exaggerated at the expense of the Home Army.[7] Like other socialist realist works, Wajda's film also has its "positive" working-class hero in the center who acquires the correct (Marxist-Leninist) knowledge about history thanks to the guidance provided by experienced communist activists.

Set in the working-class milieu, *A Generation* was shot mostly on location with young, unknown actors, who were to become familiar faces of the Polish School cinema: Tadeusz Janczar (Jasio Krone), Zbigniew Cybulski (Kostek), Tadeusz Łomnicki (Stach), and Roman Polański (Mundek). The film's opening tracking shot introduces a setting familiar from a number of neorealist films: an impoverished suburb with shacks and barren industrial buildings. The viewer sides with the most complex character in this film, Jasio (Janek) Krone, who provides a contrast to the socialist realist hero, Stach. Jasio is multidimensional and ambiguous, the type of character that anticipates other film personae such as Maciek Chełmicki in Wajda's classic *Ashes and Diamonds*. He is the prototype of Wajda's heroic protagonist: full of doubts, troubled, and tragic (Figure 4.1).

The action of *A Generation* is often set near the Warsaw Ghetto walls, and part of it takes place during the Warsaw Ghetto Uprising. In line with the political demands of the time, Wajda portrays Polish nationalistic types as treacherous and anti-Semitic. Mr Ziarno's mocking comment—"Gentlemen! Have you heard? The Yids have actually started fighting"—is quickly countered by Stach and other workers—"People are dying, Mr. Ziarno; when they are done with the ghetto, they will put the screws to us." In another scene, set in a brick tunnel where Stach and his friends have a clandestine meeting, Sekuła (Janusz Paluszkiewicz), a communist leader, comes to say goodbye to them. He also emphasizes solidarity between the communists and the fighting ghetto: "The ghetto has risen today … We must help our Jewish comrades." Sekuła's walk toward the ghetto dissolves to several shots of the burning ghetto buildings, some with flags waving on top of them (one image clearly shows a Polish flag). The scene ends with a shot of the ghetto wall that is guarded by the armed Germans. Behind them, the entire ghetto is covered by black flames.

Although not strictly a film about the Holocaust, *A Generation* includes several scenes that are relevant to our discussion. One scene in particular deserves attention. It shows an escapee from the ghetto, Abram (Zygmunt Hobot), who seeks the help of Jasio Krone. Abram is first introduced standing anxiously behind the iron bars of the gate leading to Jasio's apartment building. He opens the gate, nervously crosses the courtyard where some older women

Figure 4.1: Tadeusz Janczar as Jasio Krone in Andrzej Wajda's *A Generation* (1955).

and men are singing a religious litany, walks up the staircase, and knocks on Jasio's door. "The ghetto has risen," he states simply, almost repeating an earlier comment by Sekuła. Noticeably surprised to see his old friend and neighbor, Jasio reluctantly lets him in, but refuses him shelter ("What can I do? You see … I am just a civilian"). Dimly lit close-up images of the hiding Jew and his Polish childhood friend, who is afraid to help him, dominate the scene (Figure 4.2). Rejected by his friend, Abram leaves the apartment building and descends into a dark street, most probably after the beginning of a police curfew. Despite the comment by Jasio's father ("You're right to stay out of it. You're a journeyman, not a hero"), he rushes after Abram, but stops in front of the now locked gate. He notices a German patrol on the street and helplessly watches Abram walking in the distance.

The scene showing the rejection of Abram by his Polish friend, a sensitive "civilian" paralyzed by fear and helplessness, initiates Wajda's long-term commitment to examine Polish-Jewish wartime relations. This and several subsequent (discussed later) films by Wajda are "troubled by a kind of nagging sense of guilt over something not quite definable," as Michael Stevenson rightly notices, and deal with "a complex spectrum of problems of assimilation, integration and separation."[8] Like several other Jewish characters in films about Polish-Jewish relationships, Abram tests his fellow countrymen. Jasio, however, only witnesses the misery of his childhood friend who was marked as "other" by the Germans. The religious singing that accompanies the scene has a symbolic meaning. The litany chanted in the building's courtyard is about seeking God's forgiveness and associated with the Christian Holy Week ("Lamb of God, who takes away the sins of the world, have mercy on us …"). A careful analysis of this scene and Jasio's eventual martyrdom allows Bronisława Stolarska to compare the symbolism of his sacrifice to that of Christ who sacrificed his life on a cross for the sins of all mankind.[9] Jasio's death may be taken as atonement for his betrayal of Abram and, on a universal level, for his nation's helpless witnessing of the Jewish tragedy.

In the scene that follows Jasio's encounter with Abram, set near the ghetto wall, Stach pronounces off screen: "Smoke from the burning ghetto poisoned

Figure 4.2: Jasio (Tadeusz Janczar) and his Jewish friend Abram (Zygmunt Hobot)

the city air and hung like a heavy cloud over the carnival built by the Germans just outside the ghetto walls. Sekuła's urgent call reaches us from somewhere in that flaming quarter." Jasio Krone joins the People's Guard answering Stach's call ("we've got to help the ghetto") and, in all probability out of guilt, he volunteers to help the fighting Jews. The underground group steals a German truck and moves near the ghetto wall to rescue Jewish fighters who were escaping from the burning ghetto through the city sewers.[10] The thick smoke covers nearby buildings when Stach and Mundek remove the lid of a manhole and, helped by Stach, the ghetto fighters climb out of it, followed by the wounded Sekuła who is wearing a bloody bandage on his head (Figures 4.3, 4.4).

During the rescue mission Jasio is on the look-out on the street. He notices three approaching German patrolmen who open fire. Trying to help his comrades, he runs under fire into a narrow street in the opposite direction of the truck with Stach and the escapees from the ghetto. His white overcoat is visible for the Germans who pursue him toward a large apartment building. After exchanging fire with the growing number of German soldiers, Jasio finds himself trapped at the very top of the staircase. Wounded and short of ammunition, he stands on the railing and, shown in an extreme low angle shot, tries to balance for a while before jumping to his death.

Portraying the Warsaw Ghetto Uprising, Wajda consistently returns to the same set of images: the carousel near the ghetto wall, the heavy smoke over the ghetto observed from the Aryan side of the wall, and smoldering pieces of burned paper flying into the Polish side. As in his other films, Wajda is preoccupied with the Polish reactions to the uprising, the Polish experience of the Holocaust, and, broadly speaking, with the Polish-Jewish relationships. In *A Generation*, after the scene of Jasio's refusal to help Abram, Wajda cuts to a shot that has gained a symbolic meaning over the years—an image of a carousel operating near the wall of the burning Warsaw Ghetto (Figures 4.5, 4.6). The Polish word *karuzela*, literally translated as carousel, "implies horses with

Figure 4.3: Escape from the burning ghetto through the city sewers in *A Generation*. Tadeusz Łomnicki as Stach helps a Jewish fighter

Figure 4.4: Stach (Tadeusz Łomnicki) helps the communist Sekuła (Janusz Paluszkiewicz)

children riding in circles, while this was actually a chairoplane, with couples soaring into the sky," as poet Czesław Miłosz explains.[11]

The image of the carousel near the ghetto wall appears in a well-known poem by Czesław Miłosz, "Campo dei Fiori," which the poet wrote in Warsaw in April 1943, and which was first published anonymously in 1944, and then appeared in his 1945 collection of poems titled *Rescue* (*Ocalenie*). The poem describes the indifference of Poles to what happened in the Warsaw Ghetto at the time of the Jewish uprising. In this poem, Miłosz compares the fate of Giordano Bruno, burned to death as a heretic in the presence of an unconcerned mob at Rome's Campo dei Fiori, and the fate of Polish Jewry. He writes in stanzas three and four:

> I thought of the Campo di Fiori
> in Warsaw by the sky-carousel
> one clear spring evening
> to the strains of a carnival tune.
> The bright melody drowned
> the salvos from the ghetto wall,
> and couples were flying
> high in the cloudless sky.
>
> At times wind from the burning
> would drift dark kites along
> and riders on the carousel
> caught petals in midair.
> That same hot wind
> blew open the skirts of the girls
> and the crowds were laughing
> on that beautiful Warsaw Sunday.[12]

Figure 4.5: *A Generation*. A carousel near the wall of the burning Warsaw Ghetto

Figure 4.6: (From the left) Jasio (Tadeusz Janczar), Mundek (Roman Polański), Stach (Tadeusz Łomnicki), and Jacek (Ryszard Kotys) meet near the ghetto wall in *A Generation*

Later in the poem, Miłosz writes about "the loneliness of the dying" and about the indifference of the outside world, and ends with the image of the only witness and the uncompromising truth-teller: the poet. As stated earlier, Miłosz's commanding image of a carousel close to the ghetto wall has become very emblematic, almost the essence of the Polish indifference to the plight of their Jewish compatriots. It is therefore not a coincidence to observe similar images employed in later films, such as Janusz Kijowski's *Warszawa. Année 5703* (*Tragarz puchu*, 1992) and Wajda's own *Holy Week* (*Wielki Tydzień*, 1996), and in literary works by Adolf Rudnicki and Jerzy Andrzejewski. A short documentary film by Michał Nekanda-Trepka, *The Carousel* (*Karuzela*, 1999), also refers to Miłosz's poem.

Polish historian Tomasz Szarota devoted an extensive study to find out whether the image of a carousel near the ghetto wall is only a fitting poetic metaphor, a historical truth, or both.[13] In his research he uncovered a note published during the occupation in a German-run Polish daily, *The New Warsaw Messenger* (*Nowy Kurier Warszawski*), about the installation of a new fairground on Krasiński Square on 5 August 1942. This date, as Szarota writes, coincided with the transports to the extermination camp at Treblinka from the *Umschlagplatz*, which was located not far from the fairground square. Szarota adds that the presence of the fairground near the ghetto wall was most probably of propaganda value for the Germans, testifying "to the complete lack of interest by the Christian Poles in the plight of their Jewish co-citizens."[14] Szarota stresses that the liquidation of the Warsaw Ghetto by the Germans also coincided with their propaganda effort to link the Katyń massacre of Polish officers by the Soviets with the NKVD officers of Jewish origin.[15] His research also shows that "the Krasiński Square was used by the underground fighters as an observation point that enabled them to follow the struggles in the ghetto." Szarota refers to one of the Polish underground fighters, Jan Krok-Paszkowski, who went to the square and who used the swing near the carousel in order to get a better view of what was going on in the ghetto, the image later employed by Wajda in *Holy Week*.[16]

In the discussion among Marek Edelman, Czesław Miłosz, and a literary scholar Jan Błoński, organized on the occasion of the fiftieth anniversary of the Warsaw Ghetto Uprising and published in 2005 by the influential Catholic weekly *Tygodnik Powszechny*, Edelman remembers that the carousel was in operation since the second day of the uprising, and was seen clearly by the Jewish insurgents. Edelman's recollection offers images that are similar to Miłosz's portrayal.[17] In line with Miłosz and Edelman, historian Joanna Beata Michlic recalls the memoirs of Edward Reicher, who was hiding on the Aryan side in Warsaw: "At Krasiński Square we were passing the market stalls. Near the merry-go-round people were in a jolly and playful mood. There was loud music and a few couples were dancing. It looked as though the rabble was celebrating the fall of the Warsaw Ghetto."[18] That image is, however, contradicted by the depiction of the same square by another eyewitness, Jerzy Andrzejewski in his *Holy Week*, published for the first time in 1946: "The deserted square now seemed even wider. In its center stood two carousels not yet completely assembled, evidently being readied for the upcoming holiday. Under the cover of their wildly colored decorations stood helmeted German soldiers."[19]

The motif of the carousel near the ghetto wall, disputed by historians who support their findings with contradictory eyewitness testimonies, will reappear later in this book. Let us now return to *A Generation* and its reception by the Polish authorities. Like other films made during the Polish School period, Wajda's film was carefully monitored. The authorities considered it a "scandalous portrayal of lumpenproletariat dressed as proletariat."[20] During the meeting of the Film and Script Evaluation Committee (Komisja Ocen Filmów i Scenariuszy) concerns were also raised regarding Wajda's representation of the Holocaust.[21] As a result, one graphic scene from the original screenplay (also present in Czeszko's novel) never made it to the screen. The scene describes the encounter between Stach and Kostek (Zbigniew Cybulski), whose prominent role in the script was reduced to a minimum in the released film. Returning from the action near the ghetto wall, Stach meets Kostek who is carrying a sack filled with Jewish heads that he stole from a Jewish cemetery, planning later to extract gold teeth.[22] One of the participants of the meeting, film historian Jerzy Toeplitz, commented on this aspect as follows:

> I think that the issue of the Ghetto Uprising, as presented in the script alone, has not been shown properly. The depiction of Kostek with the hacked-off Jewish heads is too hard to take for a viewer. One can talk or read about it, but, most likely, one shouldn't show such a scene on the screen. Nevertheless, I think that while introducing the Ghetto Uprising in the background, which is politically and artistically correct, it is necessary to emphasize the bond between the People's Guard and the insurgents. It is not enough to show the ghetto only through Kostek's perspective or, as the author proposes, through a scene of fighting in the ghetto. The key emphasis should be on the common struggle.[23]

The issue of "the common struggle" is prominently portrayed in Wajda's second attempt at representing the Holocaust, *Samson* (1961), an adaptation of a novel by a Polish writer of Jewish origin, Kazimierz Brandys, which was published in 1948. The film, produced by the Film Unit "Droga,"[24] spans several years. It starts before the war by depicting an anti-Semitic atmosphere and violent excesses at the University of Warsaw. The film's protagonist, Jakub Gold (Serge Merlin), is introduced on the university campus. He is unaware of the "hatred that was growing intensely in those days," as the voice-over commentary explains. Physically attacked by a group of right-wing nationalists, Jakub accidentally kills a fellow student who, in fact, was trying to help him (the student is played by future film director Andrzej Żuławski—not credited—who assisted Wajda on this film). While serving a prison sentence for his deed, Jakub meets a charismatic communist activist, Pankrat (Tadeusz Bartosik).

When German bombs destroy the prison in September 1939, Jakub gets out of jail but quickly finds himself in another form of prison—locked in the Warsaw Ghetto, where he works burying the dead ("I collected corpses from the street," he says). The scene showing the sealing of the ghetto becomes arguably the most memorable in the film. It begins with the march of Jews wearing the Star of David to the ghetto. Gathered in a courtyard, a group of Jews is passively facing the camera and German soldiers who quickly and almost mechanically are building a wooden wall, board by board, gradually blocking the view of the camera. The positioning of the camera behind the wall and behind the German soldiers accentuates the perspective of an outside witness that dominates this and other films by Wajda. The scene showing the creation of the ghetto wall, which is accompanied by a solemn voice-over commentary and Tadeusz Baird's classical, sorrowful musical score, shows, however, not so much detachment, but Wajda's solidarity with his Jewish compatriots.

After the death of his mother, Jakub escapes from the ghetto and hides on the Aryan side, counting on help from various people. He finds a temporary shelter in a spacious studio owned by actress Lucyna (Alina Janowska)—a Jewish woman passing as a gentile. Although Lucyna feels affection for Jakub, he rejects her love and declares his will to return to the ghetto ("Look at me," he says, "I'm one of them, and I have to share their fate"). He leaves his hiding place and, with the help of a group of Polish carolers, seeks shelter with his prison cellmate, Józef Malina (Jan Ciecierski). When the situation at Malina's place becomes dangerous (Jakub's presence becomes known to outsiders), he is moved into a cellar. After learning from Kazia (Elżbieta Kępińska), Malina's protective niece, that Jakub most probably perished, Lucyna turns herself in to the Gestapo.

The action of a large portion of the film is limited to the claustrophobic dark cellar—another place where Jakub is "imprisoned." After Malina's tragic death, Kazia continues to take care of Jakub and is clearly fascinated by his presence. Once again Jakub leaves his shelter and, despite learning from Kazia about the annihilation of the ghetto, he attempts to return there. After climbing the wall, he observes the landscape of destruction: ruins, dead bodies, and German soldiers patrolling the place. He feels alone, guilty that he did not share the fate of his people. Wandering the streets of Warsaw and struggling with a Polish *szmalcownik*, he is helped by a young communist that he met in prison, Fiałka (Władysław Kowalski), a member of the communist armed wing, the People's Guard (GL), who asks him to work for an underground communist press managed by Pankrat. In the film's final scene Jakub dies a heroic death. When German soldiers search the building housing the press, Jakub throws a bunch of grenades at them. After the dust settles, the camera portrays the ruins of the printing house, dead German soldiers, and among them Jakub-Samson crushed by the falling structure.

The first version of the film script was appraised in May 1960 by the Committee for the Evaluation of Film Scripts (Komisja Ocen Scenariuszy). The script was considered ideal material to make a psychological war film.[25] This was, among others, the opinion of two prominent writers, Stanisław Dygat and Jan Józef Szczepański, who also emphasized that *Samson* belongs to the best works ever written by Brandys (at this early stage Wajda was not yet chosen to direct the film, and was not involved in working on the script). The committee members, including filmmakers Wanda Jakubowska, Jan Rybkowski, and Tadeusz Konwicki, also endorsed the project. Konwicki, who stressed that "it is our duty to make this film," also noticed that the goal of the project is not "the portrayal of the plight of the Polish Jewry, but a psychological portrait of Jakub Gold." Szczepański suggested that the film "may cause inappropriate viewers' reactions and, possibly, will not be successful."[26]

The first version of the script as well as the nature of the literary source proved to be a problem for Wajda. Brandys produced a work typical for the socialist realist years in Poland. As Bolesław Michałek explains, when the film was released, this type of literature was no longer favored by critics, which contributed to the lukewarm reception of the film. Wajda comments on his attempts at visualizing Brandys' work as follows:

> On first reading of Kazimierz Brandys' novel *Samson*, I remembered the drawings by Gustave Doré I had seen as a child, and started dreaming of making a modern version of the great Biblical tale. What the novel demanded of a director, however, was simplicity, modesty and, above all, respect for details. From the first day of shooting to the final day of editing, I remained torn between the two extremes. As veterans of *Ashes and Diamonds* both of us, Jerzy Wójcik and myself, realized the power of narrative shortcuts and the impact of symbolism on the screen. We wanted to continue in that direction, Brandys' novel, however, contradicted and desperately resisted our concepts.[27]

Wajda also attributes the departure from Brandys' realistic depiction to his first deployment of anamorphic widescreen: "*Samson* was the first film I made in Cinemascope technique. The panoramic picture favored stylization and measured narrative, with lengthy takes and deep sets. In a word: it drew us away from what Kazimierz Brandys' *Samson* should have been: an action film ... I stylized realistic scenes from the novel to resemble biblical tableaux—static and therefore slightly annoying."[28] The film's cinematographer, Jerzy Wójcik, stresses, however, that Wajda agreed with his suggestion to shoot the film to resemble documentary materials from the ghetto produced by the Germans.[29]

The casting of French actor Serge Merlin also greatly contributed to the overall shape of the film. The way he is framed by Wójcik (the camera is often placed behind the protagonist) helps to emphasize the "otherness" and isolation of Jakub Gold. With no knowledge of the Polish language, Merlin rarely faces the camera and talks as if hiding or being afraid to be noticed (he is dubbed by Władysław Kowalski, who also plays Fiałka). The choice of Merlin also forced

Wajda to change the original concept of *Samson*. Instead of an athletic, powerful Samson, the Hebrew hero, the viewer watches a character that is slender, intellectual, and full of doubt. Defending his choice of the leading man against the accusations by some Polish critics, Wajda stated on several occasions that the choice of Merlin strengthened the film, although originally his principal candidate for the role was Henryk Grynberg, a Polish-Jewish actor at that time affiliated with the Jewish Theater in Warsaw.[30]

Like the majority of Wajda's Jewish Poles, Jakub Gold is introduced at the beginning of the film as an assimilated, non-religious Jew. In an article published in 2000, Ewa Mazierska criticizes the director for focusing in his films exclusively on "non-Jewish Jews"—the Polonized Jewish characters (a minority of prewar Polish Jews). Discussing Jakub from *Samson* as well as other Jewish protagonists populating Wajda's films, she writes that in Wajda's cinema "Jewishness is a negative concept, an identity imposed upon them by the Nazi oppressors and, to a certain extent, by the Polish anti-Semites. If they had a choice," she writes, "they would be and always remain Poles rather than Jews."[31] Wajda's characters, Mazierska argues, do not speak Yiddish, are not religious, do not observe Jewish customs, and resemble Poles. If traditional Jews ("Jewish-Jews" faithful to the Jewish tradition) are present, she continues, usually they are given negative connotations. Although at first glance Mazierska's points are compelling (the majority of Wajda's Jewish characters are, indeed, Polonized Jews), her attack on Wajda for his alleged biased representation and disregard for historical truth seems unjust. It could be easily argued that Wajda's choice of assimilated Jewish characters emphasizes not only the horror, but also the absurdity of their persecution. Furthermore, a comparative analysis of, for example, other national cinemas or the history of "the Holocaust genre" in general, would reveal that the majority of Jewish screen characters are assimilated protagonists. There is nothing unflattering or patronizing about the portrayal of "Jewish ways" in Wajda's cinema related to the Holocaust.

In her concluding remarks Mazierska emphasizes Wajda's opportunism and political conformism, his attempts to "please his audiences and boost Polish national pride, together with a measure of criticism of authority and certain segments of society without seriously offending anyone."[32] The history of Wajda's film projects, including the history of his films about Polish-Jewish relations, perhaps testifies to the opposite. It has to be stressed that throughout his career the director has shown an unusual (not only for Polish standards) interest in Jewish history and Polish-Jewish history. A career that spans more than five decades undoubtedly has required a large degree of political equilibrium and willingness to compromise on the part of Wajda. Thus, for example, the embellished picture of the (marginal in reality) communist underground in *A Generation* and *Samson* has to be seen as a "negotiated compromise" between the artist and the totalitarian state rather than as a sign of Wajda's surrender.[33]

Paul Coates is arguably right when he observes that Wajda's *Samson* "represents an uneasy cocktail of communism and existentialism."[34] The multilayered structure of Wajda's film seems to be both the source of its energy and the reason for its failure with audiences and critics alike. Wajda's reworking of the Samson myth is in line with the communist ideology with its portrayal of the prewar, bourgeois Poland as the land of anti-Semites and the communists as the only protectors of Jews. The Jewish protagonist becomes a Polish hero thanks to his (accidental in the film) association with the communist cause. Jakub, however, is passive throughout the film, a characteristic that was habitually taken by critics as a stereotypical sign of "Jewishness." For example, Klaus Eder writes that "Jakub Gold is deeply rooted in Jewish mythology. Throughout at least two-thirds of the film, his attitude toward history is passive: he experiences history and succumbs to it. Rather than act, he lets himself be carried along by events."[35] The vulnerable Jakub is helped by several Poles. His situation is accentuated by camera shots suggesting passivity and imprisonment, most apparently in the scenes when he is hiding in Malina's cellar, cut off from the outside world. The voyeuristic point-of-view shot through a small cellar window aptly defines his situation. He witnesses, for example, a female *szmalcownik* accompanied by her reluctant husband, played by Roman Polański (not credited), who are searching for hiding Jews.

Despite the apparent religious subtext of the film and its references to the communist resistance, Jakub's death is portrayed according to the Polish romantic tradition that was displayed prominently in earlier films by Wajda. Unlike, however, the death of Maciek in *Ashes and Diamonds* or Jasio Krone in *A Generation*, Jakub's death is "almost absurd, of his own choice," as Polish critic and scholar Aleksander Jackiewicz writes. Calling Wajda's film "a cold masterpiece," Jackiewicz also notices as the film's central weakness that Jakub does not relate to the "Polish fate."[36] In the film's final scene, when the Germans search the communist printing house, the voice-over addresses Jakub: "Keep them here. That will be the moment of your strength, the moment of salvation. You shall quiver the pillars. You shall bring your oppressors to their knees. For the deaths of the innocent. For all the evil you were made to suffer. Destroy the pillars. Now is the time!" Jakub thus acts like the Biblical "Samson the hero," who in a suicidal attack destroyed the pillars of the Philistine temple killing himself and numerous enemies.

To tell the story about Jewish suffering, Wajda relies heavily on symbolism and biblical associations, relegating to the margins what was earlier his forte—the historical and social background. Critics, who were previously supportive of Wajda's approach, became reluctant to embrace the abstract situation presented on the screen. Critics close to Wajda, for example Bolesław Michałek, defended the film, saying that for the first time in his career Wajda portrayed his pursued protagonist "in the socio-political context of his times."[37] Siding with Wajda, critic and scholar Stefan Morawski summarized the charges against the film as unfair. For him, the neurotic protagonist and the highly stylized narration and acting are at the service of the story. Wajda's aim is to portray "a man trapped," "a symbol of the whole nation," and "a Jew who was not allowed to exist." Morawski writes that the film's unusual, "psalm-like rhythm" and the off-screen commentary throughout the film have to be taken as logical consequences of Wajda's objectives. Therefore, Wajda's hero is "characterized as Christ from the Golgotha or a Jew – Eternal Wanderer; that is why Samson always emphasizes that he is alien."[38]

Wajda was never afraid of religious connotations in his films. For example, in 1972, he made a film in Germany with Polish actors, *Pilate and Others* (*Pilatus und Andere*, 1972), a contemporary version of the story of Christ, rarely seen in Poland or elsewhere. In *Samson*, he offers a Polish reworking of the Samson myth coupled with the Communist Party perspective. Referring to scenes when Kazia (Delilah?) takes care of Samson, historian Omer Bartov notices bitterly:

> This notion of the victimized Jew as symbolizing Christ was not uncommon in Poland at the time, and it seems to have coincided with traditional Polish anti-Semitism, on the one hand, and with the Nazi persecution of the Jews, on the other. The Jews were being punished for their murder of Christ—but at the same time, they were being crucified themselves, as the first step before the anticipated slaughter of Poland, the Christ of all nations.[39]

Despite often-voiced criticism by Polish commentators, Wajda's *Samson* deserves particular attention. It reflects the politics of the time and offers powerful images that viewers may also find in other films by Wajda as well as in several other Holocaust films. As expected, the stress is on the image of the suffering Jew, on his passivity, and eventual redemption through the association with the communist underground. Jakub seems to be ungrateful to Poles (who suffer too, as Lucyna reminds him), a trait that is also developed in Wajda's later *Holy Week* (1996). Although Wajda does not refrain from showing anti-Semitism among Poles, this characteristic is mostly limited to prewar "bourgeois Poland" and, by association, to Polish nationalists. It is foreign to "progressive forces" embodied by the communists, the true heroes of *Samson*.

Reluctant Polish Helpers in *The Beater* and *By the Railway Track*

Interestingly, although the links between the Warsaw Ghetto and the communists on the Aryan side were well-established,[40] the issue of the "common struggle," frequently voiced in Polish debates of films pertaining to the Holocaust, had never featured prominently in other Polish films. Instead of images of heroic fighters attempting to aid the ghetto insurgents, for the most part Polish films offered images of reluctant helpers, terrified bystanders, and helpless eyewitnesses to crimes committed by the German occupier on Polish soil. That is how the Holocaust and Polish-Jewish relations were presented in arguably one of the most interesting films made during this period, *The Beater* (aka *Men Hunters*; *Naganiacz*, 1964), directed by Ewa and Czesław Petelski.[41] Underestimated by critics and barely known outside of Poland,[42] the film was produced by the Film Unit "Kamera," and premiered on 10 January 1964. It received several awards after its release, including the state award for the directors and the FIPRESCI Award and the Special Jury Award at the International Film Festival in Locarno.

In an interview conducted after the film's premiere, Ewa Petelska emphasized that she was attracted to Roman Bratny's script, which was based on his short story published in 1946, because of its theme of making difficult moral choices under immense pressure.[43] This aspect of *The Beater* was also appreciated by the film officials, as revealed by the minutes from the meeting of the Film Approval Committee (Komisja Kolaudacyjna). The film authorities and noted filmmakers, among them Jerzy Kawalerowicz, Jerzy Bossak, Jan Rybkowski, and Stanisław Wohl, praised the film. For Kawalerowicz, this was a "terrifying and moving" experience, the best film ever made by the Petelskis; for Bossak, "a reminder and a warning;" for Rybkowski, a film "loaded with emotions," with scenes "as if transplanted from some documentary materials." Also, according to Rybkowski, the film captured the wartime atmosphere by demonstrating that people were reluctant to help the Jews because they were putting in danger their own lives. There was no eagerness involved in helping the Jews, stressed Rybkowski, only some basic human reactions.[44]

The Beater deals with the motif of hiding, common to many Polish Holocaust narratives, and focuses its attention on a reluctant Polish helper, the Warsaw Rising insurgent Michał (Bronisław Pawlik). Dressed in a semi-military fashion, he hides in the countryside after the tragic failure of the Rising (2 October 1944). Unlike several better-known protagonists of the Polish School period, he is not a heroic figure; rather a worn-out, almost resigned character who does not want to continue fighting, and just tries to survive the last winter of the war. Nonetheless, pressed by circumstances beyond his control, Michał helps, albeit unwillingly, a group of Hungarian Jews who are hiding in the vicinity.

The setting of *The Beater* is provincial Poland before the final Soviet offensive in January 1945. The film opens with a scene featuring the killing by German soldiers of three Jews who were trying to escape from a concentration camp transport. After the credits over the images of trucks carrying Jewish people, the circular camera pan introduces the setting of almost the entire film: a country manor surrounded by adjacent buildings, including a manor's storage—Michał's temporary shelter, and fields covered with snow. The film quickly introduces a panorama of Polish characters ranging from a resident of the manor—the wife of a Polish officer imprisoned in a POW camp in Germany (Krystyna Borowicz)—to villagers living in the surrounding area.

The first scenes also emphasize Michał's reluctance to continue an armed struggle. He refuses to join his underground unit, but then changes his mind and tries to meet the fighters, to no avail, in a forester's lodge. On his way home at night, Michał encounters a young Hungarian Jewish woman (Maria Wachowiak) in search of food for a group of Hungarian Jews who escaped from a transport to a concentration camp and are now hiding in a nearby forest. Unable to understand Michał, she follows him, however, to his place where he gives her whatever food he has. Later, he helps her to carry a heavy pot of boiled potatoes to feed her fellow citizens. "What do I owe them? Why me?" Michał later asks when the whole group silently follows him home and hides in the haystacks near the manor.

The climax of the film is a "hunting sequence." The SS officers organize a hunting party near the manor. Michał and the villagers, led by the forester Jaworek (Ryszard Pietruski), are forced to participate as beaters. The hunt for foxes and rabbits quickly turns into a massacre of Jews who, alarmed by the gun shots and the approaching beaters, leave the relative safety of their hidings. The prolonged carnage, without music and featuring only diegetic sounds (bullets, the moans of the dying, both people and animals), is a petrifying experience. The German officers are depicted as if enjoying the shooting regardless of the target, while the camera portrays the horror on the faces of some Polish beaters, the involuntary participants in the killing. Jaworek, who was earlier portrayed as a collaborator, tries to rescue a Jewish child amid the mayhem, and is killed by the Germans. At the end of the hunting, the killed animals are lying on the ground near the manor; the bodies of dead Jews are abandoned in the field. "Taking into account the difficult war conditions, the hunting went great," says the commanding German officer. "We killed forty rabbits, two foxes and, in addition, sixteen Jews." After a short laugh with his fellow hunters, he adds: "I believe that we'll hunt together once again."

The young Hungarian Jewish woman, protected by Michał, survives the massacre in the hideout. After the Germans' departure, she wanders among the dead and blames her Polish rescuer for the death of her fellow citizens. He is unable to tell her what really happened (Figure 4.7). The following morning she

Figure 4.7: *The Beater* (1964) by Ewa and Czesław Petelski. Michał (Bronisław Pawlik) and a Hungarian Jewish Woman (Maria Wachowiak)

is asleep in his room as the Germans are fleeing through the village, joined by the lady of the manor. A tired and hungry German soldier suddenly appears in Michał's room begging for food and not even paying attention to the presence of the Jewish woman. In a bizarre twist of fate, he devours boiled potatoes from the same pot that Michał earlier used to feed the Hungarian Jews.

Cinematographer Stefan Matyjaszkiewicz deserves credit for the highly stylized climactic "hunting sequence," which was, however, described by some Polish critics as "too literary" and "too spectacular" to be true.[45] The sequence brings to mind a similar powerful fragment in Jean Renoir's *Rules of the Game* (*La Règle du jeu*, 1939), portraying masters and servants united in the bloody hunting game. The sequence in *The Beater*, relying on carefully arranged long shots, may serve as a symbolic picture of the occupation in Poland. The Germans (hunters) are portrayed as both architects of the massacre and the executioners; the Poles (beaters) serve as unwilling participants in the obligatory hunt that takes place on their soil. The mourning for Jaworek, the gamekeeper whose body lies inside a house, is contrasted with the Jewish bodies left in the frozen field. The lack of communication between Michał and Hungarian Jews, although explained by the film's narrative (Hungarian and Polish languages are miles apart), can be also taken symbolically as representing distance, a symbolic wall between Poles and Jews during the war. There is only one scene when Michał is able to communicate verbally, in French, with one of the older Jews, who asks him for a pencil and explains: "I'm writing a couple of words daily because nobody is going to believe me later."

The representation of Poles as bystanders and reluctant helpers also returns in a powerful short film, *By the Railway Track* (*Przy torze kolejowym*, 1963), directed by Andrzej Brzozowski, the second director of Andrzej Munk's *The Passenger*. Made for the SE-MA-FOR (Short Film Studio) in Łódź, the film was scheduled to appear at the Kraków Film Festival in 1963, but it was banned by Wincenty Kraśko, the Communist Party apparatchik responsible for cultural affairs.[46] The film premiered as late as 1992.[47]

By the Railway Track is based on a short story with the same title written by Zofia Nałkowska (1884–1954) and included in her celebrated collection *Medallions* (*Medaliony*) written in 1945 and published in 1946.[48] Nałkowska, a Polish novelist who survived the war in Warsaw and was active during the postwar period in the Main Commission for the Investigation of Nazi Crimes in Poland (Główna Komisja Badania Zbrodni Hitlerowskich w Polsce), later also published her *Wartime Diaries* (*Dzienniki czasu wojny*).[49] Both works reveal her sense of duty to provide a witness account, to describe the occupation of Poland in realistic terms, including the plight of Polish Jews. She refers to her encounters with eyewitnesses, her own observations, as well as on-location research (she traveled extensively to different concentration camps and was able to talk to survivors as a member of the investigative committee).

Nałkowska's story of *By the Railway Track* may serve as an example of her personal, concise, fragmented, almost documentary-like style. It offers realistic dialogue and matter-of-fact observation and is devoid of any mythologization of the victims, the bystanders, and the perpetrators. The story opens with the following sentence: "Yet another person now belongs to the dead: the young woman by the railway track whose escape attempt failed."[50] Later Nałkowska describes the setting in a similar straightforward, factual manner: "When the new day broke, the woman was sitting on the dew-soaked grass by the side of the track. She was wounded in the knee. Some had succeeded in escaping. Further from the track, another lay motionless in the forest. A few had escaped. Two had died. She was the only one left like this, neither alive nor dead."[51]

Brzozowski's film, photographed by Jerzy Wójcik, aptly captures the powerful observational tone of Nałkowska's story. The scenery of the action is a cruel, rural landscape covered with snow. The wounded and shocked Jewish woman crawls toward a man lying nearby in the snow only to find out that he is dead. Later, she is approached by a young man on a bicycle and slowly surrounded by other Polish villagers who are, however, reluctant to help her. As Nałkowska comments on their behavior, "It was a time of terror. Those who offered assistance or shelter were marked for death."[52] The villagers are commenting on the whole situation, waiting for what is going to happen, unable to provide any assistance beyond a cigarette and a glass of vodka. Only a young boy seems to be compassionate, while others are just watching. With every hour, the woman is losing her hope for survival. The villagers are afraid to call a doctor, to hide her, or to take her home. "She lay among people," writes Nałkowska, "but didn't count on anyone for help. She lay like an animal that had been wounded during a hunt but which the hunters had forgotten to kill off."[53] The arrival at the scene of a Polish blue policeman, who is also uncertain what actions should be taken, marks another dramatic shift in the story. The woman, who was at first afraid of the witnesses, then started hoping for some help, now pleads for death, but the policeman is reluctant to act. The sympathetic young man volunteers, points the policeman's gun toward her, and shoots. The film ends with a freeze frame of a flock of birds leaving a tree, reacting to the shot.

The shelving of the film by the communist authorities certainly had to do with its accusatory tone, merciless portrayal of the Polish population, and with its stress on the divisions between people. The film does not focus on the perpetrators responsible for the occupation and for its harsh reality. It portrays Poles as equally guilty—the indifferent eyewitnesses who are passively observing the misery of their co-citizens. However, there was also another reason for the ban discriminatorily imposed on this film. The Jewish woman is played by Halina Mikołajska (1925–1989), one of the legends of Polish theater, and also one of the symbols of the Polish resistance against the communist regime. She was involved in the anti-communist oppositional activities since the early 1970s and, as a result, ostracized by the authorities, banned from theater and film, and interned after the introduction of martial law in December 1981.

The Fate of Children in *Ambulance* and *Birth Certificate*

Among several short films made during the Polish School period, one deserves particular attention. *Ambulance* (*Ambulans*, 1961), directed by Janusz Morgenstern (1922–2011) for the Short Film Studio SE-MA-FOR, is an outstanding, although modest, black-and-white film deprived of dialogue. Awarded in 1962 at the San Francisco International Film Festival, *Ambulance* was made with the participation of some leading contributors to the Polish School, including cinematographer Jerzy Lipman, composer Krzysztof Komeda-Trzciński, and actor Tadeusz Łomnicki, who is credited as the author of the script. Before *Ambulance*, Morgenstern served as assistant director on Wajda's *Kanal* and *Ashes and Diamonds* and, after his debut in 1960 with a lyrical contemporary drama *See You Tomorrow* (*Do widzenia, do jutra*), he directed a number of films dealing with different aspects of World War II.[54]

Interestingly, despite Morgenstern's Jewish background and the fact that he survived the war in Poland in the ghetto and then hiding in the countryside, *Ambulance* serves as his only film openly dealing with the Holocaust. In recent interviews, Morgenstern commented that he never wanted to make films that would be too close to his own story of survival. After the war, he "didn't want to remember the Holocaust at all. I told myself—that's it! I am beginning a new life."[55] In another interview, Morgenstern stated that the Holocaust has become an integral part of his life although it is not evidenced by his other films. By making *Ambulance*, he "paid the debt to those who were killed."[56]

Ambulance belongs to a small, although prominent, group of Polish war films focusing on the plight of children, both of Jewish and Polish origin. The film opens with one of Hitler's anti-Jewish speeches, followed by a German military march. The camera positioned inside a moving truck portrays a concrete road and the exhaust smoke. After the credits, the ambulance with a Red Cross sign enters a gate leading to a place that looks like a schoolyard surrounded by barbed wire. Watched by their old guardian, a group of children is at play on an almost empty square. As Annette Insdorf observes, "The first child we see is blindfolded in his game, an appropriate image for their ignorance (and ours) as to the purpose of the ambulance."[57] Like the children at play, the viewer is also unaware that the Red Cross van, a symbol of safety, help, and rescue, is a gas van—a mobile gas chamber using carbon monoxide to kill unsuspecting victims.

Similarly to Tadeusz Borowski in his prose or Andrzej Munk in *The Passenger* (also filmed in 1961), Lipman's camera captures several routine, almost mechanical actions of the German guards. An SS man fills the gas tank, connects an exhaust pipe to a pipe that runs into the back of the car, and tests the gas truck camouflaged as the ambulance. The innocent expression on the faces of children, who are playing with a German dog and a small bird, contrasts with that of their teacher, who seems to know the truth, but tries to keep the spirit of his children high. Perhaps, as many critics suggested, the situation alludes to Janusz Korczak and his children from the Warsaw Ghetto orphanage?[58] In the next scene, the children climb into the ambulance along with their guardian to the bitter tune of a Jewish song. Another point-of-view shot, this time from inside the ambulance, focuses on small birds, thus providing a contrast between the doomed group of children and the relative freedom outside. In the cold-blooded reality pictured in the film, only the German shepherd reveals some human-like qualities—the dog attempts to return a toy to a child locked inside the ambulance, but is quickly scolded by the guard.

In the last scene, the ambulance unhurriedly leaves the fenced yard. The everyday brutality is portrayed in the film with the help of images that are suggestive rather than explicit. They aptly capture not only the "banality of evil" and the industrialized killing, but also evoke the helplessness of those facing extermination. As the ambulance drives away from the loading zone, the viewer is spared images of the asphyxiated young victims, but strongly reminded of the mass gassings at Auschwitz and other death camps.

***

One of the most memorable films made during the Polish School period, Stanisław Różewicz's *Birth Certificate* (*Świadectwo urodzenia*, 1961), shows the war through the eyes of a child. In the longest, third episode of this three-part film, *A Drop of Blood* (*Kropla krwi*), a young Jewish girl Mirka (Beata Barszczewska) hides out in an orphanage where she is told by some Nazi "experts" that she has typical features of the Aryan race.

Set in 1943, the film starts with an image of desolate ghetto apartment buildings after a German raid. The camera then focuses on a lone survivor, the young Jewish girl who emerges from hiding (Figures 4.8, 4.9, 4.10). After a night spent in the apartment that belonged to her family, she leaves the deserted

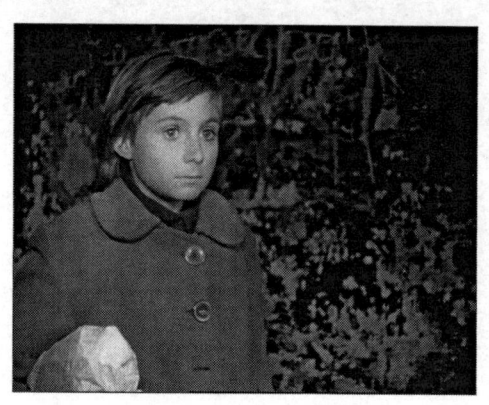

Figure 4.8: The Jewish girl Mirka (Beata Barszczewska) emerges from hiding in Stanisław Różewicz's *Birth Certificate* (1961)

Figure 4.9: *Birth Certificate*. Mirka's POV

Figure 4.10: Beata Barszczewska as Mirka in *Birth Certificate*

ghetto seeking a more permanent shelter among the Polish friends of her parents. She is being helped by a number of Poles but also threatened by their presence (for example, by the village children asking her to recite a Catholic prayer to prove that she is Polish).

Stanisław Loth's camera often captures the girl's large, frightened eyes in close-ups and emphasizes her solitude through distancing long shots, while she tries to comprehend the cruel, claustrophobic reality that surrounds her. The quiet master of Polish cinema, Różewicz, also aptly utilizes some off screen sounds, in particular distant talk in German and unanticipated knocks on the

Figure 4.11: A scene from *Birth Certificate*. (From the left) Zygmunt Zintel, Emil Karewicz, and Mariusz Dmochowski. Courtesy Filmoteka Narodowa in Warsaw. © Film Studio "Tor"

doors, which add to both suspense and the oppressive atmosphere that the child experiences.

Różewicz is not a moralizing director. Instead of criticizing the Nazi system, he exposes its madness. In the final part of the film, Mirka is presented with the new birth certificate, stating that she is a Polish girl, Marysia Malinowska, and she is being moved to a provincial Polish orphanage. This is not, however, the end of her ordeal. The tension mounts again with the arrival of a Gestapo officer, accompanied by a Nazi "racial expert," both in search of Jewish children hiding with false Polish papers. After a short examination by the "expert," Mirka is declared racially fit (having "Nordic characteristics") to be sent to a German orphanage. The film ends with a close-up image of Mirka's eyes, perhaps expressing wonder at the bizarre twist of fate. (See Figure 4.11.)

Psychologizing the Holocaust: *White Bear* and *The Passenger*

Not every film about the Holocaust succeeded despite its sometimes intriguing storyline. Jerzy Zarzycki's *White Bear* (*Biały niedźwiedź*, 1959), produced for the Film Unit "Syrena," serves as such an example. Set in early 1943, it portrays a young Jewish scientist and intellectual, Henryk Fogiel (Gustaw Holoubek), who escapes from a transport to a concentration camp and hides in Zakopane, a resort in the Tatra Mountains. He conceals his identity by wearing a white bearskin and acting as a prop for a local Polish photographer, posing with (mostly German) tourists for postcards (in German): "Greetings from Zakopane" (Figure 4.12). Despite being popular among audiences, the film received lukewarm reviews after its premiere, usually blaming the incongruities of the script (authored by as many as five scriptwriters), the improbabilities of the storyline (supposedly real, based on a true case described in a novel by

Figure 4.12: A scene from Jerzy Zarzycki's *White Bear* (1959). (From the left) Rudof von Henneberg (Adam Pawlikowski), Henryk Fogiel (Gustaw Holoubek) in a white bearskin, and Henneberg's wife (Liliana Niwińska).

Robert Azderball and Roman Frister), and Zarzycki's old-fashioned prewar directorial sensibility. The same critics, however, who complained about this failed attempt at psychological war cinema noticed the unconventional portrayal of the Germans and the relations between the victim and the victimizer.[59]

The film opens with an establishing shot of the Tatra Mountains' wintery landscape, which is followed by a long shot of a night transport train. A group of prisoners escapes and runs into the forest, despite shots being fired in their direction. Among the escapees is Henryk, a Polish Jew living in Paris since 1936, who visited his sister in Poland before the war, and was trapped by the quickly advancing Germans in September of 1939. He is captured and sent to a ghetto where he works in a stone-pit before being dispatched to a concentration camp. In Zakopane, he is sheltered in a house belonging to an old high school teacher (Stanisław Milski), who survives the occupation as a street photographer working with a young helper, Michał Pawlicki (Stanisław Mikulski), a member of the Polish underground. The teacher's house also serves as a base for some underground activities managed by Michał. The latter is reluctant to help Henryk, since above all he thinks about the safety of the house and the protection of his radio transmitter. Although the film includes a scene depicting the capture of another Jewish escapee and the killing of those who sheltered him (as well as the destruction of their property), it is not the fear of punishment for hiding a Jew but Michał's underground assignment that makes him reluctant to offer assistance. As if to reinforce the image of a noble resistance (unspecified in the film although the left-wing affiliation is implied), in a later scene a *szmalcownik* attempts to blackmail Henryk but is swiftly reprimanded by another local member of the underground.

After Michał is killed by the Gestapo, Henryk replaces him, takes on his identity, and goes out in a white bearskin, mixing with German tourists and the locals. The commanding German officer, Major Rudolf von Henneberg (Adam Pawlikowski), notices Henryk standing outside of the fence in full white bear gear and listening to a classical concert played at the officers' club. Puzzled, he invites him inside, sits him among fellow German officers, comments that Mozart's quartet charmed even such a carnivore, and calls him "my musical friend." The crucial part of the film, narrated in German, consists of the conversations between von Henneberg and Henryk, whose true identity is quickly unmasked by the German officer (Figure 4.13). Von Henneberg is portrayed as an intellectual, humanist, and connoisseur of classical music who despises brutal methods used by his fellow countrymen. He guarantees Henryk security in exchange for frank intellectual conversations. In an unconvincing finale, when Henryk's identity becomes known to other Germans, he escapes from the officer's club but Anna (Teresa Tuszyńska), the teacher's daughter, dies while trying to protect him.

The film's portrayal of the conflict was uncommon in the Polish context, in particular the presentation of an intellectual duel between the oppressor and

Figure 4.13: Gustaw Holoubek (Henryk) and Adam Pawlikowski (Major Henneberg) in *White Bear*

the oppressed, but the film suffered from several psychological improbabilities and the uncertain direction by Zarzycki. It was not even saved by Stefan Matyjaszkiewicz's cinematography and by the acting of two "intellectual Polish actors" (Holoubek and Pawlikowski). A later film, *The Passenger* (*Pasażerka*, 1963), more effectively dealt with similar issues.

***

The Passenger was made by one of the masters of the Polish School generation, Andrzej Munk (1921–1961), usually considered by critics as the leading exponent of its "rationalistic" tendency. A descendant of a Polonized Jewish family from Kraków, Munk survived the occupation in Warsaw where he did not reveal his Jewish ancestry and worked on the Aryan side. During the war, he also became a member of the socialist underground (Polish Socialist Party, PPS) and later participated in the Warsaw Rising. After the war, Munk graduated from the Łódź Film School in 1950 and began his career with a series of documentary films, elements of which one may find in his mature style. Following his feature debut, the war adventure film *The Blue Cross* (aka *The Men from the Blue Cross*, *Błękitny krzyż*, 1955), he directed three classic Polish films: *Man on the Tracks* (*Człowiek na torze*, 1957), *Eroica* (1958), and *Bad Luck* (aka *Cockeyed Luck*, *Zezowate szczęście*, 1960). In 1961, Munk was killed in a car accident on the way from Warsaw to the Łódź Film Studio where he was about to assess the set design for the next part of his new film, *The Passenger*. The project was completed by Munk's friends, including director Witold Lesiewicz and writer Wiktor Woroszylski, the latter responsible for the off-screen narration.[60] They edited the existing footage and added a voice-over commentary read by Tadeusz Łomnicki. *The Passenger* had its premiere on the

Figure 4.14: Andrzej Munk (1921–1961). *The Passenger* (1963)

second anniversary of Munk's death, 20 September 1963. It was presented as an unfinished statement by the tragically deceased director (Figure 4.14).

At the center of *The Passenger* is the relationship between the German SS woman at Auschwitz-Birkenau, Liza (Aleksandra Śląska), and the Polish inmate, Marta (Anna Ciepielewska). Years after the war, a chance meeting between the two on a luxury liner ("an island in time" as the narrator describes it) heading from South America to Europe brings back memories of the suppressed past. Munk's film is based on the story by Zofia Posmysz-Piasecka, who was incarcerated in Auschwitz from 1942 to 1945. Her radio broadcast, *The Passenger from Cabin Number 45* (*Pasażerka z kabiny 45*), aired on Polish radio on 28 August 1959. As she later revealed, the inspiration for the story came from a situation involving a group of German tourists that she encountered in Paris. One of the female voices reminded her of an SS guard from Auschwitz.[61] Munk, who listened to the broadcast, asked Posmysz-Piasecka to write a television play, which he later directed. The play aired on 10 October 1960 and starred Zofia Mrozowska as Liza, Edward Dziewoński as her husband, and Ryszarda Hanin as the silent passenger. The psychological drama was set entirely on the ocean liner; it dealt with the issue of guilt and forgetting on the part of the Germans, and offered only four comments by Liza on her Auschwitz past. In 1962, after Munk's death, Posmysz-Piasecka published her novel, *The Passenger*, one of her many attempts to deal with the legacy of Auschwitz.[62]

Munk decided to abandon the contemporary dimensions of the literary source and to focus on the past, which is revealed in his film in three powerful retrospectives. The film begins with a series of private photographs introducing director Munk at work and in a private setting, which is accompanied by a commentary on the making of the film and on the problems faced by Munk's friends after his premature death. The prologue explains that they had "no intention of adding what he had no time to say himself ... not searching for solutions, which might not have been his, nor seeking to conclude the plots which his death left unresolved." They wanted to "present what was filmed with all the gaps and reticence in an attempt to grasp whatever is alive and significant." The film proper opens with a frame story taking place on a transAtlantic liner. Employing exclusively still photographs, it depicts the chance encounter between Liza and Marta and the threat posed by Marta's presence. The shock of seeing Marta results in a sudden, quick succession of several abrupt, nightmarish, almost hallucinatory widescreen images from Auschwitz that provided a sharp contrast to the film's prologue. The flashback from Auschwitz, the uncontrolled flow of Liza's repressed memories, includes both moving images and archival stills, among them images of naked female prisoners tormented by SS guards and *Kapos*, Alsatian shepherds sitting as if ready to attack, SS dog handlers walking along an electrified barbed-wire fence, a group of prisoners pulling a road roller, and a female prisoner being tattooed.

Liza explains her strange behavior to her new husband Walter (Jan Kreczmar) by admitting that she was an overseer in Auschwitz, not an inmate. Liza's attempt at explaining the past, also for herself, introduces another flashback, this time much longer and stressing her sense of duty. In a quasi-documentary manner Krzysztof Winiewicz's camera captures images of the camp after the gassing one of the transports: the main gate leading to the camp, the railway, the barbed-wire fence, belongings left by the victims (baby carriages, suitcases, and clothing). The panning camera stops in front of the crematorium and tilts to reveal heavy black smoke from its chimneys. Liza's commentary describes her duties in the camp, her professionalism and devotion to the cause ("I just did my duty"), and her version of the relationship with Marta, whom she chose to be her clerical help ("I always tried to help these women whenever I could"). Liza comments that in Auschwitz-Birkenau she supervised a gigantic storage space, *Effektenkammer*, where goods seized from killed victims were collected and catalogued. The storage was nicknamed "Canada" by the inmates to stress its immense resources. Liza tries to distance herself from crimes committed in Auschwitz, although she admits being a witness of mass killings.

The third flashback reveals Liza's true role in the camp. From behind a fence separating the *Effektenkammer* from the crematorium, she watches the newly arrived Jewish transport walking toward the gas chamber, which is covered in black smoke (Figures 4.15, 4.16, 4.17). She observes two German guards on the roof of the gas chamber. One of them, wearing a gas mask, opens a canister with Zyklon B and methodically dumps it into the killing zone through ventilation openings (Figure 4.18). Liza's flashback also sheds new light on the relationship between her and Marta, the way she tried to control "her prisoner," and Marta's relationship with her fiancé Tadeusz (Marek Walczewski) (Figure 4.19). The flashback ends with a cut back to the liner, and the narrator concludes: "The brush with the past did not last long. Marta, or someone resembling her, disembarked at the next port of call. The ship sails on. It is doubtful if the women will ever meet again. Liza won't be challenged by truths buried in the

102 Polish Film and the Holocaust

Figure 4.15: Andrzej Munk's *The Passenger*. Aleksandra Śląska as Liza watches the newly arrived Jewish transport

Figure 4.16: A scene from *The Passenger*

Figure 4.17: A scene from *The Passenger*

Images of the Holocaust during the Polish School Period (1955–1965)   103

Figure 4.18: A scene from *The Passenger*

Figure 4.19: (From the left) Anna Ciepielewska as Marta, Marek Walczewski as Tadeusz, and Aleksandra Śląska as Liza in *The Passenger*

mud of Auschwitz. Nobody can disturb Liza's life among people indifferent to yesterday's crimes, who even today ..." The scene darkens over the long shot of a liner at sea. The ending clearly serves not so much as a reminder of what happened but, in line with the politics of the day (the Berlin Wall that had just been erected), as a warning against West German politics. Liza's attempt at self-justification, which is verified by the visuals, prompts Annette Insdorf to assert that "a major question raised by *The Passenger* is whether postwar justifications by Germans are trustworthy or merely self-serving."[63]

The narrative aspect of *The Passenger*, the reliance on flashbacks to tell the story, may be considered Munk's favorite narrative strategy, and was employed by him in two earlier films. *Man on the Tracks* tells the story of a retired train engineer who dies under mysterious circumstances while attempting to stop a train, and whose death saves the passengers of the train. Often compared to

Citizen Kane (1941) and *Rashomon* (1950), the film offers three different perspectives of the event; three different narrators complement each other and provide contradictory versions of what happened. Likewise, the story of *Bad Luck*, the last film Munk completed, is told in six flashbacks introducing an opportunist antihero and unreliable narrator who, with no luck on his side, becomes a victim of political circumstances, totalitarian systems (fascism and communism), and the war. As in *Eroica* and *Bad Luck*, in *The Passenger* Munk also introduces the perspective of a character with whom the viewer cannot identify, an unreliable narrator.

Polish film scholar and Auschwitz inmate Bolesław W. Lewicki convincingly argued in his 1968 essay that *The Passenger* functions as a polemic with Jakubowska's *The Last Stage*,[64] and this connection also preoccupied a group of critics and scholars. Definitely, there are several elements that justify such a comparison. For example, in both films the perpetrator is played by Aleksandra Śląska, but unlike her *Oberaufseherin* in Jakubowska's film, in *The Passenger* she no longer plays a pathological sadist but a psychologically complex individual, part of the killing industry. Like Marta Weiss in Jakubowska's film, Munk's Marta is a privileged prisoner who performs a similar function in the camp's structure (Figure 4.20). Both Martas are also part of the resistance (left-wing in Jakubowska's work, unspecified in Munk's film), and they smuggle information about Auschwitz to the outside world. Both have lovers in the camp named Tadeusz (Tadek). Unlike Marta Weiss, Marta in *The Passenger* is Polish and there is no indication that it was planned otherwise at an earlier stage. Similar to Jakubowska, Munk (in his own words) had to "solve a difficult problem—how to show Auschwitz without depicting its realistic dimension ... A realistic portrayal would be unbearable."[65] Like Jakubowska, he doesn't show the process of killing graphically. Instead, he relies on images that he also singled out for emphasis in his last interview, conducted on 18 September 1961, and published after his death: "masses of female prisoners, groups of naked people, small baby carriages, barbed wires, posts."[66]

Figure 4.20: Anna Ciepielewska as Marta in *The Passenger*

In *The Last Stage*, Jakubowska incorporated somber classical music to comment on the action, to emphasize the inhuman conditions of the camp, and to stress the devilish nature of the German perpetrators. Unlike Jakubowska, Munk relies on diegetic sounds of the camp and on the almost surreal, yet historically accurate, diegetic music, for example the march from *Carmen* by Bizet, which is played by the Auschwitz orchestra near the gate leading to the camp. The exception is the framework with still photographs, which is illustrated by Tadeusz Baird's musical score. Like Jakubowska, Munk decided to shoot his film on location at Auschwitz-Birkenau to enhance verisimilitude (he stayed in the commandant's office), which also had an enormous impact on the film's crew. Like Jakubowska, Munk was surrounded by people who experienced Auschwitz first-hand, for example co-scriptwriter Posmysz-Piasecka and production manager Wilhelm Hollender, who also worked on *The Last Stage*.[67] In Andrzej Brzozowski's documentary tribute to Munk, *The Last Pictures* (*Ostatnie zdjęcia*, Polish Television 2000), actress Ciepielewska commented on the "unbearable noise of the barbed wire" on the set of the film. "I'm listening to Bach to calm down," wrote Munk in a letter to his wife. He was also reading Rudolf Höss' memoirs that were published for the first time in Polish in 1956, and this certainly contributed to his portrayal of Liza.[68] The horrors of the not-so-distant past were also emphasized in press reports from the film's set. One of them (published after Munk's death) had the following fragment: "On the ground, near the crematorium, there was a small metal object. My guide [Wilhelm Hollender] picked it up carefully. This was an authentic key that was used to open tin canisters with Zyklon B."[69]

Today, it is difficult to say whether the film's ambiguity, embraced by scholars, was intentional or simply has to do with the film's incompleteness. The film's prologue already invites comments on the unfinished nature of the film ("we merely wish to present what was filmed with all the gaps and reticence in an attempt to grasp whatever is alive and significant"). The film's introductory comment about Munk also invites statements such as this one by a writer and former Auschwitz inmate Tadeusz Hołuj who declared: "This is a film about Munk, not Auschwitz."[70]

The uncompleted, fragmentary *The Passenger* "resembles antic sculptures damaged by the passing of time," writes Tadeusz Szyma fittingly.[71] The film's unfinished status elevates it to another level; it helps to make this film complex, mysterious, and multilayered. While the majority of writers consider this to be its strength,[72] others, for example Stuart Liebman, regard the film's unfinished nature as its weakness ("merely a torso"). Pointing out "quasi-Sartrean" elements in the film, Liebman adds: "Knowing what we know about life in the camps, this tale of victim and guard seems naïve and contrived."[73] The point Liebman is making is important because *The Passenger* is often discussed in the context of Holocaust films that deal with "homoerotic fascination" or "homoerotic desire."[74] The struggle for dominance, the focus on the relationship between the victim and the victimizer was noticed by critics soon after the film was released.[75] The "sexualization of the Shoah," the role of repressed memories, and the portrayal of what is almost a sexual attraction between the victimizer and the victim, to a certain extent carry associations with later exploitative works, such as Liliana Cavani's *The Night Porter* (*Il portiere di notte*, 1974).

Regardless of the problematic portrayal of the relationship between the Auschwitz perpetrator and the victim, the strength of Munk's film, however, lies in its powerful camp imagery, "one of the most terrifying images of Auschwitz," as Andrzej Wajda comments on Munk in Brzozowski's documentary. In particular, scenes heavily borrowing from Tadeusz Borowski's depiction of Auschwitz belong to the most powerful ones, for example, a "love scene" featuring a fragment from a violin concerto by Johann Sebastian Bach performed by the camp orchestra. Separated by SS guards, Marta and Tadeusz exchange glances and move slowly toward each other with the help of other prisoners. The sudden whistles and sounds of a transport train approaching the Auschwitz ramp mark the intrusion of brutal reality. The camp concert is adjourned and the guards anxiously rush to perform their duties. The whole situation resembles a scene from Borowski's short story "The People Who Walked On," which describes a Sunday soccer game at Auschwitz. Playing as a goalkeeper, the narrator has his back toward the ramp. Running to retrieve a ball near the barbed wire, he observes a transport train that has just arrived, and people walking away from the cattle cars. Later, retrieving the ball once again, he notices that the ramp is empty and concludes: "Between two throw-ins in a soccer game, right behind my back, three thousand people had been put to death."[76]

Like Jakubowska, in *The Passenger*, Munk de-emphasizes the issue of nationality. His film features images of the Jewish transport walking toward gas chambers, the search for a hidden Jewish newborn in Liza's commando, but its focus is on political prisoners, mostly Poles. Jews are relegated to the role of passive victims. Such a representation of Auschwitz, in particular the choice of a Polish character, Marta, prompted Omer Bartov to comment about Munk: "One can only assume that he meant to make a statement also about the celebration of Polish heroism and victimhood and the denial of the specific Jewish memory of the war."[77] Bartov argues that Munk's suppression of Jewish traces in the film was done as if he anticipated the 1968 anti-Semitic wave in Poland. He writes:

> One would like to believe that he was already conscious of that potential when he made *The Passenger*, and that in the final version this other aspect of the past, not merely the suppression of Jewish victimhood but the appropriation of Jewish heroism, the transformation of Marta from Jew to Pole, would have been given the kind of wry and ironic expression of which Munk was such a master.[78]

Why does the "Jewish aspect" of Auschwitz not play a more prominent role in a film made by a filmmaker of Jewish origin, something expected by Bartov and other scholars? Perhaps, like Polański, Munk was lacking the right literary material? Munk definitely was not afraid to question some aspects of Polish mythology, to introduce antiheroic characters during the period when heroism and class consciousness mattered. Munk, however, was more interested in a universal dimension of his story, therefore the lack of emphasis on the question of nationality of Auschwitz prisoners. It has to be stated that Munk also deemphasizes the issue of an "anti-fascist struggle" led by the communist underground, which was expected by the authorities and, possibly, also by those who were familiar with the director's left-wing, socialist leaning.[79]

Latent References to the Holocaust

Holocaust references can be also traced in films that, after the first viewing, seem to have little in common with the Holocaust or Polish-Jewish relations. For example, Roman Polański's very well-received short film, *Two Men and a Wardrobe* (*Dwaj ludzie z szafą*, 1958), is sometimes discussed as featuring two Holocaust survivors. Carrying their burden (a wardrobe), they return to their hometown and face a crowd of hostile inhabitants, their former neighbors.[80] Such readings certainly are justified given Polański's Jewish background and his story of survival, the open nature of the storyline, and the postwar atmosphere in Poland. As Polański writes in his autobiography, he was certainly aware that his actors "look Jewish" to Polish audiences (in fact, both lead actors, Henryk Kluba and Jakub Goldberg, were Jewish). According to Polański's anecdotal comment, Kluba "complained that the beard I'd made him grow had earned him insults while commuting by train to see his girlfriend in Gdańsk—some fellow passengers had called him a dirty Jew—and that it was blighting his love life."[81]

Another case is even more concealed. Discussing the complexities of representation of "the other" in Polish cinema, Paul Coates singles out for emphasis a scene from Jerzy Kawalerowicz's classic film, *Mother Joan of the Angels* (*Matka Joanna od Aniołów*, 1961), which he calls "the most intriguing—and baffling—of the images of Polish-Jewish relations thrown up by the cinema of People's Poland."[82] This classic tale about demonic possession is loosely based on the well-known story about the possessed nuns at the seventeenth-century monastery in Loudun (France), but set in eighteenth-century eastern Poland. The story deals with a young ascetic and devout exorcist, Father Suryn (Mieczysław Voit), who tries to understand the nature of evil in order to free Mother Joan (Lucyna Winnicka) and the possessed nuns from demons. He visits a Jewish rabbi (also played by Voit) to seek his advice. The manner of portraying this encounter indicates Suryn's journey into the self (Figures 4.21, 4.22). Later, when Father Suryn exhausts the traditional methods (prescribed rituals, prayers, self-flagellation), he consciously commits a horrid crime (the killing of two stable boys) to liberate Mother Joan and the convent's sisters from demons and place them under his care. For Coates, this is an example of an

Figure 4.21: Jerzy Kawalerowicz's *Mother Joan of the Angels* (1961). Father Suryn (Mieczysław Voit)

Figure 4.22: The Rabbi (Mieczysław Voit) in *Mother Joan of the Angels*

Aesopian film, which presents contemporary problems disguised as costume drama: "The place where Jews still exist is only imaginary, as imaginary for Kawalerowicz as it is for the priest, who is thus not really a seventeenth-century priest at all but a contemporary Pole able to imagine 'the Jew' by casting himself in his role, since he now occupies his place."[83]

Conclusion

Despite the relative freedom during the Polish School period, the pressure of politics was overwhelming. The demands for greater independence for the film units and softer censorship were incompatible with the attempts of the communists to regain total control over the filmmaking process, which had been characteristic of the pre-October 1956 period. Already toward the end of the 1950s, the communist authorities had been sending many signals that the relative freedom of expression would no longer be tolerated. The party was disappointed with the messages and themes permeating Polish films, including its treatment of Polish-Jewish relations. Gradually, the autonomy of film units became limited, and stricter control of films was administratively implemented.

The Polish School began to lose its impetus at the beginning of the 1960s. The Resolution of the Central Committee Secretariat of the Polish United Workers' Party, issued in June 1960, explicitly objected to the pessimism of a number of Polish films, their lack of compliance with the party line, and the strong role played by Western cinema in Poland.[84] As a remedy, the resolution imposed more strict limits and more rigorous criteria on imported films from the West. This same party document also postulated making political and educational films needed in the process of "building socialism," films that reflected current problems from the socialist perspective, and inspired by the "progressive tendencies" in Polish history. The document postulated the production of films stressing the common struggle of Polish and Soviet soldiers with Nazi Germany, and the role of the left wing partisans. It recommended increasing the number of pro-party writers and party functionaries in the processes of scriptwriting and script approval, and proposed to develop "socialist entertainment films."

The 1960 party resolution did not specifically mention films dealing with the Holocaust or Polish-Jewish relations, but the harsh criticism of the ideologically improper interpretations of the war and the occupation in Polish cinema could not go unnoticed. Polish filmmakers were criticized for their pessimistic portrayal of Polish reality and their abandonment of links "between the martyrology and heroism of the nation and the determined struggle for People's Poland."[85] Due to communist censorship, Polish filmmakers were unable to voice their real concerns regarding recent national history, politics, and social issues. Instead, they retreated to safer adaptations of the national literary canon and popular cinema.[86]

Notes

1. Jaff Schatz. *The Generation: The Rise and Fall of the Jewish Communists of Poland* (Berkeley: University of California Press, 1991), 228.
2. Bożena Szaynok, *Z historią i Moskwą w tle. Polska a Izrael 1944–1968* (Warsaw: Instytut Pamięci Narodowej, 2007), 353.
3. The importance of the "Polish October" and its impact on literature and film is discussed in Mariusz Zawodniak and Piotr Zwierzchowski, eds., *Październik 1956 w literaturze i filmie* (Bydgoszcz: Wydawnictwo Uniwersytetu Kazimierza Wielkiego, 2010).
4. Aleksander Jackiewicz, "Ostatniego etapu ciąg dalszy," reprinted in his *Moja filmoteka: kino polskie* (Warsaw: Wydawnictwa Artystyczne i Filmowe, 1983), 196.
5. During the Polish School period, Jerzy Lipman, an assimilated Polish Jew, worked as a cinematographer on Wajda's *Kanal* (1957) and *Lotna* (1959), Jerzy Kawalerowicz's *Shadow* (1956) and *The True End of the Great War* (1957), Jerzy Passendorfer's *Answer to Violence* (1958), and Roman Polański's *Knife in the Water* (1962), among other films. Jerzy Hoffman's *Pan Michael* (released in 1969) became Lipman's last Polish production. In 1968, a year of anti-Semitic events in Poland, he left for West Germany where he worked until 1982, mostly for television. He also worked with Aleksander Ford on *Dr. Korczak, the Martyr* (1974). Details from Lipman's eventful life are included in Tadeusz Lubelski, ed., *Zdjęcia: Jerzy Lipman* (Warsaw: PISF, SFP, WAiF, 2005).
6. In an interview accompanying the Criterion edition of *A Generation*, titled *Andrzej Wajda: On Becoming a Filmmaker*, Wajda stresses that it was not his intention to caricature the Home Army and blames his lack of knowledge and limited experience for such a portrayal.
7. Works by a Jewish-Polish communist historian, Bernard Mark, may serve as a good example of politicizing the Warsaw Ghetto Uprising. Mark's books, including his best known *Powstanie w getcie warszawskim na tle ruchu oporu w Polsce. Geneza i przebieg* (Warsaw, 1953), reflect the meanders of the communist interpretation of history. He writes: "The uprising was a part of a general struggle for liberation, which was fought by the nation under the leadership of PPR [Polish Workers' Party]. It was an element in the universal struggle of humanity, under the leadership of the Soviet Union, against Hitler's Germany," 319. Quoted from Joanna Nalewajko-Kulikov's biographical portrait of Mark, "Trzy kolory: szary. Szkic do portretu Bernarda Marka," *Zagłada Żydów. Studia i Materiały* 4 (2008): 278.

8. Michael Stevenson, "Wajda's Filmic Representation of Polish-Jewish Relations," in *The Cinema of Andrzej Wajda: The Art of Irony and Defiance*, eds. John Orr and Elżbieta Ostrowska (London: Wallflower Press, 2003), 83.
9. Bronisława Stolarska, "Pokoleniowe doświadczenie 'sacrum.' O debiucie Andrzeja Wajdy," in *Filmowy świat Andrzeja Wajdy*, eds. Ewelina Nurczyńska-Fidelska and Piotr Sitarski (Kraków: Universitas, 2003), 243–248. Stolarska writes that Wajda emphasizes the religious meaning of the scene by situating it during the Holy Week. In Bohdan Czeszko's novel, Jasio Krone joins the communist underground cell in the fall of 1943, after being inspired by Alexei N. Tolstoi's novel referring to the Bolshevik Revolution. Ibid., 246.
10. Several communists, who escaped from the Warsaw Ghetto after July 1942 (the first transports to Treblinka), joined the communist military organization, the People's Guard (GL). Its members were able to smuggle some weaponry to the ghetto and planned to join the Ghetto Uprising, which was later reduced only to minor actions near the ghetto wall. Piotr Wróbel, "An NKVD Residentura (Residency) in the Warsaw Ghetto, 1941–42," in *Secret Intelligence and the Holocaust*, edited by David Bankier (New York: Enigma Books, 2006), 269–270. The help provided by the People's Guard, stressed in Wajda's film, was modest compared to that provided by the Home Army. See Richard C. Lukas, *Forgotten Holocaust: The Poles under German Occupation 1939–1944* (New York: Hippocrene Books, 2005), 175. Another book, edited by younger generation historians, portrays the communist underground as a criminal organization. They argue that despite the loudly proclaimed pro-Jewish stand, the communists often killed Jews, as well as non-communist underground members. See: Marek J. Chodakiewicz, Piotr Gontarczyk, and Leszek Żebrowski, *Tajne oblicze GL-AL. Dokumenty* (Warsaw: Bouchard Edition, 1997–1999).
11. Czesław Miłosz, *A Year of the Hunter*, trans. Madeleine G. Levine (New York: Farrar, Straus and Giroux, 1994), 4.
12. Czesław Miłosz, "Campo dei Fiori," in *New and Collected Poems 1931–2001* (New York: Harper Collins, 1988), 33–34. [Originally published in 1944 in the underground anthology *Z otchłani (From the Abyss)*, composed by poets living on the Aryan side and dedicated to the Warsaw Jews.] Also in 1943, Miłosz wrote another well-known poem about the Warsaw Ghetto, "A Poor Christian Looks at the Ghetto."
13. Tomasz Szarota, *Karuzela przy Placu Krasińskich. Studia i szkice z lat wojny i okupacji* (Warsaw: Oficyna Wydawnicza Rytm, 2007).
14. Ibid., 149–151.
15. Ibid., 150. In April 1943, Nazi Germany announced the discovery of mass graves of Polish officers killed by the Soviet security forces. Following this announcement, Joseph Goebbels began to use it for propaganda purposes in order to discredit the Soviets and their allies. In 1989, the Soviet government admitted that approximately 22,000 Polish officers had been executed by the NKVD on Stalin's order. Andrzej Wajda's powerful film *Katyń* (2007) portrayed the massacre for the first time on Polish screens.
16. Ibid., 165.
17. "'Campo di Fiori' po pięćdziesięciu latach. Ludzkość, która zostaje," edited by Joanna Gromek-Ilg, *Tygodnik Powszechny* 18 (2005). Quoted online: http://www.dialog.org/dialog_pl/campo-di-fiori.html.
18. Joanna Beata Michlic, *Poland's Threatening Other: The Image of the Jew from 1880s to the Present* (Lincoln: University of Nebraska Press, 2006), 188.
19. Jerzy Andrzejewski, *Holy Week. A Novel of the Warsaw Ghetto Uprising* (Athens: Ohio University Press, 2007), 9.
20. Tadeusz Lubelski, *Wajda: Portret mistrza w kilku odsłonach* (Wrocław: Wydawnictwo Dolnośląskie, 2006), 60.
21. "Protokół z posiedzenia Komisji Ocen Filmów i Scenariuszy. Warsaw 18 June 1953." Andrzej Wajda Film Archive in Kraków.

22. The scene between Łomnicki and Cybulski is described in detail as a "duel between two great actors" in Kazimierz Kutz's book, *Portrety godziwe* (Kraków: Znak, 2004), 76–79. Kutz served as assistant director on Wajda's *A Generation*.
23. Jerzy Toeplitz, "Ocena scenariusza filmowego 'Staż kandydacki' na podstawie powieści 'Pokolenie' B. Czeszki, Warsaw, 8 July 1953." Andrzej Wajda Archive in Kraków.
24. Wajda decided to produce his new film outside of his usual studio Kadr due to his disappointment with the fact that the script of a historical epic, *Teutonic Knights*, which was assigned to him, had been given by the studio to Aleksander Ford. Lubelski, *Wajda*, 89. However, among several documents pertaining to the making of *Samson* and preserved at the Andrzej Wajda Archive in Kraków there are contracts with studio "Droga" (dated 29 July 1960) and "Kadr" (17 August 1960). They indicate that the film was made initially in those two studios.
25. "Samson. Protokół Komisji Ocen Scenariuszy w dniu 3 maja 1960 roku." National Film Archive in Warsaw, A-214/158.
26. Ibid.
27. Andrzej Wajda's official website: www.wajda.pl/en/filmy/film06/html.
28. Quoted from Janina Falkowska, *Andrzej Wajda: History, Politics, and Nostalgia in Polish Cinema* (New York: Berghahn, 2007), 85. Originally published in Jerzy Płażewski, Grzegorz Balski, and Jan Słodowski, *Wajda Films I* (Warsaw: WAiF, 1996), 110.
29. "Samson," *Filmowy Servis Prasowy* 7 (1961): 5.
30. See Lubelski, *Wajda*, 88–89; Falkowska, *Andrzej Wajda*, 86.
31. Ewa Mazierska, "Non-Jewish Jews, Good Poles and Historical Truth in the Films of Andrzej Wajda," *Historical Journal of Film, Radio and Television* vol. 20, no. 2 (2000): 217.
32. Ibid., 225.
33. This representation in Wajda's cinema changed after the transition to democracy, with the images of Polish nationalists/Catholics in the center of *Holy Week*.
34. Paul Coates, *The Red and the White: The Cinema of People's Poland* (London: Wallflower Press, 2005), 163.
35. Klaus Eder, *Andrzej Wajda* (Munich: Claus Hanser, 1980). Quoted from Falkowska, *Andrzej Wajda*, 86.
36. Aleksander Jackiewicz, *Moja Filmoteka: kino polskie* (Warsaw: Wydawnictwa Artystyczne i Filmowe, 1982), 35–36.
37. Michałek, *The Cinema of Andrzej Wajda*, 68.
38. Stefan Morawski, "Psalm o prześladowanych," *Ekran* 42 (1961): 7. Another prominent critic, Konrad Eberhardt, summarized many charges against Wajda's film in his article, "Samson wśród Filistynów," *Film* 42 (1961): 6.
39. Omer Bartov, *The "Jew" in Cinema: From* The Golem *to* Don't Touch My Holocaust (Bloomington: Indiana University Press, 2005), 153.
40. For example, Richard L. Lukas stresses that prior to the Warsaw Ghetto Uprising, some of the Jewish fighting units were organized by the communists. He writes: "Little wonder the AK regarded the Jewish resistance groups with suspicion and questioned their loyalty; after all, left-wing Zionists and Communists had been less than friendly toward the Polish government and its representatives in Poland." Lukas, *Forgotten Holocaust*, 172. Marek Edelman mentions the help the ghetto fighters received from one of the communist leaders, Franciszek "Witold" Jóźwiak (1895–1966). In: Hanna Krall, *Shielding the Flame: An Intimate Conversation with Dr. Marek Edelman, the Last Surviving Leader of the Warsaw Ghetto Uprising*, translated by Joanna Stasinska and Lawrence Weschler (New York: Henry Holt, 1986), 73.
41. Czesław Petelski (1922–1996) and Ewa Petelska (1924–) directed several films together that form the canon of Polish cinema. At the beginning of their career, the Petelskis were interested in "ordinary people," often placed in the midst of tragic political events that seemed to dwarf them, for example a group of Warsaw inhabitants buried in the cellar of a collapsed building in *A Sky of Stone* (*Kamienne niebo*, 1959), common soldiers during the postwar civil war in *The Artillery Sergeant Kaleń* (*Ogniomistrz Kaleń*, 1961), and provincial logging-truck drivers

in arguably the Petelskis' best film, *Damned Roads* (aka *Depot of the Dead, Baza ludzi umarłych*, 1959). Later, the Petelskis never repeated the success of their first films, although they produced big-budget historical films, such as *Copernicus* (*Kopernik*, 1973). Czesław Petelski, a Communist Party activist, also headed the Film Unit "Iluzjon" from 1963 to 1980 and from 1982 to 1987.

42. For example, *The Beater* is not mentioned in Annette Insdorf's seminal book, *Indelible Shadows: Film and the Holocaust* (Cambridge: Cambridge University Press, 2003).
43. "Naganiacz," *Filmowy Serwis Prasowy* 20 (1963): 2. During the war, Ewa Petelska was involved in helping Jews and was arrested by the Gestapo. See Krzysztof Kornacki, "Ewa i Czesław Petelscy—w krainie PRL-u," *Autorzy kina polskiego*, edited by Grażyna Stachówna and Bogusław Żmudziński (Kraków: Wydawnictwo Uniwersytetu Jagiellońskiego, 2007), 37.
44. "Protokół z kolaudacji filmu *Naganiacz* w dniu 29 VI 1963," National Film Archive in Warsaw, A-216/4.
45. Andrzej Werner, "Film fabularny," in *Historia filmu polskiego 1962–1967*, vol. V, ed. Rafał Marszałek (Warsaw: Wydawnictwa Artystyczne i Filmowe, 1985), 37.
46. J.W., "Prawda i gorycz. Przy torze kolejowym—28 lat na półce," *Rzeczpospolita* (31 October 2000): A10.
47. See also Michał Nekanda-Trepka's documentary on Brzozowski film, *By the Railway Track* (*Przy torze kolejowym*, 2000).
48. Zofia Nałkowska, "By the Railway Track," in *Medallions*, trans. Diana Kuprel (Evanston: Northwestern University Press, 2000), 23–27. All quotes from this edition.
49. Zofia Nałkowska, *Dzienniki czasu wojny* (Warsaw: Czytelnik, 1970).
50. Nałkowska, "By the Railway Track," 23.
51. Ibid., 24.
52. Ibid., 25.
53. Ibid., 25.
54. Morgenstern became particularly known for several television films about the war, some that form the canon of Polish television film, for example series such as *Columbuses* (*Kolumbowie*, 1970) and *The Polish Ways* (*Polskie drogi*, 1976). The former deals with the Warsaw Rising, the latter portrays a vast panorama of Polish characters under the German occupation.
55. Katarzyna Bielas and Jacek Szczerba, "Życie raz jeszcze," *Gazeta Wyborcza* 29 (21 November 2002): 18.
56. Rafał Świątek, "Spłaciłem dług wobec tych, co zginęli: Rozmowa z Januszem Morgensternem, gościem honorowym festiwalu," *Rzeczpospolita* (17 April 2008). Quoted online: www.rp.pl/artykuł122214.html.
57. Insdorf, *Indelible Shadows*, 50.
58. See the discussion on Janusz Korczak in chapter 7.
59. For example, Stanisław Janicki, "A mogło być świetnie," *Film* 1 (1960): 4. Also Andrzej Werner's comment in "Film fabularny," 36–37.
60. According to Andrzej Wajda, Munk's assistant directors were deeply affected by his tragic death and unable to continue with the project. Wajda was approached by Jerzy Bossak, head of the Film Unit "Kamera," the film's producer, and asked to finish the film. He declined the offer after evaluating the materials left by Munk. "I'm afraid," commented Wajda, "that Andrzej [Munk] believed too much in improvisation, which was meant to get from the script more than it was written there, and that he started to doubt the result." See Wajda's introduction to Marek Hendrykowski's book, *Andrzej Munk* (Warsaw: Więź, 2007), 10.
61. Paulina Kwiatkowska, "Obrazy czasoprzestrzeni w filmie *Pasażerka* Andrzeja Munka," *Kwartalnik Filmowy* 43 (2003): 31.
62. Details about the early stages of *The Passenger* come from Ewelina Nurczyńska-Fidelska's book, *Andrzej Munk* (Kraków: Wydawnictwo Literackie, 1982), 131–144. The television drama cannot be examined—the broadcast was not recorded (which was the standard practice at that time). Zofia Posmysz (b. 1923 in Kraków) returned to her camp experiences in several radio broadcasts, plays, and, in addition to *The Passenger*, three novels: *Holidays on the*

Adriatic Sea (*Wakacje nad Adriatykiem*, 1970), *The Same Doctor M.* (*Ten sam doctor M.*, 1982), and *To Freedom, to Death, to Life* (*Do wolności, do śmierci, do życia*, 1996). *Holidays on the Adriatic Sea* has a similar narrative structure: a small incident occurring during the holidays triggers painful memories from the past.

63. Insdorf, *Indelible Shadows*, 56.
64. Bolesław W. Lewicki, "Temat: Oświęcim," *Kino* 6 (1968): 16–18. Professor Lewicki (1908–1981) taught at the University of Łódź since 1959 and was also head of the Łódź Film School from 1968 to 1969. In 1974, he published his Auschwitz memoirs titled *You Know How It Is* (*Wiesz, jak jest*). It has to be noted that *The Passenger* also shares a number of similarities with another accomplished film produced in 1961, a short drama *Ambulance*.
65. Stefania Beylin, [untitled talk with Munk], *Film* 41 (1961): 11.
66. Ibid., 11.
67. Accomplished production manager Wilhelm Hollender (1922–1994) was imprisoned at Auschwitz. In 1994 Włodzimierz Gołaszewski made a documentary film initiated and co-scripted by Hollender, *Inspection at the Scene of the Crime—We Shouldn't Be Among the Living* (*Wizja lokalna—nie powinno nas być wśród żywych*), which introduced several former Auschwitz prisoners.
68. Nurczyńska-Fidelska, *Andrzej Munk*, 129.
69. Zdzisław Dudzik, "Ostatni film Andrzeja Munka," *Film* 41 (1961): 11.
70. Tadeusz Hołuj, "Jak powstawał *Koniec naszego świata*," *Film* 14 (1964): 6. On another level, however, one could argue that *The Passenger* is also a film about filming.
71. Tadeusz Szyma,"Szkic do portretu Andrzeja Munka," *Kino* 9 (2001): 9.
72. For example, Ewa Mazierska's essay, "*Passenger* (*Pasażerka*)" in a booklet accompanying the 2006 Second Run DVD edition of the film (p. 4).
73. Stuart Liebman, "Man on the Tracks, Passenger, Bad Luck, Eroica," *Cineaste* vol. 32, no. 2 (2007): 64.
74. See Elżbieta Ostrowska's discussion, "Caught between Activity and Passivity: Women in the Polish School," in Ewa Mazierska and Elżbieta Ostrowska, *Women in Polish Cinema* (New York: Berghahn Books, 2006), 83–84.
75. James Price, "*The Passenger* (*Pasazerka*) by Andrzej Munk," *Film Quarterly* vol. 18, no. 1 (1964): 42–46.
76. Tadeusz Borowski, "The People Who Walked On," *This Way for the Gas, Ladies and Gentlemen* (New York: Penguin, 1976), 84. I owe this observation to Marek Hendrykowski, *Andrzej Munk* (Warsaw: Więź, 2007), 7.
77. Omer Bartov, *The "Jew" in Cinema: From* The Golem *to* Don't Touch My Holocaust (Bloomington: Indiana University Press, 2005), 177. The film was shown on Polish television the day before the first visit to Auschwitz by John Paul II in 1979.
78. Ibid., 178–179.
79. During and immediately after the war, Munk was an active member of the Polish Socialist Party (PPS). His older sister, Joanna Munk-Leszczyńska, was briefly married to Józef Cyrankiewicz before he became the Polish prime minister; Munk's wife, Halszka Próchnik, was a daughter of a known prewar socialist activist. Munk was also briefly a member of the Communist Party (PZPR) until 1952.
80. See, for example, Herbert J. Eagle's analysis, "Power and the Visual Semantics of Polanski's Films," in *The Cinema of Roman Polanski: Dark Spaces of the World*, ed. John Orr and Elżbieta Ostrowska (London: Wallflower Press, 2006), 40–41.
81. Roman Polanski, *Roman by Polanski* (New York: William Morrow, 1984), 147.
82. Paul Coates, *The Red and the White* (London: Wallflower Press, 2ic05), 186.
83. Ibid., 187.
84. "Uchwała Sekretariatu KC w sprawie kinematografii," reprinted in *Syndrom konformizmu? Kino polskie lat sześćdziesiątych*, ed. by Tadeusz Miczka and Alina Madej (Katowice: Wydawnictwo Uniwersytetu Śląskiego, 1994), 27–34.
85. Ibid., 28.

86. The imposition of more strict censorship at the beginning of the 1960s, and the difficulties of making films about the Holocaust after the decline of the Polish School, make the situation in Gomułka's Poland different than that of neighboring Czechoslovakia. The flourishing Czech and Slovak film industry in the 1960s was responsible for a number of classic Holocaust films, among them *The Shop on Main Street* (*Obchod na korze*, 1965), Ján Kadár's and Elmar Klos's Oscar-winning film. The group of important Czech and Slovak films includes *Romeo, Juliet and Darkness* (*Romeo, Julie a tma*, 1960) by Jiří Weiss, *Diamonds of the Night* (*Démanty noci*, 1964) by Jan Němec, and *Transport from Paradise* (*Transport z ráje*, 1963) and *The Fifth Horseman Is Fear* (*A pátý jezdec je strach*, 1965), both films by Zbyněk Brynych.

Chapter 5

YEARS OF ORGANIZED FORGETTING (1965–1980)

In the second part of the 1960s, the leader of the Polish Communist Party, Władysław Gomułka, had been gradually losing political control. Exploiting the growing disappointment with Gomułka's regime to their advantage, the nationalistic (so-called "partisan") faction of the Communist Party, led by General Mieczysław Moczar, started to gain the upper hand. A Ukrainian national (true name Mykoła Demko), and according to several sources an NKVD agent, Moczar became one of the leading communist apparatchiks, the minister of interior affairs (1964–1968), and head of the state audit body—the Supreme Chamber of Control (Najwyższa Izba Kontroli, NIK).[1] Since 1964, he was also in charge of the Union of Fighters for Freedom and Democracy (Związek Bojowników o Wolność i Demokrację, ZBOWiD), which under his direction had changed from an inconsequential veterans' organization to an influential political weapon.

Moczar and his clique tried to get rid of their political competition by appropriating a peculiar brand of nationalist, xenophobic, and anti-Semitic rhetoric. Piotr Gontarczyk writes in his book about the Polish Communist Party road to power that the Moczarists were united by their partisan past and their alleged role as victims of repressions during Stalinism, which they attributed to the Jewish segment of the security apparatus. Gontarczyk characterizes them as "by and large primitive, often deprived of any ethical and moral principles, and perceiving politics as an art of making a proper list of participants of the next alcoholic party ... Attempting to gain power at all cost, on the one hand they tried to please Moscow; on the other they eagerly used chauvinistic and anti-Semitic slogans."[2] A personal memoir by Moczar, *Scenes of Battle (Barwy walki)*, published for the first time in 1962 and adapted for the screen in 1965 by Jerzy Passendorfer, was designed to elevate the status of the Moczarists and to present them as nationalist communists.

The mid-1960s were also characterized by the gradual deterioration of relations between Poland and Israel, which culminated in 1967. After the Israeli-Arab Six-Day War, Poland followed the Soviet example and broke off diplomatic relations with the state of Israel on 12 June 1967. One week later, Gomułka criticized those who showed support for Israel and stressed that "every Polish citizen should have only one country: the Polish People's Republic."³ In a two-hour speech he also added a line that is now often-quoted by historians, but which did not appear in a printed version of his speech: "We do not want a fifth column in our country."⁴ (The term "fifth column" designates in the Polish context internal enemies, and was mostly used to describe those segments of the German minority in Poland that actively worked for Nazi Germany as spies, saboteurs, and provocateurs.) Gomułka's speech marked the beginning of open anti-Semitic campaign under the disguise of an "anti-Zionist" crusade that employed "anti-Zionist" slogans such as "Zionists, go to Zion" (*Syjoniści do Syjonu*).

The year 1968 in Poland, as with elsewhere in Europe, was marked by student demonstrations. The ban on Adam Mickiewicz's classic romantic drama *Forefathers* (*Dziady*), directed by Kazimierz Dejmek at the National Theater (Teatr Narodowy) in Warsaw, and the brutality of the police provoked student protests at the University of Warsaw on 8 March 1968. Two days later, students at the Łódź Film School, who were supported by their teachers, expressed their solidarity with the Warsaw students. Gomułka responded at the party gathering in Warsaw on 19 March by condemning "anti-socialist elements" and singling out for criticism a prominent group of Warsaw professors, several of them of Jewish origin.

The "March Events" were exploited by the Moczar's group to get rid of old-guard communists, a number of them Jewish, who during the war escaped to the Soviet Union and later returned as officers with the Red Army. The so-called "Zionist elements" (both university students and professors) were blamed for the eruption of political protests directed against the Communist Party, for the "Zionist conspiracy." They were also accused of defaming Poland and serving the interests of "American imperialists and German revanchists." As Jaff Schatz writes, "the subjects of anti-Semitism and the Holocaust were increasingly used to construct an image of internal and external threat to Poland and to Polish honor."⁵ For example, according to Schatz, the number of the Jewish victims of German extermination camps (99 percent) included in the Polish *Great Universal Encyclopedia* (*Wielka Encyklopedia Powszechna*, published from 1962 to 1969) was "interpreted as a purposeful attempt to depreciate the plight and offend the memory of the non-Jewish Polish victims of the Nazi occupation."⁶ The editorial staff of the *Encyclopedia*, which included a number of former Jewish party functionaries, was accused of acting on behalf of Poland's enemies. The anti-Semitic campaign forced a number of Polish citizens of Jewish origin to leave Poland, nominally for Israel, but more often for Scandinavian countries, West Germany, and the USA. Between 1967 and 1970, more than thirteen thousand permanent emigrants left Poland with one-way tickets, deprived of their Polish citizenships.⁷

The "anti-Zionist" campaign resulted not only in purges within the party, but also in attacks on people of Jewish origin in other spheres of life, including the film industry. The meeting of party activists working in the Polish film industry condemned the actions of the Łódź Film School professors who supported the striking students in March 1968. A noted film historian Jerzy Toeplitz (an assimilated Polish Jew), one of the founders of the school and its head since 1957, was dismissed on 4 April 1968.[8] Also removed were two deputy heads: Stanisław Wohl and Roman Wajdowicz.[9]

As a consequence of the anti-Semitic campaign, between 1968 and 1970 several filmmakers of Jewish origin left Poland, including the most influential postwar film director and film administrator Aleksander Ford. Among those who left Poland were accomplished cinematographers who greatly contributed to the success of the Polish School phenomenon, for example Władysław Forbert (1915-2001), who moved to Denmark, and Kurt Weber (1928-) and Jerzy Lipman (1922-1983), who both migrated to West Germany. Also leaving for West Germany were Anatol Radzinowicz (1911-2003), an expert set designer whose credits include *Forbidden Songs*, *Border Street*, and *Three Women*, and documentary filmmakers Marian Marzyński and Edward Etler (Grossbaum). They were joined by actor-director Jakub Goldberg (1924-2002), perhaps best known for his appearance in Roman Polański's *Two Men with a Wardrobe*, who worked mostly as a second director or assistant on several prominent films, among them works by Andrzej Munk (*Man on the Tracks*, *Eroica*, *Bad Luck*) and Polański (*Knife in the Water*). Several seasoned production managers also left Poland, among them Ludwik Hager (1911-1985), from 1955 to 1968 the manager at the most accomplished Film Unit "Kadr" and the producer of several films by Jerzy Kawalerowicz, such as *Mother Joan of the Angels* and *The Pharaoh* (*Faraon*, 1966), and the co-producer of some canonical films by Andrzej Wajda such as *Kanal* and *Ashes and Diamonds*. Among the prominent producers who left Poland were also Zygmunt Szyndler (?-1983), the production manager of film unit "Rytm" (1955-1968), who worked on, among others, Jan Rybkowski's films, such as *The Hours of Hope*, and Mieczysław Wajnberger, head of the Film Unit "Start" (1955-1968), the producer of *The Last Stage* and several films by Janusz Morgenstern, such as *Life Once Again* (*Życie raz jeszcze*, 1964).

The December 1970 workers' strikes in the Baltic ports, which were violently suppressed by the communist authorities, led to the downfall of Gomułka, and also to the marginalization of Moczar and his clique. The more pragmatic Silesian first party secretary, Edward Gierek, became the new party leader, and introduced some minor economic reforms. With the help of foreign loans, he focused on economic investments and consumer goods. The first part of the 1970s also brought changes to film practice in Poland. Another reorganization of the film units granted them more artistic freedom. This period of relative prosperity, heightened by the so-called "propaganda of success" (propaganda sukcesu) in Poland, ended in the late 1970s. The workers' protests in 1976 (caused by food price increases) spotlighted the growing problems of the Gierek administration: mismanagement of foreign credits, corruption, and a deepening economic crisis that was barely masked by the triumphant propaganda.

The period between 1965 and 1980, despite some relaxation of censorship in the 1970s, may be called the time of organized forgetting about the Holocaust.[10] This was an era characterized by projects that were rejected at the script stage, films that were unfinished or shelved, and by the imposition of state-controlled silence over sensitive issues. Many censoring decisions were made early, at the script stage, by the Committee for the Evaluation of Scripts (Komisja Ocen Scenariuszy, KOS) that became influential in the 1960s. The committee was chaired by the head of Polish film, usually the deputy minister of culture, and consisted of film and party apparatchiks, filmmakers, and critics. Crucial decisions at several stages of film production, in particular when the film was completed and awaited its seal of approval from the state, were made by the Communist Party functionaries, cultural and ideological instructors, and, in particular, by the heads of the cultural department of the Central Committee of PZPR, such as Wincenty Kraśko (1961–1968), Lucjan Motyka (1968–1977), and Bogdan Gawroński (1977–1981). Film bodies, such as the Film Approval Committee (Komisja Kolaudacyjna) and the Main Office for the Control of the Press, Publications, and Public Performances (Główny Urząd Kontroli Prasy, Publikacji i Widowisk, GUKPPiW), made sure that filmmakers obeyed the rules set by the Communist Party.

In the 1960s, with the advent of the Moczarists, several filmmakers adopted the party line and started to portray on the screen the struggles of communist partisans and Polish soldiers fighting alongside the Soviets during World War II. Passendorfer's *Scenes of Battle* celebrated the communist partisans in the spirit of Polish Romantic literature and bluntly attempted to ascribe the Home Army ethos to the marginal left-wing partisans. Other films by Passendorfer, such as *Bathed in Fire* (*Skąpani w ogniu*, 1964), *Direction Berlin* (*Kierunek Berlin*, 1969) and its sequel *The Last Days* (*Ostatnie dni*, 1969), portrayed regular Polish soldiers on their way to Berlin with the Red Army. Among several productions that belonged to this new trend appropriating the Home Army legend are two television series that became exceptionally popular during the late 1960s: *Four Tankmen and a Dog* (*Czterej pancerni i pies*, 21 episodes, 1966–1967) and *More Than Life at Stake* (*Stawka większa niż życie*, 18 episodes, 1967–1968).[11]

In the second part of the 1960s, the Polish communist authorities became paranoid about national image and representation of Polish-Jewish relations; they insisted on portrayals stressing wartime Polish help for Jews. Interestingly, their eventual ban on films dealing with Polish-Jewish history coincided with the growing world-wide interest in the Holocaust. In the second part of the 1960s, several film projects were abandoned or suspended by the authorities, for example, Jerzy Kawalerowicz's *Austeria* co-scripted by Tadeusz Konwicki, who worked on this project with Julian Stryjkowski, the Jewish-Polish author of the novel. After the suspension of his *Austeria* project by the authorities, Kawalerowicz left Poland for Italy (where he made *Maddalena* in 1971). "Had I made *Austeria* back in 1969, my career would have taken a different turn," he commented toward the end of his life.[12]

There were also other casualties of the political situation in 1968. The project about Dr. Korczak was terminated once again in March of 1968 despite some initial work that had been done in 1967 by Aleksander Ford. Another suspended project became an adaptation of Jerzy Andrzejewski's novel about the Warsaw Ghetto Uprising, *Holy Week* (see chapter 7 for more details).

Perhaps one of the most original abandoned projects was based on Jerzy Lipman's adventurous life during the war. A prominent cinematographer whose name is associated with several great achievements of the Polish School (*A Generation*, *Kanal*, *Knife in the Water*, among others), Lipman was born in an upper middle class, assimilated Jewish family.[13] During the war he escaped from the Wołomin ghetto before its liquidation and hid in Warsaw with false papers. Later, to survive, he started to wear a German uniform of the TODT organization and, from late 1942, a stolen uniform of a Luftwaffe Lieutenant. Lipman also established contacts with the Polish underground, and, masquerading as a German officer Georg Liebich, traveled extensively to the occupied Soviet Union, Berlin, and several Italian cities smuggling goods and weaponry.

In the mid-1960s, the leading scriptwriter of the Polish School, Jerzy Stefan Stawiński (1921–2010), prepared a script of a war adventure film loosely based on Lipman's wartime survival. The script was abandoned in 1968 when it became clear for Stawiński that any film with Jewish themes, not to mention a film featuring a Jewish character as a positive wartime hero, would not be allowed by the authorities after the advent of the Moczarists.[14] Jerzy Hoffman's *Pan Michael* (*Pan Wołodyjowski*, 1969) became Lipman's last Polish production. In 1968, he left for West Germany where he worked until 1982, mostly for television.

Given the pressure of communist censorship, the majority of Polish films released in the late 1960s and the 1970s avoided open discussions about Polish-Jewish relations and the Holocaust as politically "delicate." Several films, however, referred to German concentration camps located on the occupied Polish territories without making any specific references to the extermination of Jews. For example, Zbigniew Chmielewski's *The Face of an Angel* (*Twarz anioła*, 1970) is set in a concentration camp for Polish children in Łódź and focuses on an eleven-year-old boy, Tadek Raniecki (Marek Dudek), who survives the war and attempts at Germanizing him by a German guard, Augustin (Jiři Vrstala).

In another film, a Polish-Soviet Union coproduction *Remember Your Name* (*Zapamiętaj imię swoje*, 1974), directed by Sergei Kolosov, a Russian mother (Ludmila Kasatkina), who survived Auschwitz, tries to find her son from whom she was separated in the camp. Twenty years later she learns that he is alive, adopted by a Polish family after the war. The story of *Remember Your Name* most probably owes its inspiration to a ten-minute documentary, *Children of the Ramp* (*Dzieci rampy*, 1963, Andrzej Piekutowski), which consists of interviews with those who survived Auschwitz as children, among them a young woman who, several years after the war, found her real parents in the Soviet Union. A fragment of this documentary is used as a citation in an earlier psychological film, *Julia, Anna, Genowefa* ... (1968), directed by Anna Sokołowska. It deals with a young woman, Anna Wilimska (Wanda Neumann), who learns that she has been an adopted child and tries to find her biological parents. Her posted old photograph attracts attention—different people contact her, thinking that she is their Julia, Anna, or Genowefa. Despite the frequent use of this universal motif (the search for the parent/child of a former camp inmate), Polish cinema never applied this narrative pattern to Jewish survivors until Jan Jakub Kolski's 2000 film, *Keep Away from the Window* (*Daleko od okna*) (see chapter 6).

The echoes of the Holocaust are also apparent in Andrzej Wajda's *Landscape after Battle* (*Krajobraz po bitwie*, 1970). The film opens with a memorable sequence that sets the tone for the whole film—the liberation of a German concentration camp by American troops. Lacking dialogue and accompanied by Antonio Vivaldi's *Four Seasons*, the sequence portrays the first minutes of freedom. The prisoners in their striped camp clothing run through a snow-covered field, finally encountering a barbed-wire fence. They wait, confused and tired, before one of them (Mieczysław Stoor) touches it and discovers that it is not electrified. A sharp contrast follows when the prisoners avenge their misery by killing a *Kapo*. They literally stamp him into the dirt after the lofty speech of an American officer-liberator. The camera then introduces the film's protagonist, writer Tadeusz (Daniel Olbrychski), who has the low number "105" tattooed on his arm, indicating a long stay in the camp. He appears to be an almost stereotypical young intellectual: wearing wire-rimmed glasses, absent-minded, and rescuing books from fire while others search for food and clothing (Figure 5.1).

The film's action is set in a displaced persons camp, organized in a former SS barracks. The concentration camp prisoners, POWs, Jewish refugees from Poland, and survivors from other camps live in this place under the watch of American soldiers. Although Wajda deals with the Polish suffering and portrays

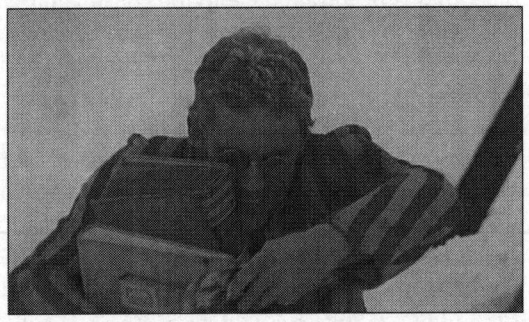

Figure 5.1: Daniel Olbrychski as Tadeusz in Andrzej Wajda's *Landscape after Battle* (1970)

Figure 5.2: Nina (Stanisława Celińska) and Tadeusz (Daniel Olbrychski) in *Landscape after Battle*

political differences among the Poles, he is primarily concerned with the love that surfaces between two survivors: Tadeusz and Nina (Stanisława Celińska), a Jewish refugee from Poland (Figure 5.2). As it often happens in Wajda's films, the sudden manifestation of love serves only as a romantic interlude before death. Ironically, while returning with Tadeusz to the camp, Nina is accidentally killed by an American guard ("We are used to it," Tadeusz tells the commanding officer) (Figure 5.3). As in Wajda's later film *Birchwood* (*Brzezina*, 1970), the death of a loved one enables the protagonist to awaken psychologically and regain some human emotions. In the film's finale, Tadeusz boards a train to Poland with numerous other refugees.

Film historian Rafał Marszałek commented that Wajda's film "is the first film about a concentration camp that, instead of an illustration, provides moral and psychological depiction of the past."[15] The situation represented in the film, however, also includes some apparent references to the late 1960s in Poland. Not only does Wajda seem to mock the nationalist communists in a bombastic scene featuring a recreation of the national past (the Battle of Grunwald), but also Nina's character has to be taken in the context of the political atmosphere preceding the release of Wajda's film. She is an escapee from the post-March

Figure 5.3: Nina's death in *Landscape after Battle*

1968 Poland who wants to study and live a quiet life somewhere in the West. As another Jewish refugee from Poland, Professor (Aleksander Bardini) remarks, "That woman just ran away from the living body of the nation." Preoccupied with his own painful story of survival, Tadeusz cannot comprehend Nina's past: "What could you know about fear? You don't even know what fear is." And later he asks: "Why did you escape from Poland. Because of fear?" Nina responds: "It wasn't fear at all. I ran away from love." Paul Coates convincingly argues that Wajda's representation of the relationship between Nina and Tadeusz serves to exemplify Polish-Jewish relations:

> Whereas Tadeusz defines himself as Polish first and foremost, Nina rejects her Jewish identity, denying ethnicity. It is the Pole who is obsessed with Nazi-inflicted suffering, not the Jew. Indeed, Nina is far less traumatized than Tadeusz, viewing some of his behaviour as deranged. Wajda's reckoning with Polish nationalism does not address the extent of its responsibility for Jewish suffering.[16]

References to the Holocaust also can be seen in several films that deal with the occupation and the actions of the Polish underground. For example, in Jan Łomnicki's *Operation Arsenal* (*Akcja pod Arsenałem*, 1978), a Polish underground fighter spontaneously intervenes when seeing a German soldier kicking an escaping young Jewish man. Similar references can also be found in a popular television series *The Polish Ways* (*Polskie drogi*, 1976–1977, eleven episodes), directed by Janusz Morgenstern. Scripted by Jerzy Janicki, the series portrays the panorama of the occupation while revolving around the wartime accounts of two characters, Władysław Niwiński (Karol Strassburger) and Leon Kuraś (Kazimierz Kaczor). With its focus on the Polish fate, the film refers to Auschwitz, the plight of Jewish children (one of them adopted by Kuraś), and the communist resistance (GL) providing help for the Jewish insurgents in the ghetto.

The only narrative film made between 1971 and 1982 that significantly incorporates the Holocaust motif is, interestingly, a film for young adults, *Salad Days* (*Zielone lata*, 1980), directed by Stanisław Jędryka (b. 1933). Best known for his popular films for children, Jędryka recreates the political atmosphere before and at the beginning of World War II in southern Poland, in the town of Sosnowiec (his place of birth). The film follows the friendship between a young Polish boy Wojtek, a German girl Erna, and a Jewish boy Abramek that survives the test of time and overcomes the barriers erected by the hostile world after September 1939. During the forceful relocation to the ghetto, Abramek's father is killed and the boy wounded. He survives thanks to the help provided by Erna and Wojtek.

An intriguing comment on Auschwitz can be found in *A Journey into the Unknown* (aka *Across the Unknown*, *Wycieczka w nieznane*, 1968), directed by an accomplished documentary filmmaker, Jerzy Ziarnik (1931–1999). This psychological drama focuses on a young and carefree writer Andrzej Miller (Ryszard Filipski), for whom a chance trip to Auschwitz, to watch a production of a film based on his friend's script, forever changes his perspective on life

Figure 5.4: Ryszard Filipski as the writer Andrzej Miller in Jerzy Ziarnik's *A Journey into the Unknown* (1968)

(Figure 5.4). Based on Andrzej Brycht's short story "Excursion: Auschwitz-Birkenau" ("Wycieczka: Auschwitz-Birkenau"), Ziarnik's film, among others, deals with the issue of memorialization of Auschwitz—the complex status of the museum as a place of both martyrdom and "the Holocaust tourism." The young writer observes what Tim Cole labels as "the tourist Auschwitz," which "threatens to trivialise the past, domesticate the past, and ultimately jettison the past altogether."[17] The writer watches the inept film crew at work on location in Auschwitz and the touristy aspect of the Auschwitz museum. A film-within-a-film segment of *A Journey into the Unknown*, the fictionalization of the camp experience, includes several pointed observations and appears to be the strongest part of the film, although it was not taken as such by Polish critics. One of them, Rafał Marszałek, commented that "instead of being a commentary on memorialization and memory, it demonstrates the known weaknesses of narrative camp films."[18] Ziarnik's work, however, is not a "camp film" although it comments on some of the most recognizable elements of the Auschwitz museum such as gas chambers and the gateway with *Arbeit Macht Frei*. Like István Szabó in *Father* (*Apa*, 1966), Ziarnik interweaves the past (photographs and names of the murdered) with the present; he also comments on role playing/reversal showing the film crew in action: extras playing SS guards flirt with "female prisoners" during the break in shooting (Figure 5.5). Although never appreciated in Poland, Ziarnik's film deserves attention. Made in the French New Wave spirit (Jan Laskowski's cinematography), this black-and-white film shares a number of stylistic elements with Wojciech Solarz's *Jetty* (*Molo*, 1969), another underappreciated film, also starring Filipski, which deals with the middle-age crisis of a ship designer from the Gdańsk shipyard for whom his fortieth birthday serves as a reminder of things he missed in life.

The reality of a Nazi concentration camp is present in one of the most unusual films ever made in Poland, *The Roll Call* (*Apel*, 1970), a classic black-and-white animated short film. Its author, an accomplished director of animated

Figure 5.5: A scene from *A Journey into the Unknown*

films Ryszard Czekała (1941–2010), portrays a nightmarish roll-call that ends in a slaughter of prisoners. Czekała's cut-out animation, which became the recipient of several international awards, was also praised in Poland and compared favorably to *The Last Stage* and *The Passenger*.[19]

Several films made in the late 1960s and the 1970s also deal with the reality before the Holocaust, but their characters and stories often invite readings through the prism of the Holocaust. For example, *Unloved* (*Niekochana*, 1966), directed by Janusz Nasfeter (1920–1998) and based on a short story by Adolf Rudnicki (Adolf Hirschhorn, 1909–1990), deals with the unhappy, obsessive and damaging love of a Jewish woman, Noemi (Elżbieta Czyżewska), for a Polish fine arts student. Set before the war, the film portrays the story of their separations and reunions, and her mental breakdown, set against the background of claustrophobic corridors, streets, and unappealing rooms. Noemi's love destroys her life; in the last scene of the film, she faces the outbreak of the war alone and depressed. The Holocaust seems to loom over the unhappy love story, making it even more impossible.

Adaptations of Bruno Schulz (1892–1941), works depicting a Jewish community in southeast small-town Poland before the war, have often been analyzed by Polish critics as narratives referring to the Holocaust since Konrad Eberhardt's 1973 essay published in monthly *Kino*.[20] *Sanatorium under the Sign of the Hourglass* (*Sanatorium pod klepsydrą*, 1973), inspired by Schulz's short stories published in 1937[21] and directed by Wojciech J. Has, deserves closer attention. Has's film deals with the theme of childhood recollections and offers a moody evocation of the lost Jewish world. Like Schulz, Has created a poetic, almost surreal landscape peopled by characters that move as if in a dream.[22] The film's protagonist, Józef (Jan Nowicki), travels in time. The film blends the past and the present, the living and the dead. The richness of the images, the panorama of characters, and the lyricism of this vision, permeated by nostalgia, contributed to this film's artistic success. *Sanatorium under the Sign of the Hourglass* is not, strictly speaking, about the Holocaust. The viewer, however, is compelled to look at this film through the prism of Schultz's tragic death in 1942, and cannot ignore what happened to the Jews of Drohobycz and other towns in former eastern Poland. The dream-like world created by Schultz in a way foretold the nightmarish future. As Daniel R. Schwartz writes in the spirit of Siegfried Kracauer's classic psycho-sociological study *From Caligari to Hitler*: "It is as if in the 1930s Schultz intuitively understood the moral illness hanging over Europe, and subsequent events brought grotesque life to his feverish imagination."[23]

Apart from *Sanatorium under the Sign of the Hourglass*, two other notable films made in 1973 were based on well-known literary works that featured either a "Jewish world" or prominent Jewish characters: *The Wedding* (*Wesele*), an adaptation of the canonical drama by Stanisław Wyspiański, a film abundant with references to Polish mythology, history, and national complexes, and *Jealousy and Medicine* (*Zazdrość i medycyna*, 1973), based on Michał Choromański's novel. In the latter, Ewa Krzyżewska (known for her role in Wajda's *Ashes and Diamonds*) appears in the role of Rebeka Widmar, an object of desire of two men: her husband (Mariusz Dmochowski) and lover (Andrzej Łapicki). Krzyżewska's portrayal of Rebeka shares a number of similarities with other female Jewish characters in Polish cinema, often portrayed as attractive, sexual, and competing for a Polish man with a plain, down to earth Polish woman (sometimes represented by an iconic figure of a Polish Mother).[24]

Włodzimierz Boruński, who appeared in a supporting role as tailor Gold in *Jealousy and Medicine*, also became known for playing a number of memorable Jewish characters on the Polish screen. His finest film characters include Goldapfel in *All Souls Day* (*Zaduszki*, 1961) and Blumenfeld in *Somersault* (*Salto*, 1965), both directed by Tadeusz Konwicki. Another film, made by Konwicki in 1972, *How Far from Here, How Near* (*Jak daleko stąd, jak blisko*), is a dream-like film essay full of autobiographical historical, and political references. The film's protagonist, film director Andrzej (Andrzej Łapicki), Konwicki's alter ego, ventures into his past, participates in a Jewish burial, warns his childhood friend Szloma about the impending Holocaust. The film ends with a Chagall-like image of a "flying Jew." Several images refer indirectly to the Holocaust and the Jewish presence in Polish life (both, as the film's title puts it, "far" and "near").[25]

Representation of a more distant Polish-Jewish history, read through the experience of the Holocaust, can be problematic for some reviewers. The landmark film from 1975, Andrzej Wajda's *The Promised Land* (*Ziemia obiecana*), serves as a good example.[26] It is based on Władysław Stanisław Reymont's novel about the birth of Polish capitalism in Łódź. Its action, set in the fast-growing industrial city of Łódź, introduces three protagonists/friends: a Pole, Karol Borowiecki (Daniel Olbrychski); a Jew, Moryc Welt (Wojciech Pszoniak); and a German, Max Baum (Andrzej Seweryn), all of whom attempt to build a textile factory. The film tells how the three young entrepreneurs try to establish themselves in Łódź, yet it is essentially the story of the city: multicultural, dynamic, vulgar, and tempting. Wajda paints an almost Marxist image of the city-Moloch devouring its children. He follows Reymont's portrayal of the end of the romantic era on the Polish territories, the loss of traditional values, and the triumphant march of uncouth and dynamic nineteenth-century capitalism. Like Reymont, Wajda portrays Łódź as having energy, potential, wealth, and national/class diversity. He also deals with the plight of the remnants of the pauperized nobility, who are forced to move from their country manors—the bastions of traditionally understood Polishness—to newly developed industrial cities. Łódź, the land of promise for many, means destruction for others in this film, which was well received by critics and audiences alike.

The Promised Land received an Oscar nomination in the Best Foreign Film category; it also won the Festival of Polish Films in Gdańsk and film festivals in Moscow, Valladolid, and Chicago. In addition, Wajda's film was chosen the best film in the history of Polish cinema in a popular plebiscite in the Polish monthly *Film* in 1996.[27] Despite the critical acclaim, its unfavorable portrayal of the Jewish bourgeoisie resulted in accusations of anti-Semitism. Commenting on his film's negative reception in the United States, Wajda stated bitterly that he: "understood that American Jews do not want to come from the aggressive Łódź capitalists. They prefer to think of themselves as descendants of the romantic *Fiddler on the Roof*."[28]

Facing the Holocaust

Given the political climate after 1965, very few films attempted to deal with the Holocaust directly, by referring to the wartime reality, rather than providing thinly veiled messages to the Holocaust in films set in distant history. Janusz Nasfeter's *The Long Night* (*Długa noc*), produced in 1967, immediately shelved by the authorities, and not released until 1989, is a rare example of such.[29] The film was adapted from Wiesław Rogowski's novel *Night* (*Noc*), published in 1961. In his novel, Rogowski, a regional Communist Party activist, included several scenes critical of Polish behavior during the war. In 1961, they did not cause any protests or even discussions. Rogowski's passages made it to the film version, which evoked an uproar.

The film is set one week before Christmas of 1943 in a small Polish town. Like several other Polish films, it opens with an image reminding the viewers about the uniqueness of the occupation of Poland. Over the credits, an older man is putting up bilingual (Polish-German) posters, the decree of the General Governor Hans Frank, issued on 15 October 1941. The decree specifies that Jews leaving the ghetto without authorization will be punished by death and, likewise, the same punishment applies to those who knowingly provide shelter to Jews. The film's story, limited to just one day and night, revolves around a young Pole, Zygmunt Korsak (Józef Duriasz), who hides a Jewish escapee from the ghetto (Zygmunt Hobot) in his small flat (Figures 5.6, 5.7). The building belongs to Mrs. Piekarczyk (Ryszarda Hanin), who is in mourning, about to bury her recently deceased husband.

The film has several layers. It deals with the psychological and emotional links between some of the characters, in particular between Korsak and Mrs. Piekarczyk's daughter Marta (Jolanta Wołlejko), and between Korsak and another tenant, Katarzyna Katjan (Anna Ciepielewska), whose husband is in the Gestapo prison. The story of fear and jealousy also involves Józef Katjan (Ludwik Pak), who is in love with his sister in-law Katarzyna and resentful of Korsak. The extended curfew implemented by the Germans threatens Korsak, who has to deliver weapons to the partisans, and other inhabitants of the house who have just discovered a hiding Jew in Korsak's room. Terrified by what might happen to them if his presence becomes known to the German police,

Figure 5.6: (From the left) Józef Duriasz as Zygmunt Korsak and Ryszard Pietruski as blue policeman Wasiak in Janusz Nasfeter's *The Long Night* (1967/1989)

Figure 5.7: Zygmunt Hobot as the Jew in hiding in *The Long Night*

Figure 5.8: A scene from *The Long Night*. (From the left) Mrs. Piekarczyk (Ryszarda Hanin), her daughter Marta (Jolanta Wołłejko), and Katarzyna (Anna Ciepielewska)

they bitterly argue what shall be done with the (nameless in the film) Jew (Figure 5.8). Their arguments contain stereotypical anti-Semitic comments ("That is the end of them for what they had done to Jesus Christ," says Katjan). Some terrified inhabitants of the house express horror after learning about the hiding man, but are against informing the police. For example, Katarzyna, portrayed as a respectable Polish woman (her husband had been arrested four months earlier for anti-German activities), first discovers the hiding man and shouts in horror that Korsak is hiding a Jew. Later, however, she is against revealing his presence to the Germans.

The inhabitants of the house are not forced to take any action. Under the cover of the night, Korsak and the hiding Jew leave for the forest to the partisans. According to Iwona Kurz in her essay titled "'This Picture is a Little Horrific:' The Story of a Film, or the Polish Nation Face-to-Face with the Jew," the ending adds a symbolic dimension to the film: "The unnamed visitor of Jewish descent cannot find shelter under the Polish roof. As a result, the viewers cannot identify themselves with the only righteous character—because he is leaving—and they cannot call him the nation's representative. The nation stays at home."[30]

Roman Włodek convincingly argues that Korsak might serve as director Nasfeter's alter ego, a fact also noticed by some participants of the meeting of the Film Approval Committee.[31] A look at Nasfeter's biography certainly justifies such a perspective. In an interview conducted in 1992, Nasfeter stated that Aleksander Ford encouraged him to make this film, and that he committed himself quickly because the story was close to his personal experiences under the occupation—he witnessed the war atrocities. In addition, his brother was a member of the Home Army unit that punished blackmailers and those who denounced Poles and Jews.[32] The director also extensively commented on this aspect of his biography in a documentary film directed by Grzegorz

Królikiewicz, *Beautiful Years of Slavery* (*Piękne lata niewoli*, 1996). Like Zbigniew Cybulski's Maciek in Andrzej Wajda's *Ashes and Diamonds*, Korsak represents more his contemporaries rather than the wartime generation. The tall, blond, well-informed protagonist does not look like a typical villager; he resembles a Polish artist from the 1960s in a desperate clash with the merciless political system. The attempts at modernizing and thus universalizing the protagonist were, however, criticized at the meeting of the Film Approval Committee, particularly by Wanda Jakubowska, who by and large praised the film's realistic and truthful portrayal of the wartime period.[33]

The Long Night contained several images that the censor did not want to release, chiefly the representation of some segments of Polish society as anti-Semites. The film also openly questioned the myth of generous Polish wartime help for the Jews, thus making Poles morally responsible for what happened. In addition, the Six-Day War between Israel and the Arab states in June 1967 and the tense situation within the Soviet bloc contributed to the shelving of the film. Nasfeter's minor changes, mostly dealing with the dialogue, weakened the accusatory tone of the film but did not save the work. The Film Approval Committee gathered after the Six-Day War, three days after Poland broke off diplomatic relations with Israel. Present at the meeting, the director could only defend his film by saying that it was not his intention to produce a film that might be used to criticize the Polish nation. The inevitable was to come—the banning of his film. The majority of the twenty-four participants of the meeting, chiefly communist apparatchiks (Tadeusz Zaorski, Wincenty Kraśko, and others), but also some prominent filmmakers (Aleksander Ford, Wanda Jakubowska, Tadeusz Konwicki), expressed their reservations about Nasfeter's portrayal of Polish-Jewish relations. While not negating the truthfulness of the represented reality, their primary concern remained the image of the Polish nation tarnished by the film's representation. One scene, in particular, proved objectionable to the committee: the search for gold after Korsak and the hiding man left the house. In that scene, Mrs. Piekarczyk is caught by her daughter while looking for the valuables in the Jewish man's hiding place; the implication being that if Poles offered shelter to the Jews, they did it for money.

The participants of the meeting also repeatedly referred to the international political situation, the Arab-Israeli war in particular; they were aware that the sympathies of Poles were often with the Jews ("our Jews") who were fighting "their" (Soviet) Arabs. The concern of the committee members was not so much the verisimilitude of the reality represented on the screen, but the possible reception of the film in the West. As almost always happened during similar gatherings, aesthetic issues as well as the question of historical accuracy were overshadowed by issues such as "how Poles are represented?," "is the film anti or pro-Polish?," and "could it be used against Poland?" Krzysztof Teodor Toeplitz (KTT), a respected cultural critic of Jewish origin, bluntly stated that the film's representation "is a little horrific," as was the historical reality. He worried that images that appear on the screen are critical of the Polish society and "in line with what is being said about the Polish attitude toward the Jews during the occupation."[34] KTT rightly stressed that Nasfeter's film demolished several noble myths about the occupation. He also pointed out a certain tendency in Polish cinema to portray a hiding Jew as a horrified, forlorn character who can only arouse pity. His presence almost always is portrayed as a burden for Poles.[35] The issue of representation of Jews in Polish war films was also raised by several other discussants. Some, for example Tadeusz Konwicki, agreed with KTT and also objected to the portrayal of the Jews as a "horrifying presence" in Polish cinema. Aleksander Ford referred to the approval of his *Border Street* and analogous comments about his representation of some Jewish characters (like old Liberman) that were not in line with the official communist policy.

The vital comments and the final decision, as always at such gatherings, belonged to the communist apparatchiks. The head of the cultural department of the Communist Party, Wincenty Kraśko, expressed the official concerns. While praising some aesthetic aspects of the film and stressing its harsh portrayal of the occupation, he stated that, given the recent political situation during which several Poles "unfortunately express solidarity and sympathy toward the successes of Israel," Nasfeter's film "should not be shown in the West."[36] Kraśko elaborated:

> Propaganda represented and still represents Poles as a nation that helped Hitler to kill the Jewish people. It has been said that there was an anti-Semitic attitude in Poland during the occupation. Beyond doubt, such propaganda is slandering the Polish nation because Ringelblum clearly writes about these issues in his memoirs, in his ghetto chronicle. He stresses that people, the working class, the decisive majority of the society were very sympathetic to the Jewish question. There we often encounter accusations of intelligentsia and the lower middle-class as far as their stance toward Jews is concerned. Since we are talking about propaganda issues, it is difficult to thrust aside what is going on in the Middle East. All sorts of information that appears in our press may lead to nothing else but anti-Semitic sentiments. The leadership of the party is alarmed by those anti-Semitic sentiments and by the stance of the Polish nation to the issue of the Middle East. Frequent are cases of taking a pro-Israeli stand. As a result, it is necessary to carry out a reasonable propagandist policy.[37]

Kraśko and minister Zaorski, who was then responsible for the Polish film industry, never specified the sources that "slander" the Polish nation. Instead, they referred to generic "propaganda" or "Western propaganda," and they employed terms such as "it has been said." The main concern of the communist bureaucrats became the perceived danger that Nasfeter's representation of the Polish-Jewish relations may create in the West. As Minister Zaorski put it, comments that "Poles did not help Jews are nothing else but an expression of the Western propaganda."[38] The communist apparatchiks also worried about the film's impact on Polish audiences. For them, the negative portrayal of the Jewish characters and the Polish-Jewish history could stir some unwanted anti-Jewish reactions. On the other hand, the positive representation was also not welcomed, given the current political situation in the Middle East, because it could only increase support for the state of Israel. That propagandist equilibrium was voiced chiefly by Zaorski who singled out for emphasis Czech and Slovak films from that period, in particular the acclaimed *The Shop on Main Street* (*Obchod na korze*, 1965), directed by Ján Kadár and Elmar Klos. For him, this and other Czechoslovak films never portrayed the brutality of the Germans, but transplanted the responsibility for wartime killings on the occupied nations. He implied that such a portrayal contributed to the popularity of those films abroad. The Oscar-winning *The Shop on Main Street*, set in the fascist Slovak state during World War II, focuses on "ordinary people" whose insensitivity and opportunism contribute to the tragedy of the Jews. For minister Zaorski, there was no place for such a representation within the context of "Polish cultural policy, particularly in cinema."[39]

***

Jan Rybkowski's *Ascension Day* (*Wniebowstąpienie*, 1969), an adaptation of Adolf Rudnicki's short story, became another film that was affected by the political situation in the late 1960s. Like Nasfeter's *Unloved*, also based on Rudnicki's narrative, Rybkowski tells a story about obsessive, damaging love that can only bring unhappiness and death. The film opens on 22 June 1941 with a pre-credit long shot image of a group of SS men on motorcycles in a rural landscape, cut to a medium close-up of goggled riders over the credits (Figure 5.9). The commentary reminds the viewer that on that particular day Hitler's Germany attacked the Soviet Union, and portrays the situation in Lwów (modern Lviv) without (of course) mentioning that the town was occupied by the Soviets since September 1939.

After several brief scenes showing the chaotic evacuation of the Lwów population, Rybkowski's intimate psychological drama revolves around two Jewish protagonists: a beautiful music student, Raisa Wolkowa (Małgorzata

Figure 5.9: Jan Rybkowski's *Ascension Day* (1969)

Braunek), and a promising scientist with psychological problems, Sebastian Goldstein (Andrzej Antkowiak) (Figure 5.10). Against all odds, they decide to get married in a traditional ceremony and to stay in the occupied town (Figure 5.11). After the murder of Sebastian's parents (his father was a professor at the University of Lwów[40]), the couple leaves Lwów and stays at the outskirts of Warsaw assuming a Polish identity. Raisa's "Aryan looks" allow her to work and to take care of her ailing husband. Sebastian's recklessness, however, and his growing isolation—the result of his mental illness—endanger not only him, but also the life of Raisa and those who offer them shelter and help. An old friend from Lwów who has been in love with Raisa, Feliks Bukin (Piotr Wysocki), suggests poisoning Sebastian to save her and others. He convinces Raisa that desperate times require desperate measures. Referring to the Warsaw Ghetto Uprising, he says: "During the Holy Week mothers strangled their children with pillows so their cry wouldn't attract the Germans. The same mothers three years ago were saying 'Go ahead—spit out Benuś, spit on your mum. Show that you can spit out.'" Raisa, however, is unable to take her husband's life; he is later killed by German soldiers during one of his escapades to "live normal life" and to test the limits of his freedom. In the film's epilogue, taking place after the war, Bukin, who is about to leave for the West, explains to Raisa's father the circumstances of Sebastian's and Raisa's deaths. Raisa's father, who survived the war in the Soviet Union, embraces the new political reality. Outside of the coffee shop, where they talk, the viewer can see images of Warsaw being rebuilt, perhaps the only hopeful sign in this tragic story.

Ascension Day, like the short story by Rudnicki, is deprived of a larger social and political context. The recurrent images of the SS men on motorcycles—"the emissaries of hell" as they were called by a Polish film reviewer[41]—serve as constant reminders about the impending danger. To portray the unique nature of the occupation of Poland, the film features scenes that are characteristic in Polish war cinema: German posters and announcements displayed on the

Figure 5.10: Małgorzata Braunek as Raisa Goldstein and Andrzej Antkowiak as Sebastian Goldstein in *Ascension Day*

Figure 5.11: The wedding in *Ascension Day*. (From the right) Mrs. Goldstein (Zofia Mrozowska), Raisa (Małgorzata Braunek), and Sebastian (Andrzej Antkowiak)

streets that capture the grim reality of the war (death sentences, the creation of the ghetto) (Figure 5.12). Rybkowski also employs recurrent images of the Jewish people being led at night by the SS men, places of public executions, infrequent signs of resistance, and professors at the university being arrested. Although the reality portrayed in the film is sketchy, Poles are shown as helping Jews. Trying to get some assistance from a Jewish fund, Raisa comments that she has already received help from Poles who know the identity of the hiding couple and the risk involved in helping them (one scene depicts the arrest of their landlady by the Gestapo).

The versatile director Jan Rybkowski (1912–1987) experienced problems with communist censorship before *Ascension Day*. His debut, the occupation drama *House in the Wilderness* (*Dom na pustkowiu*, 1949), was mutilated by the censor. His Polish-West German co-production about forbidden love, *When*

Figure 5.12: *Ascension Day*. Małgorzata Braunek as Raisa

Love Was a Crime (*Rassenschande*; *Kiedy miłość była zbrodnią*, 1968), released on 1 March 1968, faced severe criticism. Despite the fact that Rybkowski was a Communist Party activist and the recipient of several state honors, he was attacked by "the communist patriots" who organized meetings in factories denouncing his and other films that were allegedly defaming Poland. His *Ascension Day* experienced similar problems due to its timing. Rybkowski started working on his project about the Jewish newlywed couple trying to survive the Holocaust in March/April of 1968. The pressure of politics and the ongoing criticism of *When Love Was a Crime* affected his new film, which was also produced by Rybkowski's own Film Unit "Rytm" for West German television.[42]

During the meeting of the Film Approval Committee in June of 1968, its members generally praised the film but had several reservations concerning the portrayal of Polish assistance for the Jews.[43] It was bluntly stated by the political apparatchik Wincenty Kraśko: "After seeing the film one may get an impression that, basically, Poles did not face any danger, that almost always the Jews were endangered, that there was no death penalty for Poles at any time. The Jewish experience had been to a certain degree isolated from the experience of all inhabitants of Poland that lived under the occupation."[44] Kraśko also criticized the film's ending "from the artistic point of view," but acknowledged that the film is needed from "the political point of view," since it will be shown in the West.

For the Communist Party bureaucrats, every film about Jews was in fact a film about Poles. They objected to the representation of Poles portrayed as if they lived comfortable lives during the occupation. Ryszard Frelek, a prominent Secretary of the Central Committee of PZPR, stressed the film's usefulness for propaganda purposes:

> I think that this film serves our side well but, given the current political situation, I am not sure if its reception will be good. I think, however, that from the point of view of our propaganda toward foreign countries, this film is on our side, because we show that those who murdered were the Germans exclusively, that they sentenced to death Jews and Poles, and that Poles are shown as those who are helping, who are doing their best to help the Jews to survive the occupation.[45]

Frelek was convinced that Rybkowski's film will be attacked abroad because of its portrayal of the Polish help, which, in his opinion, was contradicting Western propaganda. To put emphasis on the Polish help, there was even a suggestion that one of the Jewish characters, a member of the Jewish underground organization helping Jews, should be changed into a representative of a Polish organization helping both Poles and Jews. The underlying concern of the members of the committee was to emphasize the martyrology of Poles who, despite persecutions, helped the Jews. As Kraśko put it, "It is necessary to show that during the occupation Poles were dying, that they had been killed, but despite that they helped the Jews."[46]

The head of the committee, Deputy Minister of Culture and Art Czesław Wiśniewski, who replaced Tadeusz Zaorski a few weeks earlier, concluded that the Jewish isolation and suffering cannot be shown without the images of suffering Poles. He also added that the Polish help for the Jews should be properly accentuated. At the next meeting of the committee, taking place at the beginning of July 1968, Minister Wiśniewski decided to shelve the film for the time being and to screen it at a later date, when there will be another film released about the occupation that will offer a different perspective.[47] Rybkowski's Film Unit "Rytm" (which he managed since 1955) was disbanded in December 1968. Earlier, on 30 April 1968, he was also removed from his post as the Secretary of the Communist Party cell (Podstawowa Organizacja Partyjna, POP) within the Polish Film Units (Zjednoczone Zespoły Realizatorów Filmowych), and replaced by Jerzy Passendorfer. Rybkowski's later films consisted mostly of safe literary adaptations.[48]

***

The 1970s in Poland were characterized by the communist policy of marginalizing the Holocaust and silence over the mutual Polish-Jewish history. Attempting to present the new communist leadership under Edward Gierek as more open, progressive, and Western-oriented, the Communist Party tried to suppress any discussion concerning the ethnic aspect of Poland's past; instead, the party propagandists emphasized the image of Poland as a one-nation state. Any reference to the extermination of the Polish Jewry proved to be uneasy for the new communist leadership since it could also open discussions about the embarrassing anti-Semitic campaign of 1968 and tarnish the image of Gierek's triumphant policy known as "propaganda of success" (propaganda sukcesu). Any reference to the Holocaust could also open the issue, which was already present in discussions abroad, namely the issue of complicity of Poles for the wartime events that happened on their soil.[49]

Marcin Zaremba argues that the 1977 publication of two celebrated books, Hanna Krall's *Shielding the Flame* and Kazimierz Moczarski's *Conversations with an Executioner*, heralded changes that became discernible in the 1980s.[50] They resulted in the release of several films that dealt with a topic that was pushed into oblivion for more than a decade: the Holocaust and Polish-Jewish wartime relations.

Notes

1. See Krzysztof Lesiakowski, *Mieczysław Moczar "Mietek": Biografia polityczna* (Warsaw: Oficyna Wydawnicza Rytm, 1998).
2. Piotr Gontarczyk, *PPR. Droga do władzy 1941–1944* (Warsaw: Fronda, 2003), 420.

3. Published in the main communist daily, *Trybuna Ludu* (20 June 1967): 3–4. Quoted from Bożena Szaynok, *Z historią i Moskwą w tle. Polska a Izrael 1944–1968* (Warsaw: Instytut Pamięci Narodowej, 2007), 414. The year 1968 is discussed extensively in Jerzy Eisler, *Polski rok 1968* (Warsaw: Instytut Pamięci Narodowej, 2006).
4. Jaff Schatz, *The Generation: The Rise and Fall of the Jewish Communists of Poland* (Berkeley: University of California Press, 1991), 304. Also, Szaynok, *Z historią i Moskwą w tle*, 412–413.
5. Schatz, *The Generation*, 295–296.
6. Ibid., 296.
7. Ibid., 454.
8. Jerzy Toeplitz went to Australia in 1970 as a consultant for the Interim Council for the National Film and Television Training School. Between 1972 and 1973, he lectured as a Visiting Professor at La Trobe University in Melbourne. From 1973 to 1979, he headed the Australian Film, Television, and Radio School (AFTRS).
9. Details in: Jolanta Lemann-Zajiček, "Marzec '68 w szkole filmowej w Łodzi. Wydarzenia i konsekwencje," *Kino polskie: Reinterpretacje*, ed. Konrad Klejsa and Ewelina Nurczyńska-Fidelska (Kraków: Rabid, 2008), 47–58; Krzysztof Krubski, Zofia Turowska, and Waldemar Wiśniewski, *Filmówka: Powieść o Łódzkiej Szkole Filmowej* (Warsaw: Tenten, 1992): 187–192. Jerzy Toeplitz was replaced by Dr. Bolesław W. Lewicki who, under pressure, suffered a heart attack several months later and never returned to the school.
10. I am influenced by the text about "the organized forgetting during the Gierek's decade" published by a Polish historian Marcin Zaremba: "Zorganizowane zapominanie o Holokauście w dekadzie Gierka: Trwanie i zmiana," *Kwartalnik Historii Żydów* 2 (2004): 216–224. Zaremba acknowledges that the term is coined by Shari J. Cohen in his *Politics Without a Past: The Absence of History in Postcommunist Nationalism* (Durham: Duke University Press, 1999).
11. *Four Tankmen and a Dog* is an adventure war film featuring the tank "Rudy" and its crew on the road to Poland from the Soviet Union. *More Than Life at Stake*, also set during the war, offers an equally cartoonish, simplified, and stereotypical version of history. The film narrates the story of Hans Kloss (Stanisław Mikulski), a Polish superspy dressed in a German uniform and working for the Soviets. The popularity of these two television series prompted their makers to release their theatrical versions in 1968 and 1969. Both films never mentioned the fate of Jews.
12. *My Seventeen Lives* (*Żyłem 17 razy*, 2009), documentary directed by Tadeusz Bystram and Stanisław Zawiśliński, produced by Film Studio "Kadr" and PISF in 2009.
13. Details are from *Zdjęcia: Jerzy Lipman*, ed. Tadeusz Lubelski (Warsaw: PISF, WAiF, 2005)—in particular, the chapter by Eugenia Lipman (Jerzy Lipman's wife), "Czas pociągów: Wojna Jerzego Lipmana," 110–144.
14. Jerzy Stefan Stawiński's script, *The Man Who Made Fun of the Third Reich* (*Człowiek, który zakpił sobie z III Rzeszy*), is reprinted in Lubelski, ed., *Zdjęcia: Jerzy Lipman*, 149–183.
15. Rafał Marszałek, "Film Fabularny," in *Historia Filmu Polskiego 1968–1972*, vol. 6, ed. Rafał Marszałek (Warsaw: Wydawnictwa Artystyczne i Filmowe, 1994), 133.
16. Paul Coates, *The Red and the White: The Cinema of People's Poland* (London: Wallflower, 2005), 156.
17. Tim Cole, *Selling the Holocaust: From Auschwitz to Schindler: How History is Bought, Packaged, and Sold* (New York: Routledge, 1999), 110.
18. Rafał Marszałek, "Piekło inscenizowane," *Kino* 6 (1968): 21.
19. Jerzy Giżycki, "Apel," *Kamera* 5 (1971): 24. See also Andrzej Kossakowski, *Polski film animowany 1945–1974* (Wrocław: Ossolineum, 1977), 108.
20. Konrad Eberhardt, "Sny sprzed potopu," *Kino* 12 (1973): 12–19.
21. English edition in 1978: Bruno Schultz, *Sanatorium under the Sign of the Hourglass*, trans. Celina Wieniewska (New York: Walker and Company, 1978).
22. For a detailed analysis, see Małgorzata Jakubowska, *Laboratorium czasu: Sanatorium pod klepsydrą Wojciecha Jerzego Hasa* (Łódź: PWSFTviT, 2010).
23. Daniel R. Schwartz, *Imagining the Holocaust* (New York: St. Martin's Press, 1999), 318.

24. Elżbieta Ostrowska discusses the otherness of Jewish women in her "Otherness Doubled: Representations of Jewish Women in Polish Cinema," in *Gender and Film and the Media: East-West Dialogues*, ed. Elżbieta Oleksy, Elżbieta Ostrowska, and Michael Stevenson (Frankfurt/Main: Peter Lang, 2000), 120–130.
25. See Paul Coates' discussion under the title "Polish and Jewish Eschatologies: How Far from Here, How Near?" in his book *The Red and the White*, 167–168.
26. Andrzej Wajda prepared a slightly different version of the film in 1995. He also produced a television series of *The Promised Land*, eight one-hour-long episodes that premiered on Polish television in 1975 and 1976.
27. See *Film* 7 (1996): 10.
28. Maria Malatyńska, "Siedmioramiennie" [interview with Andrzej Wajda], *Tygodnik Powszechny* 9 (1996): 7.
29. A director and scriptwriter renowned for films for children, Nasfeter established himself with films such as *Small Dramas* (*Małe dramaty*, 1958) and *Colored Stockings* (*Kolorowe pończochy*, 1960). Later he continued to write and direct films, primarily addressed to children but with a universal meaning, such as *Abel, Your Brother* (*Abel, twój brat*, 1970). Mostly known as the master of films for young adults, for which he received several international festival awards, Nasfeter was, however, a versatile filmmaker. In the 1960s, he succeeded in making a partisan war film, *The Wounded in the Forest* (*Ranny w lesie*, 1964), a psychological war drama, *Weekend with a Girl* (*Weekend z dziewczyną*, 1968), as well as a crime film, *The Criminal and the Maiden* (*Zbrodniarz i panna*, 1963), starring Ewa Krzyżewska and Zbigniew Cybulski.
30. Iwona Kurz, "'Ten obraz jest trochę straszliwy': Historia pewnego filmu, czyli naród polski twarzą w twarz z Żydem," *Zagłada Żydów. Studia i Materiały* 4 (2008): 481.
31. Roman Włodek, "Janusz Nasfeter—dziecko też człowiek," in *Autorzy kina polskiego*, ed. Grażyna Stachówna and Joanna Wojnicka (Kraków: Rabid, 2004), 16. "Stenogram z posiedzenia Komisji Kolaudacyjnej w dniu15 VI 1967: *Noc*." National Film Archive in Warsaw, A-216/132. References to the published minutes in *Iluzjon* 1 (1993): 77–86. The working title of Nasfeter's film, *Night* (*Noc*), was later changed to *The Long Night*, probably to avoid connotations with an earlier film by Michelangelo Antonioni, *Night* (*La notte*, 1961), which was signaled at the meeting of the Committee for Film Approval.
32. Katarzyna Bielas "Jeszcze tylko ten film. *Długa noc* Janusza Nasfetera—ostatni 'półkownik,'" *Gazeta Wyborcza* (28 April 1992): 9.
33. "Stenogram z posiedzenia Komisji Kolaudacyjnej w dniu15 VI 1967: *Noc*," *Iluzjon*, 80–81.
34. Ibid., 77.
35. Ibid., 77.
36. Ibid., 79, 83.
37. Ibid., 83.
38. Ibid., 85.
39. Ibid., 85.
40. At the beginning of July 1941, the Germans executed dozens of Polish professors working at the University of Lwów (Uniwersytet Jana Kazimierza we Lwowie).
41. Danuta Karcz, "Requiem dla obłąkanego," *Kino* 12 (1060): 22.
42. Jolanta Lemann-Zajiček, "Jan Rybkowski—baron polskiej kinematografii," in *Autorzy kina polskiego 3*, ed. Grażyna Stachówna and Bogusław Żmudziński (Kraków: Wydawnictwo Uniwersytetu Jagiellońskiego, 2007): 25–26.
43. "*Wniebowstąpienie*. Stenogram z posiedzenia Komisji Kolaudacyjnej w dniu 17 VI 1968." National Film Archive in Warsaw, A-344/441.
44. Ibid., 6.
45. Ibid., 17.
46. Ibid., 25.
47. *Wniebowstąpienie*. Stenogram z posiedzenia Komisji Kolaudacyjnej w dniu 2 VII 1968. National Film Archive in Warsaw, A-344/442.
48. Lemann-Zajiček, "Jan Rybkowski—baron polskiej kinematografii," 26.

49. See Zaremba, "Zorganizowane zapominanie o Holokauście w dekadzie Gierka," 218–219.
50. Ibid., 224. Hanna Krall, Zdążyć przed Panem Bogiem (Kraków: Wydawnictwo Literackie, 1977). This book is translated into English as *Shielding the Flame: An Intimate Conversation with Dr. Marek Edelman, the Last Surviving Leader of the Warsaw Ghetto Uprising*, trans. Joanna Stasińska and Lawrence Weschler (New York: Henry Holt, 1986). Kazimierz Moczarski, *Rozmowy z katem* (Warsaw: Państwowy Instytut Wydawniczy, 1977), translated as *Conversations with an Executioner: An incredible 255-day-long interview with the man who destroyed the Warsaw ghetto*, edited by Mariana Fitzpatrick (Englewood Cliffs: Prentice Hall, 1981).

Chapter 6

Return of the Repressed: "The Poor Poles Look at the Ghetto" (1981–)

The Polish approach to the common Jewish-Polish history changed toward the end of the 1980s. The television screening of Claude Lanzmann's *Shoah* (1985) had a profound effect and stimulated a heated debate in the Polish media.[1] Although generally praised for his forceful account of the Holocaust, Lanzmann has also been accused by many Polish commentators of being biased in his selection of material and, thus, of presenting an incomplete picture of the occupation in Poland. As some authors observed, Lanzmann's emphasis on anti-Semitic traits in Polish society prevented him from telling a more balanced version of what really happened.[2]

Lanzmann often stressed that his film is not a documentary per se, but "a fiction of the real."[3] Uncharacteristically for Holocaust documentaries, it excludes archival footage from the period, and offers a series of powerful, staged, and manipulated interviews. The Polish side of the story is by and large represented by unsophisticated interlocutors, mostly semi-literate peasants. Jan Karski's testimony, albeit featured prominently in the film, is deprived of several crucial elements (for example, his failed efforts to alert the world leaders about the extermination of Jews). The film's stress on "the widespread hostility of Poles toward Jews"[4] and the unsubstantiated claims about Christian anti-Semitism that led to the Nazi extermination of Jews were widely criticized in Poland. Several films produced after 1985 in Poland, beginning with the documentary *Living in Memory* (*Ocalałe w pamięci*, 1986, Zbigniew Raplewski), and stressing the other side of the story—the Polish help for the Jews during the war—may be treated as Polish responses to Lanzmann's *Shoah*.

Another important event that initiated the national debate on Polish-Jewish relations and the memory of the Holocaust was the publication of an essay by Jan Błoński (1931–2009), "The Poor Poles Look at the Ghetto," which appeared on 17 January 1987 in the Catholic weekly *Tygodnik Powszechny*.[5] Błoński, Professor of Polish Literature at the Jagiellonian University in Kraków, explores the repression of the Jewish tragedy by the Poles and the degree to which the Polish people are morally responsible, as "silent witnesses," for what happened on their soil. In this now classic text, the title of which directly refers to Czesław Miłosz's poem, "A Poor Christian Looks at the Ghetto," Błoński focuses on the question of repressed national memories and the necessity of mourning the dead. He also poses a crucial question: can the Poles be blamed for their indifference? Błoński pronounces that the Polish soil was tainted, desecrated, and needs to be exculpated from guilt. What remains now, he says, is to see the Polish past truthfully.[6]

Partly as a response to the renewed interest in Polish-Jewish history, several major literary works published toward the end of the 1980s in Poland dealt with the theme of the Holocaust. The past returned in a number of critically acclaimed books later translated into English, for example in *The Final Station: Umschlagplatz* by Jarosław Marek Rymkiewicz, *The Beautiful Mrs. Seidenman* by Andrzej Szczypiorski, *Who Was David Weiser?* by Paweł Huelle, and *Annihilation* by Piotr Szewc.[7] Szczypiorski's novel, in particular, as one of the reviewers appropriately noticed, comprises, "in a symbolic sense, an act of national catharsis. It is a powerful work that reflects upon the Polish national character: its strengths, its many flawed perceptions, and its prejudices fully exposed."[8] In *The Beautiful Mrs. Seidenman*, Szczypiorski attempts to portray the solidarity and harmony of the traditionally good Jewish-Polish relations, yet he depicts both cultures' disparity and prejudices as well. The book is peopled with a collection of Polish, Jewish, and German characters. This broad spectrum of viewpoints enables Szczypiorski to produce, in a sense, a treatise on the complexities of Central European history.

***

Several films about Polish-Jewish relations and the Holocaust were made during one of the darkest years in postwar Polish history, following the introduction of martial law by General Jaruzelski on 13 December 1981. Some of those projects originated during the Solidarity period (1980–1981) and by and large were not affected by the communist ban on "unwanted" films after the declaration of the martial law. As many as four films dealing with the Holocaust were presented at the 1984 Festival of Polish Films in Gdańsk (the first festival since 1981): *Austeria* (1983) by Jerzy Kawalerowicz, *A Postcard from the Journey* (*Kartka z podróży*, 1984) by Waldemar Dziki, *Down Carrier* (*Tragarz puchu*, 1983, television production) by Stefan Szlachtycz, and *According to the Decrees of Providence* (*Wedle wyroków Twoich*, 1983) by Jerzy Hoffman.

Holocaust references can also be found in other films, for example in *Lynx* (*Ryś*), made by Stanisław Różewicz in 1981, and released in March 1982, three months after the introduction of martial law. Based on Jarosław Iwaszkiewicz's short story, "The Church in Skaryszewo,"[9] Różewicz's film is set in a small town after the deportation of the local Jewish community to a concentration camp. The story revolves around a Polish craftsman, Alojz (Franciszek Pieczka), who receives a death sentence from the Polish underground for allegedly collaborating with the occupier. A young local parish priest, Konrad (Jerzy

Radziwiłowicz), learns about the sentence from an underground fighter nicknamed "Ryś" (Piotr Bajor) during his confession. After learning that Alojz is hiding a Jewish family who evaded the transport, and thus has to be an honest person, the priest tries to postpone the execution at all cost (Figure 6.1). In the last sequence, the hiding Jewish family is arrested by the Germans when Alojz is preparing a dugout for them in the forest. The priest and Alojz have no other choice but to escape to the partisans.[10]

Perhaps the most accomplished film made at the beginning of the 1980s is Kawalerowicz's *Austeria* (aka *The Inn*, 1983). Based on Julian Stryjkowski's novel of the same title published in 1966,[11] it offers a nostalgic account of a lost Jewish world. The director confessed in an interview that he "fantasized a film about an extinct world, a community now dead, its culture, customs, habits, religion."[12] Born in a small town of Gwoździec (now Ukraine), where "the three ethnic

Figure 6.1: Stanisław Różewicz's *Lynx* (1982). Jerzy Radziwiłowicz (Priest Konrad) and Franciszek Pieczka (Alojz). Courtesy Filmoteka Narodowa in Warsaw. © Film Studio "Tor"

groups [Poles, Jews, and Ukrainians] coexisted symbiotically."[13] Kawalerowicz knew the Jewish minority first hand. He attended the junior high (*gimnazjum*) in the town of Stanisławów where all his teachers were later killed by the Germans. Writer Julian Stryjkowski (1905–1996) was born Pesach Stark in Stryj (now Ukraine) in a family of Hasidic Jews. A convert to communism, he survived the war in the Soviet Union working for the propagandist Polish-language paper *Red Banner* (Czerwony Sztandar). In several books published after the war and dealing with the lost Jewish world, Stryjkowski produced not only references to the Holocaust, but also commemorated the vanished Galician Jews.

In *Austeria*, Kawalerowicz portrays an idealized Jewish world of a small eastern Galician town at the outbreak of World War I. Its protagonist, Tag (Franciszek Pieczka), the innkeeper at "Austeria," witnesses diverse communities who gather in his inn on the eve of the war (Figure 6.2). The last scene of this stylized film shows the destruction of Jews, in a sense heralding events that would happen thirty years later. Some critics justly argued that the characters and the world represented in *Austeria* were shaped by the Holocaust experience and ought to be analyzed in such a manner. For example, in her comparative study of *Austeria* and Michał Waszyński's prewar Yiddish classic *The Dybbuk* (*Der Dibuk*, 1937), Gabriella Safran looks at the "relationship between the themes of dancing and dying in these two films."[14] For Daria Mazur, despite Kawalerowicz's comments that his film is not a part of the "Holocaust genre," it belongs there with its "metaphoric visualization of dying."[15]

After the meeting of the Commission for Film Approval (Komisja Kolaudacyjna) in May 1982, where the film received the highest category, the Soviet embassy objected to the film's alleged anti-Russian bias. The Soviet cultural attaché discussed the issue with the Cultural Department of PZPR on 1 December 1982. The embassy expressed disappointment that such an anti-Russian film was made by a Communist Party member (Kawalerowicz) and that the film was gaining recognition in Poland and abroad. The embassy

Figure 6.2: The innkeeper Tag (Franciszk Pieczka) in Jerzy Kawalerowicz's *Austeria* (1983)

demanded that *Austeria* should be released in a limited number of copies, and that the final scene ought to be changed. In the original scene, the Tsarist Cossacks approach the river where the Hasidim are bathing and spray them with bullets until the water is red. The report issued after the meeting by a communist apparatchik Stanisław Stefański, while generally defending the film, suggested some revisions: "The last scene may be treated as a metaphor anticipated the future tragedy of European Jews during the fascist period ... However, given the possibility of imposing an anti-Soviet interpretation on the film by anti-socialist elements, it is necessary to eliminate accents that enable such an interpretation of the work."[16] Following the instructions, Kawalerowicz changed the last fragment to a scene of a distant artillery fire hitting the water and killing the bathing Hasidim.

Austeria premiered on Polish screens in March 1983, won the Grand Prix at the 1984 Festival of Polish Films in Gdańsk, and was shown outside of Poland. Iwona Irwin-Zarecka suggests that General Jaruzelski's government used the film outside of Poland as "both an 'ambassador' and an important component of the regime's celebration of Jewish culture."[17] Gabriella Safran comments in a similar manner: "In the capacity of a quasi-official expression of Polish regret at the passing of Jews, and perhaps as a demonstration of liberalism aimed at the western critics of the new regime, *Austeria* was widely promoted and exported to film festivals abroad."[18] *Austeria* was screened in the second part of 1982, before its Polish premiere, in several Western countries; it was also shown during the Chicago International Film Festival. The question whether its screenings outside of Poland were part of a larger public relations scheme by the Jaruzelski regime is, however, difficult to validate without more archival research.

Another film released after the martial law, *According to the Decrees of Providence* (1984), is Jerzy Hoffman's only film dealing with the Holocaust. Born in 1932 into a secular, assimilated Jewish family, Hoffman survived the war in Siberia where his family was deported by the Soviets in 1940. He returned to Poland in 1945 (his father served in the Tadeusz Kościuszko division), but studied at (and in 1955 graduated from) the Moscow Film School (WGiK). Later he became chiefly known for his popular epic adaptations of Henryk Sienkiewicz's novels such as *Pan Michael* (*Pan Wołodyjowski*, 1969) and *The Deluge* (*Potop*, 1974).[19]

Hoffman's *According to the Decrees of Providence* is a story of survival of a thirteen-year-old girl Ruth (Rut), played convincingly by Sharon Brauner. The script by Hoffman and Jan Purzycki, which is based on several sources, stresses the almost miraculous nature of Ruth's survival and focuses on her odyssey through war-ravaged Poland. The film opens with images of her happy childhood in a small town, punctuated by symbolic freeze frames, and ending with the voice-over commentary about the invasion of Poland on 1 September 1939. Another scene introduces the reality of the occupation—the voice from a loudspeaker announces the deportation of Jews to the ghettos. In the next scene, Ruth is thrown by her mother from a truck that transports the town's Jewish population to an extermination place. What follows is a series of episodes about Ruth seeking help, being helped as well as betrayed, and surviving against all odds. For example, she is sheltered by a Polish farmer who is betrayed by his wife out of fear and, perhaps, for the prize money. With his help, however, she escapes from a dugout prison and hides in the forest. There she witnesses Jewish people being transported by the Germans. She gazes in horror at an older Jewish man, tired and unable to walk, being killed by a soldier. After meeting a group of Jewish children who, risking their life, escaped from the Warsaw Ghetto in search of food, she joins them and enters the ghetto through a hole in the ghetto wall. Hoffman resorts here to black-and-white archival footage from the ghetto, such as images of a German soldier punishing young food smugglers, naked bodies lying on the street, the *Umschlagplatz* (a place of deportation to extermination camps), and deportations, among others.

The bulk of Hoffman's drama features a number of discernible clichéd images familiar from previously made Polish films. For example, when Ruth reaches her family in the ghetto before the Warsaw Ghetto Uprising, the viewer is reminded about similar scenes in Aleksander Ford's classic *Border Street*. The young Jewish fighters receive help from the communist Poles via the sewer system and start the uneven struggle with the Germans. Unpersuasive images of that struggle, with the overriding image of heroic fighters enclosed by flames, are, however, inferior to Ford's portrayal. The film cuts abruptly to a scene in a Polish Catholic orphanage when Ruth escapes the inferno in the ghetto. This segment reminds the viewer of Stanisław Różewicz's novella *A Drop of Blood* in his *Birth Certificate*. Although Ruth gets a new birth certificate and learns the new prayers, she has to flee the place before the search for hiding Jewish children by the Gestapo. In another segment, Ruth escapes to a mountain resort where, among other things, she is masquerading in a white bear skin, posing with the Germans for a local photographer. Unlike, however, in Jerzy Zarzycki's *White Bear*, the street photographer is not a member of the Polish underground but a *Volksdeutch* who is unaware that Ruth takes on a role usually performed by a Polish boy. With its stock characters and situations, the last segment of the film borrows heavily from adventure war films, such as the popular television series *More Than Life at Stake*. For example, the character of Ruth's aunt Rachel (Anna Dymna), introduced earlier during the Warsaw Ghetto scenes as an insurgent, reappears later in the film dressed in a German uniform—serving as a secretary (and a lover) to a civilized German commandant of the city, and also being a member of the Polish underground. She sacrifices her life throwing a grenade at a cartoonish SS officer, Walter Knoch (Mathieu Carriere), who is commanding the execution squad, thus saving the life of Ruth and Polish hostages from the town. (See Figure 6.3.)

As expected, *According to the Decrees of Providence* received lukewarm reviews after its premiere. Tadeusz Sobolewski bluntly called this co-production between West Germany (Artur Brauner) and Poland (Film Unit "Zodiak") a

Figure 6.3: A scene from Jerzy Hoffman's *According to the Decrees of Providence* (1984). Courtesy Filmoteka Narodowa in Warsaw

"kitsch work" on the Jewish theme.[20] Other critics also did not hide their disappointment with the film and emphasized its clichéd aspects and numerous wasted opportunities.[21] Several reservations were already raised during the meeting of the Committee for Film Approval on 28 December 1983.[22] The film, however, was approved without any major changes and described by the head of the committee as "mature" and "needed."[23]

***

A different Holocaust film, also released in 1984, received critical acclaim at the Festival of Polish Films in Gdańsk. *A Postcard from the Journey*, an impressive debut by Waldemar Dziki (b. 1956), received the Andrzej Munk Award for Best Debut and Best Actor award for Władysław Kowalski. Dziki's film is based on a novel by an accomplished Czech writer Ladislav Fuks (1923–1994) titled *Mr. Theodore Mundstock* (*Pan Theodor Mundstock*, 1963). The story about a Prague Jew who fears deportation to a concentration camp was adapted for the Polish situation. The film is set in 1941 in a Jewish ghetto and portrays a middle-aged office worker, Jakub Rosenberg (Władysław Kowalski), now degraded to a street cleaner, who tries to cope with the growing fear with dignity.[24] While awaiting inevitable deportation, he methodically, almost obsessively, pays attention to small practical details in order to battle his fear and to prepare for death. He knows what awaits him; although he has a chance to leave the ghetto, he stays and prepares every aspect of his way to a concentration camp. Rosenberg's friends and neighbors in the ghetto go to the *Umschlagplatz*. Some commit suicide, others have nervous breakdowns or try to escape to the Aryan side. Unlike them, Rosenberg attempts to separate himself from the external world. He exercises, psychologically as well as physically, so he is prepared for deportation, transport, and stay in a camp. He wants to be ready when the day comes. He also trains a young boy, David (Rafał Wieczyński), who was left behind by his deported parents.

In Fuks's novel, Mundstock's attempts to battle his fear and, consequently, to survive, are useless—he dies, accidentally run over by a truck. In Dziki's film, Rosenberg's actions have to do with not so much with survival but with "dignified death." Comparing the novel and the film, a Polish reviewer emphasized that Mundstock's roots are in Jewish culture, but Rosenberg's mentality is by and large a clerk-like mentality: incapability to rebel and tendency to obey orders.[25]

Preoccupations with detail, slow pace, limited dialogue, and emotional distance make Dziki's film an uneasy experience. Wit Dąbal's camera does not emphasize elements that viewers habitually associate with Holocaust cinema—deaths on the streets, overwhelming brutality, mass executions. Instead, it mostly captures images of claustrophobic and dilapidated interiors. This was pointed out as the film's weakness by a communist official during the meeting of the Film Approval Committee.[26] His reservations, however, which were mildly voiced, were negligible given the overwhelming praise the film received from established filmmakers such as Wanda Jakubowska ("outstanding debut") and Janusz Morgenstern, who noticed the film's Kafkaesque spirit.

***

In the mid-1980s, two other films were released that dealt with Polish-Jewish wartime relations: *There Was No Sun That Spring* (*Nie było słońca tej wiosny*, 1984), directed by Juliusz Janicki, and *In the Shadow of Hatred* (*W cieniu nienawiści*, 1986), directed by Wojciech Żółtowski. In addition, in 1985 Wanda Jakubowska made the last installment of her sequence of films about Auschwitz, *Invitation* (discussed in chapter 2). Like several other Polish films released after the martial law, these films were virtually ignored by local audiences. That period was characterized by a steady decline in attendance and audiences' preference for commercial cinema, often seen on pirated videos. Several established Polish critics saw the growing dominance of commercial cinema as a cynical move on the part of communist film authorities to divert the attention of Polish viewers to matters of secondary importance.[27]

There Was No Sun That Spring, directed by a documentary filmmaker Juliusz Janicki (1931–2011), is based on a debut novel published in 1972 by a popular actor, writer, and stand-up comedian Jerzy Ofierski (1926–2007), who also co-scripted the film with Janicki. Its action is set in the winter of 1943 and follows a young Jewish woman, Chaja (Ernestyna Winnicka), a physician who escapes from a transport to a concentration camp and gets safely to a house at the outskirts of a nearby village. Her quick action saves the lives of a young farmer, Piotr (Maciej Kozłowski), and his family who suffered carbon monoxide poisoning. Despite strong objections of his pregnant wife Monika (Krystyna Wachełko-Zaleska) as well as his parents, Piotr decides to shelter Chaja. The local innkeeper (Bogusław Sochnacki), also a German collaborator, learns about the hiding Jewish woman and blackmails Piotr. When Piotr refuses to bribe him, he is beaten up by a blue policeman Wiśniewski (Zdzisław Kuźniar) and taken to the German gendarmes. He is rescued by another villager, Mazurek (Henryk Bista), who is working for a local Polish partisan unit. The rest of the film revolves around Piotr's growing affection for Chaja, which is slowly reciprocated (Figure 6.4). The doomed romance with the Holocaust in the background is interrupted by Piotr's distressed wife who is able to convince the partisans to take Chaja as their doctor. Days after Chaja's departure, following one of the actions by the partisans, the village is surrounded by the Germans and Piotr's farmhouse is burned to the ground. When he emerges from a shelter where Chaja previously was hiding, he witnesses the image of destruction—the bodies of his wife, young son, and parents.

Figure 6.4: Chaja (Ernestyna Winnicka) and Piotr (Maciej Kozłowski) in Juliusz Janicki's *There Was No Sun That Spring* (1984). Courtesy Filmoteka Narodowa in Warsaw

The two leading female characters in Janicki's film, Jewish Chaja and Polish Monika, are portrayed in line with the formulaic representation of women in Polish culture, in particular with the image of "otherness" that permeates the representation of Jewish women. Such a representation was carefully examined by Elżbieta Ostrowska in several films "that depict Jewish women as being in opposition to the construction of femininity created and developed in the Polish national discourse, which has its perfect embodiment in the myth of the Polish Mother."[28]

The narrative of Janicki's film, revolving around a difficult love between a sophisticated Jewish woman from a city and a simple, uneducated farmer, brings to mind Agnieszka Holland's 1985 film made in West Germany, *Angry Harvest* (*Bittere Ernte*). This well-received film (an Academy Award nomination for Best Foreign Film), examines the psychological and social mechanisms behind the relationship between a Polish farmer, Leon Wolny (Armin Mueller-Stahl), and a Jewish fugitive from a train heading for an extermination camp, Rosa Eckart (Elisabeth Trissenaar). Holland's portrayal prompted Karen Jaehne to write that the film "explores the peasant/Jew relationship with more insight and less self-righteousness than all nine and a half hours of *Shoah*."[29]

Like Holland's film, the comparatively modest and virtually unknown outside of Poland *There Was No Sun That Spring* also portrays a doomed Polish-Jewish relationship. Unlike Holland, however, Janicki pays more attention to a realistic portrayal of a Polish province under the occupation. His film was praised by critics for its detailed and nuanced depiction of Polish peasantry during the war. Novelist and scriptwriter Ofierski knew the depicted reality first-hand—during the war, he was fighting in a Polish partisan unit in the Lublin district.

Released after Hoffman's film, and in a limited number of copies, *There Was No Sun That Spring* never had proper distribution and today is largely absent in discussions about the screen representation of Polish-Jewish relations. The film did not encounter any problems at the meeting of the Film Approval Committee that gathered in June of 1983. Its participants noticed the historical credibility of the film despite some minor "sociological stereotyping" and "linguistic problems." They also emphasized, which was a recurrent motif during such gatherings, the importance of screening the Polish-Jewish wartime relations, given some "false rumors in America and the West concerning the role of Poles in the extermination of Jews during the occupation."[30]

The issue of Polish help for the Jews features prominently in a cinematic debut by Wojciech Żółtowski (b. 1947), *In the Shadow of Hatred*, which premiered on 18 April 1986. Several members of the Film Approval Committee that gathered in December 1985 commented that this film had been made too late and that it looks like a Polish response to Lanzmann's *Shoah*. In spite of that, the committee emphasized the importance and indispensable character of Żółtowski's film.[31] Its weaknesses were negligible, they argued, compared to the historically accurate images of Poles offering assistance to the hiding Jews, as evidenced by the number of Polish citizens named the Righteous among the Nations by the state of Israel. Despite sporadically voiced mild criticism, such as "too many good Germans in this film; it is enough to have one good German,"[32] members of the Film Approval Committee embraced the film. After its release, *In the Shadow of Hatred* received a Special Award of the Polish Cinematography.

Produced by the Film Unit "Profil" and Polish Television, *In the Shadow of Hatred* is based on Jan Dobraczyński's short story "Ewa," written and set in 1943. A Catholic writer and political activist (member of the pro-communist secular Catholic organization PAX), Dobraczyński became infamous in the 1980s for his role as a Chairman of the Patriotic Movement for National Rebirth (Patriotyczny Ruch Odrodzenia Narodowego, PRON), a communist organization created by General Jaruzelski in 1982, after the introduction of martial law. PRON, which was dissolved in 1989, consisted of representatives of different pro-communist organizations, and served as a way of showing legitimacy and support for the Jaruzelski regime. Dobraczyński's political activities in the 1980s undoubtedly overshadow his earlier accomplishments. During World War II, he was a member of the Home Army, a participant in the 1944 Warsaw Rising, and a prisoner at Bergen-Belsen. In the occupied Warsaw, he worked for the city municipal Health and Social Welfare Department and was in charge of Division for Abandoned Children. He worked closely with the Council for Aid to the Jews, which was established in September 1942 by the Polish Government in Exile. The organization, which used the code name Żegota, included representatives of Polish as well as Jewish political organizations providing assistance to the Jews. For his actions during the war, Dobraczyński received awards in Poland and Israel (the Righteous among the Nations in 1993).

Like Dobraczyński's short story, Żółtowski's *In the Shadow of Hatred* takes place in 1943. To stress verisimilitude, the film opens with comments that it is based on true events involving a group of workers of the Warsaw Health and Social Welfare Department, one of whom was Irena Sendler (1910–2008) who rescued some 2,500 Jewish children from the Warsaw Ghetto and placed them in foster homes and Catholic orphanages.[33] The first scenes introduce the reluctant hero, Zofia (Bożena Adamek), a middle-class mother of a young son who just tries to survive the occupation and hopes to see her husband-officer released from a POW camp. The opening scenes also establish the grim image of the occupation. Returning home on a city tram that goes near the ghetto wall, Zofia witnesses someone throwing a loaf of bread over the ghetto wall, a fact also noticed by German soldiers. Thanks to her "good papers" (as a worker in the municipal offices), she is spared arrest and possible incarceration in a camp. Walking near one of the entrances to the ghetto, she watches Jewish policemen beating young food smugglers. As in other films, the glimpses of the ghetto life, including heavy smoke covering the ghetto during the Warsaw Ghetto Uprising, are almost always seen from the Aryan side of the wall.

Despite her initial unwillingness, Zofia risks her life to save a Jewish child, a ten-year old girl Ewa (Aleksandra Cezarska). Her mother, Róża Korngold (Róża Chrabelska), secretly leaves the ghetto and begs Zofia to save her daughter who is hiding on the Aryan side with a Polish family sheltering the child for money and demanding more (Figure 6.5). Although Róża insists on giving her money ("You Poles have sometimes too much honor"), Zofia proudly refuses. Reluctantly, after an extended talk between the two mothers, Zofia goes to the place where Ewa is hidden and takes her home (Figure 6.6). She provides shelter and gradually becomes attached to the Jewish girl. Zofia also becomes involved in clandestine help that her department provides to Jewish children. Later, when the situation becomes dangerous at work (arrests) and at home (*szmalcownik*), Zofia decides to place Ewa in an orphanage outside of Warsaw, run by Catholic nuns. Traveling there by train, they accidently cross the border between *Generalgouvernement* and *Warthegau* (Polish western district incorporated into the Reich), but are allowed to return. The last scene portrays Ewa in the orphanage, playing alone, but safe, in the convent's garden.

The film presents a panorama of Polish characters and their attitudes toward Jews. It focuses on patriotic Poles involved in anti-German conspiracy. Despite the above, Żółtowski's film strives for a balanced image of the occupation. Images of those who risk their lives to offer assistance to the Jews are juxtaposed with actions of those who blackmail the hiding Jews. The danger involved in Zofia's activities is emphasized by images of the Germans arresting municipal workers, including the head of the department where Zofia is employed. The presence of an anti-Jewish housekeeper is countered by actions of several people who, at first, are introduced as possibly collaborating with the occupier, but later prove to be decent persons, for example, a female neighbor *Volksdeutsch* (Barbara Brylska) or a caretaker Marciniak. The character of Zofia may serve as a modernized version of the mythical figure of the Polish Mother (*Matka Polka*). Her everyday struggle is heroicized, her strength and dignity are intact

Figure 6.5: Bożena Adamek as Zofia (left) and Róża Chrabelska as Róża in Wojciech Żółtowski's *In the Shadow of Hatred* (1986)

Figure 6.6: *In the Shadow of Hatred.* Ewa (Aleksandra Cezarska) and Zofia's Aunt (Wanda Łuczycka)

despite the hardships she has to face to keep up the household on her own. Bożena Adamek's theatrical performance emphasizes exactly that aspect of the protagonist's character, a fact also noticed by the members of the Film Approval Committee.[34]

One of the better-known films from this period is Mitko Panov's *With Raised Hands* (*Z podniesionymi rękami*, 1985), a six-minute black-and-white student étude, the recipient of many awards at international festivals of short films. Panov, born in 1963 in the former Yugoslavia, studied at the Łódź Film School where he made his student film under the supervision of director Wojciech Jerzy Has and cinematographer Jerzy Wójcik, among others. In his narrative film, Panov offers a fictitious cinematic interpretation concerning one of the most iconic World War II photographs. It pictures the final days of the Warsaw Ghetto Uprising and shows a terrified young boy (possibly Tsvi Nussbaum) wearing a large cap and with his hands raised. The boy and other Jewish people are surrounded by armed German soldiers, one of them pointing a machine gun in the boy's direction. The photograph was later included in the report sent to Heinrich Himmler by the SS General Jürgen Stroop ("the Stroop Report"). Panov depicts the circumstances of the archival photograph by focusing on the boy before and after the photograph was taken. Panov's camera also reveals the presence of a German cameraman trying to capture images of the ghetto and establishes the relations between him, the boy, and the German soldier with a gun. The flow of the film is brought to a halt with a freeze frame that closely resembles the archival photograph. When the action resumes, the gusty wind blows off the boy's cap. He runs after it away from the group, leaves the scene, and the next shot portrays him walking down the street. The film ends with the image of the iconic photograph.[35]

Arguably the film best known internationally from the 1980s dealing with Polish-Jewish relations is the eighth entry in Krzysztof Kieślowski's celebrated television series *Decalogue* (1988) that contributes to the discourse on memory and forgiveness.[36] Unlike the other parts of *Decalogue*, this morality tale returns to the past and deals with a sense of guilt and the complexities of history. The story introduces a respected professor of ethics at the University of Warsaw, Zofia (Maria Kościałkowska), who is visited by the Holocaust survivor Elżbieta (Teresa Marczewska), a New York-based translator of her works. Although they met earlier abroad, only now does Elżbieta reveal the story of her survival (Figure 6.7). During World War II, Zofia and her husband refused to shelter her, then a six-year-old Jewish girl who escaped from the Warsaw Ghetto to search for sanctuary on the safer side of the wall. "The false witness they were about to commit consciously was incompatible with their [Christian] principles," Elżbieta says bitterly. Luckily for her, she was able to stay with other Poles, with whom she moved to America after the war. Knowing that the child survived helps Zofia rid herself of the burden of the past. She comments that "there is nothing more important than the life of a child."

Zofia is also offered a chance to describe the complexities of the wartime situation and the real reasons for not taking care of Elżbieta. As she explains, her family was active in the Polish underground Home Army, and her husband was an officer in one of the most important sections of that army that targeted collaborators and high-profile Gestapo and SS officers, and successfully freed several prisoners. The Gestapo tried to infiltrate the organization. Information that the man who brought the child to Zofia was a suspected collaborator, and the fear that it might gravely endanger the Polish resistance, prevented Zofia from offering a hideout to Elżbieta. The person unjustly suspected of collaborating with the Nazis and almost executed for a crime he never committed, the tailor (Tadeusz Łomnicki) whom Elżbieta later visits, prefers not to talk about this painful past. In the last scene of the film, from his shop he watches Zofia and Elżbieta on the street, talking to each other, but he cannot share their sense of closeness. The window bars physically and symbolically separate him from the two women.

Unlike other Polish films about the Holocaust and Polish-Jewish relations, *Decalogue 8* is set in the present and focuses on the confrontation with the dark

Figure 6.7: Teresa Marczewska as Elżbieta in Krzysztof Kieślowski's *Decalogue 8* (1988)

and intricate past. Elżbieta visits Poland for the first time since the war ("People don't like witnesses of their humiliation," she reveals to Zofia), bringing back not only memories but also a possibility for reconciliation. The opening scene, shown over the credits, signals this preoccupation with national and personal memory. It introduces a young girl and a man walking together through a labyrinth of old houses. Andrzej Jaroszewicz's camera captures the close-up shots of their hands. Zbigniew Preisner's music, which later reappears throughout the film, adds to the murky and melancholy tone of this opening, and refers to the situation in occupied Warsaw. This sharply contrasts with the bright scenery of the subsequent scene, which is set in a blossom-filled park where Zofia is jogging.

Zofia is portrayed as a successful Polish academic, revered by students and translated into English. Her past complements this picture—during the war she was a member of the Home Army and rescued several Jews. Nevertheless, like the painting on the wall of her room that never hangs straight, the spotless picture of Zofia's life reveals one major stain that cannot be easily fixed. The person, who during the war gave false witness against the tailor, changed her life and the lives of others.

The Return of Democracy

Prior to 1989, films dealing with the Holocaust and Polish-Jewish relations were mostly made by filmmakers who were born before the war. Some of them experienced concentration camps, lived under the German or Soviet occupations, and survived the Holocaust hiding and changing their identities. Beginning in the 1980s, a new, "second generation" of filmmakers emerged who took up the subject of the Holocaust. They were born after the war but affected by the war stories of their parents as well as by the films made by their mentors (Jakubowska, Munk, Wajda), and influenced by the torrent of literary and historical works. Scholar Marianne Hirsch, the daughter of Holocaust survivors, developed the much quoted term "postmemory" to describe the experiences of those who carry the memories of the preceding generation.[37]

The return of democracy has enabled Polish filmmakers to freely explore areas that were taboo or marginalized under the previous political order. Like its Central European neighbors, Poland has always been a history-conscious nation—films dealing with the past were and are the core of serious mainstream cinema. Marcia Landy reminds us that "like museums and mausoleums, the films become part of a storehouse of images for the remains of the dead."[38] Polish films about the Holocaust, part of national memory, serve as insightful indicators whether the shared knowledge of the past matches or is influenced by historical knowledge.

After an uneasy but peaceful transition to democracy, a prominent group of feature films about Jewish-Polish history has been released, among them *Korczak* (1990) and *Holy Week* (1996) by Andrzej Wajda (discussed in the next chapter), *Warszawa. Année 5703* (*Tragarz puchu*, 1992) by Janusz Kijowski, *Farewell to Maria* (*Pożegnanie z Marią*, 1993) by Filip Zylber, *Just Beyond this Forest* (*Jeszcze tylko ten las*, 1991) by Jan Łomnicki, and *Deborah* (1996) by Ryszard Brylski. The Holocaust theme also appears in films such as *Kornblumenblau* (1989) by Leszek Wosiewicz, *The Burial of a Potato* (*Pogrzeb kartofla*, 1991) by Jan Jakub Kolski, and *All That Really Matters* (*Wszystko, co najważniejsze*, 1992) by Robert Gliński.

The transitional stage of Polish politics and economy after 1989, as well as audiences' preference for Western narratives during the first part of the 1990s, partly explain why Polish films about the wartime Polish-Jewish relations were modestly successful at the box-office and, with the exception of Andrzej Wajda's films, did not stir any consequential debates. For example, the relatively popular *Farewell to Maria* had 90,000 viewers in 1993 and was distributed in eight copies (the most popular four Polish films that year had between 112,000 and 170,000 viewers and were distributed in 16–20 copies).[39] Other films achieved much worse results. *Deborah*, released in five copies, had only 4,700 viewers. *Warszawa. Année 5703*, released in ten copies, had 9,600 viewers.[40]

It is also essential to mention foreign films shot in Poland and with strong Polish involvement, most notably Steven Spielberg's *Schindler's List* (1993), and several documentaries shot on location in Poland.[41] Another group of works, only signaled in this book, are films made abroad by Polish filmmakers, for instance Agnieszka Holland's *Europa, Europa* (1991, a French and German co-production), which received a Golden Globe award for Best Foreign Film. The subject matter of this factual odyssey of the survival of Solomon Perel, with its blending of humor and horror and its almost absurdist yet true story, perhaps prompted German film authorities to decline the nomination of *Europa, Europa* for an Academy Foreign Film Award.[42] In addition to Holland, Jerzy Kawalerowicz directed *Bronstein's Children* (*Bronsteins Kinder*, *Dzieci Bronsteina*, 1991) in Germany. His psychological drama, based on Jurek Becker's novel published in 1982, was never released on Polish screens (it was shown only on television). Kawalerowicz's film, narrated in a series of flashbacks, deals with the issue of responsibility for the Holocaust. The action is set in the 1970s in East Germany and follows a group of former concentration camp prisoners, German Jews, who capture, imprison, and torture their former SS guard from Neuengamme. They want him to admit his guilt. The film revolves around conversations about guilt and punishment between Aaron Bronstein (Armin Mueller-Stahl) and his son Hans (Matthias Paul), the film's narrator, who discovers the imprisoned man in his father's home.

The Holocaust theme is not limited to the aforementioned films. It also appears in a biographical film about the Franciscan saint Maksymilian Kolbe— *Life for Life* (*Życie za życie, Maksymilian Kolbe*, 1990), a Polish-German production directed by Krzysztof Zanussi. Father Kolbe was beatified in 1971 and canonized in 1982 by John Paul II, which was seen by some scholars as an attempt to "Catholicize Auschwitz."[43] Scripted by Zanussi and writer Jan Józef

Szczepański, the film opens in Auschwitz in 1941 with the scene of an escape of a prisoner. The escapee, Jan Tytz (Christopher Waltz), later hides in a monastery and learns that, as a reprisal for his action, the Auschwitz guards randomly selected ten prisoners and sentenced them to death in a hunger cell. He also learns that one of the selected prisoners was replaced by a volunteer, Father Kolbe (Edward Żentara). Jan tries to learn about Kolbe and what prompted him to sacrifice his life. The film tells the story of Kolbe by employing a flashback structure, through testimonies of those who knew him. It ends with a scene of Kolbe's beatification that is witnessed by Jan, now living in the United States.

The title of an earlier international co-production by Zanussi, *Wherever You Are* (*Gdzieśkolwiek jest, jeśliś jest ...*, 1989, Poland-West Germany-Great Britain), quotes elegy number ten, part of the *Laments* (*Treny*) by a Polish Renaissance poet Jan Kochanowski (1530–1584). The poems were written in 1580, after the death of his beloved young daughter Urszula, and they masterly express the poet's grief and a sense of loss. Zanussi's film tells the story of an honorary consul of Uruguay in Poland, and also a businessman, Julian Castor (Julian Sands). He moves to Poland before the outbreak of World War II with his wife Nina (Rene Soutendijk), an amateur photographer. Suffering from mental illness after an accident, Nina begins to perceive the world as slowly revealing its hidden, terrifying dimension. When she looks at the faces of photographed people she has macabre visions—a premonition about the future genocide. "My female protagonist has a premonition that she will be a victim of the forthcoming war," says Zanussi about his multilayered film, "she is already experiencing it ... These Jewish women, who disappear from photographs, although they are still alive."[44] Several attempts to cure Nina fail. When her husband has to leave Poland on business, the war begins and Nina is doomed— she is killed by the Germans while being hospitalized in a psychiatric hospital.

Among other films with references to the Holocaust, and released at the beginning of the 1990s, two deserve particular notice. The winner of the 1992 Festival of Polish Films, *All That Really Matters*, directed by Robert Gliński, offers an examination of the fate of Polish citizens deported to Kazakhstan by Stalin after the outbreak of World War II. Specifically, the film focuses on the Jewish-Polish family of writer Aleksander Wat, and their struggle for survival under the Soviet rule. In a more complex film, *The Case of Pekosinski* (*Przypadek Pekosińskiego*, 1993), directed by Grzegorz Królikiewicz, Polish history is seen through the eyes of a handicapped, alcoholic man in an unsuccessful search for his unknown mother. He has no knowledge of who he is: his date of birth is at the outbreak of the war; his place of birth is the Nazi concentration camp where he miraculously survived being pushed through a barbed wire fence by his (most probably Jewish) mother; and his surname is an acronym of a Polish charitable institution (PKOS). Taking this into account, the protagonist serves as another Central European victim of history. Known for his bold cinematic experiments, director Królikiewicz is not afraid to employ the authentic person to reconstruct episodes and scenes from his life and, consequently, to block the viewer's identification with the protagonist. Pekosiński does not act in the film (apart from some basic tasks): he is only the object of actions and manipulations of several people who surround him.

Screening the Year 1968

This book, which looks at the representation of the Holocaust chiefly through the prism of Polish-Jewish relationships, should also briefly take into consideration the first two narrative films that addressed the 1968 anti-Semitic campaign in Poland: *March Almonds* (*Marcowe migdały*, 1990) by Radosław Piwowarski (b. 1948) and *1968: Happy New Year* (*1968: Szczęśliwego Nowego Roku*, 1993) by Jacek Bromski (b. 1946). Although both films make no direct references to the Holocaust, they examine the complexities of Polish-Jewish relations in the 1960s. Both films try to re-create the events of 1968 through the perspective of young protagonists, high school and university students, respectively, who experience their political initiation and are forced to make their first adult choices.

In *March Almonds*, Piwowarski tells the story in his usual, lyrical and nostalgic style, a style that had already emerged in his earlier films, such as *Yesterday* (1985)—a film that considers the Beatles phenomenon in Poland. The film's narrator, Tomek (Olaf Lubaszenko), introduces the peaceful atmosphere of his small town that ends abruptly with the intrusion of politics. One of the protagonists, Marcyś (Piotr Siwkiewicz), learns that he is of Jewish origin and is eventually forced to leave the country with his father. At the beginning of the film, Marcyś, supposedly unaware of his Jewishness, carries an anti-Semitic slogan at the small-town gathering in support of the official party line. Gradually, politics completely takes over Marcyś's life: anonymous voices in the local paper point out "the others" who are disguised as "true Poles," but plot against them; an anonymous hand paints the word "Żyd" (Jew) on the doors of Marcyś's home. There are also clear political allusions in the film's final scene at the town's railway station. While Marcyś's train is about to leave, his school is awaiting its patron, a partisan nicknamed Leśny Władek (Władek from the Forest)—a reference to the advent of the Polish communist nationalists headed by Mieczysław Moczar. Soon after Marcyś's expulsion, a likable but conformist high school teacher remarks that "now, only amongst us, everything will work." At the film's end, the song "Ta nasza młodość" (That Our Youth) is heard, and a brief postscript describing the fates of the nonfictional characters who inspired their screen counterparts passes before the viewer.

In many respects, the atmosphere created in *March Almonds* resembles that of some Czech films of the 1960s: the characters are likable, warm, mildly grotesque but not villainous. This is, after all, a nostalgia film for the 1960s, Piwowarski's generation. Despite the director's hazardous tendency to sentimentalize, the film may serve as a good example of the new political films emerging in Poland at that time. Contrary to pre-1989 works, *March Almonds* avoids martyrological gestures and clear divisions between good and bad. It also offers a satirical look at political opportunism, primitive indoctrination, and doublespeak.

In a more politically explicit film, *1968: Happy New Year*, Bromski focuses on the turbulent March of 1968—the strike at the University of Warsaw. The story revolves around a young student from a privileged communist family, Agnieszka Bergman (Jolanta Cackowska), who is in love with a dissident fellow student Piotr (Tomasz Kozłowicz). Her involvement with Piotr and other student protesters is used during the internal struggle within the Communist Party to get rid of her high-ranked Polish-Jewish communist father, Jerzy Bergman (Krzysztof Kolberger), member of the Central Committee of PZPR. Breaking all the family ties, Agnieszka decides to accompany Piotr, who is arrested, persecuted, and eventually forced to leave Poland. Interestingly, the character of Jerzy Bergman, also played by Kolberger, appeared in an earlier film scripted and directed by Bromski, *Polish Cuisine* (*Kuchnia polska* (1991), about the ruthlessness of the Stalinist period. In that film, made somewhat in the spirit of the famous *Interrogation* (*Przesłuchanie*, 1982/1989, Ryszard Bugajski), and also starring Krystyna Janda, Bergman is introduced as a manipulative UB (security service) colonel.

Searching for a Voice

In 1991, veteran director Jan Łomnicki (1929–2002) made his *Just Beyond this Forest*—low budget, anti-spectacular, with an ordinary hero performing ordinary deeds in exceptional circumstances. Beginning in 1954, Łomnicki produced sixty-four documentary films. He also became known for a series of films referring to the war and occupation: *Contribution* (*Kontrybucja*, 1966), *To Save the Town* (*Ocalić miasto*, 1976), and *Operation Arsenal* (*Akcja pod Arsenałem*, 1978). Although in his previous films there are references to the Holocaust, *Just Beyond this Forest* deals exclusively with that subject and with the Polish attitudes to the plight of Polish Jewry.

The film's opening scenes, set in the Warsaw Ghetto in June 1942, show an elderly woman wandering fearfully through impoverished streets. The impassioned camera portrays an overcrowded ghetto in an almost semi-documentary manner. A washerwoman, Kulgawcowa (the outstanding Ryszarda Hanin, the recipient of Best Actress Award at the Festival of Polish Films in Gdynia), is introduced clearly as an outsider, an observer of a world that is far removed from her own (Figure 6.8). This simple woman, previously employed by a rich Jewish doctor and his family, is now about to help them. She is asked to take their only child, the young girl Rutka (Joanna Friedman), out of the ghetto. Reluctantly, she agrees because she knows the danger involved. Also, she is prejudiced against the Jews.

Figure 6.8: Ryszarda Hanin as Mrs. Kulgawcowa in Jan Łomnicki's *Just Beyond this Forest* (1991)

The film follows Kulgawcowa and Rutka's dangerous journey beyond the ghetto wall and their short stay at Kulgawcowa's home. Facing an open hostility of Kulgawcowa's grown-up daughter, they are forced to continue their journey to a village where Kulgawcowa hopes to hide Rutka. Conversations with fellow passengers on a train reveal Polish attitudes toward the Jews (Figure 6.9). Kulgawcowa and Rutka are blackmailed by one of the passengers and rescued by another. When they continue walking toward the village that is "just beyond the forest," they encounter a German gendarme. During a routine control, Rutka drops a photograph of her parents that she smuggled out of the ghetto, and her identity is revealed. In the last scene, Kulgawcowa accompanies Rutka to the police station where, most probably, awaits them death (Figure 6.10).

Just Beyond this Forest does not portray a favorable picture of Polish reality. The Poles in the film are presented as poorly educated people, as a collection of low Polish types, blackmailers, and often anti-Semites. Łomnicki's aim is not to

Figure 6.9: *Just Beyond this Forest.* Rutka (Joanna Friedman) and Mrs. Kulgawcowa (Ryszarda Hanin)

Figure 6.10: *Just Beyond this Forest.* (From the left) Rutka (Joanna Friedman), Mrs. Kulgawcowa (Ryszarda Hanin), and the German soldier (Bogusław Sochnacki)

present a well-known figure (like Korczak in Wajda's film). Rather, he is interested in small, insignificant people like Kulgawcowa who are overwhelmed by history. Whereas Wajda gives a lesson (presented sometimes in an almost didactic manner) on history and Jewish-Polish relations, Łomnicki creates characters and situations entrenched in realism and with seemingly contemporary dilemmas. The scriptwriter, Anna Strońska, comments on this aspect of the film:

> [We] did not want to make a film about the martyrology of a nation. This had to be a matter between people, between particular people, yet typical, like the situation between the Irish and the English, the Palestinians and the Israelis. Contrary to our expectations, the world of the twentieth century has become an arena of nationalisms and chauvinisms. This human aspect was the core of our film, not as somebody unwisely has said that Poles have anti-Semitism coded in their genes.[45]

***

Several other films made at the beginning of the 1990s also tried to offer a new perspective on the Holocaust. Two cinematic debuts produced at that time warrant attention: *Farewell to Maria* (*Pożegnanie z Marią*, 1993) by Filip Zylber (b. 1960) and *The Burial of a Potato* (*Pogrzeb kartofla*, 1991) by Jan Jakub Kolski (b. 1956), the latter quickly becoming one of the most important and the most original film directors who emerged during the post-communist period.

Zylber's *Farewell to Maria*, loosely based on a classic, powerful short story by Tadeusz Borowski,[46] differs from other Polish films dealing with the war and Polish-Jewish relations. Modern jazz compositions by Tomasz Stańko and stylized photography by Dariusz Kuc, often employing slow motion, stress the morbid melancholy initially introduced by edifying dialogues about love, war, and poetry. This is not to say that Zylber builds an atmosphere at the cost of aestheticizing the Holocaust. The film offers a new reading of a classic text and of history. Zylber does not follow the partly autobiographical, laconic, and verging-on-cynical vision of Borowski. In Borowski's world, there is no distinction between good and evil; all characters are infected by the devastating degeneration of human values. Everyday existence is marked by compromises, resignation, and the adoption of pragmatic personal philosophies useful in the struggle for survival.

The film revolves around the story of two Jewish women who manage to escape from the ghetto. The older of the two, Mrs. Doktorowa (Danuta Szaflarska), escapes from the ghetto thanks to her prewar connections on the Aryan side but later, choosing inevitable death, returns to be with her friends and relatives.[47] In *Farewell To Maria*, the young and beautiful Sara (Katarzyna Jamróz) performs a different role than Szaflarska's character. According to Zylber, she "propels the action, circles like a moth, perturbs people. In a sense, she provokes her own death."[48] Like Irena in Wajda's *Holy Week*, Sara serves as a reminder of what is going on behind the ghetto wall. She "upsets" her Polish hosts by her very presence and with comments such as this one: "One day, on the Aryan side, there will also be a ghetto. And there will be nowhere to run."

Tadeusz Lubelski calls Zylber's film "a drama of helplessness" and Borowski's short story "a drama of mutual responsibility."[49] According to Lubelski, Zylber's adaptation creates two distinct realms: the realm of private rituals and the realm of death. Young Polish intellectuals who are attending the wedding of their friends obviously know the existence of the nightmarish world behind the ghetto walls, but they are unable to do anything about it. Insulated from the realm of death by their artificial rituals, they can only powerlessly watch the death of Sara, harassed and killed by a drunken Polish *granatowy* (blue) policeman Cieślik (Sławomir Orzechowski).[50]

***

The Holocaust does not appear explicitly in Kolski's debut film, *The Burial of a Potato*. In this film that combines poetic metaphors with grotesque images of Polish postwar reality, a former concentration camp prisoner, Mateusz Szewczyk (Franciszek Pieczka), faces a hostile village after his unexpected and unwanted return several years after his incarceration. The village had already taken possession of his belongings and is after his land (the action is set immediately after the war, during the collectivization). Mateusz is rejected by his fellow villagers as an alien and as a Jew, although he is neither. He faces constant harassment; the villagers threaten him, attempt to burn his property, and even try to kill him. "Don't burn the living," shouts outraged Mateusz. In one poignant scene, he puts on a concentration camp striped uniform with a number 23423 and a letter "P" inside a triangle (indicating that he is Polish), and stands half naked, with his pants down, in front of his neighbors to prove that he is not a Jew. He says, "People! I am not a Jew. If I were, it would be less painful because I would be dead. I am standing on the *Appelplatz* that you've made before your home, and I'm saying: I'm not a Jew. And I regret that I am not."

The essence of Kolski's film is Mateusz's struggle for acceptance, not the political reality of postwar Poland (portrayed powerfully, albeit in an uncanny manner). Kolski is not afraid to demythologize Polish peasants. While in several Polish literary and filmic works, they function as the defenders of traditional nationalistic and Catholic values, in *The Burial of a Potato* they are portrayed as brutal, superficially religious, xenophobic, and anti-Semitic caricatures, almost in the manner of Jerzy Kosiński's representation in his controversial novel *The Painted Bird*.[51] Their expressions of xenophobia and anti-Semitism are frequent, and can be summed up by one of the lines delivered by one of the villagers: "That whole war was caused by you, Judases." Hungry for their own land and ready to do anything to get it, they are united in their victimization of Mateusz.[52]

Mateusz's wife is dead; his son, a Home Army combatant, died earlier in unclear circumstances, most probably killed by the villagers. In the film's final scenes, the culpable farmers are forced by Mateusz to take the body of his son and to give him a proper burial. In a fitting conclusion, Mateusz takes care of a Jewish orphan, Dawid, whose mother threw him from a transport train heading to an extermination camp. Interestingly, a similar motif appears in Kolski's later film, *Miraculous Place* (*Cudowne miejsce*, 1995), which introduces another character marginalized by a backward village, Staszko nicknamed "Indorek" (Mariusz Saniternik), who escaped from a train heading for a concentration camp and found shelter among Polish villagers.

Director Kolski stressed in an interview that the story presented in *The Burial of a Potato* is authentic and happened to his grandfather, Jakub Szewczyk, a Home Army (AK) officer who survived Auschwitz and was marginalized by the village after his late return in 1946.[53] The film's protagonist wears the concentration camp striped uniform with Jakub's actual number from the camp. The subplot regarding Mateusz' son, an officer in the AK killed after the war, is also authentic along with the names of several villagers. The film was also shot in the village of Popielawy, the actual place of the postwar drama and a mythologized space in several later films made by Kolski.

Kolski, however, sees his film as more than just a painful biographical story. He states that "this is a story about a specifically Polish anti-Semitism that does not need the Jews."[54] The film's protagonist, although of Polish origin, is stigmatized as the "Other." In several interviews and published books, Kolski returns to this issue citing his family story as an example. His Jewish grandmother perished during the occupation in the Łódź (Litzmannstadt) Ghetto with her Polish husband. In Kolski's semi-autobiographical novel, *A Bread Pellet* (*Kulka z chleba*), there is the following comment: "Our blood cannot be divided. The person, who has half, a quarter, or even a half-quarter of it, has the blood of the whole Jewish nation."[55] In an interview Kolski comments on that aspect of his biography: "I have in me one drop of Jewish blood. One, just that. Much too little for Halacha to consider me a Jew ..., but enough to consider my fate as part of the Jewish fate."[56]

* * *

In *Kornblumenblau* (1989), Leszek Wosiewicz (b. 1953) offers a different look at World War II and wartime sufferings. *Kornblumenblau* (the title of a German song) also works against the generally accepted set of conventionalized representations of concentration camps that permeate Polish films, with the exception of *The Passenger*. Moreover, since the film is set in a concentration camp (in Auschwitz, although the name is not uttered on the screen), and its protagonist's name is Tadeusz, it is inviting to treat it as another reading of the postwar prose of Tadeusz Borowski. Like Borowski, Wosiewicz also focuses not on the psychology but on the physiology of the dehumanized hero. Tadeusz Wyczyński (memorable Adam Kamień) survives by instinct—he tries to be loyal to the guards and to stay on good terms with other inmates. For them, he remains an enigma. "Is he a sly dog or an imbecile?" wonders one of his fellow prisoners. "The saintly cretin," comments another.

The film starts with a skillfully edited pre-credit, slapstick-like sequence that summarizes the early stages of Tadeusz's life. Wosiewicz employs old documentary footage and fragments of a Polish prewar film intercut with footage (also in sepia tones), showing the protagonist's parents, his birth, and the beginnings of his career as a musician. This silent part of the film (only a few captions are employed) ends with the outbreak of the war and Tadeusz being sent to a concentration camp for political activities. With luck on his side, he survives hunger, being close to death as a *Muselmann*, and selection to the gas. Thanks to the help of a friendly *Kapo*, he endures the typhoid ward in the camp hospital and is transferred to a "food preparation commando." Protected by his homosexual German *Kapo* (Krzysztof Kolberger), for whom Tadeusz plays "Kornblumenblau" and other popular musical pieces, he rises in rank and learns the camp. Although he loses his privileged status (preparing food for the Germans and entertaining them on piano), he survives again, this time the death bunker, being rescued by the commandant's wife who needs a musician for the Christmas performance for officers' children. Later, until the end of the war, he plays in the camp orchestra.

It is tempting to read *Kornblumenblau* in broader terms, as a parable on the situation of an artist in a totalitarian state, about art and everyday survival, as well as about "the misery of art."[57] Artists are, as one of the prisoners in the film puts it, "cockroaches with golden outer shells." The film's protagonist, however, is quite pragmatic, a chameleon-like person able to fit into different situations, an amiable conformist. Tadeusz fulfills his parents' dream by becoming an artist, but to secure his future, he also becomes an engineer. As if to emphasize this aspect of his personality, in the last symbolic scene, after the liberation of the camp, he voluntarily joins a group of Soviet soldiers and starts entertaining them to the tune of *Kalinka*. Tadeusz tries to survive at all costs, as if detached from the grim reality surrounding him. Art that helps Tadeusz, however, is useless for the Jews. For example, a Jewish-Hungarian virtuoso violinist, with the commandant's personal approval, lives only as long as he is able to perform. Similarly portrayed is a young Jewish girl who is dancing her last dance at the ramp.

The film's protagonist, Tadeusz, acts like a voyeur. Hidden in a storage building, he witnesses an execution of a prisoner, an elaborate grotesque spectacle organized for the German officers and their wives. In a different montage sequence, deprived of dialogue, he is watching a group of newly arrived young Hungarian Jewish women. One of them (Adrianna Biedrzyńska) catches his eye. Every morning his column of male prisoners passes near the Jewish women on their way to work. Each morning he witnesses their gradual deterioration. Similar scenes are recalled by a film scholar and former Auschwitz prisoner Bolesław W. Lewicki: "I remember the arrival of the first female transport ... We, the first numbers, hadn't seen women for three years; it was as if the meadow of flowers was thrown from the carriages on the station platform. These were, if I remember correctly, Hungarian Jewish women. In a couple of days these flowers with shaved heads, with men's striped clothing, barefoot—and the winter was cold—tragically broken, sad, frozen were passing every morning in front of the old prisoners."[58]

Although the film's focus is on Tadeusz's survival, the Jewish tragedy is present throughout the film in brief, laconic, but powerful scenes. For example, one of the prisoners remarks casually, in the spirit of Borowski, "Do you know that yesterday they set a new record? They gassed and burned 25 thousand Jews." Like Borowski, Wosiewicz depicts the camp without attempting to elevate the history of suffering.[59] Unlike his predecessors, chiefly Wanda Jakubowska, Wosiewicz mixes horror and banality, tragedy and farce. The depiction of an "insolent concentration camp reality that ridicules both the executioner and the victim," as Marta Wróbel writes, produces "the Auschwitz carnival of people changed into numbers."[60] An unusual film soundtrack emphasizes that aspect of the camp—a blend of songs, cries, whispers, clapping boots, and magnified sounds of people devouring food, among others.

Libby Saxton writes that "to avoid the gas chambers is arguably to avoid the Holocaust."[61] In *Kornblumenblau*, Wosiewicz breaks the taboo by depicting the industrialized killing in a scene set inside the gas chamber, a scene that has never been portrayed in Polish cinema and is generally avoided in Holocaust narratives. Interestingly, this is a single scene that is deprived of tragicomic dimensions that characterize the film.

It is worth noting that Wosiewicz's interest in ordinary people entangled in totalitarian systems was also earlier reflected in his documentary film, *The Case of Herman, the Stoker* (*Przypadek Hermana—palacza*, 1986), the winner of the Oberhausen Film Festival. Its protagonist (who died in 1985 in Poland) was immensely devoted to his profession. The film follows his career as a stoker that started in a mental asylum and ended in Adolf Hitler's headquarters. Wosiewicz also stressed the grotesque, absurdist nature of history in the underappreciated *Scurvy* (*Cynga*, 1993), a film about the fate of Poles who found themselves in the Soviet-occupied territories after 17 September 1939 and were deported by Stalin to Siberia.

Holocaust Melodrama

Like films made elsewhere, recent Polish films about the Holocaust have also been dominated by melodramatic representations. They were also often criticized for trivializing the Holocaust, which served as backdrop for melodrama in *Warszawa. Année 5703* (aka *Warszawa, Year 5703, Tragarz puchu*, 1992), *Deborah* (*Debora*, 1996), and *Keep Away from the Window* (aka *Far from the Window*; *Daleko od okna*, 2000).

The mixing of melodrama and history is particularly explicit in *Warszawa. Année 5703*, a Polish-French-German co-production directed by one of the leading figures of the Cinema of Distrust (Moral Concern), Janusz Kijowski (b. 1948). The film deals with events taking place in 1943 and tells the story of a young couple escaping through the sewers from the Warsaw Ghetto. They find refuge on the Polish side of the wall in an apartment owned by Stefania (Hanna Schygulla), a half-German, middle-aged woman whose Polish husband is in a POW camp. Stefania is allowed "freedom" because she gives blood to make a vaccine against typhus. Alek (Lambert Wilson), who first gets to the hiding place, becomes Stefania's lover. To prolong his and his wife Fryda's (Julie Delpy) stay at Stefania's place, and because he is afraid to tell the truth, he pretends to be Fryda's brother, in spite of her violent objections ("I can't live over there and here I don't want to"). In the film's finale, Alek follows a desperate, unstable Fryda back into the sewers to return to the burning ghetto, while Stefania's apartment is searched by the Gestapo, the result of Fryda's incriminating letter.

Warszawa. Année 5703 opens with several negative images showing mysterious faces and characters. It then cuts to an image of a photographer surreptitiously taking pictures of the horrors transpiring in the ghetto. He gives the negatives to Alek, hoping that he will deliver them to a Polish photographer on the Aryan side. The photographer, however, had been arrested (and probably killed) for hiding a Jew, and this situation forces Alek to accept Stefania's help. After these brief, promising initial scenes, the action moves to Stefania's apartment. From this point on, the film relies heavily on the three leading stars, and more and more resembles a theatrical play: most scenes are set in brownish interiors. The camera rarely ventures outside of Stefania's apartment. If it does, the results are sketchy and unconvincing, for example, in the two scenes set in the city underground sewers, which invite comparisons with Wajda's *Kanal* or Ford's *Border Street*. The nightmarish external circumstances only serve to bring the three characters more intimately, claustrophobically together. *This is Our Last Sunday* (*To ostatnia niedziela*), a famed nostalgic prewar song enhances the film's melodramatic atmosphere. Composed by Jerzy Petersburski to the "suicidal lyrics" of Z. Friedwald, the song expresses anguish about being separated forever as well as hope for the last chance (for the last Sunday). What might work in a typical melodrama, however, is indeed troubling in Kijowski's film. As Annette Insdorf notices, to have a character (Fryda) who "inspires such hatred on the part of the audience" is disconcerting in a film about the Holocaust.[62]

The image of the carousel on the Krasiński Square near the ghetto wall appears several times throughout the film. The carousel, which separates Stefania's apartment building from the ghetto wall, is in operation almost all the time—during the Warsaw Ghetto Uprising it is covered with smoke, but still running. Unlike Wajda in *Holy Week*, Kijowski employs the shots of the carousel exclusively as a symbol of the indifference of the outside world, more specifically a symbol of the indifference of Poles living on the Aryan side of the wall that divides the city.

The subtle Polish title of Kijowski's film, *Tragarz puchu*, means, in direct translation, "a person who carries downy feathers." Such a title would be more appropriate for this intimate psychological drama than the adopted English title *Warszawa. Année 5703*, which suggests a film of almost epic proportions. An earlier, modest television film with that same Polish title, directed by Stefan Szlachtycz (b. 1930), was also based on the script by Jerzy Janicki. Made in 1983, it was presented the next year at the Festival of Polish Films in Gdańsk and forgotten since despite good performances by Krzysztof Gosztyła, Elżbieta Kijowska, and Ewa Sałacka-Krauze (Fryda).[63]

Kijowski's multinational production, though far superior to Szlachtycz's television production in almost every aspect, shares the same weaknesses as its predecessor. Promoting his film, the director stressed that "the time has come for a film about people who simply were Jewish, Polish, and German during that terrible war, and not a film about Jews, Poles, and Germans who fulfil the roles ascribed to them by the 'spirit of history.'"[64] Despite, however, Kijowski's comments about the "universal nature" of his "drama of passions," the result is a schematic psychological melodrama, a love triangle set in the atypical circumstances of the Holocaust.

***

Like Kijowski in *Warszawa. Année 5703*, Ryszard Brylski (b. 1950) also attempts to incorporate the Holocaust into mainstream cinema's melodramatic formulae in his debut film *Deborah* (1996). Based on Marek Sołtysik's novel titled *Debora* (1988), Brylski's film was, however, barely noticed by critics in Poland after its premiere, weeks after Wajda's *Holy Week*. The action of *Deborah* is set before the outbreak of World War II in a provincial Polish town with a significant Jewish population. The film's Polish protagonist, painter Marek Wawrowski (Olgierd Łukaszewicz), is preoccupied with restoring the newly uncovered renaissance frescoes in a local Catholic church. Rumors about war enhance the feeling of fear in the sleepy town. The Jewish population is afraid of what looms ahead. At the outbreak of the war, with his wife and son away in a mountain resort, the painter begins an affair with a young, beautiful Jewish woman, Deborah Grosman (Renata Dancewicz). After the war begins, he hides Deborah in an empty apartment, then in a cellar, while the Jewish population of the town, including Deborah's father and friends, are being sent to death camps. The film ends with the death of the painter who is shot by the Germans.

Brylski is preoccupied with the vision of the end of a certain world—he aims at the creation of an atmosphere of despair. The imminent war and then its reality overshadow the characters' actions. Poles are generally shown to be sympathetic to the plight of the Jews; the majority are depicted helping the Jews, with many being killed by the Germans as a result. The theme of deeply rooted anti-Semitism, however, is introduced by an anti-Jewish tale portrayed in the church's frescoes ("We work on the same theme," says the Nazi officer to the Polish painter). In *Deborah*, however, the Holocaust functions as the background for a tale about passionate love, doomed from its very inception. According to Brylski, his film is in fact about the "forbidden love," not about Polish-Jewish relations or the Holocaust.[65]

***

Since his well-received mainstream debut in 1991, *The Burial of a Potato*, Kolski made a number of highly original films, such as *Johnnie the Aquarius* (*Jańcio Wodnik*, 1993). In 1998, he won the Festival of Polish Films with *The History of Cinema Theater in Popielawy* (*Historia kina w Popielawach*). The direct political references present in *The Burial of a Potato* disappeared from his later works made in the 1990s, replaced by metaphysical meditation and folk wisdom combined with a unique version of lyricism and humor. During the early stage of his career, Kolski was interested in oversensitive, weird, and marginalized rural characters whose worlds are limited to their village and end with the horizon. His prolific nature and his obsession with the private world led inevitably to a certain mannerism. Writer-director Kolski (all scripts were his own) favored the same picturesque landscapes and characters, and dealt with the presence of the religious/supernatural element in the lives of his down-to-earth yet unique characters. In 2000, attempting to broaden his *oeuvre*, Kolski directed the Holocaust drama *Keep Away from the Window*. Three years later, he also adapted Witold Gombrowicz's novel *Pornography* (*Pornografia*), saturating the latter with references to the Holocaust.

Cezary Harasimowicz's script of *Keep Away from the Window* is based on Hanna Krall's short story *That Woman from Hamburg* (*Ta z Hamburga*), published in 1994 and based on real events. The story revolves around a young woman, Helusia, born in 1943 in Lwów. Several years later she learns that her biological mother was a Jewish woman, Regina, who was hiding in her parents' apartment during the war. The childless couple, Jan and Barbara, sheltered Regina since early 1943. When she got pregnant with Jan, Barbara faked her own pregnancy and pretended to be an expecting mother for the outside world. After the birth of a baby girl, she took the child as her own. In July 1944, before the Soviets entered the city, Regina disappeared. The Polish couple raised the child and refused to give it to the mother who settled in Hamburg after the war. Later, the mature Helusia tried to establish a relationship with her birth mother but was rejected by Regina who stressed that she wants to forget that nightmarish part of her life. Hanna Krall comments on the protagonist's behavior: "Escaping from her daughter, Regina was escaping the memory of her humiliation. The whole Poland reminded her about this humiliation, although Poland was not the guilty party."[66]

Krall's laconic, restrained, and matter-of-factly narrated short story was a difficult match for Kolski, given his predilection for stylized (often labeled "magic realist") worlds.[67] Typical for Krall's Holocaust prose, the survivor's perspective dominates the narrative. Interestingly, Krall embraced the adaptation although the final result, as expected, is much different from the literary source. She emphasized that prior to Kolski's film the dominant trend in Polish cinema had been to offer an external perspective on the Jewish suffering. Praising Kolski's work, she stressed that in his film "we are inside the wardrobe with the Jewish protagonist."[68]

Kolski moves the action of a short story from Lwów closer to his own interests, to an unnamed small town. As he mentioned on several occasions, *Keep Away from the Window* is not a film with the stress on the Holocaust. Instead, it tells the story "about love, motherhood, freedom, and humanity."[69] Krall remarks in a similar fashion that Kolski's film is about relationships during the wartime period: "This is the story about three people: two women who were in love with the same man ... Other aspects are just scenery."[70]

The bulk of Kolski's film is set in the claustrophobic interiors of a house belonging to Jan (Bartosz Opania) and Barbara (Dorota Landowska). The first scenes, taking place before the war, introduce the couple for whom the lack of a child appears to be the main concern. Jan is a painter who also earns a living as a sign-maker. In his studio, he proudly stores a baby carriage with the couple's wedding portrait painted by him. The film opens with a symbolic image of his unfinished painting of the Madonna with Child whose face still waits to be painted. The painting is as incomplete as the couple's union without a child. The film moves quickly to the war period, which is announced by a brief scene with jerky images of an empty baby carriage and fleeing people, among them Hassidic Jews, and a German folk tune in the soundtrack. The image of German flags flowing over the town signals the occupation and sets the tone for the film. The grim reality of the occupation is introduced when Jan is forced to repaint the site of an execution—to cover blood on a building's wall with fresh paint. From the ground, he picks up an armband with the Star of David. In the next scene, he is shown with the armband in his hand, cutting his palm through it, perhaps in a sign of grief and solidarity, or as Elżbieta Ostrowska convincingly argues, in "a symbolic act of miscegenation."[71]

In the following scene, Jan brings home a young Jewish woman, Regina (Dominika Ostałowska). As if sensing resistance, he swiftly introduces her to Barbara ("This lady is Jewish"). The viewer never learns the circumstances of their meeting and how she survived. Despite Barbara's objections, Jan shelters Regina in his studio and in a huge wardrobe that occupies the center of their living room. Regina is informed to keep away from the window and to hide in the wardrobe when guests are coming, in particular during the often unexpected visits by a policeman, Jodła (Krzysztof Pieczyński). Several point-of-view shots employed throughout the film (Arkadiusz Tomiak's cinematography) reflect Regina's perspective from inside the wardrobe. Later, the vulnerable Regina has an affair with Jan and becomes pregnant. The outraged Barbara wants to get rid of Regina. Despite Jan's warnings that she should not do anything to endanger the household, she walks toward the police station repeating the phrase in German that exposes the hiding Jewish woman. At the last moment, however, she changes her mind and tells Jodła that she is pregnant. From this point on, Barbara takes the matter into her own hands—she acts as if pregnant, imitating the look and the behavior of Regina for the townsfolk as well as for herself. She even feels the baby's movements during a Sunday stroll with her husband. After Regina gives birth at home to Helusia, Barbara is in control of the situation and allows Regina only to feed the baby girl. When the child is baptized in the church, the camera symbolically focuses on an image of the Madonna with the child.

The war reality intrudes throughout the film and poses a constant threat. The policeman Jodła, who is attracted to Barbara, learns about the hiding Jewish woman and has to be kept quiet with bribes. When he demands more and makes indirect threats, Jan kills him in desperation. Regina disappears one day, probably to not endanger Helusia, and perhaps also being unable to endure Barbara's harsh treatment. The end of the war, marked by the change of flags, does not, however, bring liberation to Jan and Barbara. Once more, they are limited to their interiors, fearing the world, and separated from each other. Barbara is preoccupied with maternal tasks. Jan gradually sinks into alcoholism, and later dies revealing the truth about Regina to Helusia. The past seems to dwarf the characters and to overshadow their actions. Ironically, the wardrobe is still used by Helusia who hides there during the visit of Regina's emissaries from Hamburg. Later, when Helusia tries to contact her birth mother, she feels rejected ("You remind me of everything: fear, shame, darkness"). The film ends with interior shots of Barbara and her daughter talking about Helusia's pregnancy.

Kolski interrupts the realistic narrative of his film to insert three highly-stylized, dream-like images of a *shtetl*. When Regina hides in a wardrobe and starts calmly singing, two flashbacks take her back in time to images of a dwarfed *shtetl* community—a girl is standing among miniature houses, half her size. The scenery may resemble Chagall's paintings. It may also symbolize Regina's mental landscape: her yearning for a happier place, nostalgic return to her roots (although she is an assimilated Jewish woman). Similar images of the *shtetl* life appear for the third time when Regina gives birth to Helusia.

In the film's center is the representation of two women, shown atypically for Polish cinema dealing with Jewish-Polish relations.[72] The assimilated Jewish woman is blonde, suffering, and determined to survive ("I will live!" she says to Jan after revealing that her husband was killed in a concentration camp). The dark-haired Barbara acts like a jealous woman, not necessarily an anti-Semite, although from the beginning she addresses Regina like a nonperson ("let her sit down," "perhaps she is hungry"). Regina has to remain silent, suffering out of sight, in a wardrobe. Joanna Preizner writes that her portrayal bears resemblance to a traditional, symbolic way of representing the suffering and heroic Polish icon—the Polish Mother:

> Regina behaves as if she thinks that after losing a part of herself, some aspects of her life are closed to her. The stillness, withdrawal of Regina is a form of mourning—also after herself. There is some goodness and enormous dignity that gives the Jewish woman, usually seen by Poles as a colorful, but utterly alien element of the local landscape, some archetypal features of the Polish Mother.[73]

Kolski's complex film never clearly addresses the issue of guilt. Jan and Barbara risked their lives and managed to save Regina, but they did not treat her like a fellow human being. Regina later expresses her anger during a meeting with her daughter: "I had to. I had to do everything! I wanted to live ... I don't want to know anything about your father! I don't want to remember him or those years, nor you. You remind me of everything: fear, shame, darkness. I don't want them." For writer Hanna Krall, "nobody is at fault. Everybody tried, was a victim."[74] This treatment of the Holocaust was generally praised in Poland, and Kolski's film was often hailed as the best film released locally in 2000. Several critics, however, found some aspects of Kolski's film problematic, for example, his predilection for stylized images (such as characters' extensive comments on the symbolism of colors, the dream-like flashbacks, the unfinished painting of the Madonna and Child), and also the film's laconic and artificial dialogue, and detached acting.[75]

Keep Away from the Window premiered in Poland on 17 November 2000. It was distributed in barely five copies and seen only by 6,700 viewers.[76] The film also never received much deserved exposure at the international film festival circuit partly due to its unfortunate timing. It was released soon after the Polish premiere of an Oscar-nominated Czech film, *Divided We Fall* (*Musíme si pomáhat*, 2000), directed by Jan Hřebejk. Both films are domestic dramas sharing a number of similarities. The Czech film also tells the story of a young childless couple, Josef and Marie, hiding a Jewish man, their former neighbor David, whose family perished, but he escaped from a concentration camp. Hřebejk's film introduces a Nazi collaborator who is attracted to Marie. To protect herself from his advances, she lies about her pregnancy. Later, to avoid problems, she gets pregnant with the help of David, who reluctantly serves as a surrogate father for Marie's sterile husband. *Keep Away from the Window* is noticeably different than Hřebejk's black comedy that stresses the absurdist aspect of a war-torn town and features a hopeful ending. Unlike Hřebejk, Kolski offers a drama of human suffering that continues beyond the confines of the war.

Kolski followed *Keep Away from the Window* with another adaptation, this time an almost irreverent rendition of Witold Gombrowicz's classic novel *Pornography*, published in 1966. The film's action takes place during the German occupation, in 1943, in a country manor house. It revolves around two middle-aged Warsaw *literati*, the film's narrator Witold (Adam Ferency) and his companion Fryderyk (Krzysztof Majchrzak), who are visiting their friend Hipolit (Krzysztof Globisz), involved in underground activities. Playing eccentric games, Witold and Fryderyk try to prevent the wedding of sixteen-year-old Henia, Hipolit's daughter, to a local lawyer by orchestrating her amorous interest in an equally young Karol. To bring them closer together, the young couple is manipulated into murdering Colonel Siemian (Jan Frycz), a psychologically disturbed underground fighter who is potentially dangerous for other conspirators, and who was sentenced to death by the underground.

Kolski infuses Gombrowicz's narrative with references to the Holocaust by adding scenes with German soldiers and Polish partisans, Jewish people hiding in the vicinity of the manor and being caught and executed, and with over-the-credits archival footage from the Warsaw Ghetto that features a collection of a dead body. Above all, however, Kolski moves Fryderyk's character to the center of the film. By providing references to his dark, troubling past, he also tries to elucidate his present actions as marked by trauma, mourning, and a sense of guilt. As the viewer learns toward the end of the film, Fryderyk failed to save his half-Jewish daughter Hela who died in a concentration camp. After her arrest by the Germans, he managed somehow to follow her to the camp on the same transport train. When she recognized him at the entrance to the camp, however, he hid from his own child. Paralyzed by fear and brutalized by the whole ordeal, he could not admit that she was his daughter. After a successful escape from the camp, all his encounters were marked by the burden of the past. Toward the end of the film, he is shown attempting to erase the camp number on his arm (Figure 6.11). Unable to carry on, and trying to redeem himself, he commits suicide. The lush photography by Krzysztof Ptak abruptly changes into a black-and-white mode when Fryderyk cuts his wrist. The viewer follows him in the film's last scene on the road to his private Golgotha (Figure 6.12).

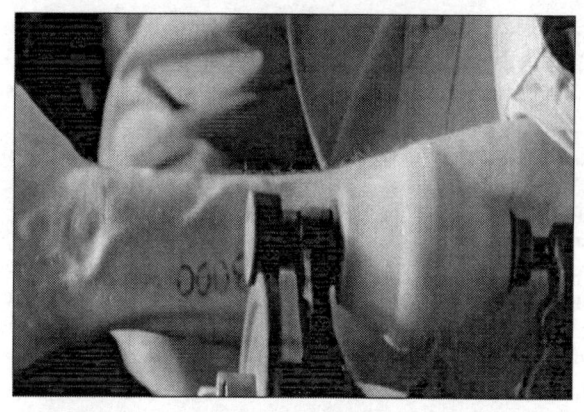

Figure 6.11: Erasing the camp number. Jan Jakub Kolski's *Pornography* (2003)

Figure 6.12: Krzysztof Majchrzak as Fryderyk in Jan Jakub Kolski's *Pornography*

"The Jedwabne Controversy"

After the 1989 transition to democracy, several major historical works published in Poland explored Polish-Jewish history, including wartime and postwar relations, the 1946 Kielce pogrom, and the 1968 anti-Semitic campaign (see bibliography).

Due to its impact, the publication in 2001 of Jan Gross's *Neighbors: The Destruction of the Jewish Community in Jedwabne, Poland* deserves a special mention. The book chronicled the massacre of a Jewish population by their Polish neighbors. It took place on 10 July 1941 in the small Polish town of Jedwabne (northeastern Poland) occupied by Nazi Germany.[77] The Polish edition of Gross's book, which appeared one year earlier, sparked a heated discussion about Polish complicity in the crime and revived the debate on Polish-Jewish wartime relations.[78] That debate, as Piotr Wróbel explains, "demonstrated clearly a conflict between collective memory and history in Poland."[79] Wróbel writes that, like several historians, he always had serious methodological reservations about Gross's approach, which "accuses but does not explain too much."[80] Despite the above, Wróbel admits that initially he belonged to Gross's defenders, and describes his book in the following way:

> A brilliant historical essay, stimulating and provocative; that shows clearly once again that the history of Poland and most Eastern European nations have to be rewritten. Occupied and persecuted for centuries, the Poles believed during World War II that they were threatened with extinction. In defense, they have developed a simplified, bipolar interpretation of their wartime history, which shows them as victims and depicts everybody else as oppressors and enemies. Gross has demonstrated that the victims can also be victimizers.[81]

According to Wróbel, the reception of Gross's book in Poland not only demonstrates a huge gap between Polish "collective memory and history," but also a conflict between Jewish and Polish memories of the war. Dorota Glowacka and Joanna Zylinska expressed it lucidly in the introduction to their anthology about *Imaginary Neighbors*: "Polish narratives of heroism, oppression, and liberation have yielded stories of sacrifice for the fatherland, including tales of the selfless rescue of the Jews. They stand in stark contrast to the Jewish narratives of suffering, senseless death, and betrayal."[82]

Gross acknowledged that his research about the "Jedwabne controversy" owes its inspiration to Agnieszka Arnold's documentary film, *Neighbors* (*Sąsiedzi*, 2001). Arnold started the work on her documentary in 1998 and allowed Gross to see the footage from Jedwabne.[83] She also referred to the Jedwabne tragedy in her earlier film, *Where Is My Older Son Cain?* (*Gdzie mój starszy syn Kain?* 1999), the title borrowed from one of Paul Celan's poems. This multilayered film offered many perspectives regarding Polish-Jewish relationships and presented Poles as victims, helpers, betrayers, xenophobes, and anti-Semites. It also emphasized the political circumstances surrounding the massacre. The broadcast of Arnold's film on Polish Television did not stir any debates about the past.[84] This should not be, however, surprising in the Polish context. Generally, the impetus for debates about Polish-Jewish relations in Poland is provided by a book or a film that originates abroad and portrays Poles and their wartime past in an unflattering, often painful manner.[85]

Despite the frequent critical voices questioning Gross's methodology and his merciless destruction of a generally accepted and rarely questioned version of recent Polish history, the impact of his *Neighbors* has been lasting. It has prompted a new examination of the Polish national past and, as if to counter the accusatory work by Gross, the publication of numerous studies that time and again emphasize the Polish wartime help for the Jews. It has also resulted in the proliferation of documentary films about the Polish Righteous, including films about prominent and largely unknown figures such as Irena Sendler and Henryk Sławik (see chapter 8). The impact of Gross's book, nonetheless, is difficult to discern in recent Polish narrative films.

International Co-productions: *Edges of the Lord* and *The Pianist*

The beginning of the 1990s proved to be very difficult for a number of Polish filmmakers. The nationalized and centralized film industry, entirely dependent on government funding, was transformed after 1989 into a free market economy subsidized by the state. Film units, the core of the local film business since 1955, were replaced by independent studios. The move toward a market economy in Poland coincided with the universalization of co-productions in Europe and the incorporation of American popular cinema into that market. Multinational enterprises, competition with Hollywood, and a plurality of styles and genres have changed the film landscape in Poland. Increasingly, Polish studios and independent producers have been looking for financing for their films abroad, and they have been participating in multinational co-productions, especially since 1992, when Poland joined the Eurimages Foundation. That trend has continued in the last decade. Two prestigious co-productions dealing with the Holocaust, *Edges of the Lord* (*Boże skrawki*, 2001) and *The Pianist* (*Pianista*, 2002), were made by two Polish émigré directors, Yurek Bogayevicz and Roman Polański respectively, on location in Poland, and with substantial Polish involvement.

Actor turned director Yurek Bogayevicz (b. 1948) left Poland in 1976 for the United States where he made, among others, two well-received films—*Anna* (1987) and *Three of Hearts* (1992). His first film made in Poland, an American-Polish co-production *Edges of the Lord*, shares a number of similarities with other Polish Holocaust narratives about hiding, in particular with films featuring a child's point of view of the war, for example, *Birth Certificate* and *According to the Decrees of Providence*. Set in 1942, the story of *Edges of the Lord* follows an eleven-year-old Jewish boy Romek (Haley Joel Osment), who is sent away by his parents from the Kraków Ghetto to the countryside.[86] The blond boy is smuggled out of the ghetto by a Polish farmer Gniecio (Olaf Lubaszenko). Pretending to be the farmer's nephew from the city, Romek stays in the village with Gniecio, his wife, and two sons. In order to not raise any suspicions, he has to pass for a Catholic. A local priest (Willem Dafoe) knows the child's secret but allows Romek to participate in preparations for the first communion. Portrayed unconventionally in the context of Polish cinema, the priest teaches Romek the Catholic catechism but respects his Jewish background. The priest also encourages children to replay some scenes from the life of Jesus to learn their catechism. To their surprise, the children discover that Jesus was Jewish, but are unaware of Romek's Jewishness.

Instead of playing one of the apostles, Gniecio's youngest son Tolo (Liam Hess) takes on the role of Jesus. Despite Hess's superb performance, however, heavy-handed symbolism dominates the second part of the film, in particular during the "crucifixion scene," and later, when the boy joins a group of Jewish prisoners and is loaded with them on a transport train heading for a death camp. Bogayevicz stressed that the film had a therapeutic value for him, and that he was referring to images he remembered from his childhood. According to him, "Tolo is a saint, but for American audiences he serves as an extreme case of child schizophrenia."[87]

Edges of the Lord focuses primarily on the relationship between Romek and his new Polish family and friends. In its presentation of Polish-Jewish relationships, Bogayevicz opts for a carefully balanced picture. Polish characters are evenly divided. The treacherous neighbor Kluba (Andrzej Grabowski) is juxtaposed with the parish priest, with Gniecio (who is later murdered by Kluba), and with other members of the rural community. The film's negative character, Kluba, profits from the war with the help of his two sons by robbing the Jewish escapees from the nightly transport trains to Auschwitz. Romek and other children witness the frantic Jewish people jumping from the trains and being captured and robbed.

Polish critics praised Bogayevicz's ability to work with child actors, but voiced their reservations concerning the film's clichéd storyline, superficiality of the characters, as well as some artificiality regarding the representation of the rural community.[88] At the Festival of Polish Films in Gdynia in 2001, the film was perceived as an American product: in English (with the exception of a Polish prayer in the church), with (often) fake Polish accents, recognizable American stars, and offering an "external look" at the Polish countryside that is captured by Paweł Edelman's camera in a picturesque manner, as if evoking distant childhood memories. Interestingly, Bogayevicz received Best Screenplay Award at the Gdynia festival and the film also received nominations in several categories for the Polish Film Awards "Eagles" (Orły), an annual film award granted since 1999 by the members of the Polish Film Academy (Polska Akademia Filmowa). *Edges of the Lord* was theatrically released in Poland and several other Western European countries. In the United States, the film was released only on DVD and as late as 2005, which is surprising given the presence of two American stars, Osment and Dafoe.

***

The Pianist (2002), Roman Polański's celebrated Holocaust drama, is based on the memoirs written by Polish-Jewish composer and pianist Władysław Szpilman (1911–2000), and published for the first time in an abbreviated, censored version in 1946.[89] Polański's Polish, French, and British co-production in English premiered at the Cannes Film Festival where it won the Golden Palm.[90] Among numerous awards that *The Pianist* later received are three Academy Awards, for Best Director (Polański), Best Adapted Screenplay (Ronald Harwood), and Best Actor (Adrien Brody). In addition, the film won eight Polish Film Awards "Eagles," including best film, director, cinematographer (Paweł Edelman), set designer (Allan Starski), music (Wojciech Kilar), costume designer (Anna Sheppard), and editor (Jean-Marie Blondel). The film also won three BAFTA awards, seven French César Awards, and cinematographer Edelman won the European Film Award for Best Cinematography.

Szpilman's powerful yet laconic and understated story of survival also provided an inspiration for one of the earliest projects in the history of Polish postwar cinema, Jerzy Zarzycki's film titled *The Warsaw Robinson* (*Robinson Warszawski*), which focused on the last stages of Szpilman's (Rafalski's in the film) survival. The first draft of the script, linking the story of one man's survival amid the ruins of Warsaw with the novel by Daniel Defoe (*Robinson Crusoe*), was written by Czesław Miłosz and Jerzy Andrzejewski in the spring of 1945, and was based on their conversations with Szpilman. They portrayed the Warsaw Robinson as a desperate loner who witnesses the destruction of his city. Later, the protagonist is accompanied by a young woman whom he had been able to rescue. The final scenes of the early version of the project pictured Rafalski accidentally killed before Warsaw had been "liberated" by the Soviets.

The project was discussed on 24 June 1945 at the meeting of the Committee for Evaluating Film Scripts. The committee, chaired by Aleksander Ford (head of Film Polski), rejected the project because of its alleged apolitical stand. The head of the Scriptwriting Office, Jerzy Toeplitz, stated that "the danger of the film is a certain passivity of the protagonists; their fate is not decided by them but by the forces beyond their control." The committee members recommended several revisions to overcome the "passivity" of the main character. In particular, they postulated grounding the story within the proper (communist) ideological and political framework.[91]

The film authorities decided to shelve the project until 1948. Several changes introduced during this year (but without Czesław Miłosz, who abandoned the project) included, among others, linking the fate of the characters surviving among the ruins of Warsaw with the Red Army's attempt to liberate the city, emphasizing the role of the Polish communist underground, and stressing the brutality of the Germans (in scenes showing the high-ranked German officers discussing the annihilation of the city). *The Warsaw Robinson* was shown in November 1949 at the congress of filmmakers at Wisła, during which the doctrine of socialist realism was officially enforced in Poland. Attacked for its lack of "revolutionary spirit," Zarzycki's film underwent further modifications (such as highlighting the role of the Soviet army and the addition of a Soviet soldier amid the ruins), and was released in December 1950 under the more politically appropriate title, *The Unvanquished City* (*Miasto nieujarzmione*).[92] The film had more than five million viewers in Poland, and is number seventy-two on the list of the box-office hits on Polish screens from 1945 to 2000.[93] Undoubtedly, the desire of Polish audiences to see a local film was greater than the film's noticeable weaknesses and its grave distortion of recent history.

The Unvanquished City should be seen as a travesty of Szpilman's memoirs. It is at the service of the communist ideology by viciously attacking the nationalist forces represented by the Home Army. The earlier version of the film, *The Warsaw Robinson*, opens with a voice-over narration offering the

Stalinist interpretation of the Warsaw Rising: "The film tells the story of five people who remained in the capital city that was shamelessly betrayed by the fascist commanders of the Home Army (AK) and given away to the German fascists." After the camera introduces the main character, Rafalski (Jan Kurnakowicz), the voice-over stresses his close links with the communist underground. The film is intended, as the narrator explains, "as a document of the fascist crime and fascist barbarity," and also as "a call to fight with all forms of fascism."

The theatrically released version, *The Unvanquished City*, tones down the vicious opening comment about the "fascists AK commanders," but also bluntly accuses the AK leadership of destroying the city hand in hand with the Germans. The film then follows not a surviving Jewish man (Szpilman), but a Polish working class character who witnesses the destruction of Warsaw (Figure 6.13). He rescues and then takes care of a young woman, Krystyna (Zofia Mrozowska), who later falls in love with one of the communist underground fighters. In line with the tenets of socialist realist cinema, Rafalski also works closely with a group of Polish communists and a Soviet paratrooper who operates the radio transmitter and informs his commanders about German positions. The Soviet soldier dies a heroic death. Surrounded by the Germans, he directs distant Soviet artillery fire onto his house. The film ends with the liberation of Warsaw, the parade of Soviet and Polish troops before their march toward Berlin (which is witnessed by Rafalski), and an uplifting commentary that encourages everybody to rebuild the country. It is important to note that the casting of a Jewish protagonist in order to remain true to the spirit of Szpilman's memoirs was never considered. His story of survival had to wait for more than fifty years to be faithfully adapted for the screen by Polański.

The Pianist, Polański's second film made in Poland since his 1962 debut, *Knife in the Water* (*Nóż w wodzie*), also marks his first cinematic return to his own wartime childhood experiences. Polański was born in 1933 in Paris in a family of Polonized Jews who returned to Poland two years before World War

Figure 6.13: Jan Kurnakowicz as Rafalski in Jerzy Zarzycki's *Unvanquished City* (1950)

II. He survived the war by escaping from the Kraków Ghetto and hiding in the Polish countryside (his mother died in a concentration camp). After the war, he studied at the Łódź Film School, graduating in 1957. His career started with a series of very well-received short films, including *Two Men and a Wardrobe* (*Dwaj ludzie z szafą*, 1958), *When Angels Fall* (*Gdy spadają anioły*, 1959), and *Mammals* (*Ssaki*, 1962). He also acted in several films, including Andrzej Wajda's *A Generation* (1955). In 1962, Polański directed his first feature-length film, *Knife in the Water* (*Nóż w wodzie*), for which he received the first Polish nomination for an Academy Award in 1963. Following the criticism of his film by the communist authorities, he left Poland.[94]

Szpilman's full, uncensored story appeared in Polish in 2001, with the foreword by his son Andrzej Szpilman, and with additional excerpts from memoirs written by the German Captain, Wilhelm Hosenfeld.[95] Polański often stated that he became attracted to Szpilman's account of survival because the book described events that he remembered from his own childhood in the Kraków Ghetto, the experiences he extensively discussed in his memoirs titled *Roman by Polanski*.[96] Earlier, Polański never cinematically revisited the places associated with his childhood trauma, although several of his films were analyzed by critics through the prism of his biography. Certain elements of his cinema, namely the prevailing images of the violent and the grotesque, were often attributed by critics to darker sides of Polański's life (such as surviving the Holocaust and the murder of his wife, Sharon Tate). Like *The Pianist*, where Szpilman and his family lose control over their fate and experience entrapment in the ghetto, some of Polański's earlier films, most notably *Repulsion* (1965) and *The Tenant* (*Le Locataire*, 1976), deal with the loss of personal space and its impact on the protagonist. Similar to *The Tenant*, Polański infuses *The Pianist* with situations that come from his biography and are detailed in his memoirs. For example, he describes images of erecting the ghetto wall ("They are walling us in") and the early stages of life in the ghetto ("During these early months the ghetto was—despite periodic bouts of terror—a self contained town where people went courting, got married, and even entertained").[97]

The Pianist opens with a brief documentary prologue featuring black-and-white shots of prewar Warsaw, and then introduces the twenty-eight-year-old Szpilman (in Adrien Brody's memorable performance) playing Chopin in the final broadcast of the Polish Radio on 23 September 1939. The concert continues despite the bombardment of the city and is abruptly terminated only when a bomb hits the station. Polański's film continues to narrate the linear story of Szpilman's survival in the Warsaw Ghetto, the separation from his family at the *Umschlagplatz*, his escape from the ghetto and hiding on the Aryan side, and his ordeal after the Warsaw Rising in the city that became destroyed and desolate. *The Pianist* ends with postwar scenes portraying Szpilman resuming his work for the Polish Radio and trying to learn about the fate of Captain Hosenfeld (Thomas Kretschmann), one of many people who helped him to survive.[98] (See Figure 6.14.)

178 Polish Film and the Holocaust

Polański's film is sincere and simple, a fact emphasized by numerous critics, for example by Leonard Quart who notices "a striking lack of theatrics or emotional manipulation."[99] *The Pianist*'s linear action introduces several scenes familiar from earlier Polish narrative films as well as from well-known documentary footage: triumphant German soldiers marching on the streets of Warsaw, the announcement of anti-Jewish decrees resulting at first in the imposition of a number of restrictions on the Warsaw Jews that slowly take away their rights, the creation of the ghetto, images of the Jewish population being forcefully relocated to the ghetto, scenes showing the building of the wall that separates them from the Poles, images of poverty, overcrowding, hunger, German cruelty, brutalization, divisions between the rich and the poor inside the ghetto, young smugglers bringing food to the ghetto, the throwing of bread over the wall, and random executions witnessed by the protagonist. Polański also portrays a German crew filming in the ghetto, and he also recreates some of the iconic images of the Warsaw Ghetto Uprising, for example the photograph of General SS Jürgen Stroop from May 1943 (Figure 6.15).

Following the majority of Polish Holocaust films, in *The Pianist* Polański portrays an assimilated middle-class Jew who, like Korczak, is both Polish and Jewish, proudly bearing the emblems of the two nationalities and being respected by both. The beginning of the occupation separates him from the

Figure 6.14: Adrien Brody as Szpilman (center) and his family in Roman Polański's *The Pianist* (2002)

Figure 6.15: A scene from *The Pianist*

Poles, brutally reminds him of his Jewishness, castigates him as the "other," and imperils his life. His friends, "the poor Poles" from the Aryan side, watch his misery and try to help him. In the film, Szpilman is portrayed not as a heroic man, but as a character overwhelmed by the reality that surrounds him. He survives due to a combination of blind chances and sheer luck. He is portrayed as a helpless eyewitness to the horrors that are difficult for him to comprehend. Brody's understated performance brings to mind Borowski-like detachment and irony. The camera is on Brody when he wanders the streets of Warsaw; it registers his transformation from a successful middle-class musician to a hunted fugitive in desperate search for shelter and food. With luck on his side, he survives random executions and is able to meet some honest people—Poles, Jews, and a German officer—who make his survival possible.

Polański resorts to long shots to portray Szpilman's loneliness. For example, after the separation from his family at the *Umschlagplatz*, where he witnessed them and other Jewish people being herded onto the train, he walks in despair on a desolated street, surrounded by belongings left behind by those who were sent to death camps (Figure 6.16). Another memorable shot, an extreme long shot, depicts Szpilman crawling over the ghetto wall and entering the almost completely destroyed part of Warsaw. The camera portrays him as a twentieth-century urban Robinson Crusoe amid the ruins of Warsaw (Figure 6.17).

Figure 6.16: Szpilman (Adrien Brody). *The Pianist*

Figure 6.17: A scene from *The Pianist*

Figure 6.18: Adrien Brody as Szpilman in *The Pianist*

In *The Pianist*, Szpilman seems almost detached "as if he himself was watching a film."[100] He "meanders through the confined space of the ghetto and of Warsaw and he looks obliquely through windows, small gaps and around corners at the catastrophe, he never sees the totality of the action, the complete picture, and neither do we."[101] The viewer follows Szpilman during his odyssey through Warsaw and witnesses the horror of destruction. Szpilman is a passive observer of atrocities in the ghetto, and later, from his shelter on the Aryan side, he watches the Warsaw Ghetto Uprising (Figure 6.18). The passivity of Szpilman's character, so vehemently criticized by the communist authorities immediately after the war, still seems to trouble some critics who would rather see a "man of action" rather than a passive spectator. Comments stressing that Szpilman's character "learns nothing from his horrific experiences" follow this line of criticism, which prevented Szpilman's story from being adequately portrayed in 1950.[102]

Instead of a faithful adaptation of Szpilman's account of survival, several Polish critics expected Polański to imprint his artistic stamp on his version of the Holocaust drama. Given Polański's manipulation of generic rules and the strong presence of an authorial self, these critics hoped that *The Pianist* would exhibit Polański's personal thematic obsessions. They were slightly disappointed that he produced a conventional Holocaust film—well narrated, visually powerful, but conventional in its representation of the Holocaust.

Notes

1. See, for example, an essay by Jean-Charles Szurek, "Shoah: From the Jewish Question to the Polish Question," in *Claude Lanzmann's Shoah: Key Essays*, ed. Stuart Liebman (Oxford: Oxford University Press, 2007), 149–169.
2. For example, André Pierre Colombat, *The Holocaust in French Film* (Metuchen: Scarecrow Press, 1993), 299–344; Stefan Korboński, *The Jews and the Poles on World War II* (New York: Hippocrene Books, 1989), 107–125.
3. Quoted from Dominick LaCapra, *History and Memory after Auschwitz* (Ithaca: Cornell University Press, 1998), 96.

4. Lawrence Baron, *Projecting the Holocaust into the Present: The Changing Focus of Contemporary Holocaust Cinema* (Lanham: Rowman and Littlefield, 2005), 8.
5. Jan Błoński, "Biedni Polacy patrzą na getto," *Tygodnik Powszechny* vol. 41, no. 2 (11 January 1987): 1 and 4. For the translation of Błoński's essay and the discussion it initiated in Poland see *"My Brother's Keeper?" Recent Polish Debates on the Holocaust*, ed. Antony Polonsky (London and New York: Routledge, 1990), 34–52.
6. The debates about Poles and Jews were also stirred by the controversies surrounding the Carmelite Convent founded in 1984 at Auschwitz. A symbol of Polish as well as Jewish trauma, Auschwitz once again became a major point of disagreement. Geneviève Zubrzycki writes about the "memory war" in her illuminating study *The Crosses of Auschwitz: Nationalism and Religion in Post-Communist Poland* (Chicago: University of Chicago Press, 2006), 139. See also Władysław Bartoszewski, *The Convent at Auschwitz* (London: Bowerdean Press, 1990) and Carol Rittner and John K. Roth, eds., *Memory Offended: The Auschwitz Convent Controversy* (New York: Praeger, 1991).
7. Jarosław Marek Rymkiewicz, *Final Solution: Umschlagplatz*, trans. Nina Taylor (New York: Farrar, Straus and Giroux, 1994) [originally published in Polish as *Umschlagplatz* (Paris: Instytut Literacki, 1988)]; Andrzej Szczypiorski, *The Beautiful Mrs. Seidenman*, trans. Klara Główczewska (New York: Grove Weidenfeld, 1989) [originally published as *Początek* (Paris: Instytut Literacki, 1986)]; Paweł Huelle, *Who Was David Weiser?* trans. Michael Kandel (Orlando: Harcourt, 1994) [originally published in Poland as *Weiser Davidek* (Gdańsk: Wydawnictwo Morskie, 1987)]; Piotr Szewc, *Annihilation*, trans. Ewa Hryniewicz-Yarbrough (Dalkey Archive Press, 1993) [originally published as *Zagłada* (Warsaw: Czytelnik, 1987)].
8. Robert DiAntonio's review of *The Beautiful Mrs. Seidenman*, *World Literature Today* vol. 65, no. 1 (1991): 145.
9. Jarosław Iwaszkiewicz's short story "Kościół w Skaryszewie" was published in 1968. The story was also adapted by Władysław Wasilewski in his short film made in 1969 at the Łódź Film School (PWSTiF).
10. The Holocaust references are also present in Stanisław Różewicz's later film, *An Angel in the Wardrobe (Anioł w szafie*, 1988). In this film, the protagonist meets an old Jew at a Jewish cemetery who tells him about his escape from a transport to a death camp.
11. Stryjkowski's *Austeria* appeared in 1972 in English as *The Inn*, translated by Celina Wieniewska, and published in New York by Harcourt, Brace, Jovanovich.
12. Quoted from Bolesław Michałek and Frank Turaj, *The Modern Cinema of Poland* (Bloomington: Indiana University Press, 1988), 112.
13. Quoted from the documentary film, *My Seventeen Lives (Żyłem 17 razy)*, directed by Tadeusz Bystram and Stanisław Zawiśliński, produced by the Film Studio "Kadr" and the Polish Film Institute (PISF) in 2009.
14. Gabriella Safran, "Dancing with Death and Salvaging Jewish Culture in *Austeria* and *The Dybbuk*," *Slavic Review* vol. 59, no. 4 (2000): 762.
15. Daria Mazur, "Paradoks i topika judajska. *Austeria* Jerzego Kawalerowicza," in *Gefilte film: Wątki żydowskie w kinie*, ed. Joanna Preizner (Kraków: Azolem Alejchem, 2008), 147. Several Polish reviewers emphasized the parallel between the reality portrayed in *Austeria* and the Holocaust, for example, Krzysztof Teodor Toeplitz, "Krajobraz przed Zagładą" [The Landscape Before the Holocaust], *Miesięcznik Literacki* 6 (1983): 81–85 and Michał Boni, "Przed dniem ostatnim" [Before the Last Day], *Kino* 4 (1983): 5–8.
16. Documents related to *Austeria*, and held at the archive of the Central Committee (KC) of PZPR, were recently reprinted by Przemysław Kaniecki in his "Z archiwum KC PZPR: Sprawa *Austerii* Jerzego Kawalerowicza," *Studia Filmoznawcze 30*, ed. Sławomir Bobowski (Wrocław: Wydawnictwo Uniwersytetu Wrocławskiego, 2009), 207. See also comments included in the documentary film about Jerzy Kawalerowicz's career, *My Seventeen Lives*, ibid.

17. Iwona Irvin-Zarecka, *Neutralizing Memory: The Jew in Contemporary Poland* (New Brunswick, NJ: Transaction, 1989), 119.
18. Safran, "Dancing with Death," 761.
19. Jerzy Hoffman is a versatile director. He started his career with now classic documentary films, later made comedies, transplanted the Western genre (in *Law and Fist*; *Prawo i pięść*, 1964, co-directed with Edward Skórzewski), adapted well-known literary pieces (*The Leper*; *Trędowata*, 1976 and *The Quack, Znachor*, 1982), and made a political war drama, *Till the Last Drop of Blood* (*Do krwi ostatniej*, 1978).
20. Tadeusz Sobolewski, "Czy film współczesny jest możliwy?" *Kino* 1 (1985): 8.
21. Oskar Sobański, "Opowieść o Rut," *Film* 39 (1984): 9; Henryk Tronowicz, "Obrazy okupacyjnego koszmaru," *Kino* 11 (1984): 8–10.
22. "Stenogram z posiedzenia Komisji Kolaudacyjnej Filmów Fabularnych w dniu 28 grudnia 1983," National Film Archive in Warsaw, A-344/352. The original title of the film was *You Must Live* (*Musisz żyć*).
23. Ibid.
24. Rosenberg's attempts to maintain dignity were emphasized by several Polish reviewers. For example, Bożena Janicka, "Ściana," *Film* 12 (1984): 9; Krzysztof Stanisławski, "Pan Mundstock idzie do gazu," *Kino* 9 (1983): 12–14.
25. J.T., "Kartka z podróży," *Filmowy Serwis Prasowy* 3–4 (1984): 2.
26. "Stenogram z posiedzenia Kolisji Kolaudacyjnej Filmów Fabularnych w dniu 2 marca 1983." National Film Archive in Warsaw, A-344/322.
27. I discuss the post-martial law period in my *Polish National Cinema* (New York: Berghahn Books, 2002), 164–171.
28. Elżbieta Ostrowska, "Between Fear and Attraction: Images of 'Other' Women," in Ewa Mazierska and Elżbieta Ostrowska, *Women in Polish Cinema* (New York: Berghahn Books, 2006), 33.
29. Karen Jaehne, "Angry Harvest," *Cineaste* vol. 15, no. 1 (1986): 39.
30. "Stenogram z posiedzenia Komisji Kolaudacyjnej Filmów Fabularnych w dniu 28 czerwca 1983 r." National Film Archive in Warsaw, A-344/337.
31. "Stenogram z posiedzenia Komisji Kolaudacyjnej Filmów Fabularnych w dniu 21 grudnia 1985," National Film Archive in Warsaw, A-344/424.
32. Ibid.
33. In 2009, John Kent Harrison directed a film about Irena Sendler, *The Courageous Heart of Irena Sendler*, with Anna Paquin in a Golden Globe nominated performance.
34. "Stenogram z posiedzenia Komisji Kolaudacyjnej Filmów Fabularnych w dniu 21 grudnia 1985," ibid.
35. For an insightful analysis and interview with the director, see the online Danish film journal *P.O.W.* no. 15 (March 2003), http://pov.imv.au.dk/Issue_15/POV_15cnt.html. The history of the famous archival photograph is thoroughly discussed by Richard Raskin in his *A Child at Gunpoint* (Aarhus: Aarhus University Press, 2004).
36. For comments on *Decalogue* see my *The Cinema of Krzysztof Kieślowski: Variations on Destiny and Chance* (London: Wallflower, 2004), 75–107. I use fragments of a subchapter on *Decalogue 8* published there, 101–103.
37. Marianne Hirsch, *Family Frames: Photography, Narrative, and Postmemory* (Cambridge: Harvard University Press, 1997). Hirsch writes that "Postmemory is distinguished from memory by generational distance and from history by deep personal connection. Postmemory is a powerful and very particular form of memory precisely because its connection to its object or source is mediated not through recollection but through imaginative investment and creation. This is not to say that memory itself is unmediated, but that it is more directly connected to the past. Postmemory characterizes the experience of those who grow up dominated by narratives that preceded their birth, whose own belated stories are evacuated by the stories of the previous generation shaped by traumatic events that can be neither understood nor recreated" (p. 22).

38. Marcia Landy, *Cinematic Use of the Past* (Minneapolis: University of Minnesota Press, 1996), 250.
39. Krzysztof Kucharski, *Kino Plus. Film i dystrybucja kinowa w Polsce w latach 1990–2000* (Toruń: Oficyna Wydawnicza Kucharski), 384.
40. Ibid., 383, 385. It has to be stressed that the low number of cinema theaters in Poland and the very low average number of theater visits per inhabitant after 1989, coupled with the growing production costs, made it difficult for Polish filmmakers to compete with Hollywood films. One hundred thousand viewers for a single Polish film had been considered high by Polish standards. For example, out of 140 Polish films released in theaters from 1991 to 2000, only 45 received such a comparatively modest result.
41. Allan Starski and Ewa Braun won Oscar awards in the Best Art Direction—Set Decoration category for their work on Spielberg's *Schindler's List*.
42. See Susan Linville, "*Europa, Europa*: A Test Case for German National Cinema," *Wide Angle* vol. 16, no. 3 (1995): 38–50.
43. See Andrew Charlesworth, "Contesting Places of Memory: The Case of Auschwitz," *Environment and Planning D: Society and Space* 12 (1994): 585.
44. Iga Czarnawska, ed. *Krzysztof Zanussi. Sylwetka artysty* (Warsaw: Oficyna Wydawniczo-Poligraficzna "Adam," 2008), 227.
45. Tadeusz Sobolewski, "Rozmowy po kinie: Przełamywanie obcości," *Kino* 7 (1991): 20.
46. Tadeusz Borowski, "Pożegnanie z Marią," the title piece of a collection of short stories, *Pożegnanie z Marią*, first published in Warsaw in 1947.
47. Interestingly, in 1985 Zylber made a medium-length film, *Don't Be Afraid* (*Nie bój się*), which focuses on a young Jewish boy who is hiding with the Polish Catholic family. Unable to cope with the new situation and the new religion, he decides to give himself up to the Germans.
48. Bożena Janicka, "Coś zostało w powietrzu—mówi Filip Zylber," *Kino* 3 (1994): 13.
49. Tadeusz Lubelski, "Borowski na dziś," *Kino* 3 (1994): 15.
50. In Borowski's short story the emphasis is on the old Jewish woman; the nameless young one performs only a marginal role. This characterization was repeated by Jerzy Antczak in his memorable 1966 television adaptation with Ida Kamińska (the star of *The Shop on Main Street*) in the leading role. Kamińska was accompanied by some iconic Polish actors, such as Tadeusz Łomnicki, Jan Świderski, and Zbigniew Zapasiewicz.
51. Jerzy Kosiński, *The Painted Bird* (New York: Harcourt Brace Jovanovich, 1970). Kolski admitted on several occasions that he was unaware of Kosinski's novel when he was working on his film.
52. Kolski's film also deserves to be analyzed in the context of rapid post-1989 privatizations, threats of losing properties gained during the communist period.
53. Marek Hendrykowski, ed., *Debiuty polskiego kina* (Konin: Wydawnictwo "Przegląd Koniński," 1998), 312.
54. Jerzy Kapuściński, "Czas przyczyn" [interview with Jan Jakub Kolski], *Kino* 8 (1991): 43.
55. Jan Jakub Kolski, *Kulka z chleba* (Warsaw: Twój Styl, 1998), 366.
56. Quoted from Natasza Koczarowska, "Mechanizm kreowania 'tożsamości żydowskiej': *Pogrzeb kartofla* Jana Jakuba Kolskiego," in *Gefilte film: Wątki żydowskie w kinie*, ed. Joanna Preizner (Kraków: Szolem Alejchem, 2008): 224. Originally published in Katarzyna Janowska and Piotr Mucharski, eds, *Rozmowy na nowy wiek* (Kraków: Znak, 2002).
57. Polish reviewers often emphasized that *Kornblumenblau* is a parable on an artist in a totalitarian system, a film about "the misery of art." See Mirosław Przylipiak, "Nędza sztuki" [The Misery of Art], *Kino* 3 (1990): 13–16; Janusz Wróblewski, "Karaluchy w złotych pancerzykach" [Cockroaches with Golden Outer Shells], *Kino* 11 (1989): 12–15.
58. Bolesław W. Lewicki, "Temat: Oświęcim," *Kino* 6 (1968): 16. An Auschwitz survivor, Lewicki later became one of the founders of Film Studies in Poland. He was professor at the University of Łódź and the Łódź Film School, and head of the latter (1968–1969). Lewicki also published his camp memoirs *Wiesz jak jest* (Łódź: Wydawnictwo Łódzkie, 1974).

59. Kazimierz Tymiński, the author of the literary source—memoirs from Auschwitz titled *To Calm Down the Sleep* (*Uspokoić sen*, 1985)—commented during the Film Approval Committee meeting that Wosiewicz's work could have been stronger and his images harsher. He noticed that in Auschwitz at some point his weight was only 39 kilograms. "*Kornblumenblau*. Stenogram z posiedzenia Komisji Kolaudacyjnej Filmów Fabularnych, 2 sierpień 1988." National Film Archive in Warsaw, A-344/566. It has to be said that, despite some obvious references, the name Auschwitz is not uttered on the screen.

60. Marta Wróbel, "Tadzikowe perypetie z totalitaryzmem. Metaforyzacja rzeczywistości lagrowej w filmie *Kornblumenblau* Leszka Wosiewicza," *Kwartalnik Filmowy* 29–30 (2000): 105.

61. Libby Saxton, *Haunted Images: Film, Ethics, Testimony and the Holocaust* (London: Wallflower Press, 2008), 71. Saxton writes that "In breaking the taboo on showing industrialized mass murder, Wosiewicz's harrowing reconstruction raises questions about the ethical position of the spectator face to face with suffering, violence and death. Furthermore, by casting its protagonists as observers and witnesses and by representing looking as a political and ethical act, *Kornblumenblau* invites us to consider the responsibilities conferred on viewers by the spectacle of violence, whether we are witnessing it first-hand, without mediation, or watching it on a screen." Ibid., 69.

62. Annette Insdorf, *Indelible Shadows: Film and the Holocaust* (Cambridge: Cambridge University Press, 2003), 341.

63. In 1979, Szlachtycz produced two television films in Yiddish, both filmed stage performances by the State Jewish Theater in Warsaw: *The Dybbuk* (*Der Dibuk*) by S. An-ski (Shloyme Zanvl Rappoport) and *The Comedians* (*Komedianci*, *Cwaj kuni-lemel*) by Abraham Goldfaden.

64. Ewa Mazierska, ed., "Tragarz puchu," *Filmowy Serwis Prasowy* 11 (1992): 14.

65. Bożena Jędrzejczak, "Malarz aniołów" [interview with Ryszard Brylski], *Film* 3 (1996): 54.

66. Tadeusz Sobolewski, "Bajka o ludziach. Z Hanną Krall rozmawia Tadeusz Sobolewski," *Kino* 2 (2001): 7. Journalist and writer Hanna Krall was born in 1937 into an assimilated Jewish family who perished during the war. She survived the occupation hiding with several Polish families. Her major works deal with the Holocaust and Jewish life in Poland.

67. The "magic realist" dimensions of Kolski's cinema are discussed by several critics and scholars, for example, Aga Skrodzka-Bates, "The Vernacular Cinema of Jan Jakub Kolski," *Kinokultura* 2 (2005), http://www.kinokultura.com/specials/2/skrodzka.shtml.

68. Barbara Hollender, "Jeden strach, jedna miłość" [interview with Hanna Krall and Jan Jakub Kolski], *Rzeczpospolita* 267 (16 November 2000): 10.

69. Katarzyna Bielas, Od środka" [interview with Jan Jakub Kolski], *Gazeta Wyborcza* 264 (13 November 2000): 14.

70. Sobolewski, "Bajka o ludziach, 7.

71. Ostrowska, "Between Fear and Attraction," 142.

72. Elżbieta Ostrowska offers a detailed discussion concerning the representation of Polish and Jewish women in Kolski's film in her "Between Fear and Attraction," 141–146.

73. Joanna Preizner, "Macierzyństwo w czasach Zagłady: *Daleko od okna* Jana Jakuba Kolskiego i *Wybór Zofii* Alana Pakuli," *Kultura Popularna* vol. 2, no. 12 (2005): 85.

74. Hollender, "Jeden strach, jedna miłość," 10.

75. See Anita Piotrowska, "Opowieść o kobiecie z szafy," *Tygodnik Powszechny* 48 (2000): 17.

76. Kucharski, *Kino Plus*, 387.

77. Jan T. Gross, *Neighbors: The Destruction of the Jewish Community in Jedwabne* (Princeton: Princeton University Press, 2001).

78. Jan T. Gross, *Sąsiedzi. Historia zagłady żydowskiego miasteczka* (Sejny: Fundacja Pogranicze, 2000). For debates in Poland on Gross's book see Antony Polonsky and Joanna B. Michlic, eds., *The Neighbors Respond: The Controversy over the Jedwabne Massacre in Poland* (Princeton: Princeton University Press, 2003). Also, several essays in Dorota Głowacka and Joanna Zylinska, eds., *Imaginary Neighbors: Mediating Polish-Jewish Relations after the Holocaust* (Lincoln: University of Nebraska Press, 2007).

79. Piotr Wróbel, "Polish-Jewish Relations and *Neighbors* by Jan T. Gross: Politics, Public Opinion, and Historical Methodology," in *Lessons and Legacies: The Holocaust in International Perspective*, ed. Dagmar Herzog (Evanston: Northwestern University Press, 2006), 396.
80. Ibid., 389.
81. Ibid., 388.
82. Glowacka and Zylinska, *Imaginary Neighbors*, 4.
83. Jan T. Gross, "Annals of War, 'Neighbors,'" *The New Yorker* (12 March 2001): 64.
84. Earlier, Agnieszka Arnold made two documentary films that referred to the Holocaust: *Small Town* (*Miasteczko*, 1995) and *The Rescued* (*Ocalona*, 1996).
85. For insightful comments see Joanna Tokarska-Bakir, "Jedwabne: History as Fetish," in *Imaginary Neighbors*, 40-63. Also, Michał Bilewicz, "Nie tylko o *Strachu*: Psychologia potocznego rozumienia historii," *Zagłada Żydów. Studia i Materiały* 4 (2008): 517-526.
86. Several Polish reviewers noticed that the choice of the main character's name, Romek, is not accidental in the film and bears strong resemblance to Roman (Romek) Polański's story of survival.
87. Łukasz Maciejewski, "Autoterapia" [interview with Yurek Bogayevicz], *Kino* 11 (2001): 9.
88. See Tadeusz Lubelski, "Neighbours and Brothers," *Kino* 10 (2001): 44-45.
89. Władysław Szpilman, *Śmierć miasta. Pamiętniki Władysława Szpilmana*, edited by Jerzy Waldorff (Warsaw, 1946). Fragments of Szpilman's memoirs appeared earlier, in 1946, in a Polish journal *Przekrój*. The censor changed the nationality of Captain Hosenfeld from German to Austrian. Born in Sosnowiec, Władysław Szpilman established himself as a composer, pianist, and author of memoirs. Before World War II, he worked in Polish Radio. During the war, he performed in a duet with Artur Goldfeder in the Warsaw Ghetto cafés. Since 13 February 1943, he was hiding on the Aryan side, where he survived the Warsaw Rising and its aftermath until January 1945, when the Soviets entered the city. After the war, he returned to the radio, founded the Warsaw Quintet, and performed in Poland and abroad. He is also the author of dozens of popular Polish songs. In 2004, Marek Drążewski made a biographical, medium length documentary about Szpilman's life, *Władysław Szpilman 1911-2000: In His Own Words* (*Władysław Szpilman 1911-2000—własnymi słowami*).
90. Poland contributed only 7 percent to the film's overall budget, which is estimated at 36 million Euros. Iwona Cegiełkówna, "Nie strzelać do *Pianisty* [interview with Lew Rywin]," *Kino* 9 (2002): 12.
91. "Protokół z posiedzenia Komisji Kwalifikującej Scenariusze z dnia 24 czerwca 1945 roku." Reprinted by Alina Madej in *Kino* 9 (1990): 16.
92. The early stages of Zarzycki's film are discussed by Barbara Mruklik in her "Film Fabularny," in *Historia filmu polskiego vol. 3*, ed. Jerzy Toeplitz (Warsaw: Wydawnictwa Artystyczne i Filmowe, 1974), 223-226.
93. Kucharski, *Kino Plus*, 389.
94. Polański's films made outside of Poland include works made in England, France, and the United States. For *Repulsion* (1965), starring Catherine Deneuve, he won the Special Award and the FIPRESCI award at the Berlin Film Festival. He won that festival the next year with a grotesque drama that he directed in England, *Cul-de-sac*. His first American film, an adaptation of Ira Levin's bestselling horror novel *Rosemary's Baby* (1968), starring Mia Farrow and John Cassavetes, brought him respect and popularity. In 1969, following the murder of his pregnant wife, actress Sharon Tate, he left the United States. In 1974, he returned to America to direct another classic Hollywood film, *Chinatown*, starring Jack Nicholson. After his conviction for statutory rape, he fled to France, where he directed a series of films, most of them with American involvement, for example *The Tenant* (*Le Locataire*, 1976), *Tess* (1979), *Frantic* (1988), and *The Ninth Gate* (2000). Polański received several Polish honors, including an honorary doctorate from the Łódź Film School in 2000 and The Polish Film Award "Eagle" for Lifetime Achievement in 2003.
95. Władysław Szpilman, *Pianista. Warszawskie wspomnienia 1939-1945* (Kraków: Znak, 2001).

96. Roman Polanski, *Roman by Polanski* (New York: William Morrow, 1984), 21–35.
97. Ibid., 23, 24.
98. The sad irony of Hosenfeld's life, the officer who died in 1952 in a Soviet camp, as *The Pianist*'s postscript informs the viewer, was covered later in a documentary film by Marek Drążewski, *We Owe Him Our Lives (Dzięki niemu żyjemy,* 2008).
99. Leonard Quart, "The Pianist," *Cineaste* vol. 28, no. 3 (2003): 43.
100. Wojtek Kość, "Weirdness Through Simplicity: Roman Polanski's *The Pianist*," *Kinoeye* vol. 2, no. 20 (2002). http://www.kinoeye.org/02/20/kosc20.php (accessed 18 February 2008).
101. Michael Stevenson, "*The Pianist* and Its Contexts: Polanski's Narration of Holocaust Evasion and Survival," in *The Cinema of Roman Polanski: Dark Spaces of the World*, ed. John Orr and Elżbieta Ostrowska (London: Wallflower Press, 2006), 149.
102. Michael B. Oren, "Schindler's Liszt: Roman Polanski's Mistake about the Holocaust," *The New Republic* vol. 228, no. 10 (2003): 25.

Chapter 7

ANDRZEJ WAJDA RESPONDS: KORCZAK (1990) AND HOLY WEEK (1996)

Since the beginning of his career, Andrzej Wajda has frequently cast his films with Jewish characters. He devoted more time to Polish-Jewish relationships than any other major Polish director. Wajda has stated on several occasions that Jewish characters and topics are present in his films because they are present in Polish lives: "One cannot be a Polish filmmaker and completely disregard this matter."[1] Wajda's often proclaimed ambition has been to reconcile Poles and Jews. The scriptwriter of *Korczak*, Agnieszka Holland, explains that Wajda "keeps doing movies about that, it's his own obsession, the guilt."[2] Given the above, it should come as no surprise that he chose the story of Korczak as his first film after the 1989 return of democracy in Poland (see Figure 7.1).

Figure 7.1: Andrzej Wajda on the set of *Korczak* (1990). © Film Studio "Perspektywa"

At the beginning of the 1990s, when Wajda could freely portray Korczak's biography on the screen, Polish audiences and critics alike seemed to have grown tired of history, politics, and national martyrology. Wajda's film, an attempt to recover long-suppressed levels of national memory, failed at the box-office. Its premiere coincided with a deep economic crisis within the Polish film industry: rapid decrease of the number of cinema theaters and the dominance of heavily promoted and well-distributed American films.

"Everything I made after *Danton*, I consider films of wasted opportunities," claimed Wajda, explaining the mixed public and critical reactions to some of his films made between 1983 and 1995.[3] *Korczak* is a perfect example. This "casualty of Jewish-Polish polemics," as Lawrence Baron rightly describes it,[4] portrays a figure of great importance for both Polish and Jewish cultures—Dr. Janusz Korczak (in reality, Józef Goldszmit, 1878–1942). Korczak was a famous writer, a well-known pediatrician, and a devoted pedagogue who in his writings and in practice always stressed the dignity of childhood. He worked with Polish as well as Jewish orphans. On 5 August 1942, he marched in the Warsaw Ghetto to the *Umschlagplatz* with two hundred of "his orphans" from a Jewish orphanage, the Orphans' Home (Dom Sierot). They all died in the gas chamber of Treblinka.[5]

***

Korczak's biography belongs to one of the oldest and the most prestigious projects in postwar Polish cinema. Due to various political circumstances, it had been postponed for more than four decades. Ludwik Starski submitted his first proposal about Korczak on 14 September 1945.[6] When he was working on the script, Korczak's saintly stature had been steadily growing among both Poles and Jews. The martyrological legend of Korczak, however, started during the war, in the Warsaw Ghetto. Władysław Szlengel, a Jewish poet writing in Polish in the ghetto, created a poem devoted to Korczak on 10 August 1942, titled "A Page from the Diary of the *Aktion*" (Kartka z dziennika Akcji). In this poem he compared the death of Korczak to the heroic Polish defense of the Westerplatte outpost in September of 1939:

> On this front, where death brings no glory,
> In this nightmare dance in the midst of night,
> He was the only proud soldier
> —Janusz Korczak, the orphan's guardian.
> What do you hear, neighbors from beyond the wall,
> Who look on at our deaths through the bars?
> Janusz Korczak died so that we
> Could also have our Westerplatte.[7]

Poems about Korczak were also published by Stefania Ney ("About Janusz Korczak"), Witold Zechenter ("How Janusz Korczak Took His Children to the Country"), and Antoni Słonimski ("A Song about Janusz Korczak").[8] Korczak also featured prominently in several accounts of wartime survival. For example, Władysław Szpilman recalled seeing Korczak and his children being deported to Treblinka:

> The evacuation of the Jewish orphanage run by Janusz Korczak had been ordered for that morning. The children were to have been taken away alone. He had the chance to save himself, and it was only with difficulty that he persuaded the Germans to take him too. He had spent long years of his life with children, and now, on his last journey, he would not leave them alone. He wanted to ease things for them. He told the orphans they were going out into the country, so they ought to be cheerful. At last they would be able to exchange the horrible, suffocating city walls for meadows of flowers, streams where they could bathe, woods full of berries and mushrooms. He told them to wear their best clothes, and so they came out into the yard, two by two, nicely dressed and in a happy mood ... When I met them in Gęsia Street the smiling children were singing in chorus, the little violinist was playing for them and Korczak was carrying two of the smallest infants, who were beaming too, and telling them some amusing story.[9]

In 1946, Korczak's friends and those who knew him founded the Committee to Commemorate Janusz Korczak (Komitet Uczczenia Pamięci Janusza Korczaka) that lasted until 1948.[10] In 1956, the year of the political thaw, the Korczak's Committee (Komitet Korczakowski) was formed, which called for the Archive Committee (Komisja Archiwalna) to collect materials dealing with Korczak's life and work. After 1968, when some members of the committee emigrated from Poland, the collection was moved to the building that once housed Korczak's orphanage, now a state orphanage named after him. Today, the archival materials are part of the Warsaw Historical Museum.

For reasons explained earlier in this book, surrounding the release of *Border Street* and other films, Ludwik Starski's project had to wait. In 1959, a West German producer born in Łódź, Artur Brauner, commissioned Starski to write a new version of the script for a possible co-production between Poland and West-Germany, with Aleksander Ford in mind as a director. The script was postponed due to other commitments by Ford—he was working on a historical epic, *The Teutonic Knights* (*Krzyżacy*), which was released in 1960. In 1965, a new contract was signed with Brauner. Soon after, the originator of the script, Starski, was replaced by Aleksander (Alexander) Ramati. Later, other names of foreign collaborators were added by Brauner. According to film historian Edward Zajiček, the preparatory work accelerated in 1967, and the Polish side was pressing to finalize the project. In March 1968, Film Polski decided to terminate the contract under the pretext that Brauner missed deadlines. The decision, obviously politically motivated, was protested by Brauner who successfully sued Film Polski.[11]

According to Paul Coates, the script by Ramati, which is preserved at the National Film Archive in Warsaw, "emphasizes Jewish resistance in the manner favored by the state of Israel but not by the Polish régime." Coates also describes the script as "highly melodramatic, making far less serious effort at historical verisimilitude than Agnieszka Holland's script for Wajda's film."[12] One may find the real concerns regarding the new version of the Korczak project by Ramati in the minutes of the Program Council of the Film Unit "Studio." Given the sensitivity of the topic, the council deliberated with the invited Communist Party apparatchiks and film administrators, including the head of Polish cinema (and deputy Minister of Culture) Tadeusz Zaorski.[13] The gathered officials voiced several reservations concerning the project. For Stanisław Trepczyński, the troubling fact was that the film had been designed as a co-production between Poland and West Germany. In addition, he characterized Korczak as a "dreamer" who deserted the "progressive left" after 1905 and isolated himself from the world. In line with the dominant ideology, Trepczyński wanted to see a film accusing the "dreamer" for not seeking "proper solutions" and for not being "politically engaged." As a pedagogue, claims Trepczyński, Korczak "was supposed to take a stand, but he withdrew and—one can even say—he managed to take his concept of passivity to the very end." Trepczyński postulated a "bigger film with a multilayered protagonist," not "a melodramatic story about the righteous character." Some participants of the meeting, chiefly writer and communist activist Bohdan Czeszko, voiced concerns similar to those expressed during the earlier approval of Ford's *Border Street*. Alluding to Ford's wartime history outside of Poland, they emphasized that the script does not reveal thorough knowledge about the reality of the occupation in Warsaw.

Committees that evaluated projects dealing with Polish-Jewish relations routinely sidelined artistic as well as commercial dimensions of the script. Of crucial importance was always the representation of wartime Polish behavior, attitudes of Poles toward Jews, and the explicit, accusatory portrayal of the perpetrators—the Germans. For some participants of the meeting, Ramati's script was lacking scenes showing assistance for the ghetto provided by the Polish political organizations. The head of the Cultural Department of the Communist Party, Wincenty Kraśko, recommended additions and reworkings that would emphasize the Polish context and the left-wing help for the ghetto in order to counter "the campaign of disinformation and half-truths about Poles and their attitudes toward the Jews during the occupation." Kraśko also pointed out that, taking into account the current policy of the state of Israel, the character of Korczak must be seen as worthy of condemnation, unlike another character in the script—the ideologically correct Jakub, a left-wing Jewish underground fighter. Offering a different perspective, journalist Krzysztof Teodor Toeplitz (KTT) emphasized that this has to be a tragic film with Korczak, not the underground fighters, taking its center; that it should be a film "about the last humanist, who had to surrender to the world."

As expected, Aleksander Ford passionately defended his project by explaining the accomplishments of producer Brauner and by emphasizing the forthcoming twenty-fifth anniversary of Korczak's death and the Warsaw Ghetto Uprising. He stressed that the project would counter Western propaganda and that it would also help to fight Israeli nationalism: "In my humble opinion, if one wants to strike a blow against Israeli nationalism, the easiest way to do it is through this brand of film—like the film about Korczak." In a long conclusion that, in principle, was approving of Ramati's script, Zaorski expressed his faith in Ford: "We are all convinced that comrade Ford will make a film, which will be in line with the principles of our cinema."

The political situation in 1968 caused suspension not only of the Korczak project but also of other films dealing with the Holocaust. Living outside of Poland since 1969, director Ford was able to make his film about Korczak in 1974 in Germany, *Dr. Korczak, the Martyr* (*Sie sind frei, Doktor Korczak*). This Israeli–West German co-production, produced by Brauner, failed critically and at the box-office; it was broadcast on German television on 8 March 1976. This now almost forgotten film was co-scripted by Ramati, photographed by another celebrated Jewish-Polish émigré Jerzy Lipman, and featured Leo Genn in the role of Korczak. Wulf Kansteiner calls Ford's film "overly sentimental," one that painted "a simplistic, heroic picture of Korczak."[14] The same sentimental aspect was criticized by Vincent Canby in his review in the *New York Times*: "This movie is full of good intentions that get smothered by the sentimental, deliberate manners of a cinema style better suited to early sound films. The only moving portions of the film are provided by Mr. Ford's occasional use of black-and-white still photographs of life in the Warsaw Ghetto. They haunt the mind in the way that makes the fictional pieties look almost complacent."[15] Polish film historian Joanna Preizner, however, sees the key weakness of Ford's film elsewhere—in its portrayal of Korczak as a Christian saint. Ford's reluctance to point out Korczak's Jewish roots, argues Preizner (and I share this view), most probably disappointed both Jewish and Christian viewers.[16]

***

Wajda considered making a film about Korczak since 1982, when American producer Larry Bachman approached him with a script by John Briley, the screenwriter of *Gandhi* (1982). The role of Korczak was planned for Richard Dreyfuss who expressed interest in the film and met with Wajda.[17] In 1983, Agnieszka Holland, who then lived in France, was commissioned to produce another script with the stress on the Holocaust. That script was later bought by Regina Ziegler from West Berlin, the co-producer of Wajda's film with the Polish Film Unit "Perspektywa" headed by Janusz Morgenstern.

From the beginning, Wajda decided to cast as Korczak one of his favorite actors, Wojciech Pszoniak (Figure 7.2), best known for his roles in *The Promised*

Figure 7.2: Wojciech Pszoniak as Dr. Korczak in Andrzej Wajda's *Korczak*. © Film Studio "Perspektywa".

Land (Moryc Welt) and *Danton* (Maximilien Robespierre), for which he received critical praise and several awards. This was a crucial decision since the camera stays close to Korczak, making other characters insignificant, often passive, influenced and being led by the charismatic man. Despite Pszoniak's believable performance and the verisimilitude of most scenes (several were taken directly by scriptwriter Holland from Korczak's diary[18]), the overdue premiere of the "Korczak project" did not fulfill audiences' expectations. Vincent Canby articulated it well in his *New York Times* review: "Mr. Wajda has been quoted as saying that he wanted to make this film because 'Jewish themes in Polish culture have been virtually banned for 20 years.' This must explain, in part, why he has treated the subject with such high-mindedness and reverence that *Korczak* seems to have no life of its own."[19]

Wajda has always been chiefly interested in Korczak's martyrdom and legend, therefore he swiftly moves to the final stages of his life. The film starts immediately before the war and briefly indicates the intricacies of Polish-Jewish relations and anti-Jewish sentiments in prewar Poland. An opening scene shows the cancellation of Korczak's radio program for children. The radio manager explains that this decision has to do with the pressure from (unspecified in the film) political forces who objected to Korczak's Jewish background (although he presented his programs under the pseudonym of the Old Doctor). In another scene, picturing Korczak's children picnicking near a river, Korczak's former pupils complain that the humanistic education they received from Korczak did not prepare them adequately for life; that they are defenseless against Poles ("they beat us up and smashed our windows").

As in his other films involving Polish-Jewish relations, Wajda opts for a carefully balanced picture. Polish anti-Semites are juxtaposed with Poles who are compassionate, and also those who risk their lives to help the Jews. The comments by a Polish washerwoman working for the orphanage ("I was not hired to wash Jewish shit") are countered by the presence of another Pole, Maria Falska (Teresa Budzisz-Krzyżanowska), who used to work closely with Korczak and shelters a Jewish girl during the occupation.[20] When Korczak is evicted into the ghetto with his children, Falska says that this is "such a shame not to be able to go there with them," and later offers Korczak a chance to escape to the Aryan side. During the scene depicting Korczak's relocation to the ghetto, an older Polish couple working for the orphanage is beaten by the Germans for trying to move to the ghetto with Korczak. Later on, a Polish city tram conductor is executed by the Germans for giving bread to the Jews (Figure 7.3).

The war is announced by a few street scenes intercut with the much-cited Polish documentary footage showing the burning King's Castle in Warsaw in September of 1939. A cut to an image of marching Polish prisoners of war announces the stage of resignation and despair. "Everyone has betrayed us," remarks Korczak. "This is the uniform of a betrayed soldier," he adds and he refuses to take off his own Polish uniform (he was a major in the Polish army).

Figure 7.3: The Polish city tram conductor (Olaf Lubaszenko) is executed for giving bread to the Jews in Andrzej Wajda's *Korczak*. © Film Studio "Perspektywa"

The film cuts from the marching POWs to scenes introducing the terror of the occupation: the creation of the Warsaw Ghetto on 13 September 1940. In the ghetto, Korczak refuses to wear an armband with the Star of David, for which he is briefly imprisoned.

From the beginning Wajda insists on an almost "documentary" quality for his film, chiefly by choosing black-and-white photography and by inserting newsreels and archival footage, both Polish and German. His docudrama is filled with "realistic" images of the ghetto. Wajda intercuts Nazi propagandist documentary material from the ghetto that is frequently indistinguishable from Robby Müller's greyish photography.[21] As if taking part in a discussion concerning the ambiguity and appropriateness of images to describe the Holocaust, Wajda questions whether such material should ever be filmed. In a short scene he shows images of the German newsreel cameramen at work, attempting to frame the disarray around them, searching for "photogenic" images, and not visibly bothered by the misery and death.

According to several reviewers, the reliance on black-and-white images of the ghetto enhanced the verisimilitude of the film. Renowned literary theorist Michał Głowiński describes the color of the ghetto as he returns to his childhood experiences in the Warsaw Ghetto in his book, *The Black Seasons*: "Before my eyes remains this monochromatism of the ghetto, perhaps best described by the word 'discoloredness' ... In my memories, the color of the ghetto is the color of the paper that covered the corpses lying in the street before they were taken away."[22] He writes that he re-discovered that aspect of the ghetto in Wajda's film: "the grayness with no boundaries, no differentiation. Watching the film, I could not believe my eyes. I was seeing that discolored color—in the very form in which it had imprinted itself in my memory decades earlier."[23]

Wajda's *Korczak* introduces images of ghetto life that one may find already in *Border Street*: hunger, brutality, overcrowding, and death in the streets. Wajda, however, is not afraid to go further and to show controversial, yet historically accurate, images of the ghetto later also found in *The Pianist* that offended many (particularly French) critics: brutal actions of the Jewish ghetto police, the presence of black marketers and racketeers, the division between rich and poor, the functioning of the ghetto's Jewish Council (*Judenrat*). He also portrays the tragedy of Adam Czerniaków (Aleksander Bardini), the chairman of the *Judenrat* who committed suicide on 23 July 1942. Korczak approaches Czerniaków and others in the hope of finding help for his orphanage ("I will see the devil himself to save my children"). One of the black marketers and a former pupil of Korczak, Szulc (Zbigniew Zamachowski), collects money for the orphanage and thanks to his high-ranked connections also later tries to save Korczak from deportation. As if to portray things to come—the Warsaw Ghetto Uprising—the film also features a group of young Jewish ghetto fighters, members of the Jewish Combat Organization, attempting to assassinate some black marketers.

Throughout the film, Wajda insists on portraying Korczak as both a Polish and Jewish hero. Jean Betty Lifton writes in her biography of Korczak: "Israel and Poland both claim Korczak as their own. The Poles consider Korczak a martyr who, had he been born a Catholic, would have been canonized by now. The Israelis revere Korczak as one of the Thirty-six Just Men whose pure souls, according to ancient Jewish tradition, make possible the world's salvation."[24] Korczak is described in the film by one of his senior pupils as "the world's greatest Pole ... and the greatest Jew, too." Also emphasized is his devotion to children, regardless of their race and nationality. In one of the film's strongest scenes, taking place in a Roentgen laboratory, Korczak demonstrates to his medical students a child's heart reacting to a stressful situation. His fight for children's rights is also shown in a scene in which he is asked, "What will you do after the war?" His response is quick: "I'll look after German orphans."

On 6 August 1942, the ghetto orphanages, including Korczak's Orphans' Home, were transported to Treblinka.[25] Although there is no indication in Korczak's diary that he knew what was coming, one could assume that he was aware what fate may await his children due to his extensive personal contacts and his witnessing of the beginning of the liquidation of the ghetto (which started on 22 July 1942). Unable to save his orphans, Korczak fought for what he called the dignity of death (*godna śmierć*). Historian Ruta Sakowska nonetheless concluded after her extensive research that on the day of the deportation Korczak and his co-workers were unaware that Treblinka was an extermination camp, not a labor camp.[26]

The last sequence of Wajda's film shows the deportation of the Jewish orphans and their instructors to Treblinka. Led by Korczak and the senior teacher Stefania Wilczyńska (1886–1942, played by Ewa Dałkowska) (Figure 7.4), who refuse to abandon their children, the orphans carry a flag with the Star of David on one side and a four-leaf clover (the orphanage emblem) on the other as they march toward the ghetto's *Umschlagplatz* to meet their doom (Figure 7.5). Absent from most of the film, Wojciech Kilar's elegiac musical score bursts to the screen. In a poetic, symbolic, and emotional final scene, shown in slow motion, the children disembark from the mysteriously disconnected railway wagon and fade into a peaceful rural landscape carrying the orphanage banner (Figure 7.6). When the image whitens, a sentence appears leaving no doubt about their actual fate: "Korczak died with his children in the gas chambers of Treblinka in August 1942." With his death the legend was born.

***

Korczak had been well-received in Germany and in Israel (among other countries), but its showing stirred many controversies in France.[27] Wajda and his scriptwriter, Agnieszka Holland, were accused by some French critics and filmmakers, including Claude Lanzmann, of being anti-Semites and of

Figure 7.4: Ewa Dałkowska as Stefania Wilczyńska in *Korczak*. © Film Studio "Perspektywa"

Figure 7.5: A scene from Andrzej Wajda's *Korczak*. © Film Studio "Perspektywa"

Figure 7.6: The ending of *Korczak*. © Film Studio "Perspektywa"

misrepresenting the Holocaust, and were castigated for their choice of a Polonized Jew as a hero. Lanzmann, known for attacking films that were not in line with his version of the Holocaust representation, left the special screening organized by the wife of the French Prime Minister, after telling the hostess, "You do not know how evil this is."[28]

"Lanzmann who did *Shoah* and thinks that he is the owner of *Shoah*," as scriptwriter Agnieszka Holland put it angrily,[29] together with journalist Daniéle Heymann launched a campaign against the film that influenced its reception abroad. Wajda comments on the pages of his official website: "The official screening at Cannes during the 1990 festival, followed by the standing ovation in the Festival Palace was, regrettably, the last success of *Dr. Korczak*. By the next morning, the review in *Le Monde* had transformed me into an anti-Semite, and not one of the major film distributors would agree to circulate the film outside Poland."[30] His website also contains an excerpt from the review by Heymann:

> It is filmed in black-and-white, with a few hidden inserts from old film news to lend verisimilitude. One could almost believe it. But there is no need for all this; despite the overwhelming dexterity pervading the film, a real hero of such charismatic intensity inescapably draws us into the overall illusion of truth ... And what do we see? Germans (brutal, they must be brutal) and Jews, in collaboration. Poles—none. The Warsaw Ghetto? A matter between the Germans and the Jews. This is what a Pole is telling us. The embarrassment which accompanies us from the start of the

showing changes into distaste. Until the epilogue, which almost makes us faint. The deportation orders are signed. The liquidation of the ghetto is underway. Under the Star of David, the children and Dr. Korczak enter the sealed carriage singing. And then the doors swing open—a coda to a sleepy, disgusting dream on the edge of revisionism—and we see how the little victims, energetic and joyful, emerge in slow-motion from the train of death. Treblinka as the salvation of murdered Jewish children. No. Not at the moment of profanation of the Jewish graves in Carpentras. Not ever.[31]

According to several Polish sources, the French accusations of anti-Semitism directed against Wajda and his film served to cover up the French wartime past and their present anti-Semitic excesses, like the desecration of the Jewish cemetery in Carpentras, which happened during the release of *Korczak*. Perhaps this concern was addressed most explicitly by the strongest defender of Wajda, Agnieszka Holland, herself half-Jewish:

> The problem in France is this terrible denial, after the war, of the guilt they had during the war, being the collaborationist nation, the organized French state sending the Jews to the concentration camps by French police and gendarmes. It's a terrible experience. This denial grows in very irrational ways. French Jews deny it also because they feel very connected to France ... The Jews there want to forget what happened there in World War II; they don't want to admit it emotionally, even though they admit it rationally, the historical facts. They transferred in some way the aggression and frustration to the Poles, who have their own register of the guilt. But it's not the French problem, this Polish anti-Semitism, it's between Poles and Jews.[32]

Wajda expressed his concern in a similar manner: "It was painful to read this, but I was aware that France preferred to lecture Poles on anti-Semitism rather than deal with cases of French anti-Semitism. The French have long sought ways to avoid facing up to the fact that it was the French authorities and the French police that dispatched Jews to Auschwitz [and not the Nazi authorities and Nazi police as was the case in Poland]."[33] Interestingly, several scenes in the film that were attacked by critics as inappropriate, one may also find in Korczak's diary.

After pointing out some weaknesses of Holland's script (such as the "declamatory illustrativiness" of Korczak's *Ghetto Diary*, sentimental subplots, and problematic acting), Paul Coates writes: "Scrupulosity so stifles the film that the imaginative leap into the powerful, poignant ending may have been too surprising for the audience to handle."[34]

The last scene in particular, the fairytale-like poetic ending, stirred controversies unanticipated by Wajda. Reviewing the film, Anna Sobolewska commented that, arguably, Wajda attempted to spare us pain: "In the last scene Wajda fulfils the viewer's secret wish—he opens the heavy doors of cattle cars."[35] Several critics, however, somehow failed to see the grim statement about the death of Korczak and his children appearing over the closing shot.[36] Polish film journals reported that *Korczak* was well-received at the film festival in Jerusalem and that the dream-like conclusion was read as a metaphor for the birth of Israel soon after the Holocaust.[37] The fantasy-like ending of Wajda's film, however, also has its roots in the legend of Korczak. His biographer, Jean Betty Lifton, explains: "For some time after the war it was rumoured that the cattle cars that took Korczak's orphans to Treblinka had been derailed and that he and Stefa and the children were saved. People claimed to have seen them in small villages throughout Poland."[38] Also, in a prose poem in Yiddish, "The Last Walk of Janusz Korczak," Aaron Zeitlin provides analogous ending about "Korczak's arrival in Heaven. The difference is that, there, Korczak confronts a Jewish God."[39]

In her thorough discussion of Wajda's film and the "French controversy" initiated by Lanzmann and Heymann, Terri Ginsberg comments that the "last scene's allegorical reference to Israel, marked by the flag-like banner bearing the Star of David, led Heymann to criticize Korczak for propagating Christian (in apparent contrast to Jewish) Zionism."[40] The alleged "Christianization of Korczak" (evidenced by the final scene and by modeling him on Francis of Assisi, among others) is often taken up by scholars. After looking closely at some of the film's scenes, such as when Korczak waters his plants, it is not difficult to agree with Ginsberg who writes that "Wajda's Korczak is lent neoplatonic qualities of second-century Christian Gnosticism—charitable humility, spiritual inwardness, sexual abstinence, and pastoral communitarianism."[41] Indeed, the film looks like a hagiography. According to Anna Sobolewska, "the biography of a distinguished pedagogue indiscernibly moves into a saint's biography." Wajda is "interested not only in the biography of a great man, but also in the phenomenon of sainthood, or—to avoid religious metaphors—the phenomenon of perfection." Sobolewska justly compares *Korczak* to Richard Attenborough's *Gandhi* (1982) and Roberto Rossellini's *The Flowers of St. Francis* (aka *Francis, God's Jester, Francesco, guillare di Dio*, 1950).[42]

The alleged "Christianization" or the "Polonization" of Korczak, or of the Holocaust for that matter, brings back similar arguments employed to discuss, for example, the "Christianization" of Edith Stein (Sister Teresa Benedicta of the Cross). A convert from Judaism, a member of the Carmelite order, Stein was killed at Birkenau along with other Dutch Jews. Her beatification in 1987 and canonization in 1988 only added more controversy surrounding the nature of her martyrdom: was she a Christian martyr or a Jewish martyr? The two versions of memory seem difficult to negotiate, almost incompatible. Addressing the issue of the "Christianization" of the Holocaust Peter Novick explains:

> One of the things I find most striking about much of recent Jewish Holocaust commemoration is how "un-Jewish"—how *Christian*—it is. I am thinking of the ritual of reverently following the structured pathways of the Holocaust in the major museums, which resembles nothing so much as the Stations of the Cross on the Via Dolorosa; the fetishized objects on display like so many fragments of the True Cross or shin bones of saints; the symbolic representations of the Holocaust—notably in the climax of Elie Wiesel's *Night*—that employ crucifixion imagery. Perhaps most

significantly, there is the way suffering is sacralised and portrayed as the path to wisdom—the cult of the survivor as secular saint. There are themes that have some minor and peripheral precedent in Jewish tradition, but they resonate more powerfully with major themes in Christianity.[43]

The "Christanization" or the "Polonization" of the Holocaust and figures such as Korczak are, however, often used by those critics who equate it with Polish anti-Semitism. They seem to forget that Polish films represent Polish memory. Writing about memorialization of the Holocaust in Poland in his book, *The Texture of Memory*, James E. Young elucidates: "Polish Catholics will remember as Polish Catholics, even when they remember Jewish victims. As Jews recall events in the figures of their tradition, so will Poles remember in the forms of their faith. The problem is not that Poles deliberately displace Jewish memory of the Holocaust with their own, but that in a country bereft of Jews, the memorials can do little but cultivate Polish memory."[44]

Wajda's film may have failed as a work of art but its vision of the Holocaust, its external perspective of a mortified Pole who looks at the annihilation of the Jewish ghetto from the Aryan side of the wall was, and likely will be, defended in Poland regardless of one's background and nationality. For example, praising the film for its apt use of black-and-white images ("colorless color of the ghetto"), Michał Głowiński thanks Wajda "for that unusual and important film, which some fanatics have attacked for reasons difficult to fathom."[45] Another Polish scholar, Ewelina Nurczyńska-Fidelska, states that "the accusations of his [Wajda's] anti-Semitism, which appeared in the world press in connection with *The Promised Land* and *Korczak*, are the evidence of a curious ill-will. The plight of Polish Jews in Wajda's films is a part of Polish history without which the picture of Polish history would be incomplete."[46]

***

As if unharmed by some negative responses to *Korczak* (perhaps because of them), in *Holy Week* (1996) Wajda returned once again to an examination of Polish-Jewish wartime relations. This time he offered a more direct assessment; furthermore, he made a Christian framework even more explicit. Despite his efforts, however, *Holy Week* had a limited audience of eight thousand viewers in Poland when released in merely three copies by the Solopan Distributors.[47] As with the earlier *Korczak*, Wajda's work was virtually ignored by audiences who at that time preferred "Polish films with an American accent"[48] at the expense of long-established popular subjects such as Polish martyrology and recent history (only two of the films presented at the 1996 Festival of Polish Films in Gdynia dealt with such themes). The film's critical reception in Poland was largely unenthusiastic, stressing the conventional, bordering on clichéd, aspect of Wajda's representation and, in sporadic cases, pointing out the film's alleged anti-Polish dimension. The film also garnered mixed reviews abroad despite the award (Silver Bear) Wajda received at the 1996 Berlin International Film Festival.

Holy Week is based on a short novel written soon after the Warsaw Ghetto Uprising by a prominent Polish writer Jerzy Andrzejewski (1909–1983), perhaps best known for his novel *Ashes and Diamonds* (1948), adapted for the screen by Wajda in 1958.[49] Andrzejewski's *Holy Week* was in all probability the first literary attempt to examine the behavior of Poles faced with the Holocaust that occurred on their soil. The story focuses on a Jewish woman, Irena Lilien, who tries to survive the annihilation of the Warsaw Ghetto being sheltered on the Aryan side by her Polish friend, Jan Malecki, and his family. The first version of the novel, produced by Andrzejewski in the spring of 1943, focused more on the psychology of the characters and was deprived of the political dimensions of the revised text, published in 1945. The now lost first version referred more extensively to Andrzejewski's biography, and it was taken as such by his contemporaries. Several early readers of *Holy Week*, while praising its formal aspects, expressed problems with the narrative that used easily recognizable characters coupled with the tragedy of the Warsaw Ghetto in the background. Daughter of well-known physicist Ludwik Wertenstein, translator and film critic Wanda Wertenstein, who was romantically involved with Andrzejewski before the war, stated that she served as a model for Irena's character.[50] Andrzejewski nevertheless claimed that he modeled Irena on another known Jewish-Polish woman, Janina Askenazy, the daughter of a professor of history, Szymon Askenazy.[51]

Writer Jarosław Iwaszkiewicz notes in his wartime diary that Andrzejewski's work was received half-heartedly during the first clandestine reading; it was well-written, yet unsettling: "The ashes of the ghetto had not cooled down yet," writes Iwaszkiewicz, "and he had already been writing a story about it."[52] Literary critic and scholar Jan Kott explained differences between the early version from 1943 and the new, expanded version from 1945, first published in Andrzejewski's anthology titled *Night (Noc)*. Kott writes that the first version dealt with a personal drama of a man who is unable to demonstrate solidarity with the desperate, albeit deprived of heroism, struggle of the Warsaw Jews. Following the tenets of the postwar communist interpretation of history, Kott notices the following: "The Jewish struggle in the ghetto was no longer a mystical drama of the chosen nation; it became a fragment of a general struggle with fascism."[53] The published version broadened the political and social context by introducing a wide spectrum of Polish characters ranging from extreme anti-Semites to young Polish fighters helping the ghetto insurgents. It also moved from the characters' psychology to "a panorama of Polish characters presented according to their attitudes to the extermination of Jews behind the ghetto walls."[54]

Oscar Swan, who is responsible for the English translation of Andrzejewski's *Holy Week*, writes in the "Introduction":

It is not endearing to the public in Poland for an author to criticize either the Catholic Church or the Polish national character. Although Andrzejewski does not exactly do either, the pages of *Holy Week* are nevertheless saturated with irony of a situation in which workaday Warsaw citizens, under the canopy of an immense cloud of smoke, baked Easter loaves, bought flowers, rode merry-go-rounds, mouthed pieties, and crowded the churches against the background of constant fire and street executions of Jewish escapees.[55]

Andrzejewski describes Poles gathering near the ghetto walls in an unflattering manner: "As with all major happenings in Warsaw, when observed from the outside it was something of a spectacle. Residents of Warsaw eagerly join a fight and just eagerly observe one in progress." A few sentences later he states bluntly: "Hardly anyone pitied the Jews. The populace was mainly glad that the despised Germans were now beset by a new worry. In the estimation of the average person on the street, the very fact that fighting was taking place with a handful of solitary Jews made the victorious occupiers look ridiculous."[56] The presence of anti-Semitic characters as well as detached bystanders (the majority) is balanced in the novel by the actions of some young Polish underground fighters: "From the very beginning, the Jewish insurgency had been doomed to annihilation and the ghetto to destruction. Under such circumstances, any kind of help might seem like a reckless increase in the number of lives lost. Nevertheless, Julek and a few others had been able to convince the leadership of one of the radical organizations that, regardless of its intimate success, the armed Jewish resistance had to be given help from the Polish side."[57]

The importance and cinematic qualities of Andrzejewski's *Holy Week* encouraged Polish filmmakers to adapt it for the screen. The earliest known attempts to produce a film based on Andrzejewski's novella occurred in 1968. The first script, written for Wajda by Andrzejewski and scriptwriter/director Andrzej Żuławski, fell victim to the March Events of 1968. Andrzejewski's biographer Anna Synoradzka writes that the project had financing provided by French and West German producers, but despite several political concessions by the scriptwriters (such as stressing the left-wing help for Jews), the project was not approved by the authorities.[58] The rights to *Holy Week* were later sold by Andrzejewski to a West German producer; several directors, including Żuławski and Agnieszka Holland, later attempted to make this film.[59]

Like Andrzejewski's novella, Wajda's 1996 film is set during the Easter Week of 1943, during the first days of the uprising in the Warsaw Ghetto. The film's Jewish protagonist, Irena Lilien (Beata Fudalej), seeks sanctuary on the Aryan side of the ghetto with her Polish friend, Jan Malecki (Wojciech Malajkat), and his pregnant wife Anna (Magdalena Warzecha). The story indicates that Jan courted Irena earlier and that perhaps they were lovers. As the story develops, Irena spends several days in her hiding place, feeling constantly threatened by the outside world, in particular by the low class family of the Piotrowskis (Cezary Pazura and Bożena Dykiel), who live in the same apartment building.

After Mr. Piotrowski's attempted rape of Irena, his malevolent wife, who is afraid that hiding Irena endangers Poles living in the house (and her marriage), falsely accuses Irena and throws her out of the building. Before leaving, Irena curses the inhabitants of the house and wishes them the same fate the Warsaw Jews are meeting. The last montage sequence depicts Irena moving toward the ghetto, Anna praying in front of the symbolic tomb of Christ in a church on Good Friday, and Jan being killed by the Gestapo while attempting to recover Irena's belongings from her former hiding place. The powerful final scene portrays Irena walking toward the burning ghetto, now in flames and almost destroyed, and passing some weary German soldiers returning from their deadly shift in the ghetto and not even reacting to her presence. Everything happens on Good Friday, in the New Testament the day of Christ's crucifixion. The parallel between the Jewish tragedy and the meaning of Easter Week, present in the literary source, provides an artistic framework carefully devised and developed by Wajda.

In *Holy Week* Wajda deals with some of his favorite themes such as individuals struggling with the fate of history and the issue of sacrifice at the altar of national needs. Unlike the novel, Wajda also deals with the issue of idealistic heroism by adding a scene portraying Malecki's younger brother, Julek (Jakub Przebindowski), and his suicidal mission to help the ghetto insurgents. To paint a panorama of diverse Polish characters, Wajda introduces another member of Polish intelligentsia, the owner of the house Councillor Zamojski (Wojciech Pszoniak), who is reading Adam Mickiewicz's classic verse novel *Pan Tadeusz* that features, among others, the nostalgic images of bygone Poland with Poles and Jews living in harmony. Taking into account several Jewish characters that Pszoniak played in Wajda's films, Zamojski perhaps may be seen as another hiding assimilated Jew.[60] At the bottom of the social strata in *Holy Week*, among the blackmailers and anti-Semitic types, are the Piotrowskis. Mrs Piotrowska, the self-proclaimed "good Catholic," is, however, not so much an anti-Semitic simpleton, but a wife jealous of her younger, good-for-nothing husband who is attracted to Irena. To make the vista of the Polish society complete, Wajda also includes a member of the ultranationalist right, Zalewski (Artur Barciś), who is caricatured in the film with his Hitler-like moustache.

Like several other Polish films, *Holy Week* opens with an image stressing the unique nature of the German occupation of Poland, the only country where the death penalty had been enforced for helping the Jews. As in Nasfeter's *The Long Night*, the camera focuses on the decree by Hans Frank, the Governor General of occupied Poland (*Generalgouvernement*), announcing the death penalty for the Jews going out of the ghetto and for those who offer them shelter. The following scene in the forest introduces Irena, and her father, Professor Juliusz Lilien, watching a group with the Star of David painted on their backs led by German soldiers. Despite Irena's remonstration, her father joins his fellow countrymen.

One of the striking features of the film is that Wajda portrays Irena in an unconventional way: she is not a sympathetic character, not a typical Holocaust victim. Unlike most of the figures in Holocaust narratives, Irena refuses to remain silent and obedient, out of German sight, and she "ungratefully" questions the attitude of her Polish hosts.[61] Always elegant, which is contrasted with the plain look of Anna, Irena is portrayed as determined, aggressive, rarely polite, contemptuous, certainly not the image of a silent, suffering Jew: "The more death you see, the more you want to live," she says. "Suffering makes you a worse person, a much worse person." As with other Jewish characters in Wajda's Holocaust films, Irena comes from an assimilated family. Commenting on that choice, Oscar Swan fittingly states: "The fact that the Liliens were fully assimilated and not religiously observant, even if Semitic in appearance, underscores the senselessness of the persecution to which Irena and her family are exposed. It is made plain that her acerbic and uncharitable nature has been shaped more by her wartime traumas than by her cultural heritage."[62]

Discussing the way Polish films focus on the otherness of Jewish women, Elżbieta Ostrowska writes: "One can observe the use of given elements of mise-en-scène as signifiers of woman's sexuality and, respectively, of two different mythologized images of femininity originating from a long cultural tradition: the archetypes are Lilith from the Bible—a symbol of animal sexuality—and the Virgin Mary whose body is sublime due to the Immaculate Conception."[63] Contrasted with Irena, the pregnant Anna serves as the image of the suffering Polish Mother (Matka Polka). She lost several members of her close family during the occupation. Madeleine G. Levine rightly calls her "the real heroine of the story," because she "represents Andrzejewski's vision of the ideal Christian response to suffering in general and to the predicament of the Jews in particular. She is sensitive, pragmatic, and resolute, firmly idealistic, and totally devoid of any histrionic traits … Anna is a symbol of all that is best in the Polish people: she carries within her the seed of hope for the future."[64] When she says, "We have to do something; we Catholics should be by their side, at least in our thoughts," this may be reminiscent of a position taken during the war by a Catholic writer of historical fiction Zofia Kossak-Szczucka (1889–1968). In the summer of 1942, she published a clandestine leaflet titled "The Protest," in which she condemned the German extermination policy toward the Jews. Kossak-Szczucka was a member of the resistance, known for her efforts to help the Jews as a co-founder of the Council for Aid to the Jews (Żegota), a special branch of the Home Army (AK). For her activities she was imprisoned for more than a year at Auschwitz.

Holy Week examines Polish morality. With the ghetto insurgents off screen, it deals with the Polish experience of the Holocaust. Irena Lilien is sent among Poles to "test the nation";[65] she acts like a litmus paper to check the attitudes of her Polish hosts. The core of the film consists of conversations between Irena and the Maleckis, and between Poles themselves. As in his first films from the Polish School period, Wajda emphasizes the tragic aspect of life. However, unlike in his early films, he alleviates all emotions and reinforces, rather than questions, the myth of the Polish intelligentsia and Polish Catholicism. Oscar Swan writes that compared to Andrzejewski's novel, Wajda tones down expressions of Polish anti-Semitism. He lists several scenes from the film (some also present in the shooting script but deleted during the editing process) that differ from the novel as instances of Wajda's "seeming sanitization of the novel for easier domestic consumption."[66] It has to be said, however, that Wajda's film, scripted by the director, never aspires to be a faithful adaptation.

Holy Week dramatizes the attitudes of Poles toward their fellow citizens who were forcefully relocated by the occupier to the ghetto. It is dominated by symbolism of several images, a feature surely expected in Wajda's cinema, but often disparaged by critics. For example, Piotr Wojciechowski referring to Wajda's characters employs the term "a symbolic theme park."[67] The narrative of *Holy Week* is punctuated by an image of a group of the German soldiers on motorcycles, described by Wajda in the script as "the riders of the Apocalypse."[68] Oscar Swan comments that they "serve to reinforce the image of the German occupation as a force of nature against which no resistance is possible."[69] Their appearance in Wajda's film had been perhaps influenced by a similar portrayal of the occupation in Jan Rybkowski's *Ascension Day* (1969).

The symbolic image of the carousel in front of the ghetto wall also appears in the film to stress the Polish indifference. However, a group of young Polish fighters, probably members of the Grey Ranks (Szare Szeregi), the underground Polish scouting organization during World War II, among them Julek, employ the infamous carousel in the Krasiński's Square to look behind the wall before entering the ghetto to help the Jewish insurgents.[70] Julek, as indicated in the film, sacrifices his life helping the ghetto fighting, thus rescuing the image of his fellow Poles. Oscar Swan argues that Wajda references his earlier film, *Ashes and Diamonds*, through his portrayal of Julek as Maciek's alter ego.[71] Choosing the powerful image of the carousel near the ghetto wall during the uprising, Wajda acknowledges Czesław Miłosz's poem, "Campo di Fiori," rather than the original novel, where the non-functioning, under-construction carousel serves as a stage for a German cannon. It was taken by some critics, as Oscar Swan writes, as an attempt to "purify and redeem Miłosz's infamous symbol by associating it with Julek and his patriotic band (sic!) of adolescent freedom fighters."[72] As Swan comments, "Wajda's transformed image verges on tampering with historical reality, as indeed Andrzejewski himself does with the entire subplot of Julek and his gang (sic!), for which there is scant justification."[73] A number of historical studies, however, demonstrated that works of fiction, such as Miłosz's poem, cannot be taken as historical facts and that Wajda's image, although not representative, can be justified by the historical data.[74]

Several critics of Wajda's film and Andrzejewski's novel argued that the representation of Polish society in *Holy Week* never goes beyond the stereotypes of bad lumpenproletariat (the Piotrowskis), good but inept intelligentsia (the Maleckis and the landlord Zamojski), and heroic young fighters marked by death (Julek Malecki). An ardent supporter of several of Wajda's films, Tadeusz Sobolewski, criticized Wajda for being unable to look harshly at his nation, incapable to "look from outside at those he loves." Attempting to explain the reasons behind Wajda's representation, Sobolewski argues that the director is "too attached to traditions and stereotypes of Polishness, hides among them, and idealizes rather than questions them."[75] Wajda's longing for popular acclaim, which he received later with his adaptations of *Pan Tadeusz* (1999) and *Revenge* (*Zemsta*, 2002), prevented him from offering a harsher view, from stirring a discussion about the Polish-Jewish past. It resulted in a safe, almost educational film deprived of passion that left the Polish viewers detached.

Postscript

In a modest television film, *Franciszek Kłos' Death Sentence* (aka *The Condemnation of Franciszek Kłos*; *Wyrok na Franciszka Kłosa*, 2000), Wajda once again attempted to deal with the complexity of the occupation in Poland. The adaptation of a novel by Stanisław Rembek (1901–1985), scripted by Wajda and Zygmunt Malanowicz, centers on an unsophisticated Polish blue policeman from a small town who dutifully serves the Germans. The alcoholic anti-hero Kłos (played by Mirosław Baka, the actor known internationally for his role of a young killer in Krzysztof Kieślowski's *A Short Film about Killing*) is eager to please his German superiors by killing Jews as well as members of the Polish resistance. His cruel acts of collaboration bring him the death sentence issued by the Polish underground state. His compliant wife (Grażyna Błęcka-Kolska) finally leaves him; his religious mother (Maja Komorowska) loathes her son's actions. In a scene that may serve as a direct reference to *Holy Week*, a Polish mother (again played Magdalena Warzecha) is killed with her children for hiding Jews. Wajda's modest television drama, which relies on strong performances, attempts to go beyond the limitations of his previous two films by focusing on an unpopular and for years relegated to the margins subject (collaboration), which is portrayed with the use of the dynamic, Dogma-like camera work (by Bartosz Prokopowicz).

Notes

1. Maria Malatyńska, "Siedmioramiennie," *Tygodnik Powszechny* 9 (1996): 7.
2. Gordana P. Crnković, "Interview with Agnieszka Holland," *Film Quarterly* vol. 52, no. 2 (1998–1999): 6.
3. Tadeusz Lubelski, "Wajda: albo *Pana Tadeusza* albo *Pannę Nikt*," *Kino* 2 (1995): 9.
4. Lawrence Baron, *Projecting the Holocaust into the Present: The Changing Focus of Contemporary Holocaust Cinema* (Lanham: Rowman and Littlefield, 2005), 48.
5. For details concerning Korczak's biography see Jean Betty Lifton, *The King of Children: The Life and Death of Janusz Korczak* (American Academy of Pediatrics, 2005). Korczak's novel

for children, *King Matt the First* (*Król Maciuś I*, 1922/1923), was adapted for the screen by Wanda Jakubowska in 1958.
6. Discussed by Edward Zajiček, *Poza ekranem. Kinematografia polska 1918-1991* (Warsaw: Filmoteka Narodowa and Wydawnictwa Artystyczne i Filmowe, 1992), 62, 197-198. Like Korczak, Ludwik Starski was born into an assimilated Jewish family. He had a successful prewar career as a screenwriter and a songwriter. He scripted a number of prewar films that were directed by Michał Waszyński, Leon Trystan, and Mieczysław Krawicz. With Jan Fethke, he co-scripted a popular musical comedy, *The Forgotten Melody* (1938), directed by Konrad Tom and Fethke. For this and other films he also provided lyrics to songs composed by Henryk Wars that are popular in Poland to this day. Starski also scripted some of the most popular postwar Polish films directed by Leonard Buczkowski, including *Forbidden Songs* (1947), *Treasure* (1949), and *An Adventure at Marienstadt* (1954). He also wrote the script for Aleksander Ford's *Border Street* (1949, with Fethke). In addition to writing, Starski headed film units "Warszawa" (1948-1949) and "Iluzjon" (1955-1963). He is the father of an Oscar-winning (for *Schindler's List*) set designer Allan Starski.
7. The Polish garrison of Westerplatte near the Free City of Danzig (Gdańsk), consisting of 180 soldiers, survived for seven days against the overwhelming German force. The poem is quoted from Barbara Engelking and Jacek Leociak, *The Warsaw Ghetto: A Guide to the Perished City*, trans. Emma Harris (New Haven: Yale University Press, 2009), 547. For comments on Szlengel see pages 544-548. Also, Irena Maciejewska, "Getto warszawskie w literaturze polskiej," in *Literatura wobec wojny i okupacji*, ed. Michał Głowiński and Janusz Sławiński (Wrocław: Ossolineum, 1976), 6. This was first published in an anthology edited by Michał Borwicz, *Pieśń ujdzie cało. Antologia wierszy o Żydach pod okupacją niemiecką* (Warsaw, 1947). The relevant fragment reads in Polish: "Czy słyszycie, sąsiedzi zza murka/Co na śmierć naszą patrzycie przez kratę?/Janusz Korczak umarł, abyśmy/Mieli także swe Westerplatte."
8. Quoted from Maciejewska, p. 161. The Polish titles of the poems are as follows: Stefania Ney's "O Januszu Korczaku," Witold Zechenter's "Jak Janusz Korczak zawiózł dzieci na wieś," and Antoni Słonimski's "Pieśń o Januszu Korczaku."
9. Władysław Szpilman, *The Pianist: The Extraordinary Story of One Man's Survival in Warsaw 1939-45* (New York: Picador, 1999), 95-96.
10. Bożena Wojnowska, "Utrwalić pamięć o Januszu Korczaku," *Rzeczpospolita* (15 December 2008), http://www.rp.pl/artykul/120621,234657_Utrwalic_pamiec_o_Januszu_Korczaku.html (accessed 1 November 2009).
11. Zajiček, *Poza ekranem*, 198.
12. Paul Coates, *The Red and the White: The Cinema of People's Poland* (London: Wallflower Press, 2005), 97. Coates provides the summary of Ramati's script. Ibid., 97-98. The script by Ramati is at the National Film Archive in Warsaw, S-11131.
13. "Stenogram z rozszerzonego posiedzenia Rady Programowej Zespołu 'Studio' w dniu 6 X 1967." National Film Archive in Warsaw, A-329/57. All quotations in this and the next two paragraphs come from this document.
14. Wulf Kansteiner, *In Pursuit of German Memory: History, Television, and Politics after Auschwitz* (Athens: Ohio University Press, 2006), 121.
15. Vincent Canby, "Sie sind frei, Dr. Korczak! (1973). 'Martyr', A Film about the Nazis and Heroic Jew," *New York Times* (17 June 1976), http://movies.nytimes.com/movie/review?res=9E06E2DE143FE334BC4F52DFB066838D669EDE (accessed 1 November 2009).
16. Joanna Preizner, "Żydowski Święty—*Korczak* Andrzeja Wajdy," in *Biografistyka filmowa. Ekranowe interpretacje losów i faktów*, ed. Tadeusz Szczepański and Sylwia Kołos (Toruń: Wydawnictwo Adam Marszałek, 2007), 91.
17. Details about the early stages of Wajda's project from Tadeusz Lubelski, *Wajda: Portret mistrza w kilku odsłonach* (Wrocław: Wydawnictwo Dolnośląskie, 2006), 235. Also, Maria Malatyńska, "Andrzej Wajda na festiwalu w Gdyni," *Kino* 11/12 (1990): 12-14.

18. Janusz Korczak, *Pamiętnik*, in: *Pisma wybrane*, vol. 4, ed. Aleksander Lewin (Warsaw: Nasza Księgarnia, 1978), 299–377. English edition: Janusz Korczak, *Ghetto Diary*, trans. Jerzy Bachrach and Barbara Krzywicka (New Haven: Yale University Press, 2003).
19. Vincent Canby, "*Korczak* (1990): Of a Saintly Jewish Doctor in Poland who Died at Treblinka," *New York Times* (12 April 1991), http://movies.nytimes.com/movie/review?res=9D0CE6DD163EF931A25757C0A967958260 (accessed 1 November 2009).
20. Maria Falska and Janusz Korczak founded an orphanage for Polish children in 1928—"Our Home" ("Nasz Dom").
21. Wajda decided to hire Robby Müller, Jim Jarmusch's cinematographer, after seeing his work in *Down by Law* (1986). Malatyńska, "Andrzej Wajda na festiwalu w Gdyni," 14.
22. Michał Głowiński, *The Black Seasons*, trans. Marci Shore (Evanston: Northwestern University Press, 2005), 6–7. Published in Poland in 1999 as *Czarne sezony*.
23. Ibid., 7.
24. Lifton, *The King of Children*, 356.
25. The film's narrative suggests, most probably for the sake of creating suspense, that the death of Czerniaków and the deportation of Korczak's orphanage happened on the same day.
26. Ruta Sakowska, "Janusz Korczak wobec Zagłady: Próba interpretacji tekstów," *Kwartalnik Historii Żydów* 2 (2005): 294.
27. See André Pierre Colombat, *The Holocaust in French Film* (Metuchen: Scarecrow Press, 1993), 113–116. Also, Tzvetan Todorov, "Umrzeć w Warszawie," *Kultura niezależna* 49 (1989), reprinted in *Kino* 7 (1991): 41–42 (trans. Jagoda Engelbrecht).
28. Quoted from Michael Stevenson, "Wajda's Representation of Polish-Jewish Relations," in *The Cinema of Andrzej Wajda: The Art of Irony and Defiance*, ed. John Orr and Elżbieta Ostrowska (London: Wallflower Press, 2003), 88.
29. Crnković, "Interview with Agnieszka Holland," 7.
30. Andrzej Wajda's official website: www.wajda.pl/en/filmy/film29.html (accessed 2 October 2009).
31. Daniéle Heymann, *Le Monde* (Paris, 13 May, 1990). Quoted from Wajda's official website. Ibid.
32. Crnković, "Interview with Agnieszka Holland," 6.
33. Aleksandra Ziółkowska-Boehm, "An Interview with Andrzej Wajda," *The Sarmatian Review* 2 (2003): 961.
34. Coates, *The Red and the White*, 178.
35. Anna Sobolewska, "Do ostatniej chwili życia," *Film* 43 (1990): 11.
36. The same critics, conceivably, were disapproving of similar fantasy endings in, for example, films made by Czech and Slovak directors, such as Ján Kadár and Elmar Klos's *The Shop on Main Street* (*Obchod na korze*, 1965) and Jan Hřebejk's *Divided We Fall* (*Musime si pomáhat*, 2000). These films also "soften" the depressing reality by offering a sentimental, escapist fantasy.
37. Tomasz Jopkiewicz, "Korczak," *Film* 15 (1992): 18.
38. Lifton, *The King of Children*, 357. In her defense of Wajda's film, published in *The New York Times* (5 May 1991), Lifton writes the following: "Those critics who detect only a Christian vision in the final ethereal scene (Korczak and the children leap off the train in slow-motion and fade into a misty countryside) are unfair to Wajda. After the war there were rumors that the carriage with the transport from the orphanage became miraculously unlinked from the train. Villagers throughout Poland recognized the 'old doctor' and his children. It could be that, like Wajda, they wanted to believe that people like Korczak are indestructible. What a shame that Wajda was unable to accomplish his original idea of making a Polish *Doctor Zhivago*, showing Korczak's pioneering work in the field of children's tribunals, children's rights, and moral education. Instead of stirring up Polish-Jewish antagonisms, we should rather be thankful for the sincere sympathy with which Wajda attempts to recreate this modern Jewish hero who died—like he lived—for his children." Quoted from Wajda's official website, http://www.wajda.pl/en/filmy/film29.html (accessed 12 November 2009).

39. Jim Hoberman, "Korczak," *Village Voice* (16 April 1991): 55.
40. Terri Ginsberg, "St. Korczak of Warsaw," in *Imaginary Neighbors: Mediating Polish-Jewish Relations after the Holocaust*, ed. Dorota Głowacka and Joanna Zylinska (Lincoln: University of Nebraska Press, 2007), 111–112.
41. Ibid., 117.
42. Sobolewska, "Do ostatniej chwili życia," 11.
43. Peter Novick, *The Holocaust in American Life* (Boston: Houghton Mifflin, 1999), 11.
44. James E. Young, *The Texture of Memory: Holocaust Memorials and Meaning* (New Haven: Yale University Press, 1993), 116–117.
45. Głowiński, *The Black Seasons*, 7.
46. Ewelina Nurczyńska-Fidelska, "Romanticism and History: A Sketch of the Creative Output of Andrzej Wajda," in *Polish Cinema in Ten Takes*, ed. Ewelina Nurczyńska-Fidelska and Zbigniew Batko (Łódź: Łódzkie Towarzystwo Naukowe, 1995), 12.
47. "Popularność filmów polskich 29.12.95 – 29.08.96," *Film Pro* vol. 10, no. 18 (1996): 11. Krzysztof Kucharski provides a total of 9,740 viewers who watched *Holy Week* in Polish theaters. Kucharski, *Kino Plus: Film i dystrybucja kinowa w Polsce w latach 1990–2000* (Toruń: Oficyna Wydawnicza Kucharski, 2002), 385.
48. See chapter on "Polish Films with an American Accent" in my *Polish National Cinema* (New York: Berghahn, 2002), 243–258.
49. Jerzy Andrzejewski, *Holy Week. A Novel of the Warsaw Ghetto Uprising* (Athens: Ohio University Press, 2007).
50. Wanda Wertenstein, "To ja byłam Ireną," *Gazeta Wyborcza* (9–10 March 1996): 11.
51. Wanda Wertenstein, "W realizacji—*Wielki Tydzień*," *Kino* 7–8 (1995): 29.
52. Jarosław Iwaszkiewicz, *Notatki 1939–1945* (Wrocław: Wydawnictwo Dolnośląskie, 1991), 89.
53. Jan Kott, "Droga do realizmu," *Kuźnica* 8 (1946): 9.
54. Anna Synoradzka, *Andrzejewski* (Kraków: Wydawnictwo Literackie, 1997), 85
55. Oscar Swan, "Introduction: Jerzy Andrzejewski's *Holy Week*," in Andrzejewski, *Holy Week*, xxi.
56. Andrzejewski, *Holy Week*, 8–9.
57. Ibid., 68.
58. Synoradzka, *Andrzejewski*, 162.
59. Jacek Szczerba, "Tragedia wiosenna," *Gazeta Wyborcza* 107 (10 May 1995): 10; Barbara Hollender, "Początek *Wielkiego Tygodnia*," *Rzeczpospolita* 108 (11 May 1995), 9. Also, Lubelski, *Wajda*, 244.
60. Katarzyna Wajda, "Gdy biedni Polacy patrzą na getto: *Wielki Tydzień* Andrzeja Wajdy," *Kwartalnik Filmowy* 34 (2001): 95.
61. Omer Bartov states: "Linking Polish suffering to Jewish suffering by way of showing the former helping the latter, and often suggesting the Jews' ingratitude to the Poles, their indifference to Polish victimhood, and even their urge for revenge, is part of the Polish discourse on the German occupation and the Holocaust." Omer Bartov, *The 'Jew' in Cinema: From* The Golem *to* Don't Touch My Holocaust (Bloomington: Indiana University Press, 2005), 150.
62. Oscar Swan, "Afterword: Andrzej Wajda's Film *Holy Week*," in Andrzejewski, *Holy Week. A Novel of the Warsaw Ghetto Uprising*, 131.
63. Elżbieta Ostrowska, "Otherness Doubled: Representations of Jewish Women in Polish Cinema," in *Gender and Film and the Media: East-West Dialogues*, ed. Elżbieta Oleksy, Elżbieta Ostrowska, and Michael Stevenson (Frankfurt/Main: Peter Lang, 2000), 124.
64. Madeleine G. Levine, "The Ambiguity of Moral Outrage in Jerzy Andrzejewski's *Wielki Tydzień*," *The Polish Review* 4 (1987): 394. Levine's comments about the novel are also applicable to Wajda's film.
65. Maria Malatyńska, "Między winą a rozgrzeszeniem," *Tygodnik Powszechny* 10 (1996): 13.
66. Swan, "Afterword," 135–138.
67. Piotr Wojciechowski, "Rekolekcje w skansenie," *Tygodnik Powszechny* 12 (1996): 9.

68. Quoted from Swan, "Afterword," 132. Earlier version of Swan's text appeared as "Andrzej Wajda's Film *Holy Week*: What Is Its Problem?" *The Polish Review* 3 (2005): 343–353.
69. Ibid., 132.
70. In Wajda's earlier *A Generation*, the young underground fighters gathering on Krasiński's Square near the carousel are members of the communist People's Guard (GL).
71. Swan, "Afterword," 135.
72. Ibid., 134.
73. Ibid., 134. The erroneous comment by Swan is somehow corrected by his remarks in the endnote number 11: "Reckoning that the time was not ripe for a general insurgency, the Polish underground provided the ghetto fighters with some small arms, rifles, hand grenades, and moral support, but with scant organized human assistance. Nevertheless, a small number of non-Jews were found among the ghetto dead, catalogued by German commander SS General Jürgen Stroop as 'bandits,' lending a certain credence to Julek's depiction." Ibid., 148.
74. See, for example, Tomasz Szarota, *Karuzela przy Placu Krasińskich. Studia i szkice z lat wojny i okupacji* (Warsaw: Oficyna Wydawnicza Rytm, 2007), 165. Joanna Rostropowicz-Clark discusses that "works of fiction should not be misread as statements of historical fact" in her review of Andrzejewski's novel: "*Holy Week*: A Novel of the Warsaw Uprising," *The Sarmatian Review* 27, no. 3 (2007). Quoted from an online edition: www.ruf.rice.edu/~sarmatia/907/273clark.html (accessed 27 October 2008).
75. Tadeusz Sobolewski, "Biedni Polacy," *Kino* 11 (1995): 41.

Chapter 8

DOCUMENTARY ARCHAEOLOGY OF THE HOLOCAUST AND POLISH-JEWISH PAST

Documentary films always played a vital role in Poland. Since 1945, they have been made primarily by the Documentary Film Studio (Wytwórnia Filmów Dokumentalnych, WFD) in Warsaw, and also by the Czołówka Film Studio and the Educational Film Studio (Wytwórnia Filmów Oświatowych, WFO). The *Polish Newsreel* (*Polska Kronika Filmowa*, PKF) performed the role of a chief documentarist of Polish life from 1945 to 1995. Starting in 1958, Polish movie theaters were obliged to screen short films (documentary, animated, or educational) before the main feature, a factor of great consequence for the makers of short films (this practice lasted until the 1980s). Documentary films also featured prominently on (and were produced by) Polish Television. This type of cinema was by no means only a training ground for the future mainstream filmmakers—it was a well-established art form generously sponsored by government funding bodies and prudently analyzed by local critics.

Postwar Beginnings

Early documentary films made in postwar Poland dealt with the effects of war—human and material losses, devastation, rebuilding, and the hardship of life. In 1944, the co-founders of the Czołówka Film Unit, Aleksander Ford and Jerzy Bossak (1910–1989), the latter also the first managing editor of *Polish Newsreel* from 1944 to 1948, produced one of the classic Holocaust documentaries, *Majdanek—The Cemetery of Europe* (*Majdanek—Cmentarzysko Europy*). The film featured footage taken after 23 July 1944, when the Red Army captured the south-eastern Polish city of Lublin, along with Majdanek, the first Nazi death camp located on the Polish territories, which was situated on the outskirts of this town. As described by film historian Stanisław Ozimek, the headquarters of the Polish documentary filmmakers were in a villa that earlier belonged to the infamous SS Gruppenführer Odilo Globocnik.[1] The ill-equipped *Czołówka* camera operators (treated with suspicion by the Soviets) were unprepared for the task—they had to work with heavy and unreliable cameras and with limited supplies of film stock. Camera operator Stanisław Wohl recalled his experiences in an article published in 1969: "We entered there just a couple of minutes after the Germans' escape. In the ovens of the crematoria there were partly burned corpses; the *Muselmänner* crawled on the ground, the prisoners wanted to greet us, but they had no strength to raise their hands or shout."[2]

Although Aleksander Ford is listed as the director of *Majdanek*, in an interview conducted in 1989, Jerzy Bossak credited himself with the on-location work. He emphasized that Ford never participated in filming in the extermination camp; given the graphic nature of the camp images, Ford "could not, did not want to look at it, and I understood him."[3] The film premiered in November 1944 and included the sound added in a Moscow studio and the music provided by a Russian composer, Sergiusz J. Potocki. The film featured shots of the liberated camp (crematoria, electrified barbed-wire fences, piles of victims' belongings, dead bodies), and juxtaposed survivors' testimonies with that of the captured SS guards.

Polish film historian Jolanta Lemann-Zajiček writes that the footage produced by Polish and Soviet cameramen at Majdanek was additionally used to make two other films about the camp in Soviet Russia. *Vernichtungslager Majdanek: The Cemetery of Europe* (*Vernichtungslager Majdanek—cmentarzysko Europy*, 1944) credits Aleksander Ford as the director of this Polish-Soviet production and *Majdanek* (1944) lists Irina Setkina as the director (only Soviet cameramen were additionally credited).[4] In a detailed study published in 2006, Stuart Liebman focuses exclusively on *Vernichtungslager Majdanek* as "one of the most important films ever made about the Holocaust," a film that "has a legitimate claim to be the first such work," and "the first to develop visual and narrational strategies to dramatize the unprecedented story of German brutality in a camp."[5]

The Polish documentary about Majdanek, although being the first film that uncovered the brutality of German death camps to the world, was treated in the West with suspicion as an example of Soviet propaganda.[6] For decades little known outside of Poland, the film was overshadowed by images of the liberation of camps such as Bergen-Belsen and Dachau, captured by the Western allies. In particular, the filming of Bergen-Belsen by the British Army's Film and Photographic Unit (AFPU), after its liberation on 15 April 1945 by the British Second Army, achieved the status of the first decisive portrayal of Nazi atrocities.

Stanisław Wohl and the brothers Adolf and Władysław Forbert also photographed the trial of the Majdanek's SS guards and *Kapos* that started in November 1944, along with the public execution by hanging of six Majdanek personnel at the beginning of December 1944. This footage was later included in the special edition of the Polish Newsreel titled *The Swastika and the Gallows* (*Swastyka i szubienica*, 1945), produced by Kazimierz Czyński and edited by Wacław Kaźmierczak, the latter also responsible for editing some of the best-known postwar Polish documentaries.

Adolf Forbert was later among the first photographers and filmmakers at the site of another concentration camp, Auschwitz-Birkenau, on 28 January 1945, after it was captured by the Red Army. With limited resources at his disposal (only 300 meters of film stock, no lighting equipment, one Bell & Howell camera), he was nonetheless able to capture several images, which he sent to a laboratory for development, and which he never saw again.[7] Forbert's footage of the liberated camp most probably was lost and never resurfaced, neither in *Auschwitz* (*Oświęcim*, 1945), made by the Red Army filmmakers led by Roman Karmen, nor in other future war documentaries. Forbert's photographs from Auschwitz, however, were included in the *Polish Newsreel* number 7 (1945).[8]

Polish filmmakers also documented trials and executions of the SS guards at other German camps, for example in *The Gallows in the Stutthof Concentration Camp* (*Szubienice w Sztutthofie*, 1946), the special edition of the *Polish Newsreel* directed by Aleksander Świdwiński. The trial and hanging of SS Obergruppenführer Arthur Greiser, the German *Gauleiter* (governor) of a Polish western district incorporated into the Reich, the so-called Wartheland, was recorded in *Greiser before the Polish Court* (*Greiser przed sądem Rzeczpospolitej*, 1946), produced by Świdwiński.[9] Another special edition of the *Polish Newsreel* in 1947 was devoted to the anniversary of the Warsaw Ghetto Uprising: *The 1947 Ghetto Anniversary* (*Rocznica Getta 1947*).

Images of war atrocities and public executions were often censored in Poland and sometimes treated as classified material, though not necessarily for political reasons. For example, photographs of the hanging of the former Auschwitz commandant Rudolf Höss on 16 April 1947 were published for the first time in 1995 by Polish journalist Andrzej Gass.[10] Sentenced to death by the Polish Supreme National Tribunal (Najwyższy Tybunał Narodowy), Höss was hanged on gallows built by German POWs on the grounds of Auschwitz-Birkenau. Although Höss's trial was widely covered by Polish newspapers, which were describing with graphic details German brutality, the public was spared the image of another execution. In her insightful book, *Photographing the Holocaust: Interpretations of the Evidence*, Janina Struk comments that "Following widespread revulsion at gruesome scenes filmed at the Lublin hangings in 1944 and particularly the public hanging of Arthur Greiser, Nazi governor of Warthegau, in Poznań in 1946, it was decided that there should be no more public executions. [Rudolf] Höss's case was an exception—but the authorities did limit the attendance and suppress publication of the pictures."[11] Paradoxically, writes Struk, "while the Commandant of Auschwitz seems to have been granted a reprieve from the public display of the indignity of his final moments, the cruel fates of his victims are commonly displayed in museums around the world."[12]

Apart from recording several trials of German functionaries who committed crimes on Polish soil, the best-known examples of Polish documentaries produced after the war featured images of Warsaw and other Polish towns being rebuilt, juxtaposed with wartime images taken from various German newsreels.

Films such as *Warsaw Rebuilds* (*Budujemy Warszawę*, 1945) by Stanisław Urbanowicz, *The Last Nazi Party Rally in Nuremberg* (*Ostatni parteitag w Norymberdze*, 1946) by Antoni Bohdziewicz, and *The Warsaw Suite* (*Suita Warszawska*, 1946) by Tadeusz Makarczyński became not only passionate accusations of German war crimes, but also life-affirming documentaries.

The plight of Polish Jews, however, was not specifically addressed in those early films. Looking at the postwar documentary films, one may discern a pattern that also will be present in several (not only Polish) later documentary and narrative films about the Holocaust—the stress on the collective trauma and the marginalization of Jewish suffering. What perhaps makes early postwar Polish documentary films unique, given the ruthless implementation of communist ideology, is the visible presence of national and religious symbols, namely, the use of Christian iconography, images of Catholic clergy at funeral masses, and references to Polish heroism and martyrdom.

The Polish School

The theme of the Holocaust returns in several documentary films made during the Polish School period. The first Polish documentary film about the Warsaw Ghetto, *Under This Same Sky* (*Pod jednym niebem*, 1955), was voted Best Documentary at the Karlovy Vary Film Festival in 1956 and also became the recipient of the FIPRESCI Award at the Mannheim Film Festival. The film was made by Kurt Weber, one of the leading Polish cinematographers and also a teacher at the Łódź Film School since 1953.[13] Weber juxtaposes images of the hopeful postwar reality (Warsaw being rebuilt from ashes, children playing) with documentary images of the Warsaw Ghetto, relying on German newsreels and photographs featuring ghetto street scenes, transports to concentration camps, and images of the Warsaw Ghetto Uprising. He captures glimpses of new life near the ruins of the former ghetto. Interestingly, when he was working on the film, reviewing archival materials at the Documentary Film Studio in Warsaw, he was accompanied there by Alain Resnais, who was researching his own project about memory and the Holocaust, *Night and Fog*, also released in 1955.[14]

Polish documentary filmmakers routinely incorporated the surviving visual materials about the Warsaw Ghetto that were produced by the Germans. *Requiem for 500,000* (*Requiem dla 500 000*) is such a compilation documentary made in 1963 by Jerzy Bossak and Wacław Kaźmierczak for the Documentary Film Studio. The film opens with an inscription that is very much in line with the official communist policy stressing the common struggle with fascism: "In memory of the Polish Jews murdered by the Nazis; in memory of the Polish underground fighters who fell trying to save them." The utilized fragments of Nazi documentary films, depicting life in the ghetto, suffering and deportations, are accompanied by music by Handel and Mozart to emphasize both horror and mourning. Undoubtedly, as Krzysztof Kąkolewski put it in his review, the film creates tension by featuring characters that are captured by German cameras and unaware of their fate, juxtaposed with the viewers' knowledge about the Holocaust.[15] The film's chronological account of the annihilation of Polish Jewry won the Short Film Festival in Kraków in 1963 and the first prize at the International Festival of Ethnographic and Sociological Films in Florence in 1965.

Janusz Majewski, a director better known for his stylish film adaptations, made in 1962 a short film about neglected Jewish cemeteries, *The Rose* (*Róża*). He is also responsible for a much-discussed and awarded documentary, *The Fleischer's Album* (*Album Fleischera*, 1962), where he employs war photographs taken by a Wehrmacht officer, covering his military service in France, Poland, and Soviet Russia. This documentary, entirely relying on pictures that were accidentally uncovered in Poland, belongs to a distinct subgenre in Polish documentary cinema—films utilizing personal photographs taken by German soldiers and functionaries of the Nazi state on Polish soil.

As Mikołaj Jazdon perceptively argues, documentary films about the war that employ photographs from many sources became a Polish specialty.[16] Unlike German propaganda newsreels, photographs taken by German functionaries offer personal perspectives on the war. In Majewski's film, the ironic commentary and the soundtrack featuring popular German tunes present not only Fleischer's military history, but also provide insights into his mind.

A similar account, featuring the perpetrator's representation of the war and occupation, is provided by an accomplished documentary filmmaker Jerzy Ziarnik in his *An Ordinary Day of Schmidt, the Gestapo Man* (*Powszedni dzień gestapowca Schmidta*, 1963). Ziarnik's ten-minute film looks at hundreds of photographs uncovered at the archives of the Main Commission for the Investigation of Nazi Crimes. They were taken by Schmidt, the Gestapo officer from Kutno, and left in his apartment after his escape in 1945. The photographic album documents, among others, the Nazi atrocities committed in occupied Poland. The commentary employs only Schmidt's own captions under the photographs. Unlike Fleischer, who is portrayed as an eyewitness to the horrors that he did not openly support, Schmidt is introduced as a willing executioner of Poles and Jews, whose cruel and robotic actions did not betray any human feelings (as evidenced by his laconic labels under photographs, such as "The Action Against 6,000 Jews in Płońsk"). Mikołaj Jazdon aptly compares the representation of Schmidt to a hunter on a "macabre safari."[17]

Several other Polish School documentary films also referred either to the occupation or the prewar world of Polish Jewry. For example, Tadeusz Makarczyński's short poetic film *Night* (*Noc*, 1961) introduced images of suffering women, survivors of concentration camps, who were searching for their children lost during the war. An earlier film by Makarczyński, *Warsaw Suite*, dedicated to "women, who cannot believe that death camps took away from them what was for them the most precious," portrayed destroyed Warsaw being rebuilt from ashes. Another filmmaker, Maria Kwiatkowska employed photographs of the Jewish population of the town of Kazimierz on the Vistula in her *On the Vistula River* (*Nad Wisłą*, 1962). Kwiatkowska's film about the loss shares several similarities with post-1989 Polish documentaries uncovering the almost forgotten, often nostalgic images of prewar *shtetls*.

Years of Organized Forgetting: 1965–1980

Between 1965 and 1980, only a handful of documentary films tackled Polish-Jewish relations and the Holocaust. In 1966, Jerzy Ziarnik made a short film *The Museum* (*Muzeum*) about the Auschwitz-Birkenau State Museum. Better known internationally is the recipient of several awards, *Archeology* (*Archeologia*, 1967), made by Andrzej Brzozowski, who was the second director of Andrzej Munk's *The Passenger* and also the maker of *By the Railway Track* (see chapter 4). Made for the Educational Film Studio, *Archeology* refers to modern archeology—the camera documents excavating work at Auschwitz-Birkenau conducted by researchers affiliated with the Institute of History, Polish Academy of Sciences (PAN). In 1967, Brzozowski also produced a docudrama *Medallions* (*Medaliony*), where he revisited the characters featured in Zofia Nałkowska's classic Holocaust collection of short stories.[18] Another documentary by Brzozowski, *Tracks* (*Ślady*), started in 1967 and completed in 1982, deals with remains of Jewish culture in Polish towns and villages situated near the railway tracks leading to the Treblinka death camp.[19]

Following the "March Events" of 1968, the Holocaust theme became marginalized by the authorities. The only exception was the issue of Polish help for the Jews. The exhibition titled "Polish Assistance for the Jewish People 1939–1945" (*Naród polski z pomocą ludności żydowskiej 1939–1945*) opened in Warsaw on 1 May 1968. It was followed by two documentary films produced by Janusz Kidawa: *The Righteous* (*Sprawiedliwi*, 1968) and *The Matter of Life and Death* (*Cena życia i śmierci*, 1968). The issue of Polish help for the Jews had been particularly emphasized in several books published during this period by writers living in and outside of Poland and representing different political positions.[20]

Toward the end of the decade of "organized forgetting," as if heralding changes occurring in the mid-1980s, Jerzy Ziarnik produced *I Am Looking at Your Photograph* (*Patrzę na twoją fotografię*, 1979). His short film makes use of several family albums from 1939 that belonged, as the viewer learns later, to the Polish Jews deported to Auschwitz, where their pictures were confiscated. The photographs are divided into several thematic groups, for example "Our Wedding" or "Our Holidays," and accompanied by popular music from the 1930s, which is replaced toward the end of the film by a commentary about the fate of the people represented in the photographs. The almost nostalgic atmosphere of the film is broken by the viewers' knowledge that these people perished in the gas chambers. In an essay on Polish documentary films utilizing archival photographs, Mikołaj Jazdon writes that Ziarnik's film shifted the miraculously preserved photographs "into a new dimension of memory. It replaced the irrevocably destroyed family memory with that of public memory."[21] Several documentary films made after the 1989 return of democracy in Poland employ similar approach, for example Jolanta Dylewska's celebrated Po-lin (Po-lin. Okruchy pamięci, 2008).

Return of the Repressed: "The Poor Poles Look at the Ghetto"

The beginning of the 1980s was not abundant with Polish documentary films dealing with the Holocaust. Likewise rare were documentaries about the Polish experience of the war, for example films such as *I Happened to Be in Auschwitz* (*Bawiłem w Oświęcimiu*, 1982) directed by Józef Gębski, an account of one of Poland's most accomplished sculptors, Ksawery Dunikowski (1875–1964). In June 1940, he was deported to Auschwitz (camp number 774) where he survived until January 1945.

The attitudes toward representing the past began to change in the second part of the 1980s. In 1987, Marcel Łoziński (b. 1940), one of the leading Polish documentary filmmakers and the winner of numerous awards at the most prestigious film festivals, produced *Witnesses* (*Świadkowie*, 1987) for French television. The film examines the 1946 Kielce pogrom, the murder of forty-two Jews by a Polish mob instigated by rumors about a ritual murder. Łoziński, who is of Jewish origin, opens the film with the *Polish Newsreel* number twenty-two from 1946, reporting the funeral of the victims of the Kielce pogrom. Over the images of the funeral the narrator reminds the viewer: "Old men, women and children had been ruthlessly murdered only because they were Jews ... The whole democratic Poland unites in pain and mourning with the Jewish nation." Picturing a group of grieving women who "went through the ordeal of the Nazi camps," the commentator adds: "These women ... lost their loved ones. They lost them because of the people who call themselves Poles." Łoziński later allows the eyewitnesses to provide their accounts of what happened in Kielce. Disturbingly, they often reveal deep layers of anti-Semitism among the Poles.

After the transition to democracy in 1989, documentary films that were earlier shown as supplements to the main program in cinema theaters became the domain of television. This fact hugely increased the number of films produced, but ended one aspect that Polish documentaries were known for— metaphorical, poetic depictions of reality. The most prominent trend in contemporary films has to do with coming to terms with the communist past and uncovering historical moments buried or distorted by the communists. Polish-Soviet relations began to feature prominently in Polish documentaries, particularly the Soviet aggression against Poland on 17 September 1939, the 1940 Katyń mass execution of Polish officers by the Soviets, and the deportations of Poles to Siberia.[22] The anti-Semitic events of 1968 also found their cinematic representation in *My Seven Jewish Schoolmates* (*Siedmiu Żydów z mojej klasy*, 1991, Marcel Łoziński), *We Honestly Did Not Know* (*I naprawdę nic nie wiedzieliśmy*, 1993, Andrzej Titkow), and in *The Gdański Railway Station* (*Dworzec Gdański*, 2006, Maria Zmarz-Koczanowicz).

A large number of documentary films made after 1989 also deal with Poland's Jewish history and the Holocaust. Several films show the surviving Polish Jews returning to places where they lived before the war, re-visiting the sites of concentration and death camps where their relatives perished, and talking to Polish eyewitnesses, often people who helped them. The survivors' testimonies are sometimes supported by a combination of archival photographs and footage, usually produced by the Germans in the ghettos.

Birthplace (*Miejsce urodzenia*, 1992), produced by Paweł Łoziński (b. 1965, Marcel Łoziński's son), one of the best documentaries made at the beginning of the 1990s in Poland, belongs to the aforementioned group. The film revolves around Henryk Grynberg's return to Poland in order to learn more about the circumstances surrounding the death of his father and brother during the war. Grynberg (b. 1936) is a Jewish-Polish writer well known for his books about the Holocaust and the fate of Polish Jewry. During the war, several members of his family perished; he and his mother survived, hiding with "Aryan papers." In 1967, Grynberg defected to the United States when his theatrical company, the State Jewish Theater in Warsaw, was on tour. In 1992, accompanied by Łoziński's camera, Grynberg revisits places where his family was hiding during the occupation and meets with a number of old villagers who remember him and his family. After talking to several people, some of whom helped the Grynbergs to survive, the grim truth about his father's fate is revealed—he was killed by two brothers, village dwellers, who were hoping to prosper from the crime. Disturbingly, the truth is revealed by a villager whose identity was concealed when the film premiered on Polish television, because he feared for his life. In the film's finale, Grynberg discovers the place where his father was buried by some villagers after his body had been lying in the field for days.

Łoziński's film follows Claude Lanzmann's strategy, employed in *Shoah* (1985), of revisiting the places of the Holocaust and letting the eyewitnesses provide their own testimonies. Unlike the majority of Polish documentary filmmakers, Łoziński avoids incorporating archival footage or photographs. Praising his work, Mirosław Przylipiak writes, "The creation of a time-bridge between two points over fifty years apart is the exceptional achievement of this film. It seems that Łoziński managed to 'reverse time' without using any archival materials."[23]

Another powerful film, Michał Nekanda-Trepka's *The Last Witness* (*Ostatni świadek*, 2002), introduces a survivor of the Treblinka death camp, Samuel Willenberg, who offers a compelling narrative of his survival. Accompanied by Nekanda-Trepka's camera, Willenberg revisits several places in Poland: Opatów—his hometown, Częstochowa—a town where his family was briefly hiding during the occupation, and Treblinka—where two of his sisters were killed. Walking on the site of the former extermination site, Willenberg provides a commentary about the mechanics of the camp and attributes his survival to sheer luck. At Treblinka, Willenberg took part in the armed mutiny of the *Sonderkommando* on 2 August 1943, during which about four hundred prisoners escaped; sixty-seven of them survived the war. Willenberg managed to get to Warsaw where his father was hiding on the Aryan side. Later, he participated in the Warsaw Rising and after the war immigrated to Israel (Figures 8.1, 8.2, and 8.3).

The Last Witness employs contemporary images from Israel, the archival footage of small prewar Polish towns, wartime ghettos and transports, and the photographs of Willenberg's family. Nekanda-Trepka (b. 1947) with the help of his wife and co-scriptwriter, Elżbieta Nekanda-Trepka, greatly contributed to the exploration of the fate of Polish Jewry. The couple also made several other films featuring the testimonies of survivors who revisit places of their suffering and rescue, such as *Five Mothers of Mine* (*Pięć moich matek*, 1998) and *Reminiscent of Yesterday* (*Jakby to było wczoraj*, 2005). The former tells the story of Tamy Lavy who survived the occupation as a child after her Jewish mother died during the war. She revisits Poland and five different Polish women who

Figure 8.1: Samuel Willenberg tells his story of survival in Michał Nekanda-Trepka's *The Last Witness* (2002)

Figure 8.2: An archival image in *The Last Witness*

Figure 8.3: Samuel Willenberg (left) and a Polish helper in *The Last Witness*

took care of her during the Holocaust. Another documentary film by Nekanda-Trepka, *Chutor Konne* (2007), also deals with the theme of Polish help for the Jews during the Holocaust, this time in a small village that provides the film's title.

Like Nekanda-Trepka, in *Childhood in the Shadow of Death* (*Dzieciństwo w cieniu śmierci*, 2004) Małgorzata Imielska follows another survivor, Henrietta Kretz-Daniszewska, who travels to the places of her traumatic childhood. Imielska tells the story about ghetto life, escape, and hiding by referring to archival footage and photographs. Imielska is also responsible for several medium-length documentaries produced for Polish Television, including *Youth during the Holocaust* (*Młodość w czasach Zagłady*, 2001) and *Tell Me, Why?* (*Powiedz mi, dlaczego?*, 2005), as well as a number of short television films about the "Polish Righteous," produced in 2006 and 2007.

An unusual story of survival is portrayed in *The Cross Inscribed in the Star of David* (*Wpisany w gwiazdę Dawida—Krzyż*, 1997), Grzegorz Linkowski's film about a Catholic priest who learned about his Jewish origin at the age of thirty-two. His Jewish biological mother, locked in the ghetto, tried to save her son by giving him to a Polish family ("You will see, one day he will become a Catholic priest," she said). Today, Romuald Jakub Weksler-Waszkinel (he bears the names of his Jewish and Polish families) is a priest who mediates between the two peoples and attempts to bring together Poles and Jews. Wearing the cross inscribed in the Star of David on his chest, he faces the camera and tells the story of his life. Weksler-Waszkinel's unusual story of survival, as well as questions of identity (Jewish/Christian) posed by the film, prompted Martin Borman, the eldest son of a prominent Nazi official and the godson of Hitler, to contact the priest. Linkowski's documentary sequel, *March of the Living* (*Marsz żywych*, 2003), captures their encounter at the site of the Auschwitz museum. The camera at first portrays them individually touring the site of the camp. They meet outside of the camp, shake hands, and return to the museum site after joining the annual March of the Living.

Three internationally known Polish films have continued the long tradition of local documentaries based on archival photographs: *Chronicle of the Warsaw Ghetto Uprising according to Marek Edelman* (*Kronika powstania w getcie warszawskim wg Marka Edelmana*, 1993) directed by Jolanta Dylewska (b. 1958), *Photographer* (*Fotoamator*, 1998) by Dariusz Jabłoński (b. 1961), and *The Portraitist* (*Portrecista*, 2005) by Ireneusz Dobrowolski (b. 1964).

Dylewska's *Chronicle of the Warsaw Ghetto Uprising according to Marek Edelman* creatively employs footage shot by the Germans in the Warsaw Ghetto in 1943. The materials were brought to Poland after the war by Jerzy Bossak, who used them in his classic documentary *Requiem for 500,000*. Later, this footage appeared in many other films, but Dylewska treats it differently. She creates new images from old ones, editing within a frame; by magnifying and slowing frames, she accentuates details missed by previous filmmakers. Through this process, she transforms anonymous and deprived-of-humanity victims into suffering and dignified characters. A member of the Jewish underground leadership in the Warsaw Ghetto, Marek Edelman, candidly narrates this powerful documentary that won several international film festival awards, including the Grand Prix in Munich.[24] Edelman's face, shown in close-ups and hidden in darkness, is juxtaposed with archival materials. The film ends with images of those who fought in the ghetto alongside Edelman, among them Mordecai Anielewicz.

Another film, Jabłoński's *Photographer*, the recipient of several awards including the Grand Prix in Amsterdam, utilizes a collection of four hundred war photographs in color that were uncovered in 1987 in Vienna. Its author, Walter Genewein, was an accountant in the Łódź (Litzmannstadt) Ghetto, and also an avid photographer. The film juxtaposes Genewein's pictures taken in the ghetto after 1940, as well as his off-screen comments (read by an actor) based on his letters and other documents, with the narration by physician and writer Arnold Mostowicz who survived the Łódź Ghetto. The contrast between the past captured by Genewein in color and the present introduced in black and white structures the film and, perhaps, also adds a commentary that to see the Holocaust in color may be "inappropriate" and "causes spontaneous resistance."[25] Genewein's images do not capture the extermination of the Jewish population of Łódź. In his words, they portray the ghetto not as a *Konzentrationslager*, but as a small Jewish town (*kleine jüdische Stadt*). In an essay about Mordecai Chaim Rumkowski, chairman of the Jewish Council in Łódź from 1939 to 1944, Richard L. Rubinstein writes that "Rumkowski's basic strategy was to make the Łódź ghetto so productive for the Germans that they would understand that their wartime economic interests were best served by allowing the ghetto inhabitants to survive."[26] Jabłoński's film demonstrates the extent to which Genewein's photographs removed the grim reality of the ghetto by including the eyewitness testimony. Without Mostowicz's account, the viewer would be helpless "facing the lie of the colored images."[27]

The third acclaimed film, Dobrowolski's *The Portraitist*, tells the story of a prewar portrait photographer, Wilhelm Brasse, best known for taking thousands of Auschwitz "identity photographs" of inmates, as well as for documenting medical experiments inside the camp and taking portraits of the Auschwitz staff. Brasse was born in 1917 in Żywiec (today southern Poland) in a Polish-German family (his father was German, mother Polish). During the war he refused to co-operate with the Nazi regime who imprisoned him in Auschwitz from 1940 to 1945 (camp number 3444). Due to his prewar training in photography, he was assigned in the camp to the political department as a portraitist and forced to document all aspects of camp life. Traumatized by war experiences, he was unable to continue taking pictures after the war. Dobrowolski's film features Brasse's commentary about his life and war experiences and utilizes select archival images that he took in Auschwitz.

***

Like several earlier films, a number of recent documentaries deal with Polish assistance to Jews by focusing on the Polish Righteous, some of them relatively unknown in Poland at that time, for example Irena Sendler. Michał Dudziewicz's film, *Ms. Sendler's List* (*Lista Sendlerowej*, 2002), was followed by a group of films such as Michał Nekanda-Trepka's *A Teaspoon for Life* (*Łyżeczka życia*, 2004). The latter film tells the story of Elżbieta Ficowska's survival and also introduces an interview with the person who rescued Ficowska and hundreds of other Jewish children, Irena Sendler (Figures 8.4 and 8.5). Another film, Jan Strękowski's *Two Drawers* (*Dwie szuflady*, 2005), centers on Professor Michał Głowiński who, like Ficowska, was also rescued as a child by Sendler. He talks about communist and fascist totalitarian systems and about his autobiographical novel *Black Seasons* (*Czarne sezony*).

A number of films were also made about another overlooked war hero, Henryk Sławik (1894–1944), a politician and social worker who saved thousands of Polish and Hungarian Jews in Budapest by granting them false Polish passports. Interned by the Hungarian authorities after 17 September 1939, Sławik later served on a committee helping Polish refugees to leave Hungary in order to join the Polish armed forces in France and the Middle East. Later, together with a representative of the Hungarian government, Jozsef Antall, he began rescuing thousands of Jewish lives by issuing false papers. Sławik continued his activities after the Nazi takeover of Hungary in March 1944. Thanks to him, numerous Jewish refugees were able to leave the country. Several weeks later Sławik was arrested and sent to the Mauthausen concentration camp where he was murdered in August 1944. Films such as *My Father Henryk Sławik* (*Mój tata Henryk Sławik*, 2003, Marek Maldis and Jan Zub) and *Henryk Sławik: Polish Wallenberg* (*Henryk Sławik: Polski Wallenberg*, 2004, Marek Maldis and Grzegorz Łubczyk), rescue from anonymity this historical figure who saved thousands of lives but remained largely unknown even in his own country.

Figure 8.4: Elżbieta Ficowska in Michał Nekanda-Trepka's *A Teaspoon for Life* (2004)

Figure 8.5: Irena Sendler in Michał Nekanda-Trepka's *A Teaspoon for Life*

Several films also portray another Polish resistance hero, Jan Karski (1914–2000), a liaison officer of the Polish underground who was chosen by the Home Army authorities to deliver to the West messages about the plight of the Jewish population in Poland. They include, among others, *The Futile Mission: The Story of Jan Karski-Kozielewski* (*Daremna misja. Opowieść Jana Karskiego-Kozielewskiego*, 1993), produced by Janusz Weychert, and *The Man who Wanted to Stop the Holocaust* (*Człowiek, który chciał zatrzymać Holocaust*, 2005), produced by Jan Grzyb.

The narrative about Polish help for Jews and the Polish Righteous is also the focus of another film, *The Price of Life* (*Cena życia*, 2004), produced by Andrzej Baczyński for Polish Television in Krakow. It tells the story of Józef and Wiktoria Ulm from the village of Markowa in south-eastern Poland. During the war, they and their six children were killed along with eight Jewish people they were hiding in the attic of their home. Polish help for Jews is also at the center of a television docudrama, *The Story of the Kowalskis* (*Historia Kowalskich*, 2009), which was scripted and directed by Arkadiusz Gołębiewski and Maciej Pawlicki. The film recreates events that took place in a small Polish town of Ciepielowo in the late fall of 1942. It focuses on the story of Adam and Bronisława Kowalski who offered shelter to their Jewish neighbors. They were burned alive together with their five children and twenty-seven other villagers. The film relies heavily on eyewitness testimonies and historical accounts, but mixes those with narrative reconstructions. Explaining the focus of his film, Maciej Pawlicki commented that if one counted all the Europeans killed during the war for helping the Jews, most probably 99 percent of them would be Polish people.[28]

Some recent Polish documentary films and television programs have also attempted to recreate Jewish life in prewar Poland. For example, *The Little Town of Kroke* (*Miasteczko Kroke*, 2008, Natalia Szmidt and Kuba Karyś) presents unique documentary footage of the "Jewish Kraków"—nostalgic images of the place where the film's narrators spent their youth. Perhaps the best known example of that trend is Jolanta Dylewska's Polish-German production *Po-lin* (2008). Dylewska's film utilizes exceptional archival footage—amateur family films made in the 1930s in a number of small *shtetls* and Polish towns with a sizable Jewish population. These unique materials were originally filmed by the visiting American relatives of Polish Jews, and thus survived the war. After conducting extensive research, Dylewska went to nineteen Polish towns featured in the documentary footage and talked to the Polish inhabitants who remembered their Jewish neighbors. In addition, Dylewska had been also able to identify several people featured in the archival materials. As a result, her film introduces history with a human face; it focuses on the everyday, unhurried rhythm of prewar Jewish life in Poland.

A number of other documentary films cover various aspects of the Holocaust and Polish-Jewish relations. Their makers address, among others, the fate of Jews from different parts of Poland. For example, the plight of the ghetto in Pabianice near Łódź is portrayed in Zbigniew Gajzler's film *Sarid* (2005), in which one of the few eyewitnesses, Alexander Bartal-Bicz, tells the story of his survival. The liquidation of the Łódź Ghetto is documented by Michał Bukojemski and Marek Miller in their *Liquidation 08.1944* (*Likwidacja 08.1944*, 2009). The ghetto in Kraków, as well as Polish-Jewish relations, are presented in *The Eagle Pharmacy* (*Apteka pod Orłem*, 2006), directed by Krzysztof Miklaszewski, the story about a Polish pharmacy that after the creation of the ghetto found itself inside its borders. The participation of Polish Jews in the Warsaw Rising is debated in a documentary by Anna Ferens and Anna Kowalewska-Onaszkiewicz, *The Jews in the Warsaw Rising* (*Żydzi w Powstaniu Warszawskim*, 2004).

Several films, some of them made for the young, uninitiated viewer, focus on different Nazi extermination sites and concentration camps created on occupied Polish territories. These films also extensively address the issue of Jewish suffering. For example, *From the Auschwitz Chronicle* (*Z kroniki Auschwitz*, 2005), directed by Michał Bukojemski, consists of a series of five "chapters": *The Longest Roll, The Orchestra, The Platform Birkenau, Love* (which refers to Mala Zimetbaum and Edek Galiński's story), and *The Sonderkommando*. Bukojemski employs German newsreels, testimonies of the survivors, drawings and paintings done by inmates, and photographs. The film's version on DVD features narration utilizing the actual words of the Auschwitz survivors in seven different language versions (the English version is read by Kenneth Branagh and Miriam Margolyes). As Bukojemski writes in the promotional leaflet accompanying the DVD version of the film, "there is no single universal truth about the Auschwitz-Birkenau extermination camp. Each camp survivor has their own unquestionable truth—which may vary from the truth of their campmate from the neighboring bunk."[29]

***

This chapter has shown how rich and varied are Polish documentary films about the Holocaust. Without a doubt, they warrant more scholarly attention. Several films discussed in this chapter were never shown outside of Poland; only some of them, recipients of accolades at various festivals of documentary cinema, are known to international audiences. This is a topic that deserves a separate study.

Notes

1. Stanisław Ozimek, "The Polish Newsreel in 1945: The Bitter Victory," in *Hitler's Fall: The Newsreel Witness*, eds. K.R.M. Short and Stephan Dolezel (London: Croom Helm, 1988), 72.
2. Stanisław Wohl, "W Chełmie i Lublinie. O historycznych dniach lipca 1944 roku," *Film* 28/29 (1969): 8–9. The German camp slang word, *Muselmann* (plural *Muselmänner*), literally meaning "Muslim," designates an exhausted prisoner who has lost the will to live. In his

report, Stanisław Wohl uses the Polish term—*Muzułman*. Wohl's comment stresses that the *Polish Newsreel* crew was the first to enter Majdanek before the Soviet filmmakers led by Roman Karmen.
3. Alicja Mucha-Świeżyńska, "Myśleliśmy o kinematografii spółdzielczej" [interview with Jerzy Bossak], *Kino* 9 (1989): 6.
4. Jolanta Lemann-Zajiček, *Kino i polityka: Polski film dokumentalny 1945-1949* (Łódź: PWSFTviT, 2003), 27-29.
5. Stuart Liebman, "Documenting the Liberation of the Camps: The Case of Aleksander Ford's *Vernichtungslager Majdanek-Cmentarzysko Europy* (1944)," in *Lessons and Legacies VII: The Holocaust in International Perspective*, ed. Dagmar Herzog (Evanston: Northwestern University Press, 2006), 334. Unlike Lemann-Zajiček, Liebman does not make a distinction between the first shorter Polish version of *Majdanek* directed by Ford (570 meters in length) and the extended Polish-Soviet version of the film, *Vernichtungslager Majdanek* (with Ford being credited as the director).
6. Tobby Haggith writes that reports about Majdanek appeared widely in the British press and radio, but their documentary value was often questioned. For example, the BBC did not broadcast Alexander Werth's material on Majdanek as "Soviet atrocity propaganda." Tobby Haggith, "Filming the Liberation of Bergen Belsen," in *Holocaust and the Moving Image: Representations in Film and Television since 1933*, ed. Toby Haggith and Joanna Newman (London: Wallflower Press, 2005), 47.
7. Adolf Forbert, "W Oświęcimiu po oswobodzeniu obozu," *Przegląd Lekarski* vol. 37, no. 1 (1980): 182-184.
8. Ibid.
9. In 1970, Robert Stando made a film about Arthur Greiser, *The Extent of Arthur Greiser's Crimes* (*Granica zbrodni Arthura Greisera*, 21').
10. Janina Struk, *Photographing the Holocaust: Interpretations of the Evidence* (London: I.B. Taurus, 2004), 123.
11. Ibid., 123.
12. Ibid., 123.
13. Kurt Weber was born in 1928 in an assimilated Jewish family in Cieszyn (southern Poland) and survived the war in the Soviet Union. He started his career working on the socialist realist film *Two Brigades* (*Dwie brygady*, 1950, Eugeniusz Cękalski) and continued during the Polish School period working on Czesław Petelski's *Damned Roads* (1959), Kazimierz Kutz's *People from the Train* (1961) and Tadeusz Konwicki's *All Souls Day* (*Zaduszki*, 1961) and *Somersault* (*Salto*, 1965). In 1969, Weber immigrated to West Germany where he worked as a cinematographer on several films.
14. Piotr Litka, "Jako dziecko myślałem, że filmy powstają w kabinie projekcyjnej" [Interview with Kurt Weber], *Kino* 12 (2002): 10.
15. Krzysztof Kąkolewski, "Gen. Hans Jürgen Stroop był człowiekiem: Requiem dla 500 tysięcy," *Film* 22 (1963): 4.
16. Mikołaj Jazdon, "Fotografie w roli głównej: O polskim filmie ikonograficznym ze zdjęć," *Kwartalnik Filmowy* 54-55 (2006): 212-230. Jazdon adds that Fleischer was found after the West German premiere of the film and visited by Majewski and his crew. According to Majewski, Fleischer accepted his screen image of an "unwilling executioner," a simple man involved in the war atrocities. Janusz Majewski, *Retrospektywka* (Warsaw: Muza, 2001), 231-233.
17. Jazdon, "Fotografie w roli głównej," 215.
18. Zofia Nałkowska, *Medallions*, trans. Diana Kuprel (Evanston: Northwestern University Press, 2000). First published in Polish in 1946.
19. See Joanna Preizner, "Świadkowie. Przy torze kolejowym Andrzeja Brzozowskiego," *Postscriptum Polonistyczne* vol. 1, no. 5 (2010): 137-138.
20. See Dariusz Libionka, "Polskie piśmiennictwo na temat zorganizowanej i indywidualnej pomocy Żydom (1945-2008)," *Zagłada Żydów. Studia i Materiały* 4 (2008): 31-44.

21. Mikołaj Jazdon, "Fotografie w roli głównej," 217.
22. For example, the Katyń massacre is examined in films such as *The Katyń Woods* (*Las Katyński*, 1990, Marcel Łoziński), *The Katyń Massacre* (*Zbrodnia katyńska*, 1991, Maciej Sieński), *The Film Found in Katyń* (*Film znaleziony w Katyniu*, 1992, Józef Gębski, 1992), and docudrama *Bury Me Together with Them* (*Pochowajcie mnie razem z nimi*, 1994, Mirosław Dembiński). This important trend in Polish cinema culminated with several films that accompanied the release of Andrzej Wajda's breakthrough narrative film *Katyń* (2007), and includes, among others, *Katyń: The Truth and the Lie about the Crime* (*Katyń. Prawda i kłamstwo o zbrodni*, 2005, Grzegorz Szuplewski) and *Katyń* (2007, Józef Gębski). The Soviet attack on Poland in September 1939 and the deportations of Poles to Siberia are examined in *The Mass Murder in Kolyma* (*Zbrodnia na Kołymie*, 1993, Józef Gębski) and *I Am Not Afraid Anymore* (*Już nie lękam się nic*, 1996, Andrzej Titkow). The crimes committed by the Polish Secret Police (UB) following the implementation of the communist system in Poland after 1945 are the subject of *We Learned How to Torture from Humer* (*Uczyliśmy się torturować od Humera*, 1995, Alina Mrowińska, Jolanta Sztuczyńska) and a three-part film, *Secret Police 1994–1956* (*Bezpieka 1944–1956*, 1997, Iwona Bartólewska).
23. Mirosław Przylipiak, "Polish Documentary Film after 1989," in *The New Polish Cinema*, ed. Janina Falkowska and Marek Haltof (London: Flicks Books, 2003), 155.
24. Marek Edelman is also the narrator of one of the most powerful accounts of the Warsaw Ghetto Uprising, a book by Hanna Krall, *Shielding the Flame: An Intimate Conversation with Dr. Marek Edelman, the Last Surviving Leader of the Warsaw Ghetto Uprising*, trans. Joanna Stasińska and Lawrence Weschler (New York: Henry Holt, 1986).
25. Tomasz Łysak, "O niemożliwej wierze w dokument. *Fotoamator* Dariusza Jabłońskiego," *Kwartalnik Filmowy* 43 (2003): 72.
26. Richard L. Rubinstein, "Gray into Black: The Case of Mordecai Chaim Rumkowski," in *Gray Zones: Ambiguity and Compromise in the Holocaust and Its Aftermath*, ed. Jonathan Petropoulos and John K. Roth (New York: Berghahn Books, 2005), 301.
27. Tomasz Majewski, "Getto w kolorach Agfa. Uwagi o *Fotoamatorze* Dariusza Jabłońskiego," in *Między słowem a obrazem*, ed. Małgorzata Jakubowska, Tomasz Kłys, and Bronisława Stolarska (Kraków: Rabid, 2005), 334.
28. Marcin Rafałowicz, "Na granicy misterium," *Rzeczpospolita* (20 October 2009). http://www.rp.pl/artykul/9131,380064_Na_granicy_misterium_.html (accessed 15 January 2010).
29. *From the Auschwitz Chronicle* (*Z kroniki Auschwitz*, 2005), produced by the Digit-Film, co-produced by Polish Television 2, the edition on DVD co-financed by the Polish Ministry of Culture. The DVD is distributed by the Auschwitz-Birkenau Memorial and Museum.

Afterword

Polish films about the Holocaust form an important group within the Polish national cinema. Several of them, first and foremost *The Last Stage* and *Border Street*, also belong to the classic films of the "Holocaust genre." They serve not only as the first attempts at representing the Holocaust, but also they have shaped the future representations of Auschwitz-Birkenau and the Warsaw Ghetto Uprising respectively.

The majority of films discussed in the present book reflect in a significant way the changing political climate in postwar Poland, the pressure of politics, and the tension between the demands of the communist ideology and the artistic objectives of some Polish filmmakers. An examination of these films reveals the struggles for the historically accurate representation of the Holocaust in a country that for decades was subjected to a communist interpretation of history.

During the Polish School period in the late 1950s and at the beginning of the 1960s, several young filmmakers, including Stanisław Różewicz, Andrzej Wajda, and Andrzej Munk, significantly contributed to the representation of the Holocaust. Their films were followed by the state-imposed stage of "organized forgetting." The struggles with censorship, and the banning of several projects in the late 1960s and in the 1970s, finally gave way to a renewed interest in the subject in the 1980s.

Since the transition to democracy, Poles have tried to face some of the previously silenced aspects of their history,[1] including the complex history of the Polish-Jewish relationship. Coming to terms with the national past has been helped by the publication of numerous historical studies that often stirred heated national debates, by the proliferation of conferences and seminars on the topic, and by the meticulous research presented on the pages of academic periodicals such as *Holocaust Studies and Materials* (*Zagłada Żydów. Studia i Materiały*), published by the Polish Center for Holocaust Studies at the Institute of Philosophy and Sociology of the Polish Academy of Sciences (PAN).

The revival of Jewish culture in Poland has largely been triggered by a younger generation of Poles, who are reviving the country's multicultural past. Poland, traditionally a haven for Jews, has no significant Jewish presence now. The sense of loss of a vibrant Jewish culture appears genuine. Polish journalist Ewa Berberyusz expresses it well: "The absence of Jews, whom I still remember but who are now gone, leaves me, for one, with a sense of irreplaceable loss. I voice here not just a sentiment in which is enshrined an idealised memory of old Poland, but rather an awareness of the real, manifest impoverishment of Polish culture. Poland has lost a very important creative contribution."[2] Another journalist, Konstanty Gebert, who founded a Polish-Jewish monthly *Midrasz*, comments: "You cannot have genocide and then have people live as if everything is normal. It's like when you lose a limb. Poland is suffering from Jewish phantom pain."[3]

The growing interest in the Jewish part of Polish history is illustrated, for example, by the number of cultural events referring to the Jewish cultural heritage and the Jewish contribution to Polish culture. These events, as stated earlier, are frequently initiated and managed by non-Jewish Poles who seem to be fascinated by the missing aspect of Poland's national identity. For example, the annual Jewish Culture Festival (Festiwal Kultury Żydowskiej), since 1988 headed by Janusz Makuch, takes place in the old Jewish district of Kraków—Kazimierz. Left to deteriorate during the communist era, Kazimierz is now revitalized, fashionable with its "Jewish" restaurants and cafés, and frequented by young non-Jewish Poles. Similar, although smaller, festivals testifying to the Jewish revival in Poland are organized in several other Polish cities. The screenings of films about Jewish themes also belong to the most popular forms of remembering the Jewish past in Poland. For example, Warsaw hosts the International Film Festival "Jewish Motifs" (Międzynarodowy Festiwal Filmowy Żydowskie Motywy) presented in the "Muranów" cinema since 2004.[4]

The interest in the Jewish-Polish past has been, and most likely will be, continued in Polish cinema. It is evidenced, among other things, by the recent release of *Joanna* (2010), scripted and directed by the veteran director Feliks Falk (born 1941). It tells the story of a young Polish woman who takes care of a Jewish girl during World War II. Although the film's story may sound familiar in the context of Polish cinema, Falk intelligently narrates the complexity of the wartime situation and avoids clichéd aspects of some of the previously made films. Another director, Waldemar Krzystek (b. 1953), narrates his television series, *The Righteous* (*Sprawiedliwi*, 2010), in a similar manner. In the seven-episode series, he moves between the present and the past to deal with the Polish Righteous, members of the Council for Aid to the Jews (Żegota), who rescued the Jews during World War II.

Taking into consideration past and present attempts at representing the Holocaust and the common Polish-Jewish past, perhaps, as Erica Lehrer writes, they "should be recognized as the product of a Polish desire to bear witness to its own Jewishness."[5]

Notes

1. An immense void in the screen representation of Polish history has been filled in recent years with the release of critically acclaimed historical films, such as Andrzej Wajda's *Katyń* (2007) and Ryszard Bugajski's *General Nil* (*Generał Nil*, 2009).
2. Ewa Berberyusz, "The Black Hole: Conversation with Stanisław Krajewski, 'a Pole and a Jew in One Person,'" in *My Brother's Keeper? Recent Polish Debates on the Holocaust*, ed. Antony Polonsky (London and New York: Routledge, 1990), 108.
3. Craig S. Smith, "Non-Jews Reviving Poland's Jewish Culture," *The New York Times* (11 July 2007). Quoted from http://www.nytimes.com/2007/07/11/world/europe/11iht-poland.4.6617269.html (accessed 20 March 2010).
4. The "Muranów" cinema theater, owned by Gutek Film (Polish distributor of art cinema), is located in a district of Warsaw that was inhabited by Jews before 1939. During World War II, it became part of the Warsaw Ghetto.
5. Erica Lehrer, "Bearing False Witness: 'Vicarious' Jewish Identity and the Politics of Affinity," in *Imaginary Neighbors: Mediating Polish-Jewish Relations after the Holocaust*, ed. Dorota Głowacka and Joanna Zylinska (Lincoln: University of Nebraska Press, 2007), 103.

Filmography (Chronological Order)

(Compiled from: film credits, Polish Film Database www.filmpolski.pl, and *Leksykon polskich filmów fabularnych*, edited by Jan Słodowski, Warsaw: Wiedza i Życie, 1997.)

Feature Films

Two Hours (*Dwie godziny*) (1946/1957), 68'
  Director: Stanisław Wohl and Józef Wyszomirski
  Script: Jan Marcin Szancer, Ewa Szelburg-Zarembina (not credited)
  Cinematography: Stanisław Wohl
  Set Design: Anatol Radzinowicz
  Music: Roman Palester
  Editing: Henryk Nowicki, Czesław Raniszewski
  Production: Aleksander Pękalski; "Film Polski"
  Cast: Danuta Szaflarska (Weronika), Jerzy Duszyński (Marek), Jacek Woszczerowicz (Leon), Władysław Hańcza (*Kapo* Filip), Barbara Fijewska (Fela), Irena Krasnowiecka (Iza), Wanda Łuczycka (Filip's wife), Hanna Skarżanka (Teresa), Władysław Grabowski, Tadeusz Łomnicki, Mieczysław Milecki, Stanisław Grolicki, Józef Węgrzyn, Aleksander Zelwerowicz, Hanka Bielicka, Barbara Drapińska (not credited), Ryszarda Hanin (not credited), Maria Kaniewska (not credited), Andrzej Łapicki (not credited), Stefan Śródka (not credited), and others.

Forbidden Songs (*Zakazane piosenki*, 1947), 97'
  Director: Leonard Buczkowski
  Script: Ludwik Starski
  Cinematography: Adolf Forbert
  Set Design: Anatol Radzinowicz
  Music: Roman Palester
  Editing: Róża Pstrokońska
  Production: Franciszek Petersile; "Film Polski"
  Cast: Danuta Szaflarska (Halina Tokarska), Jerzy Duszyński (Roman Tokarski, Halina's Brother), Henryk Szweizer (Hiding Jew), Zofia Mrozowska (Jewish Street Singer), Jan Świderski (Ryszard), Jan Kurnakowicz (Cieślak), Janina Ordężanka (Tokarska), Alina Janowska (Street Singer), Zofia Jamry (Volksdeutch), Stanisław Łapiński, Hanna

Bielicka, Andrzej Łapicki, Edward Dziewoński, Kazimierz Wichniarz, and others.

Dead Track (*Ślepy tor*, aka *Powrót do życia*, 1948/1991, not released theatrically)
Director: Boživoj Zeman
Script: Adam Ważyk
Cinematography: Adolf Forbert, Seweryn Kruszyński
Set Design: Roman Mann
Music: Jerzy Harald
Editing: Czesław Raniszewski
Production: Aleksander Suchcicki; "Film Polski"
Cast: Irena Eichlerówna (Elżbieta Gruszecka), Celina Niedźwiecka (Janina Rogowiczowa), Helena Buczyńska (Aunt Anna), Alina Janowska (Ewa), Hanka Bielicka, Halina Głuszkówna, Marysia Bujańska, Feliks Chmurkowski, Tadeusz Burnatowicz, Edward Dziewoński, and others.

Our Children (*Unzere Kinder*, 1948, in Yiddish), 80'
Director: Natan Gross
Script: Natan Gross, dialogue: Rachela Auerbach
Cinematography: Leonard Zajączkowski
Music: Saul Berezowski
Production: Saul Goskind, Natan Gross; "Kinor"
Cast: Szymon Dzigan, Israel Szumacher, Natan Majzler (Teacher), Hadasa Kestin (Teacher), Israel Glanz, Luba Majzler, Niusia Gold, Nadia Kareni, Luba Stolarska, and others.

The Last Stage (aka *The Last Stop*; *Ostatni etap*, 1948), 104'
Director: Wanda Jakubowska
Script: Wanda Jakubowska, Gerda Schneider
Cinematography: Boris Monastyrski
Set Design: Roman Mann, Czesław Piaskowski
Music: Roman Palester
Editing: Róża Pstrokońska
Production: Mieczysław Wajnberger; "Film Polski"
Cast: Barbara Drapińska (Marta Weiss), Stanisław Zaczyk (Tadek), Wanda Bartówna (Helena), Tatjana Górecka (Eugenia, the Russian Doctor), Huguette Faget (Michele), Antonina Górecka (Anna, German Communist), Maria Winogradowa (Nadia), Barbara Fijewska (Anielka), Aleksandra Śląska (Oberaufseherin), Maria Kaniewska (Raportfuhrerin), Maria Redlichówna (Urszula), Alina Janowska (Dessa), Zofia Mrozowska (Gypsy Woman), Stefan Śródka (Bronek), Barbara Rachwalska (*Kapo* Elza), Anna Jaraczówna (*Kapo* Frieda), Halina Drohocka (Lalunia), Władysław Brochwicz (Lagerkommandant Hans Schmidt), Edward Dziewoński (SS

Doctor), Kazimierz Pawłowski (Head of the Gestapo), Janina Morrisówna (Aufseherin), Elżbieta Łabuńska, Jadwiga Chojnacka, Ewa Kunina, Roma Rudecka, Zofia Niwińska, Zygmunt Chmielewski, Tadeusz Bartosik, and others.

Border Street (*Ulica Graniczna*, 1949), 115'
Director: Aleksander Ford,
Script: Ludwik Starski, Aleksander Ford, Jean Forge (Jan Fethke)
Cinematography: Jaroslav Tuzar
Set Design: Stěpán Kopecký
Music: Roman Palester
Editing: Jiřina Lukešová
Production: Aleksander Suchcicki, Jaroslav Niklos; "Film Polski"
Cast: Tadeusz Fijewski (Bronek Cieplikowski), Jerzy Leszczyński (Dr. Białek), Władysław Godik (Old Liberman), Stefan Śródka (Natan), Jerzy Złotnicki (Dawidek Liberman), Maria Broniewska (Jadzia Białek), Mieczysława Ćwiklińska (Klara, Jadzia's Teacher), Władysław Walter (Cieplikowski), Jerzy Pichelski (Kazimierz Wojtan), Josef Munclinger (Kuśmirak), Robert Vrchota (German Soldier), Eugeniusz Kruk (Fredek Kuśmirak), Dionizy Ilczenko (Władek Wojtan), Janina Łukowska (Dawidek's Mother), Justyna Karpińska, Maria Żabczyńska, Irena Renard, Edward Dziewoński, Ida Kamińska (Helena, Jadzia's Aunt, not credited), and others.

Unvanquished City (*Miasto nieujarzmione*; early version: *Robinson Warszawski*, 1950), 86'
Director: Jerzy Zarzycki
Script: Jerzy Andrzejewski, Jerzy Zarzycki; loosely based on Władysław Szpilman's memoirs
Cinematography: Jean Isnard
Set Design: Roman Mann
Music: Roman Malawski, Roman Palester (not credited)
Editing: Janina Niedźwiecka
Production: Mieczysław Wajnberger; "Film Polski"
Cast: Jan Kurnakowicz (Piotr Rafalski), Zofia Mrozowska (Krystyna), Igor Śmiałowski (Andrzej, AL Fighter), Jan Rakowiecki (Jan, AL Fighter), Kazimierz Sapiński (Julek, AL Fighter), Wieniamin Trusieniew ("Fiałka"—Russian Telegraphist), Seweryn Butrym, Adam Daniewicz, Lucjan Dytrych, Jerzy Kaliszewski, Władysław Krasnowiecki, Jerzy Wasowski (German officer playing piano), Andrzej Łapicki, Henryk Borowski, Jan Świderski, and others.

A Generation (*Pokolenie*, 1955), 83'
Director: Andrzej Wajda

Script: Bohdan Czeszko; based on his novel
Cinematography: Jerzy Lipman
Set Design: Roman Mann
Music: Andrzej Markowski
Editing: Czesław Raniszewski
Production: Ignacy Taub; WFF Wrocław
Cast: Tadeusz Łomnicki (Stach), Tadeusz Janczar (Jasio Krone), Urszula Modrzyńska (Dorota), Janusz Paluszkiewicz (Sekuła), Ryszard Kotys (Jacek), Roman Polański (Mundek), Zygmunt Hobot (Abram), Ludwik Benoit (Grzesio), Zofia Czerwińska (Bartender), Zbigniew Cybulski (Kostek), Stanisław Milski (Mr. Krone, Jasio's Father), Zygmunt Zintel (Ziarno), Tadeusz Fijewski, Cezary Julski, Hanna Skarżanka, Janusz Ściwiarski, Kazimierz Wichniarz, Bronisław Kassowski, Kazimierz Kutz (not credited), and others.

Three Women (*Trzy kobiety*, 1957), 89'
Director: Stanisław Różewicz
Script: Tadeusz Różewicz, Kornel Filipowicz; based on Kornel Filipowicz's short story (not credited)
Cinematography: Andrzej Ancuta
Set Design: Anatol Radzinowicz
Music: Andrzej Dobrowolski
Editing: Czesław Raniszewski
Production: Włodzimierz Śliwiński; Film Unit "Rytm"
Cast: Anna Ciepielewska (Celina), Zofia Małynicz (Helena), Elżbieta Święcicka (Maria), Józef Nalberczak (Władysław), Tadeusz Białoszczyński (Roman Obersztyn), Jan Ciecierski (Priest), Janusz Bylczyński, Maria Gella, Wiesława Mazurkiewicz, Tadeusz Łomnicki, Władysław Sheybal, Ryszard Pietruski, Gustaw Lutkiewicz, and others.

White Bear (*Biały niedźwiedź*, 1959), 90'
Director: Jerzy Zarzycki
Script: Robert Azderball, Jerzy Broszkiewicz, Stefan Matyjaszkiewicz, Konrad Nałęcki, Jerzy Zarzycki
Cinematography: Stefan Matyjaszkiewicz
Set Design: Jerzy Skrzepiński, Maria Szafran
Music: Stanisław Wisłocki
Editing: Tomira Ancuta, Maria Karpowicz
Production: Zwonimir Feric; Film Unit "Syrena"
Cast: Gustaw Holoubek (Henryk Fogiel), Stanisław Milski (Professor), Adam Pawlikowski (Rudolf von Henneberg), Stanisław Mikulski (Michał Pawlicki), Teresa Tuszyńska (Anna, Professor's Daughter), Liliana Niwińska (Von Henneberg's Wife), Emil Karewicz (Officer Grimm), Feliks

Chmurkowski (Nowicki), Edward Dobrzański (Józek), Jerzy Horecki, Mieczysław Łoza, Wojciech Turowski, and others.

Meetings in the Twilight (*Spotkania w mroku*, 1960), 107′
Director: Wanda Jakubowska
Script: Wanda Jakubowska, based on Stanisława Fleszarowa-Muskat's novel
Cinematography: Kurt Weber
Set Design: Anatol Radzinowicz
Music: Stanisław Skrowaczewski
Editing: Lidia Pstrokońska
Production: Stanisław Daniel; Film Unit "Start"
Cast: Zofia Słaboszowska (Magdalena), Horst Drinda (Ernst Steinlieb), Erich Franz (Wenk), Charlotte Kuter (Mrs. Wenk), Emil Karewicz (Dominik), Ilona Mikke (Marysia), Albert Hatterle (Dr. Heusler), Zofia Mrozowska (Rosa Heusler), Maria Kaniewska (Mrs. Hochmmeier), Maciej Damięcki, Anna Jaraczówna, Mieczysław Pawlikowski, and others.

Birth Certificate (*Świadectwo urodzenia*, 1961), 99′
Director: Stanisław Różewicz
Script: Stanisław Różewicz, Tadeusz Różewicz
Cinematography: Stanisław Loth
Set Design: Tadeusz Wybult
Music: Lucjan Kaszycki
Editing: Czesław Raniszewski, Anna Rubińska
Production: Konstanty Lewkowicz; Film Unit "Rytm"
Cast: (1st part): Henryk Hryniewicz (Janek), Wojciech Siemion (Soldier Józef), Barbara Rachwalska, Mieczysław Stoor, Janusz Kłosiński; (2nd part): Edward Mincer (Zbyszek), Andrzej Banaszewski (Heniek), Paweł Różewicz (Jacek), Stanisław Milski, Józef Nalberczak, Tadeusz Szmidt, Maria Kaniewska; (3rd part): Beata Barszczewska (Mirka), Zofia Małynicz (Head of Orphanage), Zdzisław Mrożewski (Dr. Orzechowski), Małgorzata Leśniewska (Nurse), Mariusz Dmochowski (Gestapo Man), Emil Karewicz (German Doctor), Zygmunt Zintel (Translator), Wanda Łuczycka, Maria Ciesielska, Halina Gryglaszewska, and others.

People from the Train (*Ludzie z pociągu*, 1961), 98′
Director: Kazimierz Kutz
Script: Marian Brandys, Ludwika Woźnicka; based on Marian Brandys' short story
Cinematography: Kurt Weber
Set Design: Jan Grandys
Music: Tadeusz Baird
Editing: Irena Choryńska
Production: Tadeusz Karwański; Film Unit "Kadr"

Cast: Janina Traczykówna (Anna), Andrzej May (Piotr), Danuta Szaflarska (Polish War Widow), Małgorzata Dziedzic (Marylka), Maciej Damięcki (Teenage Boy), Gustaw Lutkiewicz (Blackmailer Kwaśniewski), Jerzy Block (Train Station Manager), Zdzisław Tobiasz (Bahnschutz) Jan Zdrojewski (Gestapo Man), Aleksander Fogiel, Bogdan Baer, Józef Pieracki, Jerzy Turek, and others.

Samson (1961), 117′
Director: Andrzej Wajda
Script: Andrzej Wajda, Kazimierz Brandys; based on Brandys' novel
Cinematography: Jerzy Wójcik
Set Design: Leszek Wajda
Music: Tadeusz Baird
Editing: Janina Niedźwiecka
Production: Stanisław Daniel; Film Unit "Droga", Film Unit "Kadr"
Cast: Serge Merlin (Jakub Gold; dubbed by Władysław Kowalski, not credited), Alina Janowska (Lucyna), Elżbieta Kępińska (Kazia), Tadeusz Bartosik (Pankrat), Władysław Kowalski (Fiałka), Jan Ciecierski (Józef Malina), Irena Netto (Jakub's Mother), Beata Tyszkiewicz (Stasia), Jan Ibel (Genio), Edmund Fetting (not credited), Zygmunt Hubner (not credited), Zofia Jamry (Malina's Blackmailer, not credited), Roman Polański (Man who accompanies the Blackmailer, not credited), Andrzej Żuławski (Student killed by Jakub, not credited), Stanisław Jaśkiewicz, Zbigniew Józefowicz, Edward Kowalczyk, Zdzisław Maklakiewicz, Zygmunt Malawski, Magda Teresa Wójcik, Krystyna Zachwatowicz (all of them not credited), and others.

The Passenger (*Pasażerka*, 1963), 58′
Director: Andrzej Munk,
Assistants to the director: Witold Lesiewicz (completed the film), Andrzej Brzozowski, Anna Dyrka
Script: Andrzej Munk, Zofia Posmysz; based on Zofia Posmysz's work
Commentary: Wiktor Woroszylski
Cinematography: Krzysztof Winiewicz
Set Design: Tadeusz Wybult
Music: Tadeusz Baird
Editing: Zofia Dwornik
Production: Wilhelm Hollender; Film Unit "Kamera"
Cast: Aleksandra Śląska (Liza), Anna Ciepielewska (Marta), Jan Kreczmar (Walter), Marek Walczewski (Tadeusz; dubbed by Stanisław Zaczyk, not credited), Janusz Bylczyński (*Kapo*), Maria Kościałkowska (Inga Weniger), Irena Malkiewicz (Oberaufseherin Madel), Leon Pietraszkiewicz (Grabner), Anna Jaraczówna (*Kapo*), Kazimierz Rudzki (Head of the Red Cross delegation), Krzesisława Dubielówna, Anna Gołębiowska, Barbara

Horawianka, Andrzej Krasicki, Izabella Olszewska, Wanda Swaryczewska, Zdzisław Szymborski, Elżbieta Czyżewska (not credited), Maria Wachowiak (not credited), Tadeusz Łomnicki (Narrator), and others.

The End of Our World (*Koniec naszego świata*, 1964), 138'
Director: Wanda Jakubowska
Script: Wanda Jakubowska, based on Tadeusz Hołuj's novel
Cinematography: Kazimierz Wawrzyniak
Set Design: Bolesław Kamykowski
Music: Kazimierz Serocki
Editing: Lidia Pstrokońska
Production: Stanisław Adler; Film Unit "Start"
Cast: Lech Skolimowski (Henryk), Teresa Wicińska (Maria, Henryk's wife), Krystyn Wójcik (Samek), Tadeusz Hołuj (Adam), Władysław Głąbik (Wiktor), Tadeusz Madeja (Bolek), Edward Kusztal (Czarny), Tadeusz Bogucki (Jan Smolik), Jerzy Przybylski (Dawid, Leader of Sonderkommando), Piotr Augustyniak (SS Doctor Wirth), Tadeusz Teodorczyk, Adam Fornal, Mieczysław Wiśniewski, Elżbieta Starostecka, Jerzy Nowak, Lech Grzmociński, Władysław Pawłowicz, Arkadiusz Bazak, Jerzy Bińczycki, Andrzej Kopiczyński, and others.

The Beater (*Naganiacz*, 1964), 80'
Director: Ewa and Czesław Petelski
Script: Roman Bratny, based on Roman Bratny's short story
Cinematography: Stefan Matyjaszkiewicz
Set Design: Wojciech Krysztofiak
Music: Tadeusz Baird
Editing: Felicja Rogowska
Production: Ryszard Straszewski; Film Unit "Kamera"
Cast: Bronisław Pawlik (Michał), Maria Wachowiak (Hungarian Jewish Woman), Ryszard Pietruski (Jaworek), Wacław Kowalski (Tomasik), Krystyna Borowicz (Lady of the Manor), Henryk Grynberg (Hiding Jew), Aleksander Fogiel (Mr. Potyka), Tadeusz Samogi (Underground Fighter), Gustaw Lutkiewicz, Stefan Bartlik, Bohdan Ejmont, and others.

The Long Night (*Długa noc*, 1967/1989), 78'
Director: Janusz Nasfeter
Script: Janusz Nasfeter, based on Wiesław Rogowski's novel
Cinematography: Antoni Nurzyński
Set Design: Jerzy Skrzepiński
Editing: Roman Kolski
Production: Marceli Nowak; Film Unit "Studio"
Cast: Józef Duriasz (Zygmunt Korsak), Anna Ciepielewska (Katarzyna Katjan), Ryszarda Hanin (Mrs. Piekarczyk), Jolanta Wołłejko (Marta

Piekarczyk), Ludwik Pak (Józef Katjan), Zygmunt Hobot (Hiding Jew), Henryk Hunko (Mr. Szymański), Zdzisław Maklakiewicz (Antoszka), Ryszard Pietruski (Policeman Wasiak), Irena Netto (Mrs. Walecka), Krystyna Feldman, and others.

A Journey into the Unknown (aka *Across the Unknown*; *Wycieczka w nieznane*, 1968), 71'
Director: Jerzy Ziarnik
Script: Jerzy Ziarnik, Andrzej Brycht; based on Andrzej Brycht's short story
Cinematography: Jan Laskowski
Set Design: Jarosław Świtoniak
Music: Jerzy Maksymiuk
Editing: Maria Orłowska
Production: Barbara Pec-Ślesicka; Film Unit "Kamera"
Cast: Ryszard Filipski (Andrzej Miller), Małgorzata Niemirska (Jolka), Janusz Guttner (Robert; dubbed by Jan Machulski, not credited), Zdzisław Leśniak (Scriptwriter Groszek), Alicja Pawlicka (Elza), Emilia Krakowska (Mirka), Jolanta Lothe (Halina), Zdzisław Maklakiewicz, Witold Skaruch, Małgorzata Braunek (not credited), and others.

Ascension Day (*Wniebowstąpienie*, 1969), 85'
Director: Jan Rybkowski
Script: Jan Rybkowski, Adolf Rudnicki; based on Adolf Rudnicki's novel
Cinematography: Mieczysław Jahoda
Set Design: Teresa Barska and Mieczysław Jahoda
Music: Andrzej Korzyński
Editing: Krystyna Rutkowska
Production: Edward Zajiček; Film Unit "Rytm"
Cast: Małgorzata Braunek (Raisa Wolkova-Goldstein), Andrzej Antkowiak (Sebastian Goldstein), Piotr Wysocki (Feliks Bukin), Zofia Mrozowska (Mrs. Goldstein), Józef Kondrat (Mr. Goldstein), Bolesław Płotnicki (Raisa's Father), Stanisław Jaworski (Landlord Kocioł), Aleksandra Zawieruszanka (Ludwika Gerson), Gustaw Lutkiewicz (narrator, not credited), Hanna Zembrzuska, Andrzej Bogucki, Piotr Fronczewski, and others.

The Face of an Angel (*Twarz anioła*, 1970), 91'
Director: Zbigniew Chmielewski
Script: Zbigniew Chmielewski, Stanisław Loth
Cinematography: Stanisław Loth
Set Design: Bolesław Kamykowski
Music: Piotr Marczewski
Editing: Zenon Piórecki
Production: Tadeusz Baljon; Film Unit "Nike"

Cast: Marek Dudek (Tadek Raniecki), Jiři Vrstala (Augustin), Zygmunt Malawski (Guard), Wojciech Pszoniak (Tadek's Father), Saturnin Żórawski (Camp's Commandant), Alicja Zommer, Andrzej Boczula, Bogdan Izdebski, Jan Sosnowski, Piotr Augustyniak, Jerzy Balbuza, Wanda Chwiałkowska, Leon Niemczyk, and others.

Landscape after Battle (*Krajobraz po bitwie*, 1970), 101'
Director: Andrzej Wajda
Script: Andrzej Wajda, Andrzej Brzozowski; based on Tadeusz Borowski's short stories
Cinematography: Zygmunt Samosiuk
Set Design: Jerzy Szeski
Editing: Halina Prugar
Production: Barbara Pec-Ślesicka; Film Unit "Wektor"
Cast: Daniel Olbrychski (Tadeusz), Stanisława Celińska (Nina), Tadeusz Janczar (Karol), Zygmunt Malanowicz (Catholic Priest), Aleksander Bardini (Profesor), Leszek Drogosz (Tolek), Stefan Friedmann (Gypsy), Jerzy Zelnik (American Officer), Mieczysław Stoor (Second Lieutenant), Bohdan Tomaszewski (Translator), Małgorzata Braunek (German Woman), Jerzy Obłamski, Anna German, Agnieszka Fitkau, Józef Pieracki, Andrzej Piszczatowski, Józef Pitorak, Józef Harasiewicz, Alina Szpak, and others.

Remember Your Name (*Zapamiętaj imię swoje*, Poland-Soviet Union, 1974), 97'
Director: Sergei Kolosov
Script: Sergei Kolosov, Ernest Bryll, Janusz Krasiński
Cinematography: Bogusław Lambach
Set Design: Mikhail Kartaszov
Music: Andrzej Korzyński
Editing: Galina Spirina
Production: Stanisław Zylewicz, Fabian Mogilewski; Film Unit "Iluzjon," "Mosfilm"
Cast: Ludmiła Kasatkina (Zinaida Worobjowa), Tadeusz Borowski (Eugeniusz Truszczyński), Ryszarda Hanin (Halina Truszczyńska), Ludmiła Iwanowa (Nadieżda), Leon Niemczyk (Captain Piotrowski), Lilia Dawidowicz (Maria), Maciej Góraj (Andrzej), Jadwiga Boryta, Elżbieta Burakowska, Anna Jaraczówna, Stanisław Jaśkiewicz, Ewa Kania, Andrzej Krasicki (SS man), Barbara Rachwalska, and others.

Salad Days (*Zielone lata*, 1980, children's film), 98'
Director: Stanisław Jędryka
Script: Jerzy Przeździecki; based on Jerzy Przeździecki's novel
Cinematography: Jacek Korcelli
Set Design: Bolesław Kamykowski

Music: Andrzej Korzyński
Editing: Barbara Kosidowska
Production: Jerzy Owoc; Zespół Filmowy "Silesia"
Cast: Tomasz Jarosiński (Wojtek), Jacek Bryniarski (Abramek), Agnieszka Konopczyńska (Erna), Małgorzata Pritulak (Wojtek's Mother), Krzysztof Kiersznowski (Wojtek's Father), Anna Chodakowska (Abramek's Mother), Zygmunt Hobot (Abramek's Father), Henryk Bista (Dr. Turowski), Stanisław Niwiński (Teacher), Janusz Paluszkiewicz, Emilia Krakowska, Irena Laskowska, Elżbieta Karkoszka, and others.

Lynx (*Ryś*, 1982), 82'
Director: Stanisław Różewicz
Script: Stanisław Różewicz; based on Jarosław Iwaszkiewicz's short story
Cinematography: Jerzy Wójcik
Set Design: Tadeusz Wybult
Music: Lucjan Kaszycki
Editing: Urszula Śliwińska
Production: Wielisława Piotrowska; Film Unit "Tor"
Cast: Jerzy Radziwiłowicz (Priest Konrad), Franciszek Pieczka (Alojz), Piotr Bajor ("Ryś"), Ryszarda Hanin (Priest's Housekeeper), Janusz Paluszkiewicz (Sacristain Józef), Ania Skuratowicz (Jewish Child), Hanna Mikuć, Henryk Machalica, and others.

Austeria (1983), 102'
Director: Jerzy Kawalerowicz
Script: Jerzy Kawalerowicz, Tadeusz Konwicki, and Julian Stryjkowski; based on Julian Stryjkowski's novel
Cinematography: Zygmunt Samosiuk
Set Design: Jerzy Skrzepiński
Music: Leopold Kozłowski
Editing: Wiesława Otocka
Production: Urszula Orczykowska, Zygmunt Wójcik; Film Unit "Kadr"
Cast: Franciszek Pieczka (Innkeeper Tag), Wojciech Pszoniak (Josele), Jan Szurmiej (Cantor), Ewa Domańska (Asia), Liliana Głąbczyńska (Jewdocha), Wojciech Standełło (Tzadik), Ernestyna Winnicka (Tzadik's Wife), Gołda Tencer (Blanka), Zofia Saretok (Baroness), Stanisław Igar (Apfelgrun), Marek Wilk (Bum Kramer), Zofia Bajuk (Mina), Izabela Wieczorek, Seweryn Dalecki, Mirosława Lombardo, Feliks Szajnert, Edward Żentara, Szymon Szurmiej, and others.

Down Carrier (*Tragarz puchu*, 1983, TV), 86'
Director: Stefan Szlachtycz
Script: Jerzy Janicki
Cinematography: Henryk Janas

Set Design: Zenon Różewicz
Music: Waldemar Kazanecki
Editing: Maria Leszczyńska
Production: Jerzy Owoc, "Poltel"
Cast: Krzysztof Gosztyła (Dalek), Elżbieta Kijowska (Jadwiga), Ewa Sałacka-Krauze (Fryda), and others.

According to the Decrees of Providence (*Wedle wyroków Twoich*, 1984), 98'
Director: Jerzy Hoffman
Script: Jerzy Hoffman, Jan Purzycki
Cinematography: Jerzy Gościk
Set Design: Maciej Maria Putowski
Music: Andrzej Korzyński
Editing: Zenon Piórecki
Production: Artur Brauner, Wilhelm Hollender; Film Unit "Zodiak"
Cast: Sharon Brauner (Ruth, dubbed by Justyna Zbiróg), Anna Dymna (Rachel, Ruth's Aunt), Günter Lamprecht (Kurt Kleinschmidt, dubbed by Leonard Pietraszak), Mathieu Carriere (Walter Knoch, dubbed by Henryk Bista), Ryszarda Hanin (Sister Teresa), Włodzimierz Boruński (Ruth's Grandfather), Alicja Jachiewicz, Emilia Krakowska, Barbara Ludwiżanka, Halina Łabonarska, Magda Teresa Wójcik, Piotr Fronczewski, Janusz Gajos, Marian Opania, Bruno O'Ya, Leszek Teleszyński, Jerzy Trela, Edward Żentara, Walentyna Hoffman, and others.

There Was No Sun That Spring (*Nie było słońca tej wiosny*, 1984), 86'
Director: Juliusz Janicki
Script: Juliusz Janicki, Jerzy Ofierski; based on Jerzy Ofierski's novel
Cinematography: Jerzy Gościk
Set Design: Andrzej Przedworski
Music: Janusz Hajdun
Editing: Mirosława Garlicka
Production: Michał Szczerbic; Film Studio "Zodiak"
Cast: Ernestyna Winnicka (Chaja), Maciej Kozłowski (Piotr Wołosz), Krystyna Wachełko-Zaleska (Monika Wołosz), Janina Nowicka (Piotr's Mother), Juliusz Lubicz-Lisowski (Piotr's Father), Henryk Bista (Mazurek), Zdzisław Kuźniar (Policeman Wiśniewski), Bogusław Sochnacki (Innkeeper), Jerzy Nowak (Josek), Jerzy Trela (Priest), Paweł Nowisz, Maria Czubasiewicz, Helena Kowalczykowa, and others.

A Postcard from the Journey (*Kartka z podróży*, 1984), 78'
Director: Waldemar Dziki
Script: Waldemar Dziki, based on Ladislav Fuks's novel
Cinematography: Wit Dąbal
Set Design: Andrzej Przedworski

Music: Zygmunt Konieczny
Editing: Marek Denys
Production: Jacek Szeligowski: Karol Irzykowski Film Studio
Cast: Władysław Kowalski (Jakub Rosenberg), Rafał Wieczyński (Dawid Grossman), Janusz Michałowski (Dawid's Father), Maja Komorowska (Dawid's Mother), Halina Mikołajska (Dawid's Grandmother), Jerzy Trela, Sława Kwaśniewska, Janina Nowicka, Mariusz Benoit, Bogusz Bilewski, Henryk Bista, Wojciech Standełło, Zygmunt Zintel, and others.

Invitation (*Zaproszenie*, 1985), 92'
Director: Wanda Jakubowska
Script: Wanda Jakubowska
Cinematography: Maciej Kijowski
Set Design: Bolesław Kamykowski
Music: Piotr Marczewski
Editing: Zenon Piórecki
Production: Tomasz Miernowski; PRF "Zespoły Filmowe"
Cast: Antonina Gordon-Górecka (Dr. Anna Górska), Kazimierz Witkiewicz (Piotr Górski), Maria Probosz (Young Anna Górska)), Kazimierz Witkiewicz (Professor Piotr Górski), Leszek Żentara (Young Piotr Górski), Wiesława Mazurkiewicz (Nurse), Ewa Jendrzejewska, Maria Nowotarska, Janusz Sykutera, Artur Barciś, Ewa Szykulska, Jan Krzyżanowski, Mieczysław Grąbka, and others.

In the Shadow of Hatred (*W cieniu nienawiści*, 1986), 111'
Director: Wojciech Żółtowski
Script: Wojciech Żółtowski, Jan Dobraczyński; based on Jan Dobraczyński's short story
Cinematography: Janusz Gauer
Set Design: Elżbieta Karwańska
Music: Andrzej Zarycki
Editing: Alina Faflik
Production: Tadeusz Urbanowicz; Film Studio "Profil", Polish Television
Cast: Bożena Adamek (Zofia), Wanda Łuczycka (Zofia's Aunt), Maria Zbyszewska (Mrs. Celińska), Magda Teresa Wójcik (Maria), Aleksandra Cezarska (Ewa), Róża Chrabelska (Róża Korngold), Barbara Brylska (Volksdeutsch Neighbour), Ireneusz Kaskiewicz (Caretaker Józef Marciniak), Barbara Połomska (Café Owner), Zygmunt Malanowicz (Head of the Department), Janusz Paluszkiewicz (Priest), Henryk Bista (Blackmailer), Ewa Szykulska, Andrzej Róg, Wiktor Matuszewski, and others.

Kornblumenblau (1989), 88'
Director: Leszek Wosiewicz
Script: Leszek Wosiewicz, Jarosław Sander; based on Kazimierz Tymiński's novel
Cinematography: Krzysztof Ptak
Set Design: Zenon Różewicz, Krzysztof Baumiller
Music: Zdzisław Szostak
Editing: Wanda Zeman
Production: Jerzy Fidler; Karol Irzykowski Film Studio
Cast: Adam Kamień (Tadeusz Wyczyński), Krzysztof Kolberger (*Kapo*), Piotr Skiba (Włodek), Marcin Troński (Moskwa), Adrianna Biedrzyńska (Hungarian Jewish Woman), Ewa Błaszczyk (Commandant's Wife), Erwin Nowiaszek, Jerzy Rogalski, Włodzimierz Musiał, Ewa Harasimowicz, Andrzej Ferenc, Jerzy Goliński, Andrzej Szenajch, Leon Niemczyk, and others.

Korczak (1990), 113'
Director: Andrzej Wajda
Script: Agnieszka Holland
Cinematography: Robby Müller
Set Design: Allan Starski
Music: Wojciech Kilar
Editing: Ewa Smal
Production: Regina Ziegler, Janusz Morgenstern, Daniel Toscan du Plantier; Film Studio "Perspektywa," Regina Ziegler Filmproduktion (West Berlin)
Cast: Wojciech Pszoniak (Dr. Janusz Korczak), Ewa Dałkowska (Stefania Wilczyńska), Teresa Budzisz-Krzyżanowska (Maria Falska), Marzena Trybała (Esterka), Wojciech Klata (Szloma), Piotr Kozłowski (Heniek), Zbigniew Zamachowski (Szulc), Jan Prochyra (Gancwajch), Jan Peszek (Max Bauer), Aleksander Bardini (Adam Czerniaków), Andrzej Kopiczyński (Head of Polish Radio), Krystyna Zachwatowicz (Szloma's Mother), Agnieszka Krukówna (Ewa), Adam Siemion (Abramek), Marek Bargiełowski (Dr. Gepner), Jerzy Zass, Michał Staszczak, Karolina Czernicka, Anna Mucha, Maria Chwalibóg, Stanisława Celińska, Edgar Hoppe, Olaf Lubaszenko, Danuta Szaflarska, and others.

Just Beyond this Forest (*Jeszcze tylko ten las*, 1991), 86'
Director: Jan Łomnicki
Script: Anna Strońska
Cinematography: Artur Radźko
Set Design: Andrzej Rafał Waltenberger
Music: Piotr Hertl
Editing: Krystyna Górnicka

Production: Andrzej Zielonka; Documentary Film Studio (WFD)
Cast: Ryszarda Hanin (Mrs. Kulgawcowa), Joanna Friedman (Rutka), Marzena Trybała (Rutka's Mother), Marta Klubowicz-Różycka (Kulgawcowa's Daughter), Marek Bargiełowski (Blackmailer), Bogusław Sochnacki (German Soldier), Jan Jurewicz, Zofia Czerwińska, and others.

The Burial of a Potato (*Pogrzeb kartofla*, 1991), 96'
Director: Jan Jakub Kolski
Script: Jan Jakub Kolski
Cinematography: Wojciech Todorow
Set Design: Jacek Turewicz
Music: Zygmunt Konieczny
Editing: Ewa Pakulska
Production: Anna Gryczyńska; Karol Irzykowski Film Studio in Warsaw
Cast: Franciszek Pieczka (Mateusz Szewczyk), Adam Ferency (Stefan Gorzelak), Mariusz Saniternik (Pasiasia), Ewa Żukowska (Mrs. Mierzwa), Andrzej Jurczak (Mr. Mierzwa), Grażyna Błęcka-Kolska (Mrs. Lachowicz), Bogusław Sochnacki (Shoemaker Mazurek), Grzegorz Heromiński (Władzio Rzepecki), Feliks Szajnert (Andrzejewski), Katarzyna Łaniewska (Mazurkowa), Irena Burawska (Kusidełka), Henryk Niebudek (Captain), Krystyna Feldman (Gorzelak's Mother), Jan Jankowski (Jurek Szewczyk, Mateusz's Son), and others.

Warszawa. Année 5703 (*Warszawa, Year 5703*; *Tragarz puchu*, 1992, Poland, France, Germany), 111'
Director: Janusz Kijowski
Script: Janusz Kijowski, Jerzy Janicki; based on Jerzy Janicki's novella
Cinematography: Przemysław Skwirczyński
Set Design: Andrzej Przedworski
Music: Jan Kanty Pawluśkiewicz
Editing: Wanda Zeman
Production: Artur Brauner, Henry Lange; Molecule, CCC-Filmkunst, Film Studio "Zodiak"
Cast: Lambert Wilson (Alek), Julie Delpy (Fryda), Hanna Schygulla (Stefania Bukowska), Krzysztof Zaleski (Gestapo Man), Władysław Kowalski (Photographer), Piotr Cieślak (Priest), Leon Niemczyk (German Officer), Paweł Nowisz (Sacristain), Tomasz Jarosz, Marek Kasprzak, and others.

Farewell to Maria (*Pożegnanie z Marią*, 1993), 87'
Director: Filip Zylber
Script: Filip Zylber, Maciej Maciejewski
Cinematography: Dariusz Kuc
Set Design: Andrzej Przedworski

Music: Tomasz Stańko
Editing: Katarzyna Rudnik-Glińska
Production: Paweł Rakowski; Polish Television
Cast: Marek Bukowski (Tadeusz), Agnieszka Wagner (Maria), Katarzyna Jamróz (Sara), Danuta Szaflarska (Mrs. Doktorowa), Sławomir Orzechowski (Blue Policeman), Jan Frycz (Manager), Rafał Królikowski (Violinist), Magdalena Gnatowska (Bride), Radosław Pazura (Groom), Bożena Adamek (Clerk), Cezary Pazura (Tomasz), Dorota Chotecka (Tomasz's Wife), Maciej Kozłowski, Agnieszka Pilaszewska, Aleksandra Woźniak, Bartłomiej Topa, Tomasz Łysiak, Paulina Młynarska, Marek Barbasiewicz, Daria Trafankowska, and others.

Deborah (*Debora*, 1996), 98'
Director: Ryszard Brylski
Script: Ryszard Brylski; based on Marek Sołtysik's novel
Cinematography: Przemysław Skwirczyński
Set Design: Andrzej Rafał Waltenberger
Music: Michał Lorenc
Editing: Ewa Pakulska
Production: Jerzy Bugajski; Karol Irzykowski Film Studio, Film Studio "Indeks," Polish Television
Cast: Renata Dancewicz (Debora Grosman), Olgierd Łukaszewicz (Marek Wawrowski), Maria Pakulnis (Anna Wawrowska), Jerzy Zelnik (Kuba Burstein), Władysław Kowalski (Deborah's Father), Bogusław Sochnacki (Shopkeeper Rotman), Marek Barbasiewicz (SS Officer Toth), and others.

Holy Week (*Wielki Tydzień*, 1996), 93'
Director: Andrzej Wajda
Script: Andrzej Wajda; based on Jerzy Andrzejewski's novel
Cinematography: Wit Dąbal
Set Design: Allan Starski
Music Consultant: Małgorzata Przedpełska-Bieniek
Editing: Wanda Zeman
Production: Lew Rywin; "Heritage Films"
Cast: Beata Fudalej (Irena Lilien), Wojciech Malajkat (Jan Malecki), Magdalena Warzecha (Anna Malecka), Jakub Przebindowski (Julek Malecki), Cezary Pazura (Mr. Piotrowski), Bożena Dykiel (Mrs. Piotrowski), Wojciech Pszoniak (Zamojski), Artur Barciś (Zaleski), Michał Pawlicki (Irena's father), Krzysztof Stroiński (Osipowicz), and others.

Franciszek Kłos' Death Sentence (aka *The Condemnation of Franciszek Kłos, Wyrok na Franciszka Kłosa*, TV, 2000), 96'
Director: Andrzej Wajda
Script: Andrzej Wajda, Zygmunt Malanowicz; based on Stanisław Rembek's novel

Cinematography: Bartosz Prokopowicz
Set Design: Agnieszka Bartold, Halina Dobrowolska
Music: Michał Lorenc
Editing: Ewa Pakulska
Production: Michał Kwieciński; Polish Television
Cast: Mirosław Baka (Franciszek Kłos), Grażyna Błęcka-Kolska (Mrs. Kłos), Maja Komorowska (Franciszek's Mother), Magdalena Warzecha (Polish Woman hiding Jews), Iwona Bielska, Bartosz Obuchowicz, Andrzej Chyra, Krzysztof Globisz, Artur Żmijewski, Anna Majcher, Daria Trafankowska, Grzegorz Warchoł, and others.

Keep Away from the Window (aka *Far from the Window*; *Daleko od okna*, 2000), 112′
Director: Jan Jakub Kolski
Script: Cezary Harasimowicz, based on Hanna Krall's short story
Cinematography: Arkadiusz Tomiak
Set Design: Michał Hrisulidis
Music: Michał Lorenc
Editing: Zbigniew Kostrzewiński
Production: Witold Adamek; Polish Television
Cast: Dorota Landowska (Barbara), Dominika Ostałowska (Regina Lilienstern), Bartosz Opania (Jan), Karolina Gruszka (Helusia), Krzysztof Pieczyński (Blue Policeman Jodła), Dariusz Toczek (Marek), Adam Kamień (Gendarme Dolke), Magdalena Mirek (Jodła's Wife), Olgierd Łukaszewicz (Regina's Envoy), Grzegorz Damięcki (Regina's Envoy), and others.

Edges of the Lord (*Boże skrawki*, 2001, Poland-USA), 94′
Director: Yurek Bogayevicz
Script: Yurek Bogayevicz
Cinematography: Paweł Edelman
Set Design: Mayling Cheng, Ewa Skoczkowska
Music: Jan A.P. Kaczmarek
Editing: Dennis M. Hill
Production: Ewa Ziułkowska; Millennium Films with the participation of Film Studio "Tor," Polish Television, Canal+Polska, Komitet Kinematografii
Cast: Haley Joel Osment (Romek), Willem Dafoe (Priest), Liam Hess (Tolo), Olga Frycz (Marysia), Olaf Lubaszenko (Gniecio Lipa), Małgorzata Foremniak (Mrs. Lipa), Richard Banel (Władek), Andrzej Grabowski (Kluba), Wojciech Smolarz (Pyra), Chiril Vahonin (Robal), Dorota Piasecka (Ela Kluba), Edyta Jurecka (Sara, Romek's Mother), Eugene Osment (German Officer), Krzysztof Pieczyński (German Officer), Krystyna Feldman, Ryszard Ronczewski, and others.

The Pianist (*Pianista*, 2002, Poland-France-United Kingdom), 142'
   Director: Roman Polański
   Script: Ronald Harwood; based on Władysław Szpilman's book
   Cinematography: Paweł Edelman
   Set Design: Allan Starski
   Music: Wojciech Kilar
   Editing: Herve De Luze
   Production: Roman Polański, Robert Benmussa, Alain Sarde
   Cast: Adrien Brody (Władysław Szpilman), Thomas Kretschmann (Captain Hosenfeld), Frank Finlay (Szpilman's Father), Maureen Lipman (Szpilman's Mother), Emilia Fox (Dorota), Ed Stoppard (Henryk), Julia Rayner (Regina), Jessica Kate Meyer (Halina), Michał Żebrowski (Jurek), Roy Smiles (Itzhak Heller, Jewish Policeman), Andrzej Blumenfeld (Benek), Zbigniew Zamachowski, Maja Ostaszewska, Krzysztof Pieczyński, Katarzyna Figura, Adam Bauman, Marian Dzięz̈iel, Rafał Mohr, Borys Szyc (not credited), and others.

Pornography (*Pornografia*, 2003, Poland-France), 117'
   Director: Jan Jakub Kolski
   Script: Jan Jakub Kolski, based on Witold Gombrowicz's book
   Cinematography: Krzysztof Ptak
   Set Design: Andrzej Przedworski
   Music: Zygmunt Konieczny
   Editing: Eitold Chomiński
   Production: Lew Rywin; "Heritage Films"
   Cast: Krzysztof Majchrzak (Fryderyk), Adam Ferency (Witold), Krzysztof Globisz (Hipolit), Grażyna Błęcka-Kolska (Maria, Hipolit's Wife), Jan Frycz (Colonel Siemian), Sandra Samos (Henia), Anna Baniowska (Weronika), Grzegorz Damięcki (Wacław Paszkowski), Irena Laskowska (Amelia), Kazimierz Mazur (Karol), Jan Urbański (Skuziak), Magdalena Różdżka, Jerzy Chojnowski, and others.

Joanna (2010), 105'
   Director: Feliks Falk
   Script: Feliks Falk
   Cinematography: Piotr Śliskowski
   Set Design: Anna Wunderlich
   Music: Bartłomiej Gliniak
   Editing: Krzysztof Szpetmański
   Production: Michał Kwieciński; "Akson Studio"
   Cast: Urszula Grabowska (Joanna), Sara Knothe (Róża), Joachim Paul Assboeck (German officer), Stanisława Celińska (Kamińska), Kinga Preis (Staszka), Halina Łabonarska (Joanna's Mother), Joanna Gryga (Róża's Mother), Monika Kwiatkowska, Arkadiusz Brykalski, Mieczysław Grąbka, Remigiusz Jankowski, Henryk Talar, and others.

Select Documentary, Short and Television Films

Majdanek—The Cemetery of Europe (*Majdanek—Cmentarzysko Europy*, 1944, Aleksander Ford), 19'

The Swastika and the Gallows (*Swastyka i szubienica*, 1945, Kazimierz Czyński), 25'

The Gallows in the Stutthof Concentration Camp (*Szubienice w Sztutthofie*, 1946, Aleksander Świdwiński), 7'

Greiser before the Polish Court (*Greiser przed sądem Rzeczpospolitej*, 1946, Aleksander Świdwiński), 15'

We Are Still Alive (*Mir, lebngeblibene*, 1947, in Yiddish, Natan Gross), 80'

The Fifth Anniversary of the Warsaw Ghetto Uprising (*Der finfter jorcajt fun ojfsztand in warszewer geto, Rocznica getta*, 1948, in Yiddish, Natan Gross), 30'

Under This Same Sky (*Pod jednym niebem*, 1955, Kurt Weber), 18'

Ambulance (*Ambulans*, 1961, Janusz Morgenstern), 9'

The Rose (*Róża*, 1962, Janusz Majewski), 10'

The Fleischer's Album (*Album Fleischera*, 1962, Janusz Majewski), 15'

Requiem for 500,000 (*Requiem dla 500 000*, 1963, Jerzy Bossak, Wacław Kaźmierczak), 29'

An Ordinary Day of Schmidt, the Gestapo Man (*Powszedni dzień gestapowca Schmidta*, 1963, Jerzy Ziarnik), 10'

Children of the Ramp (*Dzieci rampy*, 1963, Andrzej Piekutowski), 10'

By the Railway Track (*Przy torze kolejowym* (1963/1992, Andrzej Brzozowski), 13'

The Museum (*Muzeum*, 1966, Jerzy Ziarnik), 12'

Archeology (*Archeologia*, 1967, Andrzej Brzozowski), 14'

The Matter of Life and Death (*Cena życia i śmierci*, 1968, Janusz Kidawa), 19'

The Roll Call (*Apel*, 1970, animation, Ryszard Czekała), 7'

The Polish Ways (*Polskie drogi*, 1976/7, TV series), Janusz Morgenstern

I Am Looking at Your Photograph (*Patrzę na twoja fotografię*, 1979, Jerzy Ziarnik), 8'

The House (*Dom*, 1980–2000, TV series), Jan Łomnicki

I Happened to Be in Auschwitz (*Bawiłem w Oświęcimiu*, 1982, Józef Gębski), 17'

Silence (*Milczenie*, 1983, Tomasz Lengren), 12'

With Raised Hands (*Z podniesionymi rękami*, 1985, Mitko Panov), 6'

Living in Memory (*Ocalałe w pamięci*, 1986, Zbigniew Raplewski), 54'

Witnesses (*Świadkowie*, 1987, Marcel Łoziński), 26'

Decalogue 8 (*Dekalog 8*, 1988, TV film, Krzysztof Kieślowski), 56'

My Seven Jewish Schoolmates (*Siedmiu Żydów z mojej klasy*, 1991, Marcel Łoziński), 40'

Birthplace (*Miejsce urodzenia*, 1992, Paweł Łoziński), 47'

Hope Dies Last (*Nadzieja umiera ostatnia*, 1992, Tadeusz Wudzki), 47'

Chronicle of the Warsaw Ghetto Uprising according to Marek Edelman (*Kronika powstania w getcie warszawskim wg Marka Edelmana*, 1993, Jolanta Dylewska), 74'

The Carousel (*Karuzela*, 1993, Michał Nekanda-Trepka), 34'

Where Are You My Friends (*Gdzież jesteście przyjaciele moi ...?*, 1995, Mariusz Kobzdej), 53'

The Cross Inscribed in the Star of David (*Wpisany w gwiazdę Dawida— Krzyż*, 1997, Grzegorz Linkowski), 28'

Five Mothers of Mine (*Pięć moich matek*, 1998, Michał Nekanda-Trepka), 27'

Photographer (*Fotoamator*, 1998, Dariusz Jabłoński), 57'

Where Is My Older Son Cain? (*... Gdzie mój starszy syn Kain?* 1999, Agnieszka Arnold), 52'

The Miracle of Purim (*Cud Purymowy*, 2000, TV film, Izabela Cywińska), 57'

The Last Pictures (*Ostatnie zdjęcia*, 2000, Andrzej Brzozowski), 47'

Ways to Survive (*Patent na przeżycie*, 2000, Dorota Latour), 52'

Neighbors (*Sąsiedzi*, 2001, Agnieszka Arnold), 2 parts, 60'+57'

I Remember (*Pamiętam*, 2001, Marcel Łoziński), 60'

Youth during the Holocaust (*Młodość w czasach Zagłady*, 2001, Małgorzata Imielska), 46'

The Last Witness (*Ostatni świadek*, 2002, Michał Nekanda-Trepka), 51'

Ms. Sendler's List (*Lista Sendlerowej*, 2002, Michał J. Dudziewicz), 45'

March of the Living (*Marsz żywych*, 2003, Grzegorz Linkowski), 49'

A Teaspoon for Life (*Łyżeczka życia*, 2004, Michał Nekanda-Trepka), 22'

Jews in the Warsaw Rising, The (*Żydzi w Powstaniu Warszawskim*, 2004, Anna Ferens, Anna Kowalewska-Onaszkiewicz), 57'

Władysław Szpilman 1911-2000: In His Own Words (*Władysław Szpilman 1911-2000—własnymi słowami*, 2004, A. Marek Drążewski), 56'

Childhood in the Shadow of Death (*Dzieciństwo w cieniu śmierci*, 2004, Małgorzata Imielska), 35'

Reminiscent of Yesterday (*Jakby to było wczoraj*, 2005, Michał Nekanda-Trepka), 45'

Two Drawers (*Dwie szuflady*, 2005, Jan Strękowski), 54'

From the Auschwitz Chronicle (*Z kroniki Auschwitz*, 2005, Michał Bukojemski), 125'

The Portraitist (*Portrecista*, 2005, Ireneusz Dobrowolski), 52'

Sarid (2005, Zbigniew Gajzler), 49'

The Man Who Wanted to Stop the Holocaust (*Człowiek, który chciał zatrzymać Holocaust*, 2005, Jan Grzyb), 15'

Tell Me Why (*Powiedz mi dlaczego?* 2005, Małgorzata Imielska), 48'

The Eagle Pharmacy (*Apteka pod Orłem*, 2006, Krzysztof Miklaszewski), 44'

The Fugitive (*Uciekinier*, 2006, Marek Tomasz Pawłowski), 56'

Chutor Konne (2007, Michał Nekanda-Trepka), 25'

Po-lin (*Po-lin. Okruchy pamięci*, 2008, Jolanta Dylewska), 82'

Redegast (2008, Borys Lankosz), 50'

Marek Edelman. Life (*Marek Edelman: życie. Po prostu*, 2008, Artur Więcek), 56'

We Owe Him Our Lives (*Dzięki niemu żyjemy*, 2008, Marek Drążewski), 46'

The Story of the Kowalskis (*Historia Kowalskich*, 2009, TV docudrama, Arkadiusz Gołębiewski, Maciej Pawlicki), 85'

Radegast Bahnhof Memorial (*Memoriał Radegast Bahnhof*, 2009, Małgorzata Burzyńska-Keller), 20'

The Righteous (*Sprawiedliwi*, 2010, TV series—7 episodes, Waldemar Krzystek), 315'

Inventory (*Inwentaryzacja*, 2010, Paweł Łoziński), 9'

Select Bibliography

Archives

Filmoteka Narodowa (National Film Archive), Warsaw
Archiwum Andrzeja Wajdy (Andrzej Wajda Archive at the Manggha Center), Kraków
Archiwum Akt Nowych (Archive of Contemporary Documents), Warsaw
Żydowski Instytut Historyczny (Jewish Historical Institute), Warsaw
YIVO Institute for Jewish Research, New York

Books

Andrzejewski, Jerzy. *Holy Week. A Novel of the Warsaw Ghetto Uprising.* Trans. Oscar E. Swan. Athens: Ohio University Press, 2007.
Avisar, Ilan. *Screening the Holocaust: Cinema's Images of the Unimaginable.* Bloomington: Indiana University Press, 1988.
Baer, Ulrich. *Spectral Evidence. The Photography of Trauma.* Cambridge: MIT Press, 2002.
Baron, Lawrence. *Projecting the Holocaust into the Present: The Changing Focus of Contemporary Holocaust Cinema.* Lanham: Rowman and Littlefield, 2005.
Bartoszewski, Władysław, and Zofia Lewin, eds. *Righteous Among Nations: How Poles Helped the Jews, 1939-1945.* London: Earlscourt Publications, 1969.
Bartov, Omer. *Murder in Our Midst: The Holocaust, Industrial Killing, and Representation.* New York: Oxford University Press, 1996.
———. *The "Jew" in Cinema: From* The Golem *to* Don't Touch My Holocaust. Bloomington: Indiana University Press, 2005.
Bauer, Yehuda. *Rethinking the Holocaust.* New Haven: Yale University Press, 2002.
Berendt, Grzegorz, August Grabski, and Albert Stankowski. *Studia z historii Żydów w Polsce po 1945 r.* Warsaw: Żydowski Instytut Historyczny, 2000.
Błoński, Jan. *Biedni Polacy patrzą na getto.* Kraków: Wydawnictwo Literackie, 1994 [second, expanded, and revised edition in 2008].
Bobowski, Sławomir. *W poszukiwaniu siebie. Twórczość filmowa Agnieszki Holland.* Wrocław: Wydawnictwo Uniwersytetu Wrocławskiego, 2001.
Borowski, Tadeusz. *This Way for the Gas, Ladies and Gentlemen.* Trans. Barbara Vedder. New York: Viking Press, 1976.
Brandys, Kazimierz. *Samson.* Warsaw: Czytelnik, 1948.

Bren, Frank. *World Cinema 1: Poland*. London: Flicks Books, 1986.
Cała, Alina. *The Image of the Jew in Polish Folk Culture*. Jerusalem: Magnus Press, 1995.
———, and Helena Datner-Śpiewak, eds. *Dzieje Żydów w Polsce 1945–1948. Teksty źródłowe*. Warsaw: Żydowski Instytut Historyczny, 1997.
Cherry, Robert, and Annamaria Orla-Bukowska, eds. *Rethinking Poles and Jews: Troubled Past, Brighter Future*. Lanham: Rowman and Littlefield, 2007.
Chodakiewicz, Marek Jan. *After the Holocaust: Polish-Jewish Conflict in the Wake of World War II*. New York: Columbia University Press, 2003.
———. *Between Nazis and Soviets: Occupation Politics in Poland, 1939–1947*. Lanham: Lexington Books, 2004.
Coates, Paul. *The Story of the Lost Reflection: The Alienation of the Image in Western and Polish Cinema*. London: Verso, 1985.
———. *The Red and the White: The Cinema of People's Poland*. London: Wallflower Press, 2005.
Cole, Tim. *Selling the Holocaust: From Auschwitz to Schindler. How History is Bought, Packaged, and Sold*. New York: Routledge, 1999.
Colombat, André Pierre. *The Holocaust in French Film*. Metuchen: Scarecrow Press, 1993.
Cooper, Leo. *In the Shadow of the Polish Eagle: Poles, the Holocaust, and Beyond*. New York: Palgrave MacMillan, 2000.
Davies, Norman. *Heart of Europe: The Past in Poland's Present*. Oxford: Oxford University Press, 2001.
Dawidowicz, Lucy. *The Holocaust and the Historians*. Cambridge: Harvard University Press, 1981.
Dean, Carolyn J. *The Fragility of Empathy after the Holocaust*. Ithaca: Cornell University Press, 2004.
Engelking, Barbara. *Holocaust and Memory*. London: Leicester University Press, 2001.
———, and Jacek Leociak. *The Warsaw Ghetto: A Guide to the Perished City*. New Haven: Yale University Press, 2009.
Falkowska, Janina. *Andrzej Wajda: History, Politics, and Nostalgia in Polish Cinema*. New York: Berghahn Books, 2007.
———, and Marek Haltof, eds. *The New Polish Cinema*. London: Flicks Books, 2003.
Finkelstein, Norman. *The Holocaust Industry: Reflections on the Exploitation of Jewish Suffering*. London: Verso, 2000.
Figielski, Łukasz, and Bartosz Michalak. *Prywatna historia kina polskiego*. Gdańsk: słowo/obraz terytoria, 2006.
Ford, Charles, and Robert Hammond. *Polish Film: A Twentieth Century History*. Jefferson: McFarland, 2005.
Friedländer, Saul. *Memory, History, and the Extermination of the Jews of Europe*. Bloomington: Indiana University Press, 1993.
———. ed. *Probing the Limits of Representation: Nazism and the "Final Solution."* Cambridge: Harvard University Press, 1992.
———. *Memory, History, and the Extermination of the Jews of Europe*. Bloomington: Indiana University Press, 1993.
Ginsberg, Terri. *Holocaust Film: The Political Aesthetics of Ideology*. New York: Columbia University Press, 2005.

Głowacka, Dorota, and Joanna Zylinska, eds. *Imaginary Neighbors: Mediating Polish-Jewish Relations after the Holocaust*. Lincoln: University of Nebraska Press, 2007.
Głowiński, Michał, and Janusz Sławiński, eds. *Literatura wobec wojny i okupacji*. Wrocław: Ossolineum, 1976.
Goldberg, Judith N. *Laughter through Tears: The Yiddish Cinema*. East Brunswick: Fairleigh Dickinson University Press, 1983.
Goldman, Eric A. *Visions, Images, and Dreams: Yiddish Film Past and Present*. Ann Arbor: UMI Research Press, 1983.
Grabski, August. *Żydowski ruch kombatancki w Polsce 1944–1949*. Warsaw: Trio, 2002.
——. *Działalność komunistów wśród Żydów w Polsce (1944–1949)*. Warsaw: Trio, 2004.
——, Maciej Pisarski, and Albert Stankowski, eds. *Studia z dziejów i kultury Żydów w Polsce po 1945 roku*. Warsaw: Trio, 1997.
Gross, Jan Tomasz. *Revolution from Abroad: The Soviet Conquest of Poland's Western Ukraine and Western Belorussia*. Princeton: Princeton University Press, 1988.
——. *Neighbors: The Destruction of the Jewish Community in Jedwabne*. Princeton: Princeton University Press, 2001.
——. *Fear: Anti-Semitism in Poland after Auschwitz: An Essay in Historical Interpretation*. New York: Random House, 2006.
Gross, Natan. *Film żydowski w Polsce*. Kraków: Rabid, 2002.
Haggith, Toby, and Joanna Newman, eds. *Holocaust and the Moving Image: Representations in Film and Television since 1933*. London: Wallflower Press, 2005.
Haltof, Marek. *Polish National Cinema*. New York: Berghahn Books, 2002.
——. *The Cinema of Krzysztof Kieślowski: Variations on Destiny and Chance*. London: Wallflower Press, 2004.
——. *Historical Dictionary of Polish Cinema*. New York: Scarecrow Press, 2007.
Hames, Peter, ed. *The Cinema of Central Europe*. London: Wallflower Press, 2005.
Helman, Alicja, and Tadeusz Miczka, eds. *Analizy i interpretacje. Film polski*. Katowice: Wydawnictwo Uniwersytetu Śląskiego, 1984.
Hendrykowska, Małgorzata. *Kronika kinematografii polskiej 1895–1997*. Poznań: Ars Nova, 1999.
——, ed. *Widziane po latach. Analizy i interpretacje filmu polskiego*. Poznań: Wydawnictwo Poznańskiego Towarzystwa Przyjaciół Nauk, 2000.
Hendrykowski, Marek, ed. *Debiuty polskiego kina*. Konin: Wydawnictwo "Przegląd Koniński," 1998.
——. *Andrzej Munk*. Warsaw: Więź, 2007.
Hirsch, Marianne. *Family Frames: Photography, Narrative, and Postmemory*. Cambridge: Harvard University Press, 1997.
Hoberman, J. *Bridge of Light: Yiddish Film between Two Worlds*. New York: Museum of Modern Art/Schocken Books, 1991.
Holland, Agnieszka. *Korczak* [film script]. Warsaw: Wydawnictwa Artystyczne i Filmowe, 1991.
Huener, Jonathan. *Auschwitz, Poland, and the Politics of Commemoration, 1945–1979*. Athens: Ohio University Press, 2003.
Insdorf, Annette. *Indelible Shadows: Film and the Holocaust*. Cambridge and New York: Cambridge University Press, 1989.

Iordanova, Dina. *Cinema of the Other Europe: The Industry and Artistry of East Central European Film*. London: Wallflower Press, 2003.
Irvin-Zarecka, Iwona. *Neutralizing Memory: The Jew in Contemporary Poland*. New Brunswick: Transaction, 1989.
Jackiewicz, Aleksander. *Moja filmoteka: kino polskie*. Warsaw: Wydawnictwa Artystyczne i Filmowe, 1983.
Jakubowska, Małgorzata. *Laboratorium czasu: Sanatorium pod klepsydrą Wojciecha Jerzego Hasa*. Łódź: PWSFTviT, 2010.
Jakubowska, Wanda. *Ostatni etap* [film script]. Warsaw: Filmowa Agencja Wydawnicza, 1955.
Janicki, Stanisław. *Aleksander Ford*. Warsaw: Wydawnictwa Artystyczne i Filmowe, 1967.
Jankun-Dopartowa, Mariola. *Gorzkie Kino Agnieszki Holland*. Gdańsk: słowo/obraz terytoria, 2000.
Jasiewicz, Krzysztof. *Pierwsi po diable: Elity sowieckie w okupowanej Polsce, 1939–1941*. Warsaw: Rytm and Instytut Studiów Politycznych PAN, 2002.
———. *Rzeczywistość sowiecka 1939–1941 w świadectwach polskich Żydów*. Warsaw: Rytm, 2009.
Jewsiewicki, Władysław. *Polscy filmowcy na frontach Drugiej Wojny Światowej*. Warsaw: Wydawnictwa Artystyczne i Filmowe, 1972.
Kersten, Krystyna. *The Establishment of Communist Rule in Poland 1943–1948*. Berkeley: University of California Press, 1991.
———. *Polacy. Żydzi. Komunizm. Anatomia półprawd 1939–1968*. Warsaw: Niezależna Oficyna Wydawnicza, 1992.
Kobylarz, Renata. *Walka o pamięć: Polityczne aspekty obchodów rocznicy powstania w getcie warszawskim 1944–1989*. Warsaw: Instytut Pamięci Narodowej, 2009.
Kopka, Bogusław. *Konzentrationslager Warschau*. Warsaw: Instytut Pamięci Narodowej, 2007.
Korboński, Stefan. *The Jews and the Poles in World War II*. New York: Hippocrene Books, 1989.
Krall, Hanna. *Shielding the Flame: An Intimate Conversation with Dr. Marek Edelman, the Last Surviving Leader of the Warsaw Ghetto Uprising*. Trans. Joanna Stasińska and Lawrence Weschler. New York: Holt, Rinehart and Winston, 1986.
Krawczyk, Andrzej, ed. *Pierwsza próba indoktrynacji. Działalność Ministerstwa Informacji i Propagandy w latach 1944–1947. Dokumenty do Dziejów PRL*. Warsaw: ISP PAN, 1994.
LaCapra, Dominick. *Representing the Holocaust: History, Theory, Trauma*. Ithaca: Cornell University Press, 1994.
———. *History and Memory after Auschwitz*. Ithaca: Cornell University Press, 1998.
Landy, Marcia. *Cinematic Uses of the Past*. Minneapolis: University of Minnesota Press, 1996.
Lanzmann, Claude. *Shoah: An Oral History of the Holocaust*. New York: Pantheon Books, 1985.
Lemann-Zajiček, Jolanta. *Kino i polityka. Polski film dokumentalny 1945–1949*. Łódź: PWSFTviT, 2003.
Liebman, Stuart, ed. *Claude Lanzmann's* Shoah: *Key Essays*. Oxford: Oxford University Press, 2007.

Liehm, Mira and Antonin J. Liehm. *The Most Important Art: Soviet and Eastern European Film after 1945*. Berkeley: University of California Press, 1977.
Lifton, Betty Jean. *The King of Children: The Life and Death of Janusz Korczak*. American Academy of Pediatrics, 2005.
Loshitzky, Yosefa, ed. *Spielberg's Holocaust: Critical Perspectives on* Schindler's List. Bloomington: Indiana University Press, 1997.
Lubelski, Tadeusz. *Strategie autorskie w polskim filmie fabularnym lat 1945–1961*. Kraków: Rabid, 2000.
———, ed. *Zdjęcia: Jerzy Lipman*. Warsaw: Wydawnictwa Artystyczne i Filmowe, 2005.
———. *Wajda. Portret mistrza w kilku odsłonach*. Wrocław: Wydawnictwo Dolnośląskie, 2006.
———. *Historia kina polskiego. Twórcy, filmy, konteksty*. Chorzów: Videograf II, 2009.
———, and Konrad J. Zarębski, eds. *Historia kina polskiego*. Warsaw: Fundacja Kino, 2006.
Lukas, Richard C. *Forgotten Holocaust: The Poles under German Occupation 1939–1944*. New York: Hippocrene Books, 2005.
———. ed. *Out of the Inferno: Poles Remember the Holocaust*. Lexington: University of Kentucky Press, 1989.
———. *Forgotten Holocaust: The Poles under German Occupation 1939–1944*. New York: Hippocrene Books, 2005.
Lustiger, Arno. *Stalin and the Jews. The Red Book: The Tragedy of the Jewish Anti-Fascist Committee and the Soviet Jews*. New York: Enigma Books, 2003.
Madej, Alina. *Kino, władza, publiczność. Kinematografia polska w latach 1944–1949*. Bielsko-Biała: Wydawnictwo "Prasa Beskidzka," 2002.
Mąka-Malatyńska, Katarzyna. *Krall i filmowcy*. Poznań: Wydawnictwo Poznańskie, 2006.
———. *Europa, Europa*. Poznań: Wydawnictwo Uniwersytetu im. Adama Mickiewicza, 2007.
———. *Agnieszka Holland*. Warsaw: Więź, 2009.
Marcus, Millicent. *Italian Film in the Shadow of Auschwitz*. Toronto: University of Toronto Press, 2007.
Marszałek, Rafał, ed. *Historia filmu polskiego 1962–1967* (vol. 5). Warsaw: Wydawnictwa Artystyczne i Filmowe, 1985.
———. *Historia filmu polskiego 1968–1972* (vol. 6). Warsaw: Wydawnictwa Artystyczne i Filmowe, 1994.
Mazierska, Ewa, and Elżbieta Ostrowska. *Women in Polish Cinema*. New York: Berghahn Books, 2005.
Mazur, Daria. *Waszyński's* The Dybbuk. Poznań: Wydawnictwo Naukowe Uniwersytetu im. Adama Mickiewicza, 2009.
Michałek, Bolesław, and Frank Turaj, eds. *The Modern Cinema of Poland*. Bloomington: Indiana University Press, 1988.
Michlic, Joanna Beata. *Poland's Threatening Other: The Image of the Jew from 1880 to the Present*. Lincoln: University of Nebraska Press, 2006.

Minz, Alan. *Popular Culture and the Shaping of Holocaust Memory in America*. Seattle: University of Washington Press, 2001.
Misiak, Anna. *Kinematograf kontrolowany. Cenzura filmowa w kraju socjalistycznym i demokratycznym (PRL i USA). Analiza socjologiczna*. Kraków: Universitas, 2006.
Nałęcz, Daria, ed. *Dokumenty do dziejów PRL. Główny Urząd Kontroli Prasy 1945-1949*. Warsaw: ISP PAN, 1994.
Nałkowska, Zofia. *Medallions*. Trans. Diana Kuprel. Evanston: Northwestern University Press, 2000.
Novick, Peter. *The Holocaust in American Life*. Boston: Houghton Mifflin, 1999.
Nurczyńska-Fidelska, Ewelina. *Andrzej Munk*. Kraków: Wydawnictwo Literackie, 1982.
———, and Zbigniew Batko, eds. *Polish Cinema in Ten Takes*. Łódź: Łódzkie Towarzystwo Naukowe, 1995.
———, and Piotr Sitarski, eds. *Filmowy świat Andrzeja Wajdy*. Kraków: Universitas, 2003.
———, and Bronisława Stolarska, eds. *"Szkoła polska"—powroty*. Łódź: Wydawnictwo Uniwersytetu Łódzkiego, 1998.
Orr, John, and Elżbieta Ostrowska, eds. *The Cinema of Andrzej Wajda: The Art of Irony and Defiance*. London: Wallflower Press, 2003.
———, and Elżbieta Ostrowska, eds. *The Cinema of Roman Polanski: Dark Spaces of the World*. London: Wallflower Press, 2006.
Ozimek, Stanisław. *Film polski w wojennej potrzebie*. Warsaw: Państwowy Instytut Wydawniczy, 1974.
Paulsson, Gunnar S. *Secret City: The Hidden Jews of Warsaw 1940-1945*. New Haven: Yale University Press, 2002.
Piotrowski, Tadeusz. *Poland's Holocaust: Ethnic Strife, Collaboration with Occupying Forces and Genocide in the Second Republic 1918-1947*. Jefferson: McFarland, 1998.
Polanski, Roman. *Roman*. New York: William Morrow, 1984.
Polonsky, Antony, ed. *"My Brother's Keeper?" Recent Polish Debates on the Holocaust*. London: Routledge, 1990.
———, and Joanna B. Michlic, eds. *The Neighbors Respond: The Controversy over the Jedwabne Massacre in Poland*. Princeton: Princeton University Press, 2003.
Preizner, Joanna, ed. *Gefilte film: Wątki żydowskie w kinie*. Kraków: Azolem Alejchem, 2008.
———, ed. *Gefilte film II: Wątki żydowskie w kinie*. Kraków: Austeria, 2009.
———, ed. *Gefilte film III: Wątki żydowskie w kinie*. Kraków: Austeria, 2010.
Reiter, Andrea. *Narrating the Holocaust*. New York: Continuum, 2000.
Ringelblum, Emmanuel. *Polish-Jewish Relations during the Second World War*, ed. Joseph Kermish and Shmuel Krakowski. Evanston: Northwestern University Press, 1992.
Rudnicki, Adolf. *Ascent to Heaven*. Trans. H.C. Stevens. New York: Roy McLeod and Dennis Dobson, 1951.
Saxton, Libby. *Haunted Images: Film, Ethics, Testimony and the Holocaust*. London: Wallflower Press, 2008.
Schatz, Jaff. *The Generation: The Rise and Fall of the Jewish Communists of Poland*. Berkeley: University of California Press, 1991.

Shore, Marci. *Caviar and Ashes: A Warsaw Generation Life and Death in Marxism 1918-1968*. New Haven: Yale University Press, 2006.
Słodowski, Jan, ed. *Leksykon polskich filmów fabularnych*. Warsaw: Wiedza i Życie, 1996.
Smoleń, Kazimierz, ed. *KL Auschwitz*. Warsaw: Krajowa Agencja Wydawnicza, 1980.
———. *Auschwitz 1940-1945. Guide Book Through the Museum*. Oświęcim: State Museum in Oświęcim, 1991.
Snyder, Timothy. *The Reconstruction of Nations: Poland, Ukraine, Belarus, Lithuania, 1569-1999*. New Haven: Yale University Press, 2003.
———. *Bloodlands: Europe between Hitler and Stalin*. New York: Basic Books, 2010.
Sowińska, Iwona. *Polska muzyka filmowa 1945-1968*. Katowice: Wydawnictwo Uniwersytetu Śląskiego, 2006.
Steinlauf, Michael C. *Bondage to the Dead. Poland and the Memory of the Holocaust*. Syracuse: Syracuse University Press, 1997.
Struk, Janina. *Photographing the Holocaust: Interpretations of the Evidence*. London: I.B. Tauris, 2004.
Szarota, Tomasz. *Karuzela przy Placu Krasińskich. Studia i szkice z lat wojny i okupacji*. Warsaw: Oficyna Wydawnicza Rytm, 2007.
Szaynok, Bożena. *Z historią i Moskwą w tle. Polska a Izrael 1944-1968*. Warsaw: Instytut Pamięci Narodowej, 2007.
Szpilman, Władysław. *The Pianist: The Extraordinary Story of One Man's Survival in Warsaw 1939-45*. New York: Picador, 1999.
Szwagrzyk, Krzysztof, ed. *Aparat bezpieczeństwa w Polsce. Kadra kierownicza 1944-1956*. Warsaw: Instytut Pamięci Narodowej, 2005.
Tec, Nechama. *When Light Pierced the Darkness: Christian Rescue of Jews in Nazi-Occupied Poland*. New York, Oxford: Oxford University Press, 1986.
Toeplitz, Jerzy, ed. *Historia filmu polskiego 1939-1956* (vol. 3). Warsaw: Wydawnictwa Artystyczne i Filmowe, 1974.
———, ed. *Historia filmu polskiego 1957-1961* (vol. 4). Warsaw: Wydawnictwa Artystyczne i Filmowe, 1980.
Tomaszewski, Irene, and Tecia Werbowski. *Code Name: Żegota. Rescuing Jews in Occupied Poland, 1942-1945*. Santa Barbara: Praeger, 2010.
Tomaszewski, Jerzy, ed. *Najnowsze dzieje Żydów w Polsce w zarysie (do 1950 roku)*. Warsaw: Państwowe Wydawnictwa Naukowe, 1993.
Trzynadlowski, Jan, ed. *Polska Szkoła Filmowa. Poetyka i tradycja*. Wrocław: Ossolineum, 1976.
Umińska, Bożena. *Postać z cieniem: Portrety Żydówek w polskiej literaturze od końca XIX wieku do 1939 roku*. Warszawa: Wydawnictwo Sic!, 2001.
Walker, Janet. *Trauma Cinema: Documenting Incest and the Holocaust*. Berkeley: University of California Press, 2005.
Werner, Andrzej. *Zwyczajna apokalipsa. Tadeusz Borowski i jego wizja świata obozów*. Warsaw: Czytelnik, 1971.
Wiśniewska, Anna, and Czesław Rajca. *Majdanek: The Concentration Camp of Lublin*. Trans. Anna Zagórska. Lublin: Państwowe Muzeum na Majdanku, 1997.
Wróbel, Józef. *Tematy żydowskie w prozie polskiej, 1939-1987*. Kraków: Universitas, 1991.

Young, James E. *Writing and Rewriting the Holocaust: Narrative and the Consequences of Interpretation.* Bloomington: Indiana University Press, 1988.

———. *The Texture of Memory: Holocaust Memorials and Meaning.* New Haven: Yale University Press, 1993.

———, ed. *The Art of Memory: Holocaust Memorials in History.* New York: Prestel, 1994.

Zajiček, Edward. *Poza ekranem. Kinematografia polska 1918–1991.* Warsaw: Filmoteka Narodowa and Wydawnictwa Artystyczne i Filmowe, 1992.

———. *Encyklopedia kultury polskiej XX wieku: Film i kinematografia.* Warsaw: Instytut Kultury and Komitet Kinematografii, 1994.

Zaremba, Marcin. *Komunizm, legitymizacja, nacjonalizm: Nacjonalistyczna legitymizacja władzy komunistycznej w Polsce.* Warsaw: Trio, 2001.

Zeidler Janiszewska, Anna, and Tomasz Majewski, eds. *Pamięć Shoah: kulturowe reprezentacje i praktyki upamiętniania.* Łódź: Officyna, 2009.

Zelizer, Barbie. *Remembering to Forget: Holocaust Memory through the Camera's Eyes.* Chicago: Chicago University Press, 1998.

———, ed. *Visual Culture and the Holocaust.* New Brunswick: Rutgers University Press, 2001.

Ziębińska-Witek, Anna. *Holocaust: Problemy przedstawiania.* Lublin: Wydawnictwo Uniwersytetu Marii Curie Skłodowskiej, 2005.

Zimmerman, Joshua, ed. *Contested Memories: Poles and Jews during the Holocaust and Its Aftermath.* New Brunswick: Rutgers University Press, 2003.

Zubrzycki, Geneviève. *The Crosses of Auschwitz: Nationalism and Religion in Post-Communist Poland.* Chicago: University of Chicago Press, 2006.

Zwierzchowski, Piotr. *Pęknięty monolit. Konteksty polskiego kina socrealistycznego.* Bydgoszcz: Wydawnictwo Uniwersytetu Kazimierza Wielkiego w Bydgoszczy, 2005.

———, and Daria Mazur, eds. *Kino polskie wobec umierania i śmierci.* Bydgoszcz: Wydawnictwo Akademii Bydgoskiej, 2005.

Articles and Book Chapters

Baron, Lawrence. "The Holocaust and American Public Memory, 1945–1960." *Holocaust and Genocide Studies* vol. 17, no. 1 (2003): 62–88.

———. "Cinema in the Crossfire of Jewish-Polish Polemics: Wajda's *Korczak* and Polanski's *The Pianist*." 43–53 in *Rethinking Poles and Jews: Troubled Past, Brighter Future,* edited by Robert Cherry and Annamaria Orla-Bukowska. Lanham: Rowman and Littlefield, 2007.

Bartov, Omer. "Eastern Europe as the Site of Genocide." *Journal of Modern History* vol. 80, no. 3 (2008): 557–593.

Biskupski, Mieczysław B. "Poland and the Poles in the Cinematic Portrayal of the Holocaust." 27–42 in *Rethinking Poles and Jews: Troubled Past, Brighter Future,* edited by Robert Cherry and Annamaria Orla-Bukowska. Lanham: Rowman and Littlefield, 2007.

Błoński, Jan. "The Poor Poles Look at the Ghetto." 34–52 in *"My Brother's Keeper?" Recent Polish Debates on the Holocaust,* edited by Antony Polonsky. London: Routledge, 1990.

Bojko, Krzysztof. "Poland's Relations with the State of Israel." *Yearbook of Polish Foreign Policy* 1 (2006): 146–155.

Braid, Monika, "The Guilt on Both Sides: Leszek Wosiewicz's *Kornblumenblau* (1998)." *Kinoeye* 7 (2001). www.kinoeye.org/01/07/braid07.html (accessed 30 September 2003).

Bukowiecki, Leon. "Oświęcim na ekranie." *Film* 6 (1948): 5.

Cała, Alina. Kształtowanie się polskiej i żydowskiej wizji martyrologicznej po II wojnie światowej." *Przegląd Socjologiczny* vol. 49, no. 2 (2000): 167–180.

Charlesworth, Andrew. "Contesting Places of Memory: The Case of Auschwitz." *Environment and Planning D: Society and Space* 12 (1994): 579–593.

Coates, Paul. "Walls and Frontiers: Polish Cinema's Portrayal of Polish-Jewish Relations." *Polin: Studies in Polish Jewry* 10 (1997): 221–246.

———. "Notes on Polish Cinema, Nationalism and Wajda's *Holy Week*." 189–202 in *Cinema and Nation*, edited by Mette Hjort and Scott MacKenzie. London: Routledge, 2000.

———. "Observing the Observer: Andrzej Wajda's *Holy Week* (1995)." *Canadian Slavonic Papers* vol. 42, no. 1–2 (2000): 25–33.

Crnković, Gordana P. "Interview with Agnieszka Holland." *Film Quarterly* vol. 52, no. 2 (1998–1999): 2–9.

Czapliński, Lesław. "Tematyka żydowska w powojennym filmie polskim." *Powiększenie* 1–4 (1990): 171–176.

Eberhardt, Konrad. "Przeciw niepamięci." *Film* 40 (1963): 4–5.

Forbert, Adolf. "W Oświęcimiu po oswobodzeniu obozu." *Przegląd Lekarski* vol. 37, no. 1 (1980): 182–184.

Gebert, Konstanty. "The Dialectics of Memory in Poland." 121–129 in *The Art of Memory: Holocaust Memorials in History*, edited by James E. Young. New York: Prestel, 1994.

Ginsberg, Terri. "St. Korczak of Warsaw." 110–134 in *Imaginary Neighbors: Mediating Polish-Jewish Relations after the Holocaust*, edited by Dorota Głowacka and Joanna Zylinska. Lincoln: University of Nebraska Press, 2007.

Grabski, August. "Czy Polacy walczyli w powstaniu w getcie? Rzecz o polskich sojusznikach Żydowskiego Związku Wojskowego." *Kwartalnik Historii Żydów* 4 (2007): 422–434.

Gross, Natan. "Film żydowski w Polsce po wojnie. Lata 1945–1950." *Kino* 12 (1988): 21–23.

Haltof, Marek. "A Fistful of Dollars: Polish Cinema After 1989 Freedom Shock." *Film Quarterly* vol. 48, no. 3 (1995): 15–25.

———. "Everything for Sale: Polish National Cinema after 1989." *Canadian Slavonic Papers* 1–2 (1997): 137–152.

———. "National Memory, the Holocaust and Images of the Jew in Polish Cinema." 81–97 in *The New Polish Cinema*, edited by Janina Falkowska and Marek Haltof. London: Flicks Books, 2003.

———. "Return to Auschwitz: Wanda Jakubowska's *The Last Stage* (1948)." *The Polish Review* vol. 55, no. 1 (2010): 7–34.

Hansen, Miriam Bratu, "*Schindler's List* is not *Shoah*: The Second Commandment, Popular Modernism, and Public Memory." *Critical Inquiry* vol. 22, no. 2 (1995): 292–312.

Helman Alicja. "The Masters Are Tired." *Canadian Slavonic Papers* vol. 42, no. 1-2 (2000): 99-111. [Reprinted in *The New Polish Cinema*, edited by Janina Falkowska and Marek Haltof. London: Flicks Books, 2003: 37-53.]
Holland, Agnieszka. "List Agnieszki Holland do *Le Monde*." *Kino* 1 (1991): 46-47.
Jakubowska, Wanda. "Kilka wspomnień o powstaniu scenariusza (na marginesie filmu *Ostatni etap*)." *Kwartalnik Filmowy* 1 (1951): 40-47.
Janicka, Bożena. "Korczak." *Film* 4 (1990): 4-5.
Jazdon, Mikołaj. "Ograniczony punkt widzenia—filmowy obraz powstania w getcie warszawskim." *Kwartalnik Historii Żydów* 2 (2004): 225-232.
———. "Fotografie w roli głównej. O polskim filmie ikonograficznym ze zdjęć." *Kwartalnik Filmowy* 54-55 (2006): 212-230.
Jewsiewicki, Władysław. "Polscy filmowcy i Oświęcim." *Kino* 9 (1987): 26-29.
Kaniecki, Przemysław. "Z archiwum KC PZPR: Sprawa *Austerii* Jerzego Kawalerowicza." 203-209 in *Studia Filmoznawcze 30*, edited by Sławomir Bobowski. Wrocław: Wydawnictwo Uniwersytetu Wrocławskiego, 2009.
Karcz, Danuta. "Requiem dla obłąkanego." *Kino* 12 (1969): 22-24.
Koczarowska, Natasza. "Mechanizm kreowania 'tożsamości żydowskiej.'" 223-236 in Joanna Preizner, ed. *Gefilte film: Wątki żydowskie w kinie*. Kraków: Azolem Alejchem, 2008.
———. "Co się stało z Żydami z Ostrowca? *Pornografia* Jana Jakuba Kolskiego." 207-232 in *Gefilte film III: Wątki żydowskie w kinie*, edited by Joanna Preizner. Kraków: Austeria, 2010.
Konigsberg, Ira. "*Our Children* and the Limits of Cinema: Early Jewish Responses to the Holocaust." *Film Quarterly* vol. 52, no. 1 (1998): 7-19.
Kornatowska, Maria. "Nowy etap *Ostatniego etapu*." *Kino* 3 (1994): 35-36.
Kosewski, Paweł. "Pamięć o Holokauście w filmie fabularnym (analiza retrospekcji filmowej, na podstawie filmów *Pasażerka* i *The Pawnbroker*)." *Zagłada Żydów. Studia i Materiały* 5 (2009): 339-356.
Kucia, Marek. "'Jews'—The Absence and Presence of a Category in the Representations of Auschwitz in Poland, 1945-1985." *Studia Judaica* 2 (2006): 323-348.
Kurz, Iwona. "'Ten obraz jest trochę straszliwy.' Historia pewnego filmu, czyli naród polski twarzą w twarz z Żydem." *Zagłada Żydów. Studia i Materiały* 4 (2008): 466-483.
Kwiatkowska, Paulina. "Obrazy czasoprzestrzeni w filmie *Pasażerka* Andrzeja Munka." *Kwartalnik Filmowy* 43 (2003): 22-47.
Kwieciński, Bartosz. "'Iść po słonecznej stronie': Shoah jako doświadczenie cywilizacyjne w filmowej twórczości Andrzeja Wajdy. Wybrane aspekty." 315-336 in *Filmowy świat Andrzeja Wajdy*, edited by Ewelina Nurczyńska-Fidelska and Piotr Sitarski. Kraków: Universitas, 2003.
Lemann-Zajiček, Jolanta. "Marzec '68 w szkole filmowej w Łodzi. Wydarzenia i konsekwencje." 47-58 in *Kino polskie: Reinterpretacje*, edited by Konrad Klejsa and Ewelina Nurczyńska-Fidelska. Kraków: Rabid, 2008.
Levine, Madeline G. "The Ambiguity of Moral Outrage in Jerzy Andrzejewski's *Wielki Tydzień*." *The Polish Review* 4 (1987): 385-399.
Lewicki, Bolesław W. "Temat: Oświęcim." *Kino* 6 (1968): 12-18.
Libionka, Dariusz, "Polskie piśmiennictwo na temat zorganizowanej i indywidualnej pomocy Żydom (1945-2008)." *Zagłada Żydów: Studia i Materiały* 4 (2008): 17-80.

Liebman, Stuart. "Wanda Jakubowska's *The Last Stop (Ostatni etap)*." *Slavic and East European Performance* vol. 16, no. 3 (1996): 56–63.

———."I Was Always in the Epicenter of Whatever Was Going On ... An Interview with Wanda Jakubowska." *Slavic and East European Performance* vol. 17, no. 3 (1997): 16–30.

———. "Documenting the Liberation of the Camps: The Case of Aleksander Ford's *Vernichtungslager Majdanek—Cmentarzysko Europy* (1944)." 333–351 in *Lessons and Legacies VII: The Holocaust in International Perspective*, edited by Dagmar Herzog. Evanston: Northwestern University Press, 2006.

Liebman, Stuart, and Zsuzsa Berger, trans. "Béla Balázs on Wanda Jakubowska's *The Last Stop*: Three Texts." *Slavic and East European Performance* vol. 16, no. 3 (1996): 64–70.

———, and Leonard Quart. "Lost and Found: Wanda Jakubowska's *The Last Stop*. *Cineaste* vol. 22, no. 4 (1997): 43–45.

Linville, Susan E. "*Europa, Europa*: A Test Case for German National Cinema." *Wide Angle* vol. 16, no. 3 (1994): 39–50.

Litka, Piotr. "Rzecz o buchalterii zła" [interview with Dariusz Jabłoński]. *Tygodnik Powszechny* 33 (1998): 13.

———. "Tego świata już nie ma" [review of *The Photographer*]. *Tygodnik Powszechny* 33 (1998): 13.

———. "Polacy i Żydzi w *Ulicy Granicznej*." *Kwartalnik Filmowy* 29–30 (2000): 60–68.

Loewy, Hanno. "The Mother of All Holocaust Films? Wanda Jakubowska's Auschwitz Trilogy." *Historical Journal of Film, Radio and Television* vol. 24, no. 2 (2004): 179–204.

Lubelski, Tadeusz. "Generalissumus płakał" [interview with Wanda Jakubowska]. *Film* 18–19 (1990): 3–4.

———. "Dwa debiuty oddzielone w czasie. Rozmowa z Wandą Jakubowską." 10–27 in *Debiuty polskiego kina*, edited by Marek Hendrykowski. Konin: Wydawnictwo "Przegląd Koniński," 1998.

———. "Zamknięte w szafie." *Kino* 11 (2000): 36–37.

Łysak, Tomasz. "O niemożliwej wierze w dokument. *Fotoamator* Dariusza Jabłońskiego." *Kwartalnik Filmowy* 43 (2003): 66–76.

———. "Życie pośmiertne nazistowskiej propagandy. Powojenne filmy dokumentalne o getcie warszawskim." *Kwartalnik Filmowy* 54–55 (2006): 163–176.

Maciejewska, Irena. "Getto warszawskie w literaturze polskiej." 135–162 in *Literatura wobec wojny i okupacji*, edited by Michał Głowiński and Janusz Sławiński. Wrocław: Ossolineum, 1976.

Madej, Alina. "Ja po prostu swojej partii ufałam. Rozmowa z Wandą Jakubowską." *Kino* 8 (1991): 28–31.

———. "Stalinowskie panopticum." *Kino* 8 (1991): 32–33.

———. "Wielka gra [interview with Stanisław Albrecht]. *Kwartalnik Filmowy* 6 (1994): 204–206.

———. "Wielki Tydzień: Wokół opowiadania i filmu." 128–135 in *W stulecie kina: Sztuka filmowa w Polsce*. Łódź: Cenralny Gabinet Edukacji Dzieci i Młodzieży, 1996.

———. "100 lat kina w Polsce: 1946–1948." *Kino* 5 (1998): 47–50.

———. "Wanda Jakubowska: Jak powstawał *Ostatni etap*." *Kino* 5 (1998): 13–17.

———. "Proszę państwa do kina (*Ostatni etap* Wandy Jakubowskiej)." 11–32 in *Widziane po latach. Analizy i interpretacje filmu polskiego*, edited by Małgorzata

Hendrykowska. Poznań: Wydawnictwo Poznańskiego Towarzystwa Przyjaciół Nauk, 2000.
Majewski, Tomasz. "Getto w kolorach Agfa. Uwagi o *Fotoamatorze* Dariusza Jabłońskiego." 321–334 in *Między słowem a obrazem*, edited by Małgorzata Jakubowska, Tomasz Kłys, and Bronisława Stolarska. Kraków: Rabid, 2005.
Mąka-Malatyńska, Katarzyna. "Auschwitz jako symbol XX wieku. Rozważania na marginesie cyklu dokumentalnego *Z kroniki Auschwitz* Michała Bukojemskiego." *Images* vol. 4, no. 7–8 (2006): 51–60.
———. "Dzieciństwo skazane na śmierć. Bohaterowie dziecięcych polskich filmów o Zagładzie: *Dekalog VIII* i *Miejsce urodzenia*." *Polonistyka* 9 (2008): 51–57.
Malatyńska, Maria. "Między winą a rozgrzeszeniem." *Tygodnik Powszechny* 10 (1996): 13.
———. "Siedmioramiennie" [interview with Andrzej Wajda]. *Tygodnik Powszechny* 9 (1996): 13.
Maron, Marcin. "Genialna epoka Schulza i katastroficzna epoka Hasa: *Sanatorium pod Klepsydrą* Wojciecha Jerzego Hasa." 49–73 in *Gefilte film III: Wątki żydowskie w kinie*, edited by Joanna Preizner. Kraków: Austeria, 2010.
Marszałek, Rafał. "Piekło inscenizowane." *Kino* 6 (1968): 18–21.
Mazierska, Ewa. "Non-Jewish Jews, Good Poles and Historical Truth in the Films of Andrzej Wajda." *Historical Journal of Film, Radio and Television* vol. 20, no. 2 (2000): 213–226.
———. "Double Memory: The Holocaust in Polish Film." 225–235 in *Holocaust and the Moving Image: Representations in Film and Television since 1933*, edited by Toby Haggith and Joanna Newman. London: Wallflower Press, 2005.
Mazur, Daria. "Paradoks i topika judajska. *Austeria* Jerzego Kawalerowicza." 145–168 in *Gefilte film: Wątki żydowskie w kinie*, edited by Joanna Preizner. Kraków: Azolem Alejchem, 2008.
———. Miłość—obojętność—śmierć w cieniu Zagłady: *Niekochana* Janusza Nasfetera." 75–105 in *Gefilte film III: Wątki żydowskie w kinie*, edited by Joanna Preizner. Kraków: Austeria, 2010.
Mikos, Jarosław. "O niestnieniu indywidualnym Korczaka i indywidualnym istnieniu praczki." *Kino* 7 (1991): 18–19.
Miles, William F.S. "Post-communist Holocaust Commemoration in Poland and Germany." *Journal of Holocaust Education* vol. 19, no. 1 (2000): 33–50.
Misiak, Anna. "Politically Involved Filmmaker: Aleksander Ford and Film Censorship in Poland after 1945." *Kinema* 20 (Fall 2003): 19–31.
Mruklik, Barbara. "Wierność sobie. Rozmowa z Wandą Jakubowską." *Kino* 5 (1985): 4–9, 20–21.
Munk, Andrzej. "Analiza filmowa. Gra aktorów w filmie *Ulica Graniczna*." *Images* vol. 5, no. 9–10 (2007): 102–105.
Nielsen, Jakob Isak. "With Raised Hands." *P.O.V.* 15 (March 2003), http://pov.imv.au.dk/Issue_15/section_1/artc4A.html (accessed 8 March 2010).
Orla-Bukowska, Annamaria. "Presenting the Shoah in Poland and Poland in Shoah." 179–194 in *Re-presenting the Shoah for the Twenty-first Century*, edited by Ronit Lentin. New York: Berghahn Books, 2004.
———. "New Threads on an Old Loom: National Memory and Social Identity in Postwar and Post-Communist Poland." 177–209 in *The Politics of Memory in*

Postwar Europe, edited by Richard Ned Lebow, Wulf Kansteiner, and Claudio Fogu. Durham: Duke University Press, 2006.

Ostrowska, Elżbieta. "Filmic Representations of the 'Polish Mother' in Post-Second World War Polish Cinema." *European Journal of Women Studies* vol. 5, no. 3-4 (1998): 419-435.

———. "Otherness Doubled: Representations of Jewish Women in Polish Cinema." 120-130 in *Gender and Film and the Media: East-West Dialogues*, edited by Elżbieta Oleksy, Elżbieta Ostrowska, and Michael Stevenson. Frankfurt/Main: Peter Lang, 2000.

———. "Between Fear and Attraction: Images of 'Other' Women." 131-146 in *Women in Polish Cinema*, by Ewa Mazierska and Elżbieta Ostrowska. New York: Berghahn Books, 2006.

Ozimek, Stanisław. "The Polish Newsreel in 1945: The Bitter Victory." 70-79 in *Hitler's Fall: The Newsreel Witness*, edited by K.R.M. Short and Stephan Dolezel. London: Croom Helm, 1988.

Polanowska, Agnieszka. "Ukryte na marginesie kadru: *Pasażerka* Andrzeja Munka." 129-145 in *Gefilte film III: Wątki żydowskie w kinie*, edited by Joanna Preizner. Kraków: Austeria, 2010.

Portuges, Catherine. "Traumatic Memory, Jewish Identity: Remapping the Past in Hungarian Cinema." 121-133 in *East European Cinemas*, edited by Anikó Imre. New York: Routledge, 2005.

Preizner, Joanna."Macierzyństwo w krajach zagłady. *Daleko od okna* Jana Jakuba Kolskiego i *Wybór Zofii* Alana Pakuli." *Kultura Popularna* vol. 2, no. 12 (2005): 81-88.

———. "Aleksander Ford—car PRL-owskiego kina." 9-42 in *Autorzy kina polskiego*, edited by Grażyna Stachówna and Bogusław Żmudziński. Kraków: Wydawnictwo Uniwersytetu Jagiellońskiego, 2007.

———. "Trudne sąsiedztwo—obraz relacji polsko żydowskich w polskiej kinematografii po 1989 roku." 28-36 in *Kino polskie po roku 1989*, edited by Piotr Zwierzchowski and Daria Mazur. Bydgoszcz: Wydawnictwo Uniwersytetu Kazimierza Wielkiego, 2007.

———. "Żydowski Święty—*Korczak* Andrzeja Wajdy." 89-96 in *Biografistyka filmowa. Ekranowe interpretacje losów i faktów*, edited by Tadeusz Szczepański and Sylwia Kołos. Toruń: Wydawnictwo Adam Marszałek, 2007.

———. "Świadkowie. *Przy torze kolejowym* Andrzeja Brzozowskiego," *Postscriptum Polonistyczne* vol. 1, no. 5 (2010): 137-138.

———. "Żydzi z naszego miasteczka: *Marcowe migdały* Radosława Piwowarskiego." 337-368 in *Gefilte film III: Wątki żydowskie w kinie*, edited by Joanna Preizner. Kraków: Austeria, 2010.

Price, James. "The Passenger (*Pasażerka*) by Andrzej Munk." *Film Quarterly* vol. 18, no. 1 (1964): 42-46.

Przylipiak, Mirosław. "Misja, polityka, estetyka." *Film na Świecie* 11-12 (1990): 37-43.

———. "Nędza sztuki." *Kino* 3 (1990): 13-16.

———. "Polish Documentary Film after 1989." 143-164 in *The New Polish Cinema*, edited by Janina Falkowska and Marek Haltof. London: Flicks Books, 2003.

Raskin, Richard. "An Interview with Mitko Panov on *With Raised Hands*. *P.O.V.* 15 (March 2003), http://pov.imv.au.dk/Issue_15/section_1/artc3A.html (accessed 8 March 2010).

Rogerson, Edward. "Images of Jewish Poland in the Post-War Polish Cinema." *Polin: A Journal of Polish-Jewish Studies* 2 (1987): 359-371.
Safran, Gabriella. "Dancing with Death and Salvaging Jewish Culture in *Austeria* and *The Dybbuk*." *Slavic Review* vol. 59, no. 4 (2000): 761-781.
Sakowska, Ruta. "Janusz Korczak wobec Zagłady. Próba interpretacji tekstów." *Kwartalnik Historii Żydów* 2 (2005): 185-194
Shore, Marci. "Conversing with Ghosts: Jedwabne, Żydokomuna, and Totalitarianism." *Kritika: Explorations in Russian and Eurasian History* vol. 6, no. 2 (2005): 1-20.
Smolar, Aleksander. "Jews as a Polish Problem." *Daedalus* vol. 116, no. 2 (1987): 31-73.
Sobolewski, Tadeusz. "Biedni Polacy. *Wielki Tydzień* Andrzejewskiego i Wajdy." *Kino* 11 (1995): 17-19, 41.
Stachówna, Grażyna. "Elon lanler liron – śpiew z szafy. *Daleko od okna* Jana Jakuba Kolskiego." 141-157 in *Gefilte film II: Wątki żydowskie w kinie*, edited by Joanna Preizner. Kraków: Austeria, 2009.
Staines, Deborah. "Auschwitz and the Camera." *The Journal of Mortality* vol. 7, no. 1 (2002): 13-32.
Stanisławski, Krzysztof. "Pan Mundstock idzie do gazu." *Kino* 9 (1983): 12-14.
Stevenson, Michael. "Wajda's Representation of Polish-Jewish Relations." 76-92 in *The Cinema of Andrzej Wajda: The Art of Irony and Defiance*, edited by John Orr and Elżbieta Ostrowska. London: Wallflower Press, 2003.
———. "*The Pianist* and its Contexts: Polanski's Narration of Holocaust Evasion and Survival." 146-157 in *The Cinema of Roman Polanski: Dark Spaces of the World*, edited by John Orr and Elżbieta Ostrowska. London: Wallflower Press, 2006.
Stolarska, Bronisława. "Czas Apokalipsy: Świadectwa Stanisława Różewicza." 63-79 in *"Szkoła polska"—powroty*, edited by Ewelina Nurczyńska-Fidelska and Bronisława Stolarska. Łódź: Wydawnictwo Uniwersytetu Łódzkiego, 1998.
———. "Pokoleniowe doświadczenie 'sacrum': O debiucie Andrzeja Wajdy." 233-251 in *Filmowy świat Andrzeja Wajdy*, edited by Ewelina Nurczyńska-Fidelska and Piotr Sitarski. Kraków: Universitas, 2003.
Swan, Oscar E. "Andrzej Wajda's Film *Holy Week*: What Is Its Problem?" *The Polish Review* 3 (2005): 343-353. [Reprinted as "Afterword: Andrzej Wajda's Film *Holy Week*" in Jerzy Andrzejewski, *Holy Week: A Novel of the Warsaw Ghetto Uprising*. Athens: Ohio University Press, 2007: 130-144.]
Szurek, Jean-Charles. "*Shoah*: From the Jewish Question to the Polish Question." 149-169 in *Claude Lanzmann's Shoah: Key Es*says, edited by Stuart Liebman. Oxford: Oxford University Press, 2007.
Todorov, Tzvetan. "The Wajda Problem." *Salmagundi* 92 (1991): 29-35.
Tronowicz, Henryk. "Obrazy z okupacyjnego koszmaru." *Kino* 11 (1984): 8-10.
Tsiolkas, Christos. "The Atheist's Shoah—Roman Polanski's *The Pianist*." *Senses of Cinema* (2003), at http://72.14.203.104/u/AHCCA?q=cache:8mrY4zQZl6YJ:www.sensesofcinema.com/contents/03/26/pianist.html+polanski&hl=en&gl=us&ct=clnk&cd=2&ie=UTF-8 (accessed 15 October 2009).
Wajda, Katarzyna. "Gdy biedni Polacy nie tylko patrzą na getto. *Wielki Tydzień* Andrzeja Wajdy." *Kwartalnik Filmowy* 34 (2001): 78-101.
Wertenstein, Wanda. "W realizacji—*Wielki Tydzień*." *Kino* 7-8 (1995): 28-29.

Włodek, Roman. "Getto i film." *Powiększenie* 1–4 (1990): 151–164.
———. "Trzy filmy – jeden los." *Tygiel Kultury* 4–6 (2004): 153–157.
———. "Ten strach, ciągły strach." 179–207 in *Gefilte film II: Wątki żydowskie w kinie*, edited by Joanna Preizner. Kraków: Austeria, 2009.
———. "Świadectwo dojrzałości: Nowela *Kropla krwi* z filmu *Świadectwo urodzenia* Stanisława Różewicza." 147–167 in *Gefilte film III: Wątki żydowskie w kinie*, edited by Joanna Preizner. Kraków: Austeria, 2010.
Wojciechowski, Piotr. "Rekolekcje w skansenie." *Tygodnik Powszechny* 12 (1996): 9.
Wollaston, Isabel. "Sharing Sacred Space? The Carmelite Controversy and the Politics of Commemoration." *Patterns of Prejudice* vol. 28, no. 3–4 (1994): 19–27.
Woroszylski, Wiktor. "Nad *Pasażerką*." *Film* 38 (1963): 6–7.
———. "Jestem Janusza Korczaka i Andrzeja Wajdy. *Kino* 8 (1990): 1–5.
Wróbel, Marta. "Tadzikowe perypetie z totalitaryzmem. Metaforyzacja rzeczywistości lagrowej w filmie *Kornblumenblau* Leszka Wosiewicza." *Kwartalnik Filmowy* 29–30 (2000): 96–112.
———. "*Ostatni etap* Wandy Jakubowskiej jako pierwszy etap polskiego kina ideologicznego." *Kwartalnik Filmowy* 43 (2003): 6–19.
Wróbel, Piotr. "Double Memory: Poles and Jews after the Holocaust." *East European Politics and Societies* vol. 11, no. 3 (1997): 560–574.
———. "Polish-Jewish Relations and *Neighbors* by Jan T. Gross: Politics, Public Opinion, and Historical Methodology." 387–399 in *Lessons and Legacies: The Holocaust in International Perspective*, edited by Dagmar Herzog. Evanston: Northwestern University Press, 2006.
Wróblewski, Janusz. "Karaluchy w złotych pancerzykach." *Kino* 11 (1989): 12–15.
Zajiček, Edward. "Aleksander Ford – organizator kinematografii." *Miesięcznik Literacki* 2 (1985): 63–73.
Zaremba, Marcin. "Zorganizowane zapominanie o Holocauście w dekadzie Gierka: Trwanie i zmiana." *Kwartalnik Historii Żydów* 2 (2004): 216–224.
Zwierzchowski, Piotr. "Zagłada Żydów i martyrologia Polaków: *Wniebowstąpienie* Jana Rybkowskiego." 169–204 in *Gefilte film III: Wątki żydowskie w kinie*, edited by Joanna Preizner. Kraków: Austeria, 2010.

Index

A

According to the Decrees of Providence (*Wedle wyroków Twoich*, 1984), 20, 152, 155–57, 185, 252
Adamek, Bożena, 161–63, 253, 256
Adventure at Marienstadt, An (*Przygoda na Mariensztacie*, 1954), 58, 219n6
Albrecht, Stanisław, 14, 35, 55, 59, 70n12, 70n32
All Souls Day (*Zaduszki*, 1961), 125
Ambulance (*Ambulans*, 1961), 94–95, 113n64, 247
Andrzejewski, Jerzy, 9, 58, 75, 83–84, 110n19, 119, 175, 201–2, 204–5
Angry Harvest (*Bittere Ernte*, 1985), 4, 148, 182n29
Anielewicz, Mordecai, 221
Anna (1987), 173
Antkowiak, Andrzej, 132–33, 237
Archeology (*Archeologia*, 1967), 216, 247
Arnold, Agnieszka, 172, 185n84, 248
Ascension Day (*Wniebowstąpienie*, 1969), 8, 131–34, 205, 237
Ashes and Diamonds (*Popiół i diament*, 1958), 76, 79, 86, 88, 94, 117, 125, 129, 201, 205
Aszkenazy, Janina, 201
Aszkenazy, Szymon, 201
Auerbach, Rachela, 58, 231
Auschwitz (1945), 213
Auschwitz (Konzentrationslager Auschwitz-Birkenau), 3, 6–7, 25, 28–52, 77–78, 95, 100–7, 113n64, 113n67, 119, 122–24, 146, 154–55, 161–63, 174, 181n6, 183n58, 184n59, 198, 204, 213, 216–17, 220–21, 224, 227, 247, 249
Austeria (1983), 4, 118, 140–43, 181n11, 181nn14–16, 239
Avisar, Ilan, 5, 33, 62, 63, 69

B

Bachman, Larry, 191
Baczyński, Andrzej, 223
Bad Luck (*Zezowate szczęście*, 1960), 76, 99, 104, 117
Baird, Tadeusz, 85, 105, 234–36
Bajor, Piotr, 141, 239
Baka, Mirosław, 206, 245
Balázs, Béla, 33–34
Baron, Lawrence, 5, 188
Barciś, Artur, 203, 244
Bardini, Aleksander, 122, 194, 238, 242
Barszczewska, Beata, 95–96, 234
Bartal-Bicz, Alexander, 224
Bartosik, Tadeusz, 84, 232, 235
Bartoszewski, Władysław, 19
Bartov, Omer, 5, 15, 43, 56, 66, 68, 89, 106, 209n61
Bartówna, Wanda, 28–30, 33, 51n56, 231
Bathed in Fire (*Skąpani w ogniu*, 1964), 118
Beater, The (*Naganiacz*, 1964), 7, 78, 89–92, 112n42, 236
Beautiful Years of Slavery (*Piękne lata niewoli*, 1966), 129
Benita, Ina, 11, 69n5
Bergen-Belsen concentration camp, 149, 212
Berman, Jakub, 19, 55
Białoszewski, Miron, 58
Biedrzyńska, Adrianna, 163
Bierut, Bolesław, 41, 74
Birenbaum, Halina, 50n39
Birth Certificate (*Świadectwo urodzenia*, 1961), xii, 94–97, 144, 173, 234
Birthplace (*Miejsce urodzenia*, 1992), 9, 218, 248
Bista, Henryk, 147, 239–41
Błęcka-Kolska, Grażyna, 206, 245
Blondel, Jean-Marie, 174
Błoński, Jan, 8, 83, 139
Blue Cross, The (*Błękitny krzyż*, 1955), 99
Bodo, Eugeniusz, 11
Bogayevicz, Yurek, 173–74, 245
Bohdziewicz, Antoni, 214
Border Street (*Ulica Graniczna*, 1949), xi, 6–7, 25, 53–73, 117, 130, 144, 164, 189–90, 194, 227, 232

Borman, Martin, 220
Borowicz, Krystyna, 90, 236
Borowski, Tadeusz, 34, 43, 46, 58, 94, 106, 159–60, 162–63, 179, 183n50, 238
Boruński, Włodzimierz, 125, 240
Borwicz, Michał, 58
Bossak, Jerzy, 9, 13, 90, 112n60, 211–12, 214, 220, 247
Brandys, Kazimierz, 58, 75, 84, 86, 234–35
Brandys, Marian, 77
Brasse, Wilhelm, 221
Bratny, Roman, 90, 236
Braunek, Małgorzata, 131–33, 237
Brauner, Artur, 144, 189, 191, 240
Brauner, Sharon, 143, 240
Briley, John, 191
Brochwicz, Władysław, 33, 231
Brodniewicz, Franciszek, 11
Brody, Adrien, 174, 177–80, 246
Bromski, Jacek, 156–57
Broniewska, Maria, 61, 63, 232
Brycht, Andrzej, 123, 237
Brylska, Barbara, 150, 241
Brylski, Ryszard, 8, 154, 165–66, 244
Brynych, Zbynek, 114n86
Brystiger, Julia, 19
Brzozowski, Andrzej, 92–93, 105–6, 216, 235, 238, 247
Buczkowski, Leonard, 6, 13–14, 22, 58, 207n6, 230
Budzisz-Krzyżanowska, Teresa, 193, 242
Bugajski, Ryszard, 52n64, 157, 228n1
Bugayski-Prus, Władysław, 11
Bukojemski, Michał, xi, 224, 249
Bukowiecki, Leon, 60, 65
Burial of a Potato, The (*Pogrzeb kartofla*, 1991), 154, 159–61, 166, 243
By the Railway Track (*Przy torze kolejowym*, 1963/1992), 89, 92–93, 216, 247

C

Cackowska, Jolanta, 157
Canby, Vincent, 191–92
Carousel, The (*Karuzela*, 1993), 83, 248
Carriere, Mathieu, 144, 240
Case of Herman, the Stoker, The (*Przypadek Hermana – palacza*, 1986), 163–64
Cavani, Liliana, 106
Cękalski, Eugeniusz, 14
Celan, Paul, 172
Celińska, Stanisława, 121, 238
Cezarska, Aleksandra, 150–51, 241
Charlesworth, Andrew, 1, 43
Cherry, Robert, 3
Childhood in the Shadow of Death (*Dzieciństwo w cieniu śmierci*, 2004), 220, 249
Children Must Laugh (*Mir kumen on*, 1936), 54
Children of the Ramp (*Dzieci rampy*, 1963), 119, 247
Chmielewski, Zbigniew, 119, 232, 237
Chodakiewicz, Marek Jan, 15
Choromański, Michał, 125

Chrabelska, Róża, 150, 241
Chronicle of the Warsaw Ghetto Uprising according to Marek Edelman (*Kronika powstania w getcie warszawskim wg Marka Edelmana*, 1993), 9, 220, 248
Chutor Konne (2007), 220
Ciecierski, Jan, 85, 233, 235
Ciepielewska, Anna, 76, 100, 103–5, 127–28, 233, 235–36
Citizen Kane (1941), 104
Coates, Paul, 5, 88, 107, 122, 190, 198
Cole, Tim, 123
Contribution (*Kontrybucja*, 1966), 157
Council for Aid to the Jews (Rada Pomocy Żydom, Żegota). See Żegota
Cross Inscribed in the Star of David, The (*Wpisany w gwiazdę Dawida – Krzyż*, 1997), 220, 248
Cross of Valor (*Krzyż Walecznych*, 1959), 77
Ćwiklińska, Mieczysława, 72n50, 232
Cybulski, Zbigniew, 79, 84, 111n22, 129, 233
Cyrankiewicz, Józef, 41–42, 113n79
Czekała, Ryszard, 124, 247
Czerniaków, Adam, 194, 208n25
Czeszko, Bohdan, 75, 78, 84, 110n9, 190, 233
Czołówka Film Unit, 13, 55, 211
Czyński, Kazimierz, 212, 247
Czyżewska, Elżbieta, 124, 236

D

Dąbal, Wit, 146, 240, 244
Dąbrowska, Maria, 36, 58–59, 71n29
Dachau concentration camp, 212
Dafoe, Willem, 173–74, 245
Dałkowska, Ewa, 195–96, 242
Damned Roads (*Baza ludzi umarłych*, 1959), 51n55, 112n41
Dancewicz, Renata, 166, 244
Danton (1983), 188
Dawidowicz, Lucy S., 1, 9n1, 25n15
Dead Track (*Ślepy tor*, 1947/1991), 23, 231
Death of Cavalry Captain Pilecki, The (*Śmierć Rotmistrza Pileckiego*, 2006), 52n64
Deborah (*Debora*, 1996), 8, 154, 164–66, 244
Decalogue 8 (*Dekalog 8*, 1988), 8, 152–53, 248
Defoe, Daniel, 175
Dejmek, Kazimierz, 116
Delpy, Julie, 164, 243
Deluge, The (*Potop*, 1974), 143
Diary of Anne Frank, The (1959), 51n47
Direction Berlin (*Kierunek Berlin*, 1969), 118
Divided We Fall (*Musíme si pomáhat*, 2000), 169–70
Dmochowski, Mariusz, 96, 125, 234, 249
Dobraczyński, Jan, 149, 241
Dobrowolski, Ireneusz, 220–21
Dobrowolski, Stanisław Ryszard, 66
Donskoi, Mark, 38
Don't Be Afraid (*Nie bój się*, 1985), 183n47
Down Carrier (*Tragarz puchu*, 1983), 140, 239
Dr. Korczak, the Martyr (*Sie Sind Frei, Dr. Korczak*, 1974), 69, 109n5, 191

Drapińska, Barbara, 29, 33, 40, 51n56, 230–31
Dreyfuss, Richard, 191
Drohocka, Halina, 36, 231
Dudek, Marek, 119, 238
Dudziewicz, Michał, 222, 248
Dunikowski, Ksawery, 217
Duriasz, Józef, 127, 236
Duszyński, Jerzy, 24, 230
Dybbuk, The (*Der Dibuk*, 1937), 142
Dykiel, Bożena, 202, 244
Dylewska, Jolanta, 9, 217, 220, 223, 248–49
Dymna, Anna, 144, 240
Dymsza, Adolf, 13, 70n8
Dziewoński, Edward, 36, 100, 231–32
Dzigan, Szymon, 21, 231
Dziki, Waldemar, 8, 140, 145–46, 240

E

Eagle Pharmacy, The (*Apteka pod Orłem*, 2006), 226, 249
Eberhardt, Konrad, 124
Edelman, Marek, 9, 67–68, 72n62, 83, 111n40, 220–21, 248–49
Edelman, Paweł, 174–75, 245–46
Edges of the Lord (*Boże skrawki*, 2001), 173–74, 245
Eichlerówna, Irena, 23
Eichmann, Adolf, 46
End of Our World, The (*Koniec naszego świata*, 1964), 7, 45–48, 78, 236
Eroica (1958), 99
Etler, Edward, 117
Europa, Europa (1991), 4, 154

F

Face of an Angel, The (*Twarz anioła*, 1970), 119, 237
Faget, Huguette, 29, 231
Falk, Feliks, 228, 246
Falska, Maria, 193, 208n20
Farewell to Maria (*Pożegnanie z Marią*, 1993), 8, 154, 159–60, 243
Father (*Apa*, 1966), 123
Fejgin, Anatol, 19
Ferency, Adam, 170, 243, 246
Ferens, Anna, 224, 249
Fethke, Jan, 58, 71n27, 232
Ficowska, Elżbieta, 222
Ficowski, Jerzy, 58
Fifth Anniversary of the Warsaw Ghetto Uprising (*Der finfter jorcajt fun ojfsztand in warszawer geto*, 1948), 27n35, 247
Fifth Horseman Is Fear, The (*A pátý jezdec je strach*, 1965), 114n86
Fijewski, Tadeusz, 62–63, 65, 68, 232–33
Filipski, Ryszard, 122–23, 237
Film Polski (National Board of Polish Film), 14, 20–21, 32, 35, 55, 59, 175, 189, 230–32
Filmoteka Narodowa (National Film Archive), xi, xiii, 29, 54, 96, 141, 145, 147, 250
Finder, Paweł, 19

First Circle, The (*Den Foerste Kreds*, 1971), 69
Five Boys from Barska Street (*Piątka z ulicy Barskiej*, 1954), 69, 78
Five Mothers of Mine (*Pięć moich matek*, 1998), 219, 248
Fleischer's Album, The (*Album Fleischera*, 1962), 215, 247
Fleszarowa-Muskat, Stanisława, 45, 234
Flowers of St. Francis, The (*Francesco, guillare di Dio*, 1950), 199
Forbert, Adolf, 20–22, 27n35, 54, 212–13, 230–31
Forbert, Władysław, 20–21, 54, 117, 212
Forbidden Songs (*Zakazane piosenki*, 1947), 6, 22–24, 41, 49n10, 56, 58, 117, 230
Ford, Aleksander, 6–7, 13–14, 20, 25, 32, 49n19, 53–73, 76, 78, 111n24, 117, 119, 128–30, 144, 175, 189, 191, 211–12, 225n5, 232, 247
Forge, Jean. *See* Fethke, Jan
Four Tankmen and a Dog (*Czterej pancerni i pies*, 1966–67), 118
Franciszek Kłos' Death Sentence (*Wyrok na Franciszka Kłosa*, 2000), 206, 244
Frank, Hans, 126, 203
Frelek, Ryszard, 134
Frenkiel, Tadeusz, 11
Friedman, Joanna, 157–59, 243
From the Auschwitz Chronicle (*Z kroniki Auschwitz*, 2005), 224, 226n29, 249
Frycz, Jan, 170, 246
Fudalej, Beata, 202, 244
Fuks, Ladislav, 145–46, 240
Futile Mission: The Story of Jan Karski-Kozielewski, The (*Daremna misja. Opowieść Jana Karskiego-Kozielewskiego*, 1993), 223

G

Gajzler, Zbigniew, 223, 249
Galiński, Edward, 40, 224
Gallows in the Stutthof Concentration Camp, The (*Szubienice w Sztutthofie*, 1946), 213, 247
Gandhi (1982), 199
Gardan, Juliusz, 12
Garliński, Józef, 42, 52n63
Gebert, Konstanty, 2, 56, 228
Gębski, Józef, 217, 247
Gen, Leo, 191
General Nil (*Generał Nil*, 2009), 228n1
Generation, A (*Pokolenie*, 1955), 7, 68, 78–84, 87–88, 109n6, 111n22, 119, 177, 210n70, 232–33
Genewein, Walter, 221
Ghosts, The (*Strachy*, 1938), 14
Gierek, Edward, 8, 74, 117, 135
Ginsberg, Terri, 199
Girs, Anatol, 43–44
Gliński, Robert, 154–55
Globisz, Krzysztof, 170, 246
Globocnik, Odilo, 211
Głowacka, Dorota, 3, 172
Głowiński, Michał, 194, 200, 222
Godik, Władysław, 61, 64–65, 232

Index

Goldberg, Jakub, 107, 117
Goldman, Eric A., 1
Gołębiewski, Arkadiusz, 223, 249
Gombrowicz, Witold, 166, 170, 246
Gomułka, Władysław, 7-8, 17, 74-75
Gontarczyk, Piotr, 115
Górecka, Antonina, 29-30, 36, 45, 231, 241
Górecka, Tatjana, 29-30, 37, 231
Goskind, Izak, 20, 22
Goskind, Saul, 20-22, 27n35, 54, 231
Gosztyła, Krzysztof, 165, 240
Grabowski, Andrzej, 174, 245
Grabski, August, 16
Green, Joseph, 20
Greiser, Arthur, 213, 225n9
Greiser before the Polish Court (*Greiser przed sądem Rzeczpospolitej*, 1946), 213, 247
Gross, Jan T., 171-72, 184n78
Gross, Natan, 20-22, 27n35, 231, 247
Grynberg, Henryk, 87, 218, 236
Grzyb, Jan, 223
Gutman, Israel, 67

H

Hager, Ludwik, 117
Hańcza, Władysław, 24, 230
Hanin, Ryszarda, 100, 127-28, 157-59, 230, 236, 238-40, 243
Harasimowicz, Cezary, 167, 242, 245
Harwood, Ronald, 174, 246
Has, Wojciech Jerzy, 4, 76, 124, 171
Heimkehr, 70n8
Hen, Józef, 75
Henryk Sławik: Polish Wallenberg (*Henryk Sławik: Polski Wallenberg*, 2004), 222
Hess, Liam, 173, 245
Heymann, Daniéle, 197, 199
Himmler, Heinrich, 151
Hirsch, Joshua, 6
Hirsch, Marianne, 153, 182n37
Hirszbejn, Maria, 11
History of Cinema Theater in Popielawy, The (*Historia kina w Popielawach*, 1998), 166
Hitler, Adolf, 15, 61, 63, 94, 125, 130-31, 164, 203, 220
Hłasko, Marek, 75
Hobot, Zygmunt, 79-80, 127, 233, 237, 239
Hoffman, Jerzy, 8, 119, 140, 143-45, 182n19, 240
Holland, Agnieszka, 4, 148, 154, 187, 190-92, 195, 197-98, 202, 242
Hollender, Wilhelm, 105, 113n67, 235, 240
Holoubek, Gustaw, 97, 99, 233
Hołuj, Tadeusz, 46-47, 105, 236
Holy Week (*Wielki Tydzień*, 1996), 8-9, 83, 89, 119, 153, 160, 165, 187, 200-6, 209n47, 244
Hosenfeld, Wilhelm, 177, 185n89, 186n98
Hospital under the Hourglass (*Sanatorium pod klepsydrą*, 1973), 4
Höss, Rudolf, 31, 213
Hours of Hope, The (*Godziny nadziei*, 1955), 76, 117

House in the Wilderness (*Dom na pustkowiu*, 1949), 133
How Far from Here, How Near (*Jak daleko stąd, jak blisko*, 1972), 125
Hřebejk, Jan, 169-70
Huelle, Paweł, 140
Huener, Jonathan, 31, 42, 52n70

I

I Am Looking at Your Photograph (*Patrzę na twoją fotografię*, 1979), 216, 247
I Happened to Be in Auschwitz (*Bawiłem w Oświęcimiu*, 1982), 217, 247
Ilczenko, Dionizy, 62-63, 232
Imielska, Małgorzata, 220, 248-49
Insdorf, Annette, 5, 94, 103, 112n42, 165
Interrogation (*Przesłuchanie*, 1982/1989), 157
In the Shadow of Hatred (*W cieniu nienawiści*, 1986), 146, 148-51, 241
Invitation (*Zaproszenie*, 1985), 7, 45, 146, 241
Irwin-Zarecka, Iwona, 143
Iwaszkiewicz, Jarosław, 140, 181n9, 201, 239

J

Jabłoński, Dariusz, 9, 220
Jackiewicz, Aleksander, 76, 88
Jaehne, Karen, 148
Jakubowska, Wanda, xii, 6-7, 14, 25, 28-52, 59, 65, 76-77, 86, 104-6, 129, 146, 153, 162, 207n5, 231, 234, 236, 241
Jamróz, Katarzyna, 160, 244
Janczar, Tadeusz, 79-80, 82, 233
Janda, Krystyna, 157
Janicki, Jerzy, 122, 165, 239, 243
Janicki, Juliusz, 8, 146-48, 240
Janicki, Stanisław, 73n65
Janowska, Alina, 29-30, 85, 230-31, 235
Jaracz, Stefan, 70n8
Jaroszewicz, Andrzej, 153
Jaruzelski, Wojciech, 140, 143, 149
Jasiewicz, Krzysztof, 18
Jastrun, Mieczysław, 58
Jazdon, Mikołaj, 215, 217, 225n16
Jealousy and Medicine (*Zazdrość i medycyna*, 1973), 125
Jeannot, Leon, 54-55
Jędryka, Stanisław, 122, 238
Jetty (*Molo*, 1969), 123
Jews in the Warsaw Rising, The (*Żydzi w Powstaniu Warszawskim*, 2004), 224, 249
Joanna (2010), 228, 246
Johnnie the Aquarius (*Jańcio Wodnik*, 1993), 166
John Paul II, 113n77, 154
Journey into the Unknown, A (*Wycieczka w nieznane*, 1968), 122-24, 237
Julia, Anna, Genowefa... (1968), 120
Junosza-Stępowski, Kazimierz, 11
Just Beyond this Forest (*Jeszcze tylko ten las*, 1991), 8, 154, 157-59, 242
Jutzi, Piel, 58

K

Kacyzne, Alter, 12
Kaczor, Kazimierz, 122
Kadár, Ján, 72n46, 114n86, 131, 208n36
Kaden, Danny, 11
Kadr, Film Studio, 111n24, 117, 136n12, 181n13, 234–35, 239
Kalatozov, Mikhail, 32
Kamień, Adam, 162, 242
Kamińska, Ida, 72n46, 183n50, 232
Kanal (*Kanał*, 1957), 51n46, 57, 76, 94, 109n5, 117, 119, 164, 228n1
Kaniewska, Maria, 230–31, 234
Kansteiner, Wulf, 191
Karewicz, Emil, 96, 233–34
Karmen, Roman, 213
Karski, Jan, 139, 223
Karyś, Kuba, 223
Kasatkina, Ludmila, 119
Kataszek, Szymon, 11
Katyń (2007), 110n15, 226n22
Katyń Massacre (1940), 18, 26n25, 83, 110n15, 218, 226n22
Kawalerowicz, Jerzy, 4, 16–17, 30, 48n6, 51n46, 76, 90, 107–8, 109n5, 117–18, 140–43, 154, 181nn15–16, 239
Kaźmierczak, Wacław, 9, 212, 214, 247
Keep Away from the Window (*Daleko od okna*, 2000), 8, 120, 164, 166–70, 245
Kępińska, Elżbieta, 85, 235
Kersten, Krystyna, 26n27
Khrushchev, Nikita, 74
Kidawa, Janusz, 216, 247
Kielar, Wiesław, 40, 46, 51n55
Kieślowski, Krzysztof, 8, 151–53, 206, 248
Kijowska, Elżbieta, 165, 240
Kijowski, Janusz, 8, 83, 154, 164–65, 243
Kilar, Wojciech, 174, 195, 242, 246
Kinor (Kino-Organizacja), 6, 20–22, 27n35, 231
Klos, Elmar, 72n46, 114n86, 131, 208n36
Knife in the Water (*Nóż w wodzie*, 1962), 117, 119, 176–77
Kochanowski, Jan, 155
Kolbe, Maksymilian, 154–55
Kolberger, Krzysztof, 157, 162, 242
Kołodziej, Marian, 46, 52n78
Kolosov, Sergei, 119, 238
Kolski, Jan Jakub, 8, 120, 154, 159–62, 166–71, 183n52, 184n67, 184n72, 243, 245–46
Komeda-Trzciński, Krzysztof, 94
Komorowska, Maja, 206, 245
Konigsberg, Ira, 21–22
Konwicki, Tadeusz, 86, 118, 125, 129–30, 239
Kopecký, Stépán, 53, 232
Korczak (1990), 8, 153, 187–200, 208n36, 208n38, 242
Korczak, Janusz, 9, 94–95, 119, 159, 178, 187–200, 206n5, 208n20
Korewicki, Henryk, 11
Kornblumenblau (1989), 46, 154, 162–63, 183n57, 184n61, 241–42

Korotyński, Henryk, 35
Kościałkowska, Maria, 152, 235
Kossak-Szczucka, Zofia, 204
Kostecki, Józef, 25
Kott, Jan, 201
Kotys, Ryszard, 82, 233
Kowalewska-Onaszkiewicz, 224, 249
Kowalski, Adam and Bronisława, 223
Kowalski, Władysław, 85–86, 145, 235
Kozłowicz, Tomasz, 157
Kozłowski, Maciej, 147, 240, 244
Krall, Hanna, 67, 135, 167, 169, 184n66, 245
Kraśko, Wincenty, 92, 118, 129–31, 135, 190–91
Krawicz, Mieczysław, 11
Kreczmar, Jan, 101, 235
Kretschmann, Thomas, 177, 246
Królikiewicz, Grzegorz, 129, 155
Krzystek, Waldemar, 228, 249
Krzyżewska, Ewa, 125
Kuc, Dariusz, 159
Kucia, Marek, 44
Kurnakowicz, Jan, 176, 230
Kurz, Iwona, 128
Kutz, Kazimierz, 24, 76–77, 111n22, 234
Kuźniar, Zdzisław, 147, 240
Kwiatkowska, Maria, 216

L

Łabuńska, Elżbieta, 30, 232
LaCapra, Dominick, 3
Landowska, Dorota, 167, 245
Landscape after Battle (*Krajobraz po bitwie*, 1970), 8, 120–21, 238
Landy, Marcia, 153
Lanzmann, Claude, 3, 8, 139, 148, 195, 197, 199, 218
Łapicki, Andrzej, 125, 230–33
Laskowski, Jan, 123, 237
Last Days, The (*Ostatnie dni*, 1969), 118
Last Nazi Party Rally in Nuremberg, The (*Ostatni parteitag w Norymberdze*, 1946), 214
Last Pictures, The (*Ostatnie zdjęcia*, 2000), 105, 248
Last Stage, The (*Ostatni etap*, 1948), 6–7, 25, 28–52, 59, 65, 76, 78, 104–5, 117, 124, 227, 231
Last Stop, The. See The Last Stage
Last Witness, The (*Ostatni świadek*, 2002), 218–19, 248
Legion of the Street, The (*Legion ulicy*, 1932), 53, 62
Lejtes, Józef, 13
Lemann-Zajicek, Jolanta, 212
Lenartowicz, Stanisław, 76
Lesiewicz, Witold, 61, 65, 99, 232
Leszczyński, Jerzy, 61, 65, 232
Levi, Primo, 39
Levine, Madeleine G., 204
Lewicki, Bolesław W., 35, 59, 104, 113n64, 136n9, 163, 183n58
Liebman, Stuart, 5, 35, 40, 51n47, 105, 212, 225n5

Life for Life (Życie za życie, 1990), 154
Life Once Again (Życie raz jeszcze, 1964), 117
Lifton, Jean Betty, 195, 199, 206n5, 208n38
Linkowski, Grzegorz, 220, 248
Lipman, Jerzy, 78, 94, 109n5, 117, 119, 191, 233
Liquidation 08.1944 (*Likwidacja 08.1944*, 2009), 224
Little Town of Kroke, The (*Miasteczko Kroke*, 2008), 223
Living in Memory (*Ocalałe w pamięci*, 1986), 139, 248
Łódź Film School (PWSFTviT), 51n55, 55, 76, 99, 113n64, 116–17, 151, 177, 181n9, 183n58, 214
Loewy, Hanno, 47, 52n79
Łomnicki, Jan, 8, 122, 154, 157–59, 242, 247
Łomnicki, Tadeusz, 78–79, 81–82, 94, 99, 111n22, 152, 183n50, 230, 233, 236
Long Night, The (*Długa noc*, 1967), 8, 126–30, 137n31, 203, 236
Lotna (1959), 76
Loved and Hated: The Tragedy of Life and Death of the Maker of the Teutonic Knights (*Kochany i znienawidzony. Dramat życia i śmierci twórcy Krzyżaków*, 2002), 73n65
Łoziński, Marcel, 217–18, 226n22, 248
Łoziński, Paweł, 9, 218, 248–49
Lubaszenko, Olaf, 156, 173, 193, 242, 245
Łubczyk, Grzegorz, 222
Lubelski, Tadeusz, 27n39, 38, 160
Łuczycka, Wanda, 151, 230
Lukas, Richard C., 18, 111n40
Łukaszewicz, Olgierd, 166, 244
Lukešová, Jiřina, 53, 232
Lynx (*Ryś*, 1982), xii, 140–41, 239

M

Madej, Alina, 25n5, 34–36, 48n6, 59–60, 70n12
Majchrzak, Krzysztof, 170–71, 246
Majdanek (1944), 212
Majdanek concentration camp, 24, 211–12, 225n6
Majdanek – The Cemetery of Europe (*Majdanek – Cmentarzysko Europy*, 1944), 211–12, 225n5, 247
Majewski, Janusz, 215, 225n16, 247
Malajkat, Wojciech, 202, 244
Makarczyński, Tadeusz, 214
Makuch, Janusz, 228
Maldis, Marek, 222
Man who Wanted to Stop the Holocaust, The (*Człowiek, który chciał zatrzymać Holocaust*, 2005), 223
Mann, Roman, 38, 51n46, 231–33
Man on the Tracks (*Człowiek na torze*, 1957), 99, 103, 117
March Almonds (*Marcowe migdały*, 1990), 156–57
March of the Living (*Marsz żywych*, 2003), 220
Marczewska, Teresa, 152

Marek, Andrzej, 12
Mark, Bernard, 109n7
Marszałek, Rafał, 121, 123
Marten, Aleksander, 12
Marzyński, Marian, 117
Matter of Life and Death, The (*Cena życia i śmierci*, 1968), 216, 247
Matyjaszkiewicz, Stefan, 92, 99, 233, 236
Mazierska, Ewa, 87
Mazur, Daria, 142
Meetings in the Twilight (*Spotkania w mroku*, 1960), 7, 45, 78, 234
Merlin, Serge, 84, 86–87, 235
Merz, Irena, 65
Michałek, Bolesław, 86, 88
Michlic, Joanna, 19, 83
Mickiewicz, Adam, 116
Migowa, Jadwiga, 12
Miklaszewski, Krzysztof, 224, 249
Mikołajska, Halina, 93, 241
Mikulski, Stanisław, 98, 136n11, 233
Miller, Marek, 224
Milski, Stanisław, 98, 233–34
Miłosz, Czesław, 58, 82–83, 110n12, 139, 175, 205
Minc, Hilary, 19
Mintz, Alan, 6
Miraculous Place (*Cudowne miejsce*, 1995), 161
Moczar, Mieczysław, 7, 115–19, 156
Moczarski, Kazimierz, 135
Modrzyńska, Urszula, 78, 233
Monastyrski, Boris, 38, 51n45, 231
Morawski, Stefan, 88–89
More Than Life at Stake (*Stawka większa niż życie*, 1967–68), 118
Morgenstern, Janusz, 94, 112n54, 117, 122, 146, 191, 242, 247
Mosdorf, Jan, 40
Mostowicz, Arnold, 221
Mother Joan of the Angels (*Matka Joanna od Aniołów*, 1961), 107–8, 117
Mother Krause's Journey to Happiness (*Mutter Krauses Fahrt ins Glück*, 1929), 58
Mrozowska, Zofia, 22–23, 29, 100, 133, 176, 230–32, 234, 237
Ms. Sendler's List (*Lista Sendlerowej*, 2002), 222, 248
Mueller-Stahl, Armin, 148
Müller, Robby, 194, 208n21, 242
Muncliger, Josef, 61
Munk, Andrzej, 7, 24, 76, 78, 92, 94, 99–107, 112n60, 112n62, 113n79, 117, 145, 153, 216, 227, 235
Museum, The (*Muzeum*, 1966), 216, 247
My Father Henryk Sławik (*Mój tata Henryk Sławik*, 2003), 222
My Seven Jewish Schoolmates (*Siedmiu Żydów z mojej klasy*, 1991), 218
My Seventeen Lives (*Żyłem 17 razy*, 2009), 136n12

N

Nałkowska, Zofia, 34, 44, 58, 92–93
Nasfeter, Janusz, 8, 124, 126–31, 137n29, 137n31, 203, 236
Neighbors (Gross), 171–72, 184n78
Neighbors (*Sąsiedzi*, 2001, Arnold), 172, 248
Nekanda-Trepka, Michał, xi, 83, 112n47, 218–20, 222, 248–49
Nel-Siedlecki, Janusz, 43
Němec, Jan, 114n86
Neumann, Wanda, 120
Ney, Stefania, 189
Night (*Noc*, 1961), 215
Night and Fog (*Nuit et Brouillard*), 5, 10n16, 38, 45, 49n22, 214
1968: Happy New Year (*1968: Szczęśliwego Nowego Roku*, 1993), 156–57
Night Porter, The (*Il portiere di notte*, 1974), 106
Niwińska, Liliana, 97, 232
Novick, Peter, 3, 44, 57, 71n22, 199
Nowicki, Jan, 124
Nurczyńska-Fidelska, Ewelina, 112n62, 200
Nussbaum, Tsvi, 151

O

Ofierski, Jerzy, 147, 240
Olbrychski, Daniel, 120–21, 125, 238
Olszewski, Krystyn, 43
On the Niemen River (*Nad Niemnem*, 1939), 48n1
On the Vistula River (*Nad Wisłą*, 1962), 216
Opania, Bartosz, 167, 245
Operation Arsenal (*Akcja pod Arsenałem*, 1978), 122, 157
Ordinary Day of Szmidt, the Gestapo Man, An (*Powszedni dzień gestapowca Szmidta*, 1963), 215, 247
Ordyński, Ryszard, 13
Orla-Bukowska, Annamaria, 3
Orzechowski, Sławomir, 160
Osment, Haley Joel, 173–74, 245
Ostałowska, Dominika, 168, 245
Ostrowska, Elżbieta, 5, 51n57, 137n24, 148, 168, 184n72, 204
Others Will Follow (*Za wami pójdą inni*, 1949), 25
Our Children (*Unzere Kinder*, 1948), 21–22, 231
Ozimek, Stanisław, 21

P

Pak, Ludwik, 127, 237
Pakula, Alan, 38
Palester, Roman, 33, 230–32
Paluszkiewicz, Janusz, 79, 81, 233, 239, 241
Pan Michael (*Pan Wołodyjowski*, 1969), 119, 143
Pan Tadeusz (1999), 206
Panov, Mitko, 15, 248
Panufnik, Andrzej, 66
Passendorfer, Jerzy, 115, 118, 135

Passenger, The (*Pasażerka*, 1963), 7, 78, 92, 94, 97, 99–107, 112n62, 113n64, 113n70, 124, 162, 216, 235
Pawlicki, Maciej, 223, 249
Pawlik, Bronisław, 90–91, 236
Pawlikowski, Adam, 97–99, 233
Pazura, Cezary, 202, 244
People from the Train (*Ludzie z pociągu*, 1961), 77, 234
People of the Vistula, The (*Ludzie Wisły*, 1938), 14, 58, 69n5
Perski, Ludwik, 13, 55
Perspektywa Film Studio, xii, 187, 191–93, 196–97, 242
Petelska, Ewa, 7, 78, 90–91, 111n41, 112n43, 236
Petelski, Czesław, 7, 51n55, 78, 90–91, 111n41, 236
Pharaoh, The (*Faraon*, 1966), 117
Photographer (*Fotoamator*, 1998), 9, 220–21, 248
Piaskowski, Czesław, 38
Pichelski, Jerzy, 61, 64–65, 70n5, 232
Picon, Molly, 20
Pieczka, Franciszek, 140–42, 160, 239, 243
Pieczyński, Krzysztof, 168, 245
Piekutowski, Andrzej, 119, 247
Pietruski, Ryszard, 91, 127, 233, 236–37
Pilate and Others (*Pilatus und Andere*, 1972), 89
Pilecki, Witold, 42, 52n64
Piwowarski, Radosław, 156
Pogrom (Kielce, 1946), 17, 20, 26n18, 56, 171, 217
Polański, Roman, 8, 55, 79, 82, 88, 106–7, 117, 173–74, 176–80, 185n94, 233, 235, 246
Po-lin (*Po-lin. Okruchy pamięci*, 2008), 217, 223, 249
Polish Cuisine (*Kuchnia polska*, 1991), 157
Polish Newsreel (*Polska Kronika Filmowa*, PKF), 212–13, 217
Polish School, The, 7, 9, 45, 62, 74–79, 84, 94–95, 99, 108–9, 114n86
Polish Ways, The (*Polskie drogi*, 1976–77), 112n54, 122, 247
Pornography (*Pornografia*, 2003), 166, 170–71, 246
Portraitist, The (*Portrecista*, 2005), 220–21, 249
Posmysz (Posmysz-Piasecka), Zofia, 100, 105, 112n62, 235
Postcard from the Journey, A (*Kartka z podróży*, 1984), 8, 140, 145–46, 240
Potocki, Sergiusz J., 212
Preisner, Zbigniew, 153
Preizner, Joanna, 169, 191
Price of Life, The (*Cena życia*, 2004), 223
Prokopowicz, Bartosz, 206, 245
Promised Land, The (*Ziemia obiecana*, 1975), 125–26, 137n26, 191–92, 200
Prószyński, Kazimierz, 11
Przebindowski, Jakub, 203, 244
Przylipiak, Mirosław, 218

Pszoniak, Wojciech, 125, 191–92, 203, 238–39, 242, 244
Ptak, Krzysztof, 170, 242, 246
Purzycki, Jan, 143, 240

R

Rachwalska, Barbara, 35–36, 231
Radzinowicz, Anatol, 117, 230, 233–34
Radziwiłowicz, Jerzy, 141, 239
Rainbow (*Raduga*, 1943), 38
Ramati, Aleksander, 189–91
Raplewski, Zbigniew, 139, 248
Rapoport, Nathan, 56, 57
Rashomon (1950), 104
Ravensbrück concentration camp, 29, 45
Redlichówna, Maria, 32, 231
Reich, Aleksander, 12
Reicher, Edward, 83
Remember Your Name (*Zapamiętaj imię swoje*, 1974), 119, 238
Reminiscent of Yesterday (*Jakby to było wczoraj*, 2005), 219
Renoir, Jean, 92
Repulsion (1965), 177
Requiem for 500,000 (*Requiem dla 500 000*, 1963), 9, 214, 220, 247
Resnais, Alain, 5, 38, 45, 214
Revenge (*Zemsta*, 2002), 206
Reymont, Władysław Stanisław, 125
Righteous, The (*Sprawiedliwi*, 2010), 228, 249
Ringelblum, Emmanuel, 20, 58, 67, 130
Roll Call, The (*Apel*, 1970), 123–24, 247
Rogowski, Wiesław, 126, 236
Rome, Open City (*Roma città aperta*, 1945), 36
Rose, The (*Róża*, 1962), 215, 247
Rosen, Józef, 12
Rossellini, Roberto, 36, 199
Rotmil, Jacek, 12
Różański, Józef, 19
Różewicz, Stanisław, 7, 76, 95–97, 140–41, 144, 181n10, 227, 233–34, 239
Rubinstein, Richard L., 221
Rudnicki, Adolf, 58, 83, 124, 131–32, 237
Rules of the Game (*La Règle du jeu*, 1939), 92
Rumkowski, Mordecai Chaim, 221
Rybkowski, Jan, 8, 76, 86, 90, 117, 131–35, 205, 237
Rymkiewicz, Jarosław Marek, 140

S

Sabra (1933), 54
Sachsenhausen concentration camp, 45
Safran, Gabriella, 142–43
Sakowska, Ruta, 195
Salacka-Krauze, Ewa, 165, 240
Salad Days (*Zielone lata*, 1980), 122, 238
Samberg, Ajzyk, 12
Samson (1961), 7, 78, 84–89, 111n24, 235
Sanatorium under the Sign of the Hourglass (*Sanatorium pod klepsydrą*, 1973), 124–25
Sands, Julian, 155

Sarid (2005), 223, 249
Saxton, Libby, 163, 184n61
Scenes of Battle (*Barwy walki*, 1965), 115, 118
Schatz, Jaff, 17, 74, 116
Schindler's List (1993), 5, 154
Schneider, Gerda, 29, 36–37, 48n6, 231
Schochet, Simon, 18
Schulz, Bruno, 125
Schwartz, Daniel R., 125
Schygulla, Hanna, 164, 243
Scurvy (*Cynga*, 1993), 164
See You Tomorrow (*Do widzenia, do jutra*, 1960), 94
Sendler, Irena, 149, 172, 182n33, 222
Setkina, Irina, 212
Seweryn, Andrzej, 125
Sheppard, Anna, 174
Shoah (1985), 8, 139, 148, 197, 218
Shop on Main Street, The (*Obchod na korze*, 1965), 72n46, 114n86, 131, 208n36
Short Film about Killing, A (*Krótki film o zabijaniu*, 1988), 206
Sienkiewicz, Henryk, 12, 143
Siwkiewicz, Piotr, 156
Skolimowski, Lech, 46–47, 236
Słaboszowska, Zofia, 45, 234
Śląska, Aleksandra, 100, 102–4, 231, 235
Sławik, Henryk, 172, 222
Słonimski, Antoni, 58, 189
Smolar, Aleksander, 17
Smosarska, Jadwiga, 13
Snyder, Timothy, 15
Sobolewska, Anna, 198–99
Sobolewski, Tadeusz, 144, 206
Sochnacki, Bogusław, 147, 159, 240, 243, 244
Sokołowska, Anna, 120
Solarz, Wojciech, 123
Soldier of Victory, The (*Żołnierz zwycięstwa*, 1953), 45
Sołtysik, Marek, 165, 244
Somersault (*Salto*, 1965), 125
Sophie's Choice (1982), 38
Soutendijk, Rene, 155
Sowińska, Iwona, 66
Spielberg, Steven 5, 38, 51n47, 154, 183n41
Śródka, Stefan, 30, 61, 66, 72n52, 230–32
Stalin, Joseph, 15, 18, 26n28, 32, 37, 60, 74, 110n15, 164
Stańko, Tomasz, 159, 243
Starski, Allan, 71n26, 174, 183n41, 242, 244, 246
Starski, Ludwik, 13, 22–23, 58, 71n26, 188–89, 207n6, 230, 232
START (The Society of Film Art Devotees), 14, 37, 53, 65, 69n5
Stawiński, Jerzy Stefan, 75, 119
Stefański, Stanisław, 143
Stein, Edith, 199
Steinberg, Baruch, 18
Steinlauf, Michael C., 3, 15
Steinwurzel, Seweryn, 13

Stevens, George, 51n47
Stevenson, Michael, 5, 80
Stolarska, Bronisława, 80, 110n9
Stoor, Mieczysław, 120, 234, 238
Story of the Kowalskis, The (*Historia Kowalskich*, 2009), 23, 249
Strassburger, Karol, 122
Strękowski, Jan, 222, 249
Strońska, Anna, 159, 242
Stroop, Jürgen, 68, 151, 178, 210n73
Struk, Janina, 49n22, 67
Stryjkowski, Julian, 118, 141–42, 239
Suzin, Leon Marek, 56
Swan, Oscar, 201, 204–5, 210n73
Swastika and the Gallows, The (*Swastyka i szubienica*, 1945), 212, 247
Światło, Józef, 19, 74
Świdwiński, Aleksander, 213, 247
Synoradzka, Anna, 202
Szabó, István, 123
Szaflarska, Danuta, 24, 51n56, 77, 160, 230, 235, 242, 244
Szaro, Henryk, 11
Szarota, Tomasz, 70n8, 83
Szaynok, Bożena, 4
Szczepański, Jan Alfred, 48
Szczepański, Jan Józef, 86, 154–55
Szczypiorski, Andrzej, 140
Szelburg-Zarembina, Ewa, 24, 27n39, 230
Szewc, Piotr, 140
Szlachtycz, Stefan, 140, 165, 184n63, 239
Szlengel, Władysław, 188, 207n7
Szmaglewska, Seweryna, 34–35
Szmidt, Natalia, 223
Szpilman, Władysław, 8, 174–80, 185n89, 189, 232, 246
Szumacher, Israel, 21, 231
Szweizer, Henryk, 22–23, 230
Szyma, Tadeusz, 105
Szyndler, Zygmunt, 117

T

Tate, Sharon, 177
Teaspoon for Life, A (*Łyżeczka życia*, 2004), 222, 248
Tell Me, Why? (*Powiedz mi, dlaczego?* 2005), 220, 249
Tenant, The (*Le Locataire*, 1976), 177
Teutonic Knights, The (*Krzyżacy*, 1960), 69, 111n24, 189
There Was No Sun That Spring (*Nie było słońca tej wiosny*, 1984), 8, 146–48, 240
Three of Heart (1992), 173
Three Women (*Trzy kobiety*, 1957), 76
Titkow, Andrzej, 218
Toeplitz, Jerzy, 14, 37, 84, 117, 136nn8–9, 175
Toeplitz, Krzysztof Teodor (KTT), 129, 190
Tomiak, Arkadiusz, 168, 245
Tor Film Studio, xii, 96, 141, 239
To Save the Town (*Ocalić miasto*, 1976), 157
Tracks (*Ślady*, 1967/1982), 216

Transport from Paradise (*Transport z raje*, 1963), 114n86
Treasure (*Skarb*, 1948), 24, 41, 58
Treblinka extermination camp, 58, 64, 69n5, 83, 110n10, 188–89, 195, 198–99, 216, 218–19
Trepczyński, Stanisław, 190
Trissenaar, Elisabeth, 148
True End of the Great War, The (*Prawdziwy koniec wielkiej wojny*, 1957), 76–77
Trystan, Leon, 12
Tuwim, Julian, 63, 72n45
Tuzar, Jaroslav, 53
Two Drawers (*Dwie szuflady*, 2005), 222, 249
Two Hours (*Dwie godziny*, 1946/1957), 21, 23–24, 27n39, 230
Two Men and a Wardrobe (*Dwaj ludzie z szafą*, 1958), 107, 177
Tymiński, Kazimierz, 184n59, 242

U

Ucicky, Gustav, 70n8
Ulm, Józef and Wiktoria, 223
Umschlagplatz, The (Warsaw), 64, 83, 140, 144, 146, 177, 179, 188, 195
Under the Phrygian Star (*Pod gwiazdą frygijską*, 1954), 16–17
Under This Same Sky (*Pod jednym niebem*, 1955), 214, 247
Unloved (*Niekochana*, 1966), 124, 131
Unvanquished City (*Miasto nieujarzmione*, 1950), 8, 21, 175–76, 232
Urbanowicz, Stanisław, 214

V

Vernichtungslager Majdanek: The Cemetery of Europe (1944), 212
Vigo, Jean, 70n5
Voit, Mieczysław, 107–8
Vrstala, Jiři, 119, 238

W

Wachełko-Zaleska, Krystyna, 147, 240
Wachowiak, Maria, 91, 236
Wajda, Andrzej, 7–9, 24, 57, 68, 76–89, 94, 106, 109n6, 110n9, 110n15, 111n24, 111n33, 112n60, 117, 120–22, 125–26, 129, 137n26, 153–54, 159–60, 164–65, 187–210, 227, 232, 235, 238, 242, 244
Wajdowicz, Roman, 117
Wajnberger, Mieczysław, 49n10, 117, 231
Walczewski, Marek, 101, 103, 235
Walker, Janet, 6
Walter, Władysław, 61, 232
Waltz, Christopher, 155
Warsaw Ghetto Monument, 56, 57, 70n18
Warsaw Ghetto Uprising, The (1943), 7, 9, 16, 25, 39, 53, 55–57, 67–68, 79, 81, 83, 109n7, 111n40, 119, 132, 144, 149, 151, 165, 178–80, 191, 194, 201–2, 213–14, 220, 227
Warsaw Rebuilds (*Budujemy Warszawę*, 1945), 214

Index

Warsaw Rising, The (1944), 7, 11, 15, 42, 55–57, 66, 68, 90, 99, 112n54, 149, 176–77, 219, 224
Warsaw Robinson, The (Robinson Warszawski, 1950), 8, 175
Warsaw Suite, The (Suita Warszawska, 1946), 214
Warszałłowicz, Marian, 65
Warszawa. Année 5703 (Tragarz puchu, 1992), 8, 83, 154, 164–65, 243
Warzecha, Magdalena, 202, 206, 244–45
Wasilewska, Wanda, 54
Waszyński, Michał, 13, 142
Wawrzyniak, Kazimierz, 47, 236
Ważyk, Adam, 23, 231
We Are Still Alive (Mir, lebngeblibene, 1947), 20–21, 247
Weber, Kurt, 45, 117, 214, 225n13, 234, 247
Wedding, The (Wesele, 1973), 125
We Honestly Did Not Know (I naprawdę nic nie wiedzieliśmy, 1993), 218
Weksler-Waszkinel, Romuald Jakub, 220
Werner, Andrzej, 34
Wertenstein, Ludwik, 201
Wertenstein, Wanda, 201
When Angels Fall (Gdy spadają anioły, 1959), 177
When Love Was a Crime (Rassenschande; Kiedy miłość była zbrodnią, 1968), 134
Wherever You Are (Gdzieśkolwiek jest, jeśliś jest..., 1989), 155
Where Is My Older Son Cain? (Gdzie mój starszy syn Kain? 1999), 172, 248
White Bear (Biały niedźwiedź, 1959), 7, 78, 97–99, 144, 233
Wicińska, Teresa, 46,
Wiesel, Elie, 3, 199
Wilczyńska, Stefania, 195–96
Willenberg, Samuel, 218–19
Wilson, Lambert, 164, 243
Winnicka, Ernestyna, 147, 239–40
Winnicka, Lucyna, 76, 107
Winogradowa, Maria, 29–30, 231
Wiśniewski, Czesław, 135
With Raised Hands (Z podniesionymi rękami, 1985), 151, 248
Witnesses (Świadkowie, 1987), 217, 248
Włodek, Roman, 128
Wohl, Stanisław, 13–14, 21, 23, 54, 90, 117, 211–12, 224n2, 230
Wójcik, Jerzy, 86, 93, 151, 231, 239
Wojdowski, Bogdan, 62
Wołłejko, Jolanta, 127–28, 236

Woroszylski, Witold, 99, 235
Wosiewicz, Leszek, 46, 154, 162–64, 184n59, 184n61, 241–42
Woszczerowicz, Jacek, 24, 230
Wróbel, Marta, 163
Wróbel, Piotr, 1, 26n28, 110n10, 171
Wysocki, Piotr, 132
Wyspiański, Stanisław, 125
Wyszomirski, Józef, 21, 23, 230

Y

Yesterday (1985), 156
Yiddish cinema, Poland, 1, 20–22, 54, 142, 184n63, 231, 247
Yiddle with His Fiddle (Yidl mitn fidl, 1936), 20
Young, James E., 1, 70n18, 200
Youth during the Holocaust (Młodość w czasach Zagłady, 2001), 220, 248
Youth of Chopin, The (Młodość Chopina, 1952), 69

Z

Zacharewicz, Witold, 11
Zaczyk, Stanisław, 40, 231, 235
Zajiček, Edward, 49n10, 49n19, 189, 237
Zamachowski, Zbigniew, 194, 242, 246
Zanussi, Krzysztof, 154–55
Zaorski, Tadeusz, 129–31, 135, 190–91
Zaremba, Marcin, 135, 136n10
Zarzycki, Jerzy, 7–8, 14, 21, 69n5, 78, 97–99, 144, 175–76, 232–33
Zechenter, Witold, 189
Żegota (Council for Aid to the Jews), 2, 19, 58, 149, 204, 228
Zeitlin, Aaron, 199
Zeman, Božívoj, 23, 231
Żentara, Edward, 155
Zhdanov, Andrei, 32
Ziarnik, Jerzy, 122–23, 215–17, 237, 247
Ziegler, Regina, 191, 242
Zimetbaum, Mala, 39–40, 224
Zintel, Zygmunt, 96, 233–34, 241
Złotnicki, Jerzy, 61, 63, 65, 232
Znicz, Michał, 12
Żółtowski, Wojciech, 146, 148–50, 241
Zub, Jan, 222
Żuławski, Andrzej, 84, 202, 235
Zwierzchowski, Piotr, 51n59
Zylber, Filip, 8, 154, 159–60, 243
Zylinska, Joanna, 3, 172
Żywulska, Krystyna, 34, 35, 40